Conversations on Dictionaries

How did dictionaries come to be? When and how did they originate in a specific language? Who was involved in that origin story? How have they evolved over time? What is the tension between scholarly and commercial, and between prescriptive and descriptive, dictionaries? What is the politics behind each dictionary? And what is the connection between dictionaries and nation-building? This fascinating book has the answers. It brings together a collection of conversations with leading lexicographers from around the world to explore the role dictionaries have played in history, comparing the parallel histories of lexicography in some three dozen different languages. The conversations explore the way dictionaries, which preserve languages while contributing to their standardization, are always political in nature, prescribing some words while canceling others. Covering major world languages, Indigenous languages, and hybrid languages, this is essential reading for academic researchers and students of lexicography, and lovers of language and literature.

ILAN STAVANS is the Lewis-Sebring Professor of Humanities and Latin American and Latino Culture at Amherst College, the publisher of Restless Books, and an advisor to the *Oxford English Dictionary*. His recent publications include *How Yiddish Changed America and How America Changed Yiddish* (2020) and *The People's Tongue* (2023).

Conversations on Dictionaries
The Universe in a Book

Edited by
Ilan Stavans
Amherst College

CAMBRIDGE
UNIVERSITY PRESS

Shaftesbury Road, Cambridge CB2 8EA, United Kingdom

One Liberty Plaza, 20th Floor, New York, NY 10006, USA

477 Williamstown Road, Port Melbourne, VIC 3207, Australia

314–321, 3rd Floor, Plot 3, Splendor Forum, Jasola District Centre, New Delhi – 110025, India

103 Penang Road, #05-06/07, Visioncrest Commercial, Singapore 238467

Cambridge University Press is part of Cambridge University Press & Assessment, a department of the University of Cambridge.

We share the University's mission to contribute to society through the pursuit of education, learning and research at the highest international levels of excellence.

www.cambridge.org
Information on this title: www.cambridge.org/9781009392419

DOI: 10.1017/9781009392433

© Cambridge University Press & Assessment 2025

This publication is in copyright. Subject to statutory exception and to the provisions of relevant collective licensing agreements, no reproduction of any part may take place without the written permission of Cambridge University Press & Assessment.

When citing this work, please include a reference to the DOI 10.1017/9781009392433

First published 2025

Cover image: *El sueño de Jacob* (1969), by José Gurvich, from the Museo Gurvich Collection, Montevideo, Uruguay.

A catalogue record for this publication is available from the British Library

A Cataloging-in-Publication data record for this book is available from the Library of Congress

ISBN 978-1-009-39241-9 Hardback
ISBN 978-1-009-39239-6 Paperback

Cambridge University Press & Assessment has no responsibility for the persistence or accuracy of URLs for external or third-party internet websites referred to in this publication and does not guarantee that any content on such websites is, or will remain, accurate or appropriate.

For EU product safety concerns, contact us at Calle de José Abascal, 56, 1°, 28003 Madrid, Spain, or email eugpsr@cambridge.org.

I am not yet so lost in lexicography, as to forget that words are the daughters of earth, and that things are the sons of heaven.

—Samuel Johnson, Preface to *A Dictionary of the English Language* (1755)

Contents

Acknowledgments   *page* ix
List of Contributors   x

Introduction: The Universe in a Book   1

1   Ancient Greek   4
WILLIAM A. ROSS

2   Esperanto   16
ESTHER SCHOR

3   German   28
VOLKER HARM

4   Chinese   42
HAORAN TONG

5   Hybrid Languages   58
ILAN STAVANS AND MARGARET E. BOYLE

6   English   72
PETER GILLIVER

7   French   83
MARIE-HÉLÈNE DRIVAUD AND PETER SOKOLOWSKI

8   Italian   94
CARLA MARELLO AND CLAUDIO MARAZZINI

9   Arabic   107
HASSAN HAMZÉ

10   Hebrew   119
RUVIK ROSENTHAL

11   Indigenous Languages   132
MARK TURIN

12	Irish SEÁN UA SÚILLEABHÁIN	145
13	African Languages DION NKOMO AND PAUL ACHILLE MAVOUNGOU	156
14	Nahuatl JOHN SULLIVAN	172
15	Yiddish GITL SCHAECHTER-VISWANATH	184
16	Portuguese RUTE COSTA AND ANA SALGADO	195
17	Japanese YUKIO TONO	207
18	Russian MIKHAIL KOPOTEV	227
19	Quechua ODI GONZALES	241
20	Scandinavian LARS TRAP-JENSEN	248
21	Spanish FRANCISCO JAVIER PÉREZ	263

| Epilogue: The Total Dictionary | 274 |
| *Index* | 283 |

Acknowledgments

Thanks to Vinithan Sethumadhavan, project manager, and to Franklin Matthews Jebaraj, senior production editor, both at Straive; Heather Dubnick for the index; and Cheryl Hutty for copy-editing the book.

Contributors

MARGARET E. BOYLE (Hybrid Languages) is Professor of Romance Languages and Literatures and Latin American, Caribbean and Latinx Studies at Bowdoin College. A Mexican-American from Los Angeles, she directs Multilingual Mainers, an elementary program promoting intercultural conversations and the study of languages other than English in the state of Maine. Her books include *Unruly Women: Performance, Penitence and Punishment in Early Modern Spain* (2015), *Health and Healing in the Early Modern Iberian World: A Gendered Perspective* (2021, with Sarah Owens), and *Sabor Judío: The Jewish Mexican Cookbook* (2024, with Ilan Stavans).

RUTE COSTA (Portuguese), head of the Linguistics Centre of the Universidade NOVA de Lisboa, is currently leading the digitization of *Diccionario da lingua portugueza* by António de Morais. In 2011, she was honoured with the title of "Chevalier de l'Ordre des Arts et des Lettres" from France.

MARIE-HÉLÈNE DRIVAUD (French) began working at *Dictionnaires Le Robert* in 1988, learning lexicography from Josette Rey-Debove. As editorial director, she is responsible for the *Petit Robert*, among other endeavors. She teaches general linguistics at the Sorbonne.

PETER GILLIVER (English) is an executive editor of the *Oxford English Dictionary*, has been working on the *OED* for nearly forty years, and is one of the *OED*'s most experienced lexicographers. For most of that time he has also been writing and speaking about the history of the *OED*. His history, *The Making of the Oxford English Dictionary*, was published in 2016 by Oxford University Press to great critical acclaim; in 2018 he was awarded a doctorate by the University of Cambridge for his work on the history of the *OED*.

List of Contributors xi

ODI GONZALES (Quechua) is an award-winning poet and scholar of the Andean oral tradition who teaches Andean linguistic anthropology at New York University. He is the coauthor of *Quechua-Spanish-English Dictionary: A Hippocrene Trilingual Reference* (2018), which he edited with Christine Mladic Janney and Emily Fjaellen Thompson.

HASSAN HAMZÉ (Arabic) is professor emeritus at Lumière University Lyon 2 in France and professor of Arabic Linguistics and Lexicography at Doha Institute for Graduate Studies in Qatar. He is deputy chair of the Scientific Council of the Doha Historical Dictionary. This conversation delves into the tradition of Arabic dictionaries, starting with Al-Farāhīdī's first lexicon *Kitab al-'Ayn*, el-Fīrūz Abād's *Al-Qamus al-Muhit*, Muḥammad ibn Muḥammad Murtaḍá al-Zabīdī's *Taj al-Arus*, and Ahmad Mukhtar Omar's *Lexicon of the Modern Arabic Language*.

VOLKER HARM (German), a professor at Göttingen University, is chief editor of the dictionary project "Wortgeschichte digital" at the Lower-Saxonian Academy of Sciences in Göttingen. The author of several books, including *Einführung in die Lexikologie* (2015) and *Funktionsverbgefüge des Deutschen* (2021), his publications also include *Historische Lexikographie des Deutschen* (2022).

HAORAN TONG (Chinese) is a poet from Beijing, China. His work in Chinese frequently draws references from classical Chinese dictionaries such as *Erya* and assigns new meanings from the otherwise terse definitions. He graduated from Amherst College in 2023 and currently lives in Boston.

MIKHAIL KOPOTEV (Russian), an affiliate professor at Stockholm University and associate professor at the University of Helsinki, researches East Slavic languages, corpus linguistics, and computer-assisted language learning. His books include *The Palgrave Handbook of Digital Russia Studies* (2021) and *Constructions with Lexical Repetitions in East Slavic* (2024).

CLAUDIO MARAZZINI (Italian) is professor emeritus of History of the Italian Language at the University of Eastern Piedmont and honorary president of the Accademia della Crusca in Florence. He is the author of a brief history of the Italian language (2002) and director of *Studi di Lessicografia Italiana*, a journal of the Accademia della Crusca.

CARLA MARELLO (Italian) is professor emeritus at the University of Turin and a member of Accademia della Crusca. She was president of Euralex (European Association for Lexicography) and an editor of the *International Journal of Lexicography*.

PAUL ACHILLE MAVOUNGOU (African Languages) is an associate professor of the Department of Language Sciences at the University Omar Bongo in Libreville, Gabon. He has been involved in the *Dictionnaire Yilumbu-Français* (2010, with Bernard Plumel) and the *Dictionnaire des expressions idiomatiques Lumbu* (2023, with Ludwine Mbindi Aninga, et al.).

DION NKOMO (African Languages) is a professor of African language studies at the School of Languages and Literatures at Rhodes University. He occupies a research chair on Intellectualisation of African Languages, Multilingualism, and Education. A lexicographer by training, he was introduced to the field at the University of Zimbabwe. For his PhD, he studied English dictionaries there. He is one of the revolving editors of *Lexikos*.

FRANCISCO JAVIER PÉREZ (Spanish), a native of Venezuela, is a lexicographer and linguistic historian who has been a researcher at the Centro de Estudios Latinoamericanos Rómulo Gallegos and University of Augsburg, Germany. He is a member of the Academia Venezolana de la Lengua, as well as of the academies of Chile, Cuba, Dominican Republic, Guatemala, Panama, United States, and Uruguay. His books include the two-volume *Diccionario histórico del español de Venezuela* (2013). He is currently general secretary of the Asociación de Academias de la Lengua Española.

REUVEN "RUVIK" ROSENTHAL (Hebrew), an expert in Modern Hebrew, writes for the site "The Language Arena," following a weekly column on language for the Israeli daily *Ma'ariv* since 1997. The author of essays, novels, and children's books, as well as dictionaries, he is the winner of the Sokolov Award for Journalism in 2004, the Ramat Gan Award for Children's Books in 2012, and the Ariel Prize for Creativity in Hebrew Language in 2014. His doctoral dissertation examined Israeli military language.

WILLIAM A. ROSS (Ancient Greek), a native of Philadelphia, is an associate professor of the Old Testament at the Reformed Theological Seminary in Charlotte, North Carolina. He completed his doctorate at the University of Cambridge as a Cambridge Trust Scholar under the late James K. Aitken, specializing in the Septuagint, ancient Greek lexicography, and the textual history of the Bible. His books include *Septuaginta: A Reader's Edition* (2018) and *Postclassical Greek and Septuagint Lexicography* (2022).

ANA SALGADO (Portuguese), president of Instituto de Lexicologia e Lexicografia da Língua of Academia das Ciências de Lisboa, where she is the chief editor of the online dictionaries of this institution, is a researcher at the Linguistics Center of Universidade NOVA de Lisboa and is one of the editors of *Thesaurus de Ciências da Terra* of the Academia das Ciências de Lisboa.

List of Contributors

GITL SCHAECHTER-VISWANATH (Yiddish) is coeditor of *Comprehensive English-Yiddish Dictionary* (2016; revised, 2nd ed., 2021). Board chair of the League for Yiddish, founded in 1979 by linguist Mordkhe Schaechter, she serves as language editor for the Yiddish magazine *Afn Shvel*. Schaechter-Viswanath is a Yiddish poet and has published a volume of her poetry (*Plutsemdiker Regn/Sudden Rain*). Her son Arun Schaechter Viswanath, the grandson of Mordkhe Schaechter, translated *Harry Potter and the Sorcerer's Stone* into Yiddish. She worked for three decades as a nursing home consultant.

ESTHER SCHOR (Esperanto), the John J. F. Sherrerd '52 University Professor and Professor of English at Princeton, is a scholar, biographer, poet, and essayist. She is the author of *Bearing the Dead: The British Culture of Mourning from the Enlightenment to Victoria* (1994), *Emma Lazarus* (2006), and *Bridge of Words: Esperanto and the Dream of a Universal Language* (2016).

PETER SOKOLOWSKI (French) joined Merriam-Webster in 1994 as the company's first French-language editor. He has written definitions for many of Merriam-Webster's dictionaries, is active as a blogger, podcaster, and speaker on language, and has served as pronouncer for spelling bees worldwide. He was named among TIME's 140 Best Twitter Feeds of 2013.

JOHN SULLIVAN (Nahuatl) is professor emeritus in Nahuatl Language and Culture at the Universidad Autónoma de Zacatecas, Mexico, and teaches Older Nahuatl at the University of Utah and University of Warsaw, Poland. He coedited the monolingual Nahuatl dictionary *Tlahtolxitlauhcayotl* (2016). His other books include *Dialogue with Europe, Dialogue with the Past: Colonial Nahua and Quechua Elites in Their Own Words* (2018) and *Loans in Colonial and Modern Nahuatl* (2020).

ILAN STAVANS (Hybrid Languages) is the Lewis-Sebring Professor of Humanities, Latin American, and Latino Culture at Amherst College, the cofounder and publisher of Restless Books, and a consultant to the *Oxford English Dictionary*. He is known for his research on Spanglish and his book *Spanglish: The Making of a New American Language* (2003). His other books on language include his memoir *On Borrowed Words* (2001), *Dictionary Days: A Defining Passion* (2005), *Resurrecting Hebrew* (2008), *How Yiddish Changed America and How America Changed Yiddish* (2020), and *A People's Tongue: Americans and the English Language* (2023).

LARS TRAP-JENSEN (Scandinavian) holds an MA in linguistics, Greenlandic, and social studies from Aarhus University as well as an MPhil in linguistics from Cambridge University. He served as lecturer in Danish language at the University of Basel and University of Zürich. Since 1994, he has been dedicated to the field of lexicography, serving as a practical lexicographer at the Society for Danish Language and Literature in Copenhagen and, from 2003 to 2020, serving as managing editor for *Den Danske Ordbog*.

YUKIO TONO (Japanese), a professor in corpus linguistics at Tokyo University, is the coauthor, with Makoto Yamazaki and Kikuo Maekawa, of *A Frequency Dictionary of Japanese* (2013), among other books. He is past president of the Asian Association for Lexicography and was editor-in-chief of the journal *Lexicography*. This conversation delves into dictionaries in Japanese, from the first semantically collated lexicon of Chinese characters known as *Kagakushū* to the twenty-volume *Nihon Kokugo Daijiten*.

MARK TURIN (Indigenous Languages), an anthropologist and linguist who teaches at the University of British Columbia, studies Indigenous languages in North America as well as in Northern South Asia, and works with communities to support their goals for language reclamation. Among his books are *A Grammar of Thangmi with an Ethnolinguistic: Introduction to the Speakers and Their Culture* (2012; Nepali ed., 2023) and *Nepali-Thami-English Dictionary* (2004).

SEÁN UA SÚILLEABHÁIN (Irish) worked on the *Dictionary of Modern Irish* project in the Royal Irish Academy, was a scholar in the School of Celtic Studies of the Dublin Institute for Advanced Studies, and is a lecturer at University College Cork.

Introduction
The Universe in a Book

Ilan Stavans

"DICTIONARY," as Ambrose Bierce defines it, with satirical acumen, is "a malevolent literary device for cramping the growth of a language and making it hard and inelastic." He adds, however, that *this* particular one, referring to his own book *The Devil's Dictionary*, "is a most useful work."

Dictionaries, indeed, dream of being useful. That is, they seek to be orderly, practical, and expedient. Not all succeed, of course. As with anything else, there are dictionaries that are good, meaning they are precise and imaginative, and others that are plain bad because of their rigidity. Most are both: good and bad. How often do we come across a definition that seems inspired, as if the lexicographers had hit the nail on the head? Or, contrariwise, one that feels bad, as if it had missed an opportunity, producing an explanation that is hard and inelastic and just wrong?

At any rate, Bierce is correct that dictionaries "cramp the growth of a language," for by cataloging words, as they do, these instruments of language are inevitably aligned with tradition, suffusing words that are included in their pages with the stink of officialness and words that are left out with a spontaneity and freedom that is alluring.

This is a collection of twenty-two conversations – decidedly not interviews – about the endurance of dictionaries across time and space. The participants are dictionary makers, lexicographers, language scholars, newspaper columnists, bloggers, and other such authorities. They inhabit or come from different languages, at times more than one, which is the point since my overall interest in this endeavor is to understand how different dictionaries "behave" differently depending on the language they represent and how that language defines them.

Samuel Johnson, a renaissance man for whom I have enormous admiration, once portrayed lexicographers as "unhappy mortals who toil at the lower employments of life." It is an unkind portrayal, made even more obnoxious as Johnson augments that these individuals are considered by humankind "not as the pupil, but the slave of science, the pionier of literature, doomed only to remove rubbish and clear obstructions in our parlance." Truth is, the participants in the volume are quite the opposite: eloquent, passionate people interested in how 1,001 complexities of our world might be conveyed in words and vice versa.

Shakespeare, in *Hamlet* (Act 2, Scene 2), has his protagonist state that "There is nothing either good or bad, but thinking makes it so." Words too might be considered neutral until the moment we use them. Once we do, they are no longer innocent. In this volume, that use – and abuse – the way different national histories catalog words in their own way, is scrutinized in an informed, enlightening fashion. Just as no two languages are alike, nor are the lexicons.

I have known many of the participants in this book for years, in some cases decades. We have become friends. I met others after sending them an admiring letter inviting them to talk to me extemporaneously about dictionaries in their life. It might look like not only my selection of speakers but that of the languages here are completely arbitrary. No doubt unadulterated affinity brought us together. What cannot be described as arbitrary is the way these languages have shaped me: I either know them intimately or I have spent extended periods in milieus where those languages are used. In other words, these are the languages that have made me who I am.

In aggregate, the exchanges were made over a period of twelve months. A few were in person, with an iPhone recording the dialogue; others were carried out via Zoom, followed by a transcription; but the vast majority came about from intense email exchanges that ultimately coalesced into a free-flowing tête-à-tête.

Every conversation starts with a headnote offering context and mapping out the exchange. In those headnotes, I occasionally express my debt to an author or book who served me as a bridge to that language, say Dante for Italian or Goethe for German. To me, this confirms Johnson's statement that lexicographers are the pioneers of literature. Depending on the occasion, the exchanges were carried out in English, Spanish, French, Hebrew, Yiddish, and other languages. They were then translated into English, either by myself or by a trustworthy colleague, whose name is credited in the headnote. Every participant was sent various drafts of the exchange and approved the final version. Once everything was in place, they provided a list of suggested readings in the hope of inspiring readers to further explorations. The order the conversations follow is also random.

Had I had more time (we never do!), or more lives (ah, impostorship!), I would have made a dozen more of these. Or twice that amount. Or a thousand. I'm not being facetious, such has been the joy resulting from these encounters. Actually, I have always regretted the fact that, as a tool of knowledge, the dialogue, Socrates and Plato notwithstanding, is looked down upon in academia, for it is through unrehearsed conversations when information becomes knowledge. On this point, it is worth returning to Bierce.

In *The Devil's Dictionary*, he defines ERUDITION as "dust shaken out of a book into an empty skull." These one-on-ones prove him wrong.

The epilogue is the twenty-second conversation, although it is somewhat different. This one is a fictionalized narrative based on real-life events.

I want to thank all and every one of the participants in *Conversations on Dictionaries* for their energy, disposition, and generosity. I played out a number of ideas with my extraordinary students at Amherst College and with the equally inspiring campers, middle- and high-schoolers, at Great Books Summer Program. Along the way, I have received invaluable support from two student interns: Gabriel Mandereau and Ilya Nemirovsky. I also – and most emphatically – wish to express my profuse *gracias* to Helen Barton, my unwavering in-house editor at Cambridge University Press, who supported the idea from the start, and to her assistant Isabel Collins, who helped bring it to fruition.

Words are never only words; they conjure universes, which brings to mind Anatole France's inspiring image of the dictionary and grants the subtitle to the volume: *"l'univers dans un livre."*

1 Ancient Greek

William A. Ross

"I am not an Athenian or a Greek, but a citizen of the world," Diogenes is credited with having said. Thus, ancient Greek isn't exclusively the language of an empire whose foundation defined Europe; it is also a language that dreamed itself global before globalism became a concept. This conversation starts with a discussion of what constitutes a "dead language," then moves to a reflection on the role dictionaries of ancient Greek play in the study of antiquity. It looks at Johann Gottlob Schneider's *Kritisches griechisch-deutsches Handwörterbuch* (1797–98) as the foundation of future lexicons and considers other important lexicographers, such as Franz Passow, whose work influenced James Murray, the force behind the completion of the *Oxford English Dictionary (OED)*.[1] It ponders the role of online dictionaries of ancient Greek. And it concludes with an autobiographical reflection on stumbling on a copy of the Septuagint, the ancient Greek translation of the Hebrew scriptures, as an epiphanic moment that ultimately defined a scholar's path.

***

ILAN STAVANS: Does the concept of a "dead language" strike you as accurate?

WILLIAM ROSS: In some ways yes, but others no. If we adopt the notion of certain early modern German philologists and picture language as an organism, then death fits into the metaphor. We know an organism is alive if it is changing over time; growing, moving, interacting with other organisms, spawning offspring. By that logic, a language that doesn't change is a dead language. And the only sort of language that doesn't change is one that is no longer in continual spoken use among speakers. So in that sense, yes, some linguistic patients may accurately be pronounced dead; tag on the toe, freezer door shut, light out. Examples like Ugaritic or Etruscan come to mind. Those are ancient

---

[1] Johann Gottlob Schneider, *Kritisches griechisch-deutsches Handwörterbuch* (Leipzig: Friedrich Fromann, 1797–98); *OED* originally published as James A. H. Murray, *A New English Dictionary on Historical Principles; Founded Mainly on the Materials Collected by the Philological Society* (Oxford: Oxford University Press, 1884–1928).

languages spoken by ancient people, and they're certainly dead. But that brings us to a possible pitfall with the idea of a "dead" language: it is fairly easy for us to conflate *oldness* with *deadness*, when in fact the two qualities don't always coincide.

Greek, of course, is still very much in use by a large community and is constantly developing. And so the same morbid diagnosis we gave Ugaritic and Etruscan (happily) does not apply to it. At the same time, to return to the organism metaphor, precisely because Greek has been in use for well over two millennia now and continuously changing, it no longer looks like its younger self. And that younger self did some things that Greek would not attempt nowadays, and other things perhaps that it can't even remember, whether for better or worse. But that old self isn't *dead*; no more than a thirty-year-old version of yourself is dead once you turn forty-five, or sixty, or ninety. So in the case of Greek at least, it's better to think in terms of life stage than to use the living/dead binary.

IS: Let's talk about Johann Gottlob Schneider's *Kritisches griechisch-deutsches Handwörterbuch* (1797–98), an influential Greek-German volume that set the parameters for those to come.

WR: Schneider is an interesting lexicographer to begin with. Although he's not very widely known today, his influence is pretty wide-ranging, and his work draws our attention to several important threads in the history of dictionary-making for ancient Greek. First is his historical context. Schneider lived toward the end of the early modern era, which as a whole was a period of prodigious philological scholarship. It was all prompted by Renaissance Humanism with its feverish focus on reviving the cultural and intellectual achievements of classical antiquity. And that required ancient Greek, which in turn required dictionaries.

One of the things Schneider did that makes him fully part of his era is bootleg the work of his predecessors, but with enough modification to justify declaiming his intellectual proprietorship. Schneider says as much himself in the preface to his *Handwörterbuch*, where we are told that the work is based upon (and, naturally, greatly improves) the 1788 edition of the *Graecum Lexicon Manuale* compiled by Benjamin Hederich and expanded by Johann Ernesti.[2] Schneider also tells us of several other, lesser attempts at revising Hederich-Ernesti too. While we don't need to get into all of that, his comments are enough to illustrate how ancient Greek lexicography in this era was a bird's nest of borrowing, modifying, and supplementing previous works. That tradition would only continue, and Schneider's *Handwörterbuch* would itself become the foundation for the mainstream of Greek lexicons right down to today.

We can also note in passing two other things that Schneider did that place him within a broader tradition. The first is the fact that he completely ignored biblical and parabiblical texts in Greek. Although it's part of a longer story, the history of ancient Greek lexicography is largely split into two streams, one for the New Testament (and occasionally also the Septuagint), another for classical authors. Philologists in Schneider's day tended to paddle their lexicographical boats in only one stream or the other. The second thing is Schneider's approach to

---

[2] Benjamin Hederich, Thomas Morell, Johann August Ernesti, and Samuel Patrick, *Graecum Lexicon Manuale* (London: Stirling & Kenney, 1788).

representing word meaning ("Bedeutung") in his entries. Again, just like everyone else, Schneider felt that furnishing a handful of German translation options was suitable for the task. Of course, as any lexicographer worth their salt today will tell you, this method – known as glossing – is no substitute for definitions as a means of describing word meaning.

IS: I've always thought that Schneider allows us to see how dictionaries have come to take their present form. It was a slow process. I sometimes even think of it in Darwinian terms. Anyway, I'm interested in Henri Estienne's *Thesaurus Graecae Linguae* (1572).[3] He was a printer and the son of Robert Estienne, who published many classic texts – Cicero, Pliny, Virgil, et al. – as well as Greek and Latin translations of the Bible. And he was the author of *Thesaurus Linguae Latinae* (1531).[4]

WR: Yes, what a fascinating family this was. Henri's father, Robert – sometimes known as Robert Stephens, or Stephanus – was a French humanist, biblical scholar, and an influential publisher. Although the printing firm had been founded in Paris by Robert's father in 1502, Robert was forced to relocate it to Geneva in 1556, along with Henri and the rest of the family. That upheaval became necessary thanks to Robert's relatively late-blooming Protestant convictions, which cost him many former friends but earned his business a great deal of Calvinistic book sales. Among his most popular sellers were Bibles, including his editions of the *Novum Testamentum Graece*, one of which became known as the *Textus Receptus* (1550) and went on to furnish the textual basis of the 1611 King James Version.[5]

As if that weren't enough, Robert is also considered the founder of both French and Latin lexicography, thanks largely to his monumental labors to improve upon Ambrogio Calepino's Latin *Dictionarium* (1502),[6] which led ultimately to the *Thesaurus Linguae Latinae* in 1531. Robert was twenty-eight years old. As it happens, that same year saw the birth of another philological tour de force: Robert's son and intellectual heir, Henri. The story goes that, while Henri spent much of his youth learning the print trade, he learned to speak Latin conversationally, since it was the only language known by all of Robert's rather international group of employees. Apparently even the servants used it! That was life *chez Estienne*.

For his part, not long after Henri's fortieth birthday, he had successfully brought the *Thesaurus Graecae Linguae* to press in 1572. Henri was certainly the man for the task. As familiar as he was with Latin, Henri notes in the introduction to one of his books that in fact he had learned Greek earlier and that some people claimed he spoke it better even than French. Work on the *Thesaurus* was begun by Henri's father, who died at fifty-six, bequeathing the project to his son upon his deathbed. Naturally, it adopted many of the lexicographical innovations of Robert's Latin *Thesaurus*, which Henri made clear even in the title of his work, which stretched to over 60,000 Greek headwords.

---

[3] Henri Estienne, *Thesaurus Graecae Linguae* (Geneva: Henri Estienne, 1572).
[4] Robert Estienne, *Thesaurus Linguae Latinae* (Geneva: Robert Estienne, 1531).
[5] Robert Estienne, *Stephanus Textus Receptus* (Geneva: Robert Estienne, 1550).
[6] Ambrogio Calepino, *Dictionarium Latinum* (Rhegium Lingobardum, 1502).

IS: Personally, in seeing them in their historical context I not only seek to understand the dictionary makers who made great leaps through their work but, what I think is the other side of the coin, the need of an ever more linguistically curious and detailed readership. Elsewhere, I've referred to this facet of my logocentric obsession as a modality of *Rezeptionsgeschichte*. Is it possible for you to speculate on the changing nature of ancient Greek dictionaries as the *Thesaurus Linguae Latinae* is released?

WR: Oh, a lot of things were changing in the early sixteenth century. Prior to that point, virtually all dictionaries of ancient Greek were produced (and largely remained) in the eastern Byzantine Empire, far out of the reach of scholars in the Latin West. To the extent there was any purchase upon ancient Greek as a language in Western Europe during the medieval period, it was mostly limited to the New Testament writings and was sustained only meagrely by grammars written centuries earlier in Roman antiquity, along with some crude Greek-Latin glossaries.

But all of that would change, thanks in large measure to the fall of Constantinople to the Ottomans in 1453, an event that drove countless Greek refugees into Western European regions. Although it's obvious once you think about it, those Greeks rather naturally brought with them their knowledge of Greek but also a wealth of ancient Greek texts that were previously unknown in the West. So a massive geopolitical event triggered a massive intellectual event, as the influx of Greeks was the *sine qua non* for Renaissance Humanism, which as a whole was certainly an exercise in *Rezeptionsgeschichte*. It became an age driven by a manic, encyclopaedic urge to collect and organize ancient textual knowledge as a means of fashioning or refining contemporary cultural identities. And ancient Greek dictionaries were at the very center of that project.

Not only did secular humanists need them to pore over classical works by philosophers or historians like Aristotle or Herodotus, but increasingly Greek dictionaries became a critical resource in the Protestant Reformation, with its focus on the original languages of the Bible. Talk about a linguistically curious and detailed readership! It's difficult to overstate how influential such pursuits would prove to be in the course of history. I would go so far as to say that, beginning in the sixteenth century, ancient Greek dictionaries became brokers for the kind of credibility and knowledge that lay at the foundation of the strident and protracted cultural debates that would ultimately shape the intuitions and institutions of modern Europe as a whole.

IS: *A Greek-English Lexicon*, often referred to as *Liddell and Scott*, after the editors Henry George Liddell and Robert Scott, appeared in 1843.[7] How did it come about? I believe there were two other editors, Henry Stuart Jones and Roderick McKenzie. The ninth edition appeared in 1940.[8]

WR: That's right. This lexicon is *the* lexicon of classical Greek. It's the reigning champion and has been for over a century, though in recent years some challengers have finally appeared. It all goes back to Henry Liddell and Robert Scott, like

---

[7] Henry George Liddell and Robert Scott, *A Greek-English Lexicon: Based on the German Work of Francis Passow* (New York: Harper and Brothers, 1843, 1848, 1852).

[8] Henry George Liddell, Robert Scott, Henry Stuart Jones, and Roderick McKenzie, *A Greek-English Lexicon*, 9th ed., 2 vols. (Oxford: Clarendon Press, 1940).

you said. These two were Oxford graduates and later college heads but also longtime friends. Having studied Classics, a local bookseller and publisher called David Talboys commissioned the lexicon from Liddell and Scott in 1836. From the outset, it was actually meant to be a translation based upon the fourth edition (1831) of a well-known Greek-German lexicon by Franz Passow, who had died just three years earlier.[9] And this is where we come back to Schneider in a roundabout way. Because the first edition of Passow's lexicon was called *Johann Gottlob Schneider's Handwörterbuch der griechischen Sprache* (1819–24).[10]

As the title indicates, Passow's project was based on the final edition of Schneider's own *Handwörterbuch* (1819). (Schneider was still alive at that point and on board with the endeavor.) By the time that Passow's fourth edition appeared in 1831, however, Schneider's name had surreptitiously fallen out of the title. Which is actually pretty ironic, because while the first three editions of Liddell and Scott's lexicon (1843, 1848, 1852) bore Passow's name prominently in the title – *A Greek-English Lexicon based on the German work of Francis Passow* – it was gone in the fourth edition, just like Passow had done with Schneider.[11]

The new lexicon had a number of motivations and aspirations. One of the former was certainly to adopt the methodological improvements that Passow had made upon Schneider into English-speaking scholarship of ancient Greek. Perhaps the most important of these was Passow's insistence on organizing entries to provide a *Lebensgeschichte*, or "life history," of each headword. Liddell and Scott were keen to adopt this principle, adding a diachronic aspect to their lexicon. But they weren't the only ones. Passow's method was also to influence the work of the English-speaking lexicographer *par excellence* Sir James Murray, who was appointed editor of the *OED* around the time that Liddell and Scott were at work on their supposedly final seventh edition.

This influence was by no means unintentional or indirect. As John Considine (2019) has so ably shown, Passow's historical principles were well known among the members of the Philological Society who in the 1850s first began to dream of what would later become the *OED*. By then, Liddel and Scott's Greek lexicon was well respected in such circles as a lexicographical model precisely because of its adoption of Passow's method. Some of the most influential figures in the planning stages of the *OED*, such as Richard Chenevix Trench and Herbert Coleridge, had studied and even published on ancient Greek themselves. Later, when Murray became lead editor, he consulted directly with Henry Liddell, among others, on draft entries and matters both theoretical and practical.

Aside from their motivation to produce a historical dictionary of ancient Greek, Liddell and Scott also aspired for their project to solidify the role of English as a

---

[9] Franz Passow, *Johann Gottlob Schneiders Handwörterbuch der griechischen Sprache* (Leipzig: Friedrich Christian Wilhelm Vogel, 1831).
[10] Franz Passow, *Johann Gottlob Schneiders Handwörterbuch der griechischen Sprache* (Leipzig: Friedrich Christian Wilhelm Vogel, 1819–24).
[11] Henry George Liddell and Robert Scott, *A Greek-English Lexicon*, 4th ed. (Oxford: Oxford University Press, 1855).

language within classical scholarship as a discipline that historically had been undertaken only in Latin. In the 1830s, only three, smaller Greek lexicons existed in English, aimed mostly at students. But Liddell and Scott wanted to serve scholars. They acknowledge in their preface to the first edition that some may regard their decision as "an unworthy condescension to the indolence of the age," and yet they maintain that English is capable of conveying the "richness, boldness, and freedom" of Greek words. Aside from these aesthetic judgments that likely helped ward off accusations of populism, Liddell and Scott had a nationalist angle as well: "A Frenchman may have reason for using a Greek-Latin lexicon," they remark. "An Englishman can have none."

IS: Liddell and Scott's lexicon has been through a lot of editions.

WR: The duo worked constantly on improving it for four decades, up until the seventh edition in 1882, which was supposed to be final and definitive. Even so, after Scott passed away in 1887, Liddell went on to produce an eighth edition in 1897 before he died the following year, just a few weeks before his eighty-seventh birthday.[12] In time, after some abridged and intermediate editions had been spun off, Henry Stuart Jones and Roderick McKenzie were recruited to update the eighth edition, improving etymologies and adding information from recently discovered papyri and inscriptions. Their new edition began appearing in a series of fascicles in 1925 and was eventually printed in two volumes in 1940,[13] which is still the standard edition that people mean when they say "*Liddell and Scott*" or "*LSJ*." (Although personally, I prefer to remember McKenzie as well and use "*LSJM*.") Worth noting too are the two supplements that have appeared since 1940. A reviewer of the first, which appeared in 1968,[14] offered this refrain:

> Says Scott to Liddell . . .
> "Editions reach nine
> And I want to resign;
> I'm just skin and bones,
> Though we did bring in Jones."[15]

The second supplement was published in 1996 under the editorship of Peter Glare, with involvement from a number of assistants, associate editors, and scholars, including John Chadwick and Anne Thompson of Cambridge.[16] In fact, Anne is a friend of mine from my years as a doctoral student working on Septuagint lexicography in the Faculty of Divinity.

---

[12] Henry George Liddell and Robert Scott, *A Greek-English Lexicon*, 8th ed. (New York: American Book Company, 1897).
[13] Liddell et al., *Greek-English Lexicon*, 9th ed.
[14] Henry George Liddell, Robert Scott, Henry Stuart Jones, and Roderick McKenzie, *A Greek-English Lexicon*, 8th ed., 2 vols. (Oxford: Clarendon Press, 1968).
[15] Gordon M. Messing, "Review of Greek-English Lexicon: A Supplement. H. G. Liddell, Robert Scott, H. Stuart Jones, E. A. Barber," *Classical Philology* 64 (1969): 238–39.
[16] Henry George Liddell, Robert Scott, Henry Stuart Jones, and Roderick McKenzie, *A Greek-English Lexicon*, 9th ed. (Oxford: Clarendon Press, 1996).

IS: The *Cambridge Greek Lexicon* used *Liddell and Scott* as its source but then revised it thoroughly.[17]

WR: Well, yes and no. The Cambridge *Lexicon* was originally the vision of John Chadwick, who was a remarkable figure. Aside from helping to crack the Axis powers' military code in World War II and his role in the decipherment of the ancient Minoan Linear B script in the 1950s, Chadwick had also worked on a variety of projects prior to moving to Cambridge. As I mentioned too, he had worked with Peter Glare on the supplement to *Liddell and Scott* but also on the *Oxford Latin Dictionary*.[18] Sometime around 1990, Chadwick dreamed up the idea to revise Liddell and Scott's *Intermediate Lexicon*, which had appeared in 1889 and remained in print, unchanged, a century later.[19] In 1997 he pitched it to the Faculty Board of Classics at Cambridge and was soon joined by his former student and collaborator Anne Thompson. The following year, Chadwick died of a heart attack on his way to a meeting in London.

In time, the *Lexicon* project passed into the hands of James Diggle, who took things in a new direction with a team of fellow editors. It had become clear that the *Intermediate Lexicon* presented too many problems to serve as a base text; more than revision was necessary. So much more, in fact, that it took twenty years to finish the task. Nor is that much of a surprise, considering that the editorial staff of the *Lexicon* undertook a completely fresh analysis of Greek sources. In other words, unlike all the other lexicons we've discussed so far, this project didn't rely on an older lexicon as its starting point. And so the long chain of dependence stretching from Liddell and Scott all the way back to Henri Estienne was broken.

One of the most noteworthy features that distinguishes the Cambridge *Lexicon* from *LSJM*, for example, is the organization of entries according to meaning, rather than chronology, to show the development of word senses and their relationships. But in another ironic twist, although the Cambridge *Lexicon* project broke completely from its initial kinship with Liddell and Scott's *Intermediate Lexicon*, in the end both went to press without any citations as evidentiary support in word entries but included only authors' names and works. Still, the Cambridge *Lexicon* is anything but lightweight, running to two volumes with 37,000 headwords. As a final note of interest, this lexicon is also one of the first to handle obscenities without euphemism. Let's just say that words like κοπρών and ῥαφανιδόω, for which Liddell and Scott offer "a place for dung, privy, necessary" and "thrust a radish up the fundament," respectively, are not so elliptically described in the Cambridge *Lexicon*.

IS: How about the ongoing *Greek-Spanish Dictionary* project?

WR: If you can believe it, this dictionary is even grander in scope and intent than the twenty-plus-year Cambridge *Lexicon* project. In fact, this project – also known as the *Diccionario griego-español* or *DGE* – is older than I am! It has been based at the Consejo Superior de Investigaciones Científicas in Madrid since its inception in

---

[17] James Diggle, *The Cambridge Greek Lexicon* (Cambridge: Cambridge University Press, 2021).

[18] Peter Geoffrey William Glare and Christopher Stray, *Oxford Latin Dictionary* (Oxford: Oxford University Press, 1973).

[19] Henry George Liddell and Robert Scott, *An Intermediate Greek-English Lexicon* (Oxford: Oxford University Press, 1889).

1980, at which point preparation had already been underway for several years. It's slated to be something like three times as long as *LSJM* when it's finished; an *OED* for ancient Greek. To date, there are seven fascicles in publication, at a total of 1,640 pages. That's a lot, right? Well, progress has only reached partway through *epsilon*, the fifth of twenty-four letters in the Greek alphabet!

Similar to the Cambridge *Lexicon*, at the beginning this Spanish project had humbler aims. The plan was to carry on the tradition of revising the best existing lexicons to provide an updated resource for university students. But ambitions grew quickly, as *LSJM* and other existing lexicons lacked data that the Spaniards wanted to include; things like Mycenaean Greek, the Patristic corpus, personal and place-names, as well as new critical editions and data from the morass of literary and documentary texts discovered at the turn of the century. On top of that, the editors rightly wanted their work to be informed by developments in general linguistics. In sum, the *DGE* aims to be utterly exhaustive in scope, beginning with the earliest known phases of the language through the end of antiquity around 600 CE, covering Greek sources of every register, from lofty literary styles, to religious texts both canonical and obscure, to lowly receipts and letters preserved in ancient trash heaps thanks only to the arid Mediterranean climate.

IS: I just love the historical scope you're presenting: from the modest to the ambitious, almost Quixotic. In most linguistic traditions where the language (Italian, English, French, Spanish) is used on a daily basis, online lexicons have become ubiquitous, though not yet absolutely erasing the print varieties. Where are we with ancient Greek?

WR: Yes, that is an important question. The frank answer is: we are still functionally analogue. There are online lexicons. But almost none of them are supported by dynamic digital databases that are improved and expanded over time by a team of lexicographers. Instead, most of them are just digitized but static versions of print resources. To my mind, the main reason for this state of affairs is simply market pressure. As slender a margin as there is for publishers producing dictionaries of modern languages, things get even more financially risky for ancient languages. The demand comes from a passionate but problematically small group of prospective customers.

Over the past twenty years or so, one semi-solution to this situation has been to make dictionaries available through bible software. These are programs that integrate biblical texts, dictionaries, commentaries, monographs, and so on into a seamless, intuitive, and highly leveraged research experience (or so they claim). So it has become fairly standard for publishers with Greek (or Hebrew) dictionaries on their book list to license a work to the bible software companies, so that users can purchase single volumes or resources bundles. But this process is not very consistent or efficient. Sometimes publications only make the jump from print to digital years after publication, often intentionally so on the part of the publishers.

Of course, the software companies are equally concerned to maximize profit, so one approach they take is to create pledge web pages for customers to register their support for a digital version of a publication before it's even available, sort of like a Kickstarter campaign. But once a Greek dictionary is available digitally, the price is rarely much lower than a physical copy. The benefit of buying it, I suppose, is time saved by not having to flip through pages looking for a word entry.

But these digital lexicons are, like I said, only a semi-solution, since they are tied to the proprietary software platforms themselves, which are not immune from going defunct; some already have. Nor are these digitized versions of dictionaries actually updated with new information. They are essentially just e-book versions that have been souped up with some handy hyperlinks. Of course, none of this is much help to Classicists or others who aren't engaged in biblical scholarship and don't want to put money into specialist software not otherwise relevant to their research.

When it comes to digital Greek lexicons, two anecdotes come to mind. The first is about *The Brill Dictionary of Ancient Greek* (2015), an English translation of the third edition of Franco Montanari's *Vocabolario della lingua greca* (2013).[20] Its appearance was hailed as an invaluable development in Greek lexicography, with over 140,000 headwords ranging from the archaic to Byzantine periods. Now, some have had their doubts about how significant the *Brill Dictionary* really is given its chain of dependence on older resources, stretching back through the first edition of *Liddell and Scott* (1843) and behind that Passow and ultimately Schneider's *Kritisches griechisch-deutsches Handwörterbuch*! Even so, as far as I am aware, the *Brill Dictionary* is the only lexicon of ancient Greek that is not only available online but is also maintained, corrected, and even updated with new information on an ongoing basis. Finally!

Here's the rub, though: the price for access to the online version of the *Brill Dictionary* is completely prohibitive for anyone who isn't independently wealthy or part of a robustly financed academic department paying for the institutional subscription. So here we have a cutting-edge digital dictionary of ancient Greek that is operating like many online versions of modern language dictionaries but sealed behind walls that would make biblical Jericho envious.

The second anecdote relates to the *Cambridge Greek Lexicon*. As I mentioned before, that massive project is distinguished by the fresh appraisal of Greek sources undertaken by a team of lexicographers over decades. It's a massive achievement. And yet, despite having trolled through countless thousands of Greek texts, the final decision was to print the lexicon *without* even a single citation. Entries will include, for instance, "Hdt." for Herodotus or "Pi." for Pindar after a given sense to note that those authors use the word that way but without references to where in those authors the usage occurs.

Now, I recognize that economic constraints must have influenced the decision to omit references like this. But it is sour grapes for scholars and researchers. And what is especially torturous is knowing that a mountainous database containing every single reference – and other useful information besides – exists somewhere out there, inaccessible to scholars who would be eager to consult, improve, and expand upon it. It's a real pity. But such is the state of affairs for ancient Greek dictionaries.

---

[20] Franco Montanari, *The Brill Dictionary of Ancient Greek* (Leiden: Brill, 2015); Franco Montanari, *Vocabulario della lingua greca* (Turin: Loescher Editore, 2013).

IS: Lest I sound too dour on this topic, I should note that there are two important digital lexicons available online. One is the digital version of LSJM, which, although it isn't being updated, is freely available to anyone.[21] The second is the online version of the *DGE*, which is in fact kept updated, albeit only at the iceberg pace that new volumes appear.[22]

IS: I want to change gears. Tell me about your own journey as a scholar and about your love of dictionaries.

WR: What a pleasantly personal question. Thank you for asking it. Like many others, I'm sure, my journey into scholarship was perhaps less like following a sequence of clearly marked intersections and road signs, and more like navigating the set of staircases in M. C. Escher's drawing *Relativity*. When I was young, I certainly never thought I would go into academics. But looking back, I can see that I was always somewhat interested in language. Part of that, I think, was because my parents (though thoroughly monolingual themselves) hosted numerous international students in our home throughout my childhood, often for many months at a time, and the linguistic learning experience of these mysterious non-English speakers piqued my interest.

In addition to that, although he spent almost his entire career as a jeweller, my father had briefly taught English at a local school before I was born. It was a long-enough period for my mother to purchase the two-volume set of the *OED* as a gift for him. For many years, that monumental set of tomes sat regally upon a desk upstairs where my brother and I did our schoolwork. I recall many occasions on which I would laboriously extract a volume of the *OED*, open the little drawer at the top of the display case, and retrieve the magnifying glass to stare ponderously at the pages.

I'm sure I had no real reason to consult the *OED* in those years except perhaps to avoid doing my assignments. But something about its musty smell, its miniscule print, and the fact that it was my father's gave it an inexplicable allure for a young man who otherwise had no scholarly aspirations. Just before I went off to college, the *OED* took on a new and intriguingly human dimension after I read Simon Winchester's then newly published *The Meaning of Everything* (2004).[23] That was when I first met James Murray and learned something of the life of dictionaries and lexicography.

In time, I completed a Master of Divinity degree, and it was then that I began studying ancient languages in earnest, especially the Hebrew and Greek of the Bible and its related literatures. During those years, I was blissfully dependent on bilingual lexicons to give me quaintly rock-solid assurance as to word meanings. Then I stumbled upon the Septuagint, the ancient Greek translation of the Hebrew scriptures, which quickly became my academic focus. I was particularly drawn to scholarship that was investigating word meaning in the Septuagint corpus using textual evidence from ancient papyri and inscriptions, as a way of understanding the social context of the Jewish translators.

As it turns out, one of the key scholars in this area, John A. L. Lee, who I now consider a friend and mentor, had also written a monograph entitled *A History of*

---

[21] http://stephanus.tlg.uci.edu/lsj [22] http://dge.cchs.csic.es/xdge/
[23] Simon Winchester, *The Meaning of Everything* (Oxford: Oxford University Press, 2004).

New Testament Lexicography (2003).[24] After reading that book, I realized how naïvely I had been using my biblical lexicons, as if they were repositories of indisputable semantic certainty. But actually, not only is there a long, incestuous relationship among most lexicons of Hebrew or Greek (like the *Brill Dictionary* and others noted in this chapter), often their textual basis is questionable and their method is flawed, as Lee's book so painstakingly demonstrates.

When I went on to doctoral study at Cambridge, I made Greek lexicography a primary area of my research. One of the lines of investigation I began was the history of lexicography of the Septuagint, which turned up many of the same results that Lee had found for the New Testament. But perhaps even more clearly in Septuagint lexicography, I saw how the method and cultural assumptions of dictionary makers come to shape their work in significant but often subtle ways. A few years later, I had the chance to begin exploring the ways that sort of shaping has occurred in other sorts of dictionaries when I was invited to write a chapter in the *Cambridge Handbook of the Dictionary*.[25]

Although I was already fascinated by the history of Greek lexicography, this project was what pushed my interests further into the history of biblical philology, almost all of which is connected with dictionaries of some sort or another, especially bible dictionaries and what are known as theological wordbooks. Much like I had unthinkingly regarded lexicons as indices of objective knowledge, so also, I realized, do most users of bible dictionaries and theological wordbooks, whether layperson, pastor, or scholar. Yet these sorts of publications are perhaps even more liable than biblical lexicons to wrap up the ideological biases of their compilers into the package of cultural authority that is "the dictionary."

These days I am still regularly engaged in ancient Greek (and Hebrew) lexicography in various ways. But the history of biblical philology at large strikes me as an area of research that is worthy of much more attention. And yes, my father's copy of the *OED* is still around, now planted firmly in my faculty office, where I still consult it, and where my own children sometimes visit and leaf through its pages like I did thirty years ago.

Suggested Readings

Adrados, F. R., and E. Gangutia. "The Greek-Spanish Dictionary: Its Present State." In Λεξικογραφία της αρχαίας, μεσαιωνικής και νέας ελληνικής γραμματείας: Παρούσα κατάσταση και προοπτικές των σύγχρονων λεξικογραφικών εγχειρημάτων. Πρακτικά Διεθνούς Ημερίδας, edited by J. N. Kazazis, 177–85. Thessaloniki: Centre for the Greek Language, 2003.

Bortone, Pietro. *Language and Nationality: Social Inferences, Cultural Differences, and Linguistic Misconceptions*. London: Bloomsbury, 2021.

---

[24] John A. L. Lee, *A History of New Testament Lexicography*, Studies in Biblical Greek 8 (New York: Peter Land, 2003).

[25] William A. Ross, "Dictionaries in Religious History and Biblical Interpretation," in *The Cambridge Handbook of the Dictionary*, ed. Edward Finegan and Michael Adams (Cambridge: Cambridge University Press, 2024), 361–84.

Chadwick, John. "The Case for Replacing Liddell and Scott." *Bulletin of the Institute of Classical Studies* 39 (1994): 1–11.
— *Lexicographia Graeca: Contributions to the Lexicography of Ancient Greek*. Oxford: Oxford University Press, 1997.
— *Dictionaries in Early Modern Europe: Lexicography and the Making of Heritage*. Cambridge: Cambridge University Press, 2008.
— "*Liddell and Scott* and the *Oxford English Dictionary*." In *Liddell and Scott: The History, Methodology, and Languages of the World's Leading Lexicon of Ancient Greek*, edited by Christopher Stray, Michael Clarke, and Joshua T. Katz, 395–411. Oxford: Oxford University Press, 2019.
Dowling, Linda C. *Language and Decadence in the Victorian Fin de Siecle*. Princeton: Princeton University Press 1987.
Facal, L. Javier. "The New Greek-Spanish Dictionary." *Classical Journal* 76 (1981): 357–63.
Lee, John A. L. *A History of New Testament Lexicography*. Studies in Biblical Greek 8. New York: Peter Lang, 2003.
Messing, Gordon M. "Review of Greek-English Lexicon: A Supplement. H. G. Liddell, Robert Scott, H. Stuart Jones, E. A. Barber," *Classical Philology* 64 (1969): 238–39.
Murray, K. M. Elisabeth. *Caught in the Web of Words: James Murray and the Oxford English Dictionary*. New Haven, CT: Yale University Press, 1977.
Ross, William A. "Dictionaries in Religious History and Biblical Interpretation." In *The Cambridge Handbook of the Dictionary*, edited by Edward Finegan and Michael Adams, 361–84. Cambridge: Cambridge University Press, 2024.
Stray, Christopher, ed. *Classical Dictionaries: Past, Present and Future*. London: Duckworth, 2010.
Stray, Christopher, Michael Clarke, and Joshua T. Katz, eds. *Liddell and Scott: The History, Methodology, and Languages of the World's Leading Lexicon of Ancient Greek*. Oxford: Oxford University Press, 2019.

2 Esperanto

Esther Schor

Esperanto was created in the nineteenth century by the Warsaw-based ophthalmologist L. L. Zamenhof (1859–1917) as a universal second language; he called it *Lingvo Internacia*, the international language, hoping that it would foster global peace and understanding. It isn't the only constructed language (Balaibalan, Solresol, Sona, Interlingua, and Mirda *aka* Unilingua, among others), but it is the most popular; it is also the one with the richest cultural legacy and a complex history of dictionaries. Offering a comparative analysis of the dictionary tradition of Esperanto, this conversation compares that tradition to other languages. Zamenhof is discussed as the seminal figure in that tradition. It looks at translation as a force changing Esperanto that reflects on the tension between particularism and universalism, and questions Esperanto's Eurocentrism. It meditates on how the internet has changed Esperanto lexicography. Finally, it explores canonical lexicons such as the *Baza Radikaro Oficiala*, published under the aegis of the Academy of Esperanto, as well as the *Plena Vortaro de Esperanto*, released by the Sennacieca Asocio Tutmonda, Kazimierz Bein's *Vortaro de Esperanto*, and the *Plena Ilustrita Vortaro*.[1]

***

ILAN STAVANS: How did you get into Esperanto?
ESTHER SCHOR: Since I can remember, I always had a bee in my bonnet about Esperanto, but I never bothered to learn it and never met an Esperantist until I was in my fifties. The bee was still buzzing some years ago when I wrote a book proposal about three quixotic projects; Esperanto was one of them. A well-meaning agent told me to choose one project and rewrite the proposal, and Esperanto seemed to me to be the obvious choice. After reading the revised

---

[1] www.akademio-de-esperanto.org/verkoj/baza_radikaro_oficiala.html; Émile Grosjean-Maupin, *Plena Vortaro de Esperanto* (Paris: Sennacieca Asocio Tutmonda, 1930); Kazimierz Bein, *Vortaro de Esperanto* (Paris: Hachette, 1911); Gaston Waringhien, *Plena Ilustrita Vortaro de Esperanto* (Paris: Sennacieca Asocio Tutmonda, 1970).

IS:	proposal, the agent said, "I think you chose the wrong one." I decided I'd chosen the wrong agent and set out to write about the Esperanto language movement, its creator, and its community. And by the way, I no longer consider it quixotic, by any means. Esperanto, in its 135th year, with a worldwide following, is a success, not a failure.
IS:	I'm tickled. What were the other two quixotic projects?
ES:	In 1986 T. Y. Lin, the father of prestressed concrete, planned to build an "Intercontinental Peace Bridge" between the US and the USSR; to be honest, I couldn't quite manage the deep dive into prestressed concrete. The third quixotic project was the effort to capture the life of Napoleon on film, all attempts at which – until Ridley Scott's 2023 film – either failed or were severely truncated. Napoleon was not unfilmable, but he was hard to afford and hard to get right.
IS:	Were your ancestors Yiddish-speaking immigrants? Although in very different ways, Yiddish is also a universalist language.
ES:	Two of my grandparents (I hardly think of them as ancestors) were Yiddish-speaking immigrants from Poland; another was born in Palestine, from a family who had been there since the 1850s; the fourth was American-born. She was a sculptor who had lived in Europe; her English had more French phrases (*Ooh-la-la*!) than Yiddish ones.

There were certainly universalists – Socialists, Bundists, Communists – who spoke Yiddish, but like most Jewish languages, it's a very particular mix: its lexicon comprises mostly German, Slavic, and Hebrew words, written in Hebrew script. Its detractors called it a "jargon," a "mongrel" language. Ludovik Lazarus Zamenhof himself was from a Russian-speaking family, but he was comfortable speaking, reading, and writing Yiddish.

IS:	I used the term "universalist" first in this conversation, but let me ask you to explain it. What is a "universalist" language? Don't all human languages aspire to universality, however that concept is defined? What would be the opposite of a "universalist" language: a "particularist" one?
ES:	I know why you're asking, Ilan. Esperanto is known as the "universal language," but you raise an important question: Was Esperanto designed by a universalist? And was it designed for universalists? The first question would be yes, if by "universalist" we mean a vision of humanity that exceeds – but does not supersede – national, ethnic, or religious identity. The second question would be no, not by any means.

It was designed for moderns, for people who were eager to participate in transnational networks of transit, communication, and knowledge, whatever their views about humanity and identity. And it was designed in Europe, in a milieu where people of multiple ethnicities lived and died in the same cramped space. By the way, the inventor of Esperanto did not call his language "universal"; he didn't even call it "Esperanto." In the introductory pamphlet of 1887, he called it the "International Language" or simply "International," and published it under the name "Doktoro Esperanto," meaning "the hopeful one."[2] Within a year or so, it became known as "Esperanto," and the name stuck.

---

[2] Ludovik Lazarus Zamenhof, *Doctor Esperanto's International Language*, trans. R. H. Geohegan (1889); ed. Gene Keys (2000); online version (2006), www.genekeyes.com/Dr_Esperanto.html

IS: As you describe it in your book *Bridge of Words*, Esperanto is the product of the age of nationalism.[3] This constructed language, which came about in the second half of the nineteenth century, was created by Zamenhof, aka Doktoro Esperanto. Zamenhof's dream was to unite humankind. Esperanto was meant to be a universal tongue whose mission wasn't to replace, or even to eclipse, other languages; it wanted to become everyone's default second language.

You state that "with the tools of modernity – reason, efficiency, pragmatism – he handed down the plank till it was smooth; people would cross over without getting splinters from irregular verbs and knotty idioms. Unlike most language inventors, Zamenhof then renounced the privileges of a creator, without reneging on a creator's duties to his progeny. He is the only language inventor on record ever to cede his language to its users, inviting them to take the rudimentary list of roots, combine them with a handful of affixes, and invent words for new things, new occasions."[4]

My interest, as you know, is in lexicons. Did Zamenhof, shortly after coming up with Esperanto, conceive of one or more dictionaries that would safekeep the words he and his progeny concocted? That is, what role did dictionaries play in the making of Esperanto?

ES: Dictionaries, lexicons, glossaries, word lists have all been crucial to the history of Esperanto. Here's why. Before giving his language to its users, Zamenhof had a problem to solve. To survive and grow, Esperanto would have to have a flexible and expansive lexicon, one that could be adapted to new ideas, new technologies, and new groups of speakers. But what would stabilize the language while the lexicon was growing and changing? Zamenhof's solution was to balance an open, limitless lexicon with a closed set of rules – both rules of grammar and rules about how to form new words.

That's why Esperanto has a towering, dynamic lexicon and a modest, Cape Cod–style set of rules. Zamenhof launched the language in 1887 with a lexicon of some 920 roots – roots, meaning *potential* words; when roots are combined with prefixes, suffixes, other roots, and vowel endings, they blossom into words.[5] Esperanto was a language, yes; but it was also a language-making machine, primed for the creation of new words for new occasions.

IS: A language-making machine. I'm thinking of John Wilkins' proposal for a universal language and his "Essay Toward a Real Character and a Philosophical Language" (1668).[6] He also created "things and notions," which he saw as building blocks that can be endlessly combined. But I'm focusing on dictionaries. What were the sources of Zamenhof's lexicon?

ES: Zamenhof, born in Bialystok in 1859, was a practicing ophthalmologist, not a trained linguist. With a pile of dictionaries, a firm grasp of five or six languages, and an acquaintance with several others, he mined the lexicons of Europe to make his list of roots and affixes; for prepositions, he pilfered Greek and Latin.

---

[3] Esther Schor, *Bridge of Words: Esperanto and the Dream of a Universal Language* (New York: Metropolitan Books, 2016).
[4] Schor, *Bridge of Words*, 5. [5] Zamenhof, *Doctor Esperanto's International Language*.
[6] John Wilkins, "Essay Toward a Real Character and a Philosophical Language" (London: Gellibrand and Martyn, 1668).

His original lexicon has a ratio of four Romance-based roots to one Germanic-based root, with a sprinkling of Slavic elements thrown in.

I have a hunch about why he favored Romance roots. Before inventing Esperanto, Zamenhof had spent three years writing a grammar of Yiddish, which he left unfinished. The Yiddish lexicon has a ratio of four Germanic-based words to one Romance-based word, with about 10 percent of the lexicon derived from Slavic languages. Building the Esperanto lexicon, Zamenhof *reversed* the ratio in the Yiddish lexicon of Germanic to Romance words. The idea was not only to set Esperanto apart from the disparaged "jargon" of Yiddish but also to set his sights on France, rather than Germany, as the best hope for building a community of Esperantists. That said, in 1901 he also tried calling together a group of followers from the forward-thinking Jews of Russia; the attempt failed, and he focused his energies elsewhere.

IS: Dictionaries grow in complex ways. Some like Samuel Johnson's *A Dictionary of the English Language* start as a sheer proposal endorsed by subscribers, a publisher, an academic institution, or another supporter.[7] Others remain quixotic dreams for extended periods of time, for instance Eliezer ben Yehuda's Hebrew dictionary.[8] How did Zamenhof's lexicon grow?

ES: Within five years of Esperanto's launch, thirty-seven pamphlets in seventeen languages appeared, most of them containing translations of Zamenhof's 1887 lexicon. Zamenhof himself created the first multilingual "International Dictionary" of Esperanto in 1894 and revised it in 1905 for the first meeting of the Universal Esperanto Association.[9] By 1905, the original lexicon of 920 roots had grown to about 2,500. Every Esperanto root was now translated into French, English, German, Russian, and Polish.

A quick comparison of the 1887 lexicon with that of 1905 shows how the language spread its wings. The 1887 lexicon includes roots for eagle, horse, bear, and fish, but only in 1905 can we find a tiger, monkey, and giraffe. 1887 offers bread, cheese, apples, and cherries, but only in 1905 can we select grapes and apricots; not until the 1930s could Esperantists sample a banana or a pineapple – at least from the dictionary. 1887 invites us to pray, to remember, and to shed tears – in fact, there are two distinct roots for "weeping"; 1905, at the dawn of a violent century, beckons us to shoot a pistol, thrust a bayonet – or invite another Esperantist to waltz.

Of course, many additions to the dictionary were prompted by new technologies, and early dictionaries sometimes give a few options. In the 1930s, an airplane could be an *aviadilo*, an instrument for flight; an *aerŝipo*, or airship; a *flugmaŝino*, or flight machine; or even an *aeroplano*; and despite the world-domination of English, *aviadilo* prevailed. Despite – or perhaps because of – since there has always been a high value placed on forming new words

---

[7] Samuel Johnson, *A Dictionary of the English Language* (London: W. Strahan, 1755).
[8] Eliezer ben Yehuda, *The Ben-Yehuda Dictionary*, 17 vols. (1908–58), https://archive.org/details/a-complete-dictionary-of-ancient-and-modern-hebrew-eliezer-ben-yehuda-copy2-images.
[9] L. L. Zamenhof, *Esperanto: Universala Vortaro de la Lingvo Internacia* (Warsaw: Gins, 1894); L. L. Zamenhof, *Fundamento de Esperanto: Gramatiko, Ezercaro, Universala Vortaro* (Paris: Hachette, 1905).

Esperantically, that is, from Esperanto roots and affixes, rather than simply importing a word from another language, however powerful or "international." This is why an airport is still, rather quaintly, called a *flughaveno*, meaning a harbor for flights. It's thoroughly Esperantic. So is the word for computer: whereas Italian borrowed the English word computer wholesale – "il computer" – Esperanto turned it into a *komputilo*, an instrument for computing. And because -*ero* is an affix meaning "a small bit of something," the word *komputero* – a small bit of computation? – would have been a dubious choice.

IS: We are talking of dictionaries of roots, not words.

ES: Yes, roots. This was Zamenhof's strategy for achieving maximal flexibility and growth. Esperanto is an agglutinative language – meaning a language that glues parts of words (morphemes) together to make new words. For example:

>The root "manĝ-" (eat) + the affix "-ejo" (a place for) = manĝejo, a dining hall.
>The root "manĝ-" + the affix "-aĵo" (a thing) = manĝaĵo, food.
>The root "manĝ-"+ the affix "-aĉo" (bad) = manĝaĉo, lousy food.

Roots of course, can also be combined with other roots:

>The root "manĝ-" + the root "maten-" (morning) = matenmanĝo, breakfast.
>The root "manĝ-" + the root "tag-" (day) = tagmanĝo, lunch.
>The root "manĝ-" + the root "vesper-" (evening) = vespermanĝo, dinner.

And Esperanto's superpower is its capacity to turn a single root into multiple parts of speech – and multiple words – simply using a vowel ending.

>The root "nokt-" + the vowel -a = the adjective night (as in a "night light")
>The root "nokt-" + the vowel -o = the noun, night
>The root "nokt-" + the vowel -e = the adverb, nightly
>The root "nokt-" + the vowel -i = an infinitive...
>...which, if used with the affix "tra-" (across) = tranokti, to sleep over.

There are also verb endings for present, past, and future; there is no subjunctive. (You don't miss it.)

Zamenhof's original list of affixes has a special status, but many new ones have joined the lexicon; for instance, "ge-" meaning "of both sexes." Your parents are "gepatroj" – literally father-of-both-sexes. Which brings us to the issue of sexist language.

IS: How about social change, for instance racism and sexuality. How do lexicons in Esperanto respond to the times?

ES: Since Esperanto is officially a "neutral" language movement, it has a deliberately vague ideology – Zamenhof called it simply "the internal idea." For that reason, Esperanto, from the start a progressive movement, has been congenial to various vanguard social movements: communism and anarchism in the 1920s, feminism in the 1960s, gay liberation since Stonewall, anti-nuclear activism, environmentalism since the 1980s, and more recently, gender fluidity and language justice.

Sometimes intentionally, sometimes not, these vanguards changed, expanded, and nuanced the language. For instance, early dictionaries use masculine forms for most professions, requiring the feminine suffix *-ino* to designate a female doctor (*kuracistino*), professor (*professorino*), or tightrope-walker (*funambulino*). Few people use these *-ino* endings anymore; certainly not young Esperantists. It's even been suggested that *-iĉo*, a masculine equivalent of *-ino*, be implemented, but I don't hear it used very often. Most of the words that end in *-ino* these days express relationships: *patrino*, mother; *duonpatrino*, stepmother; *avino*, grandmother. Gays and lesbians have dispensed with the archaic *samseksemulo* – a lover of the same sex; now they simply say *gejoj* and *lesboj*. I've also seen *gegejoj* – meaning "gays of both sexes." And, of course, *gejradaro* means "gaydar."

Lest we forget pronouns, Esperantists were experimenting with the gender-neutral *ri* in the early 1970s, giving everyone a choice of *li* (he) and *ŝi* (she), and *ri*. It took a while, but finally we know how to say *ri* in English: they.

IS: Proof that quixotic endeavors are ahead of their time. Don Quixote himself, in Cervantes' novel, is quite uncomfortable with seventeenth-century Spain.

ES: Many Esperantists have issued their own specialized lexicons. These grassroots dictionaries expanded the language in such fields as physics, zoology, architecture, rhetoric, poetics, heraldry, and auto mechanics, among many others. A marvelous website curated by Sonja Lang – alas, it's no longer active – generated lists of ten random words at a time, many dealing with sexuality and sexual practices. (Lang is also the inventor of the feminist language Toki Pona.)

As in most languages, Esperanto dictionaries follow users, not vice versa; that said, there's a strong expectation that dictionaries have a pedagogical and normative role to play, since Esperanto is usually not a speaker's native language.

IS: Translation, in any language, is a way to bring the outside world in. But in doing so it changes the internal landscape of the language. I'm interested in how translation has changed Esperanto and vice versa.

ES: From the start, Zamenhof imagined Esperanto as a literary language.

First, it would be a language for original literary works. In fact, in 1887 Zamenhof wrote two original poems for the inaugural pamphlet – they're not bad, considering that they were the only two poems in the language. But Zamenhof also thought that Esperanto – the language itself – would inspire writers to test its expressive capacities and expand them. He was right; now in its second century, Esperanto has given rise to an entire library of original works – mainly poetry, but also novels, stories, and essays. Since it's hard to mount a theatrical production in Esperanto, there are relatively few plays, though the annual Universal Congress often features an original one-act.

Second, Zamenhof offered Esperanto as a bridge language for the translation of literary works – classic and contemporary – from all national traditions. The idea was for speakers of Bengali to be able to read the great works of, say, Albanian literature, and vice versa. Zamenhof himself translated the Hebrew Bible, as well as Shakespeare's *Hamlet*, Schiller, Hans Christian Andersen, and others. Homer, Dante, Austen – more recently, J. K. Rowling – can all be found in Esperanto translation. In fact, I know of five Esperanto translations of Lewis Carroll's "Jabberwocky," each virtuosic in its own way.

IS: That's because translation is a revitalizer of language. Returning briefly to Yiddish, aside from its astonishing literary production, which exploded beyond its confines, real and imaginary, in the eighteenth century, countless Yiddish translations were done at the time: Robinson Crusoe, Spinoza, Dickens, etc. Conversely, Judeo-Spanish, also known as Ladino, produced very few translations of world literature. *Many* more translations into Esperanto have been published than from Esperanto.

ES: True. That's partly because Esperanto was intended to be a medium for sharing the world's literary treasures, as well as ordinary conversation. It's the inverse of the wild imbalance between works translated *from* English and works translated *into* English; a popular estimate of the number of translated books published in English annually is 3 percent. Anyway, works translated into Esperanto don't just end up in a library; they end up in the minds of readers who will go on to think and talk about them in their native language. Some works have been translated into Esperanto multiple times, for the sheer joy of translation. For example, Esperanto cut its teeth on Zamenhof's own translation of *Hamlet* back in 1894, and it's been retranslated several times since.

Since you mentioned it, there are a few translations – mostly in English, but also in Russian, Spanish, and Portuguese – of works written in Esperanto by William Auld, István Nemere, Tibor Sekelj, Tivadar Soros (father of George Soros), and Anna Lowenstein, among others. For Anglophones, I'll give a shout-out to Humphrey Tonkin's fine translations of Tivadar Soros' memoirs *Crusoes in Siberia* and *Masquerade*, and to Sebastian Schulman's recent translation of Spokmenka Štimec's arresting novel/memoir, *Croatian War Nocturnal*.[10]

IS: Poetry too pushes a language in unforeseen directions, in part because poets use words in ways that emphasize their historical, semantic, metaphorical, and musical dimensions. How has poetry pushed Esperanto?

ES: You can say anything you want in Esperanto. But to make the language fly, sing, or flow, poets have taken liberties with the lexicon. That's not simply poetic license: the very feature of Esperanto that makes it generative – affixive agglutination – is a liability for poets writing in metric forms. The chief culprit is the very common prefix *mal-* which means "the opposite of." *Mola* means "soft" and *malmola* means "hard"; *sana* means "healthy" and *malsana* means "sick." But slap a few affixes together – which is precisely how you build words Esperantically - and you have words that are hard to scan at best and clunky at worst. Take *malsanulejo* – a great Esperanto word meaning "hospital" (literally, a place for unhealthy people) but far more unwieldy than *hospitalo*. Likewise, *vinbero* (literally, a wine-berry), can be bypassed by using *uvo*, from the Italian word for grape.

For connoisseurs of poetry, the conventional wisdom is that poets have to earn their neologisms, but on that question, readers will differ. Unfortunately, some Esperantists conflate poetic neologisms with the lazy borrowing of non-

---

[10] Tivadar Soros, *Crusoes in Siberia and The Fairest Judgment*, trans. Humphrey Tonkin (New York: Mondial, 2010); Tivadar Soros, *Masquerade: Dancing around Death in Nazi-Occupied Hungary*, trans. Humphrey Tonkin (New York: Arcade Publishing, 2001); Spokmenka Štimec, *Croatian War Nocturnal*, trans. Sebastian Schulman (Los Angeles: Phoneme Media, 2017).

Esperanto words. In fact, there's a website intended to rescue the language from borrowed words; beside the most common borrowings, there's a preferred, Esperantic alternative.

If this seems a bit joyless, let me assure you Esperantists like nothing more than playing with language: sometimes this is the magic of turning words into unaccustomed parts of speech, sometimes it's coining a new word. A young woman I know coined the word *jutubumi*, which means "wasting time on YouTube."

IS: You've talked about neologisms in Esperanto. The whole language, of course, could be described as made *only* of neologisms, at least in its inception. Writers are machines of neologism. Shakespeare is said to have invented around 1,700 new words, including bedroom, critic, gossip, worthless, and zany. But neologisms, in a natural (vis-à-vis a constructed) language are made by the young, by immigrants, by advertising folks, people in the tech business, science, and so on. Expand on the topic of neologisms in Esperanto.

ES: I'm thinking of those dire public service announcements from the 1960s: *Every eight minutes, someone in America dies of heart disease*. Well, every few minutes someone in Esperantujo (the world-community of Esperantists) invents a new word. Or perhaps *tries out* is more accurate; unless a word appears online in a blog or tweet, it may well disappear. That said, Esperantists were quick to coin terms for social media; Facebook is *Vizaĝlibro*, the platform formerly known as Twitter is *Tvitero*, Tinder is *Tindro*. And the slang words for gender and sexuality – *gejradaro* for gaydar – are legion. There are, of course, Esperanto words that refer to Esperantic culture, which mainly means the culture of Esperanto gatherings, whether in real life or online. *Gufujo* (an owlery) is a word for a lounge open for late-night conversation; and I've heard *kongresedzo* (congress-spouse) used to mean "the person you customarily sleep with at an Esperanto Congress." And the Potterism *mugloj* (muggles) is bandied around a lot, meaning "non-Esperantists." "*Ĝis, mugloj!*" ("So long, muggles!") is what you put on Facebook when you leave for an Esperanto congress.

IS: It is natural, I suppose, that Esperanto is a Eurocentrist language, as you put it. To what extent has this geographic worldview both stimulated and hindered its growth?

ES: Esperanto is undoubtedly Eurocentric, a situation satirized in Cynthia Ozick's short story "What Happened to the Baby?" (2006).[11] Ironically, Eurocentrism is precisely the reason that Esperanto found a following in China, as well as Japan and Korea. The rise of Esperanto in the first decades of the twentieth century dovetailed with efforts to modernize Chinese culture; proponents of Esperanto, some of whom had studied in Europe, argued that Esperanto, much more easily learned than French, English, or German, would be a very efficient way to connect China with Europe and modernize it.

The history of Esperanto in Asia and the non-Western world is too complex to summarize here; suffice it to say that since the 1960s, every third or fourth Esperanto congress has been held in a non-European country, allowing Japanese, Koreans, Brazilians, Nepalese, Vietnamese, and North American Esperantists to

---

[11] Cynthia Ozick, "What Happened to the Baby?," *The Atlantic*, Fiction 2006 issue.

IS:

ES:

IS:

ES:

participate as never before, diversifying a multicultural movement well beyond Zamenhof's original vision. Only a handful of words from Chinese, Japanese, and Korean have entered the Esperanto lexicon; most are names of places, foods, and currency.

In Ozick's story, the central character, the philanderer Uncle Simon, invents a new language, GNU, inspired by the African antelope with two curved horns turned toward each other, as if creating an impossible circle. It is a feminist tale of revenge. As in the case of some of Ozick's other stories, young women are used by older men, in this case a crazy amateur linguist with a true universalist drive. Uncle Simon, unlike Zamenhof, traveled all over the world, from China to Turkey to Africa, and there are references to languages such as Bugi, Brahui, Khowar, Oriya, Mordvinian, Yurak, Shilha, Jagatai, Tipura, Dravidian-Munda, Ilokano, and Veps. These are all real, if lesser-known, languages. Ozick's topic is the invention of new languages by utterly unreliable eccentric characters.

Ozick is not the only recent satirist of Esperanto; there's also David Ives, whose one-act play, *The Universal Language*, begins with the cheery greeting, "Velcro!"[12] But "What Happened to the Baby?" is a work of genius, since it gets the endlessness, obsessiveness, and solipsism of the endeavor to universalize language and marks it as masculine. It's classic Ozick, slipping irony and blasphemy into period costumes. By the way, the "two curved horns, each one turned toward the other, as if striving to close a circle" is a good description of the logo created in 1987 for Esperanto's jubilee.

Talk to me about *Plena Vortaro* (PV) of the 1930s vis-à-vis the *Plena Ilustrita Vortaro* (PIV) of 1970. To what extent are these endeavors defined by the moment in which they were created?

Each dictionary preserves in amber the usage and locutions of its day, as well as the cultural context in which it emerged. In 1911, the *Dictionary of Esperanto*, the first monolingual Esperanto dictionary, was published by Hachette in Paris.[13] Ever since, Francophone lexicographers, editors, and publishers have played an outsized role in the making of dictionaries.

In the 1930s, the Paris-based Sennacieca Asocio Tutmonda (SAT), a loose alliance of leftist groups, played a leading role in the Esperanto world. It was SAT that published the *Complete Dictionary of Esperanto* (known as PV) in Paris in 1930,[14] bringing out eleven more editions into the 1990s. In 1970, SAT also published the massive *Complete Illustrated Dictionary of Esperanto*, known as PIV;[15] the P stands for *plena*, meaning "complete," but Esperantists will tell you it really stands for *peza*, meaning "heavy." The title overstates the salience of images, which are few and far between; some say the "illustrations" are the examples of usage. (PIV, by the way, is fully available online.)[16]

In short, the three milestone dictionaries all emerged from France, Francophones, and the French-based SAT, which is duly proud of this tradition. And not surprisingly, each dictionary has been criticized for gallic and leftist biases. But new dictionaries still have their coming-out parties at SAT

---

[12] David Ives, *All in the Timing: Six One-Act Plays* (New York: Dramatists Play Service, 1994).
[13] Bein, *Vortaro de Esperanto*.   [14] Grosjean-Maupin, *Plena Vortaro de Esperanto*.
[15] Waringhien, *Plena Ilustrita Vortaro de Esperanto*.   [16] https://vortaro.net/

conferences, not at the Universal Congress or at the Academy of Esperanto. Without question, the lexicographical life of Esperanto owes a great debt to SAT, which in a few years will celebrate the centenary of the 1930 PV. It should be quite an event; they have a lot of experience throwing parties for dictionaries.

IS: I know that the PIV is published by the most left-wing branch of the Esperanto movement, based in Paris. What are the ideological wars at the heart of Esperanto? Could we envision a counterpart of PIV released by right-wingers? Is this a contradiction in terms? After all, all languages that are alive depend on the tension between conservatives and liberals, purists and progressives, and so on.

ES: The ideology wars, at least in the Esperanto world, are essentially over. The heyday of ideological conflict was the 1920s and 1930s when two things happened: First, a range of leftist movements in Europe – including communists, socialists, syndicalists, anarchists, and "anationalists" – seized on Esperanto as a lingua franca for the world proletariat. Second, Soviets tried to use Esperanto as a tool by which to Sovietize the European left. If the history of Esperanto has a hero, it has to be a French anarchist named Eugène Adam, who went by the name of Lanti (meaning "the oppositional one"). His stalwart resistance to the Soviets preserved the values of French republicanism within the Esperantist left. Lanti was also the uncle of Eric Blair, who lived with him for a time in Paris and who, as George Orwell, credited his Esperantist uncle with inspiring "Politics and the English Language."

The story of Lanti gets at a point I make in my book: Esperanto, contrary to its reigning mythology, is not politically neutral. No, it is *essentially* political: both a critique of imperialism and a theory of the world-polis, of human solidarity across national and ethnic boundaries. Calling it "neutral" was a move Zamenhof made in 1905 to promote Esperanto among both Dreyfusards and anti-Dreyfusards. To protect and preserve the fledgling language movement, he spoke of the "internal idea" of Esperanto without defining it. And in time, the "internal idea" became a blank screen onto which a good many different ideologies have been projected, including (I regret to say) Stalinism, Nazism, and McCarthyism.

IS: ReVo is an internet dictionary.[17] In my conversations with numerous other lexicographers, we have explored the way online lexicons have redefined the discipline.

ES: Word-play is big in the Esperanto world, and ReVo is a play on words: it's short for *RetaVortaro* (online dictionary), but in Esperanto *revo* means "dream." Some say the Esperantists dreamed up the internet in the early twentieth century, with its burgeoning network of people chatting, learning, teaching, working, and playing together.

IS: The internet is claimed by just anybody with a globalist bent. H. G. Wells in his story "The Crystal Egg" (1897) concocted a metaphor for it, as did Borges in "The Aleph" (1945).[18]

ES: ReVo itself began in 1997 and has always been crowdsourced. It's a bit like Zamenhof's first international dictionary, in that headwords appear not only with Esperanto definitions but also with translations in several languages (and it's not

---

[17] www.reta-vortaro.de/revo/dlg/index-2l.html
[18] H. G. Wells, *Tales of Space and Time* (London: Harper & Brothers, 1900); Jorge Luis Borges, *Collected Fictions*, trans. Andrew Hurley (New York: Viking, 1999), 274–86.

always easy to predict which); all in all, about twenty languages are represented, including Breton, Catalan, Bahasa Indonesia, and Farsi. It's the go-to dictionary for thematic lexicons specializing in geography, zoology, botany, medicine, computer science, music, and cooking, among other topics. It's become an institution, growing steadily; according to its Wikipedia page, twenty years ago it listed 8,473 main articles (headwords) as well as 17,825 derivative forms; in January of 2023, there were almost 50 percent more main articles, and the number of derivatives had risen by 70 percent.

IS: In the ecosystem of standardized languages, internet dictionaries aren't only outpacing printed dictionaries – one example is *Merriam-Webster* online and in physical copies – but actually threaten the existence of printed dictionaries. In the case of Esperanto, given its own fringe status as a world language as well as its universalist ambition, might the online version be seen as an evangelizing tool in its capacity to reach people everywhere at all times?

ES: Esperantists were early adapters of the internet, and getting out-of-print dictionaries onto the web was a priority from the start; going forward, PIV, the most authoritative dictionary, is going to be web-based rather than print-based.

But your question is about "evangelizing." Oddly enough, one doesn't evangelize in Esperanto; the traditional verb is "to recruit" (*varbi*) with its connotations of labor and loyalty. (In academia these days, we delicately speak of "outreach," but those were different times.) Lately the "recruiting" I've seen consists of week-long courses with sections for *komencantoj* (beginners), both in person and web-based; also on short, witty videos by many hands which are sometimes filmed twice – first in English and then in Esperanto. Sometimes they just have subtitles. Low-budget Esperanto video production is so popular that Esperanto video workshops have been offered – and are in demand.

IS: Consciously or otherwise, the issue of authority is central to the health of any language. And dictionaries are tools of authority, although they don't have to be authoritarian in nature. Other such tools are academies, which might function as "the language police." Please reflect on this aspect of Esperanto.

ES: Since its origins, Esperanto has called on the advice of experts to weigh in on linguistic change trends and reform. The original "Language Committee" of Zamenhof's day spawned an "Academy of Esperanto" and in 1948 the two entities became one.

The academy, comprising more than forty members with varied language backgrounds, meets each year at the Universal Congress, where they hold a popular public session at which anyone can submit a question: for example, "How do you say 'cluster bomb' in Esperanto?" Most are questions about new words for new technologies and social practices. I can't imagine another language community in which a public meeting of the academy is spirited, fun, and occasionally boisterous.

The academy periodically issues "Decisions and Recommendations," most famously, intricate guidelines about how to form the names of countries in Esperanto. But the academy's decisions are not binding; a "language police" they're not. In fact, these days even the academy relies on Google to see what forms predominate in everyday usage.

IS: Could we imagine, in the first third of the twenty-first century, another constructed language like Esperanto being created? Or is the age of pacifism through language long gone?

ES: Why would we need one when we have Esperanto, which is cheap to use, easy to learn, and a blast to speak and share. Esperantists like to mull over what their ever-evolving, never-finished language may yet become: some say more Anglicized; some say, Brazilified; some say rife with Sinocisms.

As for the age of pacifism through language, Ilan, it was over before it started.

Suggested Readings

Bein, Kazimierz. *Vortaro de Esperanto*. Paris: Hachette, 1911.
Benson, Peter. *Comprehensive English-Esperanto Dictionary*. El Cerrito, CA: Esperanto League for North America, 1995.
Boulton, Marjorie. *Zamenhof: Creator of Esperanto*. London: Routledge and Kegan Paul, 1960.
Forster, Peter G. *The Esperanto Movement*. The Hague: Mouton, 1982.
Grosjean-Maupin, Émile. *Plena Vortaro de Esperanto*. Paris: Sennacieca Asocio Tutmonda, 1930.
Janton, Pierre. *Esperanto: Language, Literature and Community*. Edited by Humphrey Tonkin. Albany: State University of New York Press, 1993.
Korĵenkov, Aleksander. *Homarano*. Kaunas: Sezono, 2009.
Lapenna, Ivo. *Esperanto en Perspektivo: Faktoj kaj Analizoj pri la Internacia Lingvo*. Rotterdam: Universala Esperanto-Asocio, 1974.
Lins, Ulrich. *Dangerous Language: Esperanto under Hitler and Stalin*. 2 vols. Translated by Humphrey Tonkin. New York: Palgrave, 2020.
Okrent, Arika. *In the Land of Invented Languages: Esperanto Rock Stars, Klingon Poets, Loglan Lovers, and the Mad Dreamers Who Tried to Build a Perfect Language*. New York: Spiegel and Grau, 2009.
Reta Vortaro (ReVo). www.reta-vortaro.de/revo/dlg/index-2l.html. Crowd-sourced.
Richardson, David. *Esperanto: Learning and Using the International Language*. Eastsound, WA: Esperanto League for North America, 1988.
Schor, Esther. *Bridge of Words: Esperanto and the Dream of a Universal Language*. New York: Metropolitan Books, 2016.
Sutton, Geoffrey. *Concise Encyclopedia of the Original Literature of Esperanto*. New York: Mondial, 2008.
Tonkin, Humphrey. *Esperanto, Interlinguistics, and Planned Language*. Lanham, MD: University Press of America, 1997.
Waringhien, Gaston. *Plena Ilustrita Vortaro de Esperanto*. Paris: Sennacieca Asocio Tutmonda, 1970. (Gaston Waringhien and Roland Levereaud eds., Supplement, 1987; Claude Roux and Michel Duc-Goninaz, eds., PIV 2020.)
Wells, John C. *English-Esperanto-English Dictionary*. 2nd ed. New York: Mondial, 2010.
Wennergren, Bertilo. *Kritikaj Notoj pri la Plena Ilustrita Vortaro 2002 kaj 2005*. https://bertilow.com/piv/index.html
Zamenhof, Ludovik Lazarus. *Doctor Esperanto's International Language*. Translated by R. H. Geohegan, 1889; edited by Gene Keys, 2000; online version, 2006. www.genekeyes.com/Dr_Esperanto.html
Zamenhof, L. L. *Esperanto: Universala Vortaro de la Lingvo Internacia*. Warsaw: Gins, 1894.
Zamenhof, L. L. *Fundamento de Esperanto: Gramatiko, Ezercaro, Universala Vortaro*. Paris: Hachette, 1905.

3 German

Volker Harm

Goethe believed that those who don't know foreign languages don't know themselves (*"wer fremde Sprachen nicht kennt, weiss nichts von seiner eigenen"*). Indeed, there is at the core of German civilization an attempt to engage with the world, to appreciate its nuances. Goethe argued in favor not only of world literature but of a German language attuned to globalism. Not surprisingly, one finds his echoes, one way or another, in all dictionaries. The brothers Jacob and Wilhelm Grimm are best known for their ethnographic work with folktales such as "Cinderella," "Hansel and Gretel," "Little Red Riding Hood," "Sleeping Beauty," and "Snow White." Equally influential – even radical – was their work as philologists, producing the *Deutsches Wörterbuch* (*DWB*), which they began in 1838 and began publishing in 1852 in installments.[1] This conversation explores it in the context of German dictionaries, tracing their history from the glossaries of the Middle Ages up to recent online lexicography, thereby featuring monks, schoolmasters, and linguists as their protagonists. In a tour d'horizon, a look is taken at monolingual and bilingual lexicography as well as the abundant landscape of dialect dictionaries. The place of dictionaries in German culture will be discussed and the interlocutors try to find out what might be particular about German lexicographical tradition in a European context.

***

ILAN STAVANS: What were the earliest manifestations of dictionaries in German?
VOLKER HARM: The first dictionaries of German, dating back to the Early Middle Ages, were glossaries, that is collections of Latin words with their Old High German translations. The most famous example is the so-called *Abrogans* dating back to the eighth century.[2] These glossaries were compiled by monks, in the first place in order to ensure a better

---

[1] *Deutsches Wörterbuch von Jacob Grimm und Wilhelm Grimm*, 16 vols. [1–32] (Leipzig: Hirzel, 1854–1971), www.woerterbuchnetz.de/DWB1.
[2] Bernhard Bischoff, *Die „Abrogans"-Handschrift der Stiftsbibliothek St. Gallen: Das älteste deutsche Buch* (St. Gallen: Zollikofer, 1977).

IS: understanding of the Bible (i.e. the Latin *Vulgata*). Thus, bilingual lexicography was at the beginning.

IS: I understand that German dictionaries, in rudimentary fashion, date back to the eighth century. But it wasn't until the Brothers Grimm, Jacob (1785–1863) and Wilhelm (1786–1859), embarked on the *DWB* (1838) that a full-fledged one, in the modern sense, appeared. Plenty happened in between.

VH: A lot of things happened between *Abrogans* and *DWB*, indeed. In the first place, the shape of the language itself dramatically changed. During this time-span (a millennium!), German evolved out of a West Germanic dialect continuum into a full-fledged and standardized European language. The history of German up to the nineteenth century is often described as the history of its successive emancipation from Latin, and the history of German lexicography can be described in such terms as well. Whereas in the Middle Ages and in early modern times, dictionaries *with* German (there were no such things as dictionaries *of* German) were designed and used as a tool for reading the Latin version of the Bible and for learning Latin.

This started to change in the fifteenth century, when Gerd van der Schueren, in his *Teuthonista* (1477), reversed the traditional order of dictionary entries and put the German words in the first place.[3] Many important German-Latin dictionaries of the sixteenth century, though emphasizing the importance of the vernacular in their prefaces, were still based on older Latin-German models. One example is Josua Maaler's *Die Teütsch Spraach* (1561).[4] This work is traditionally considered as the first real dictionary of German; however, it is based on the Latin-German dictionary of Fries (which, by the way, is based on the older Latin-French dictionary of Stephanus).[5]

The first dictionary which finally left behind the century-old tradition of Latin-focused lexicography is Johann Caspar Stieler's *Teutscher Sprachschatz* (1691).[6] Stieler's work is a dictionary of German from scratch. It still includes Latin, but Latin is merely used to explain German words and expressions. The last step in the long process of emancipation from Latin is made by the lexicographers of the eighteenth century, notably Christoph Ernst Steinbach and Johann Christoph Adelung. Here, the senses of German lemmata are explained by German words, meaning that Latin is no longer used.

IS: For readers unused to lexicographic terms, what do you mean by lemmata?

VH: Lemmata is a plural form of the word lemma, which is the headword of a dictionary entry.

IS: What was the reaction to Grimm's approach?

VH: Grimm's *DWB*, which was published from 1852 onwards, returns to the older tradition of illustrating the meaning of German lemmata by Latin words (next to

---

[3] Gherardus de Schueren, *Vocabularius Qui Intitulatur Teuthonistha* (Cologne: Arnoldus ter Hornen, 1477).

[4] Josua Maaler, *Die Teütsch Spraach: Dictionarium Germanicolatinum Novum* (Zürich, 1561; repr. Hildesheim: Olms, 1971).

[5] Johannes Frisius, *Dictionarium Latino-Germanicum* (Zürich, 1556); Robertus Stephanus, *Dictionarium Latinogallicum* (Paris 1552).

[6] Johann Kaspar Stieler, *Der Teutschen Sprache Stammbaum und Fortwachs oder Teutscher Sprachschatz* (Nürnberg: Hofmann, 1691).

German definitions) – Jacob Grimm was heavily criticized for what appeared to his contemporaries as a backward movement to the seventeenth century.

On the long way from *Abrogans* to *DWB*, not only the relation between Latin and German changed. Let me just mention two other things which are characteristic of the history of German lexicography in the long run: Today, we think of dictionaries as alphabetically ordered inventories of words. But this notion is rather a recent one. During the seventeenth century, many monolingual dictionaries listed morphological roots rather than words, and the most important glossaries of the Middle Ages were ordered following encyclopedic rather than linguistic criteria. When the alphabetical arrangement of words finally prevailed over alternative systems in the eighteenth century, it was somehow a return to the beginnings: The Latin lemmata of *Abrogans* were ordered alphabetically as well.

Looking at the history of lexicography in a macro perspective, there is another feature which is natural for us today but which evolved only relatively late: the idea that a dictionary should somehow mirror real language use. This, too, was an idea of the eighteenth and especially of the nineteenth century. Dictionaries before were either focused on Latin and the culture of Roman Antiquity (this was the case, e.g. for Fries and Maaler) or they tried to form an ideal German language equal with and even superior to other ancient and modern languages. This does not mean, of course, that modern dictionaries are always objective mirrors of current language use.

IS: I appreciate the historical overview. I'm also interested in the *rezeptionsgeschichte* of dictionaries. Or more fittingly, I want to explore the connection between dictionaries and their users. In what way, from the early nineteenth century, has the German public changed in connection with dictionaries? Is it possible to estimate a growth in etymological knowledge, for instance? Or in the place of dictionaries in German popular culture?

VH: The *rezeptionsgeschichte* of German dictionaries still needs to be written. So, I can only guess. There seems to be, in the German-speaking countries and certainly beyond, a general tendency to consider dictionaries as necessary evils. This clearly was the case with *Adelung* around 1800: the dictionary was widely used, but it was not loved. In the twentieth century, the attitude (e.g. toward *Duden* and the bilingual *Langenscheidt* dictionaries) remained much the same.[7]

By contrast, the connection of the German-speaking public with Grimm's *DWB* was much more emotional. As a national symbol, *DWB* was admired but hardly used by a broader audience. An event which changed that situation was the publication of an affordable paperback edition in 1984, followed by many reprints.[8] This edition sold well, and the thirty-two *DWB* volumes could now be seen on many bookshelves up and down the country.

While I don't know if this has resulted in a growth of etymological knowledge since the 1980s, the broader availability of *DWB* certainly has created a growing awareness of how rich and fascinating language is. However, the *DWB* has not

---

[7] *Duden – Die Rechtschreibung der deutschen Sprache und der Fremdwörter*, ed. Dudenredaktion (Mannheim: Brockhaus, 1986); https://en.langenscheidt.com/.

[8] *Deutsches Wörterbuch von Jacob Grimm und Wilhelm Grimm*, 16 vols. [1–32] (Leipzig: Hirzel, 1854–1971; Repr. München: dtv 1984).

found its way into popular culture. It is only the *Duden* which is more widely known as *the* dictionary. So, *Duden* has become part of many fixed expressions such as "to make it into the Duden" (*es in den Duden schaffen*) or "to be in the Duden" (*im Duden stehen*), where "Duden" is equated with "dictionary."

IS: Let's move forward. How did Petrus Dasypodius and Johannes Fries engage in comparative lexicography, Latin-German?

VH: The second edition of Petrus Dasypodius' *Dictionarium Latinogermanicum*, a school dictionary published in 1536, was a milestone in the history of German lexicography: The new edition of the dictionary included an additional part with a list of German-Latin equivalents and a new onomasiological index, both in Latin-German and German-Latin.[9]

As far as I know, Dasypodius was not engaged in any kind of comparative philology avant la lettre; as a humanist and schoolmaster, he wanted to provide a good basis for teaching classical Latin in the first place – with success, because his *Dictionarium* was reprinted many times up to the beginning of the eighteenth century. In the German-Latin parts of his dictionary, however, Dasypodius was creative as he tried to give proper equivalents of Latin words; therefore, he sometimes had to invent German words, using the rich potential of German word-formation. Some of his creations have survived for some time as lexicographical ghost words.

Johannes Fries was a schoolmaster, too. His *Dictionarium* drew on the model of Dasypodius with regard to its structure, and it relied on Robert Estienne's Latin-French dictionary with regard to the lemma inventory.[10] The time of Dasypodius and Fries, which dominated the market of Latin school dictionaries for a very long time, ended in the second half of the eighteenth century, when Egidio Forcellini and Immanuel Scheller set new standards in the field.[11]

IS: How about the *Grammatisch-kritisches Wörterbuch der Hochdeutschen Mundart* (1781)?[12]

VH: Adelung's dictionary was widely known and used around 1800, but it was also heavily disputed at the time. One reason for this was that Adelung attempted a definition of what German is or should be. In a language community like German which is characterized by many regional variants, such an attempt inevitably leads to disagreement and conflict. A second reason is that Adelung was a child of Enlightenment and Rationalism – he wrote, for example, a *History of the Human Folly* in seven volumes where he denounced superstition and bigotry.[13] Already in the 1790s, the ideas of Romanticism had gained ground and rationalistic classifications became out of fashion.

---

[9] Petrus Dasypodius, *Dictionarium Latinogermanicum: Mit einer Einführung von Gilbert de Smet*. 2. Nachdruck der Ausgabe von 1536 (Hildesheim: Olms, 1995).
[10] Frisius, *Dictionarium Latino-Germanicum*; Stephanus, *Dictionarium Latinogallicum*.
[11] Egidio Forcellini, *Totius Latinitatis Lexicon*, 4 vols. (Padua, 1771); Immanuel J. G. Scheller, *Ausführliches und möglichst vollständiges lateinisch-deutsches und deutsch-lateinisches Lexicon oder Wörterbuch*, 2 vols. (Leipzig: Fritsch 1783/1784).
[12] Johann Christoph Adelung, *Versuch eines vollständigen grammatisch-kritischen Wörterbuchs der Hochdeutschen Mundart*, 5 vols. (Leipzig: Breitkopf, 1793–1801).
[13] Johann Christoph Adelung, *Geschichte der menschlichen Narrheit*, 7 vols. (Leipzig: Weygand, 1785–89).

Against this background, it is noteworthy to see however that Adelung's standing improved increasingly during the nineteenth century: A famous illustration of his growing esteem is Jacob Grimm's entry *Adelung* in the *DWB* (1854): "Adelung, m. vir nobilis, Old High German adalunc, the well-sounding name of a man who has earned high merit for the sake of our language, especially by his dictionary." Today, we more and more see that Adelung's *Grammatisch-kritisches Wörterbuch* stands at the beginning of modern lexicography in many respects. As my colleague Ulrike Haß has put it, we owe the whole lexicographical inventory which we use today in order to describe words and their usage in our dictionaries mainly to him. Thus, Adelung certainly is of no lesser importance for German lexicography than Jacob Grimm.

IS: Was German lexicography in the eighteenth century impacted by French, Italian, and Spanish dictionaries?

VH: To my knowledge, Spanish and Italian dictionaries played no major role in the lexicography of the German-speaking countries during the eighteenth century. For German scholars, the Spanish language and literature was not part of their intellectual map until the Romanticists (re)discovered Spanish around 1800. So, the most important Spanish dictionary of the time, the *Diccionario de la lengua castellana* (1726–39), has apparently left no traces in the German lexicographical tradition.[14]

More or less the same holds for the great Italian *Vocabolario degli Accademici della Crusca* (in its edition from 1729 to 1738).[15] The *Crusca* dictionary was well-known and probably widely used since the days of the language societies from the early seventeenth century, but its impact on German lexicography unfolded as late as the middle of the nineteenth century when Jacob Grimm mentioned it as an important model for his own historical dictionary enterprise.

Although French was omnipresent in eighteenth-century Germany, neither the *Dictionnaire de l'Académie française* nor Furetière's *Dictionnaire universel* appear to have had a direct influence on Johann Leonhard Frisch, Adelung, or any other German lexicographer of the era.[16] But it is interesting to see how German lexicography, notably Adelung, realigned with the general European tradition during the eighteenth century.

First, the morphological arrangements of lemmata according to roots (*Stammwörter*), which was typical for the seventeenth-century approach to the lexicon in Germany, was left behind; with Adelung, the word eventually became the central lexicographical object, just as was already the case in French and Italian dictionaries. Second, the technique of defining word meanings by the Aristotelian principles of *genus proximum* and *differentia specifica* (e.g. by providing the genus to which a term belongs, plus the additional features) gained

---

[14] *Diccionario de la lengua castellana en que se explica el verdadero sentido de las voces: Compuesto por la Real Academia Española*, 6 vols. (Madrid: Francisco del Hierro, 1726–39).
[15] *Vocabolario degli academici della Crusca* (Venice: Tramontino, 1686).
[16] *Le dictionnaire de l'Académie française*, 2 vols. (Paris: Coignard, 1694); Antoine Furetière, *Dictionnaire universel contenant generalement tous les mots français*, 2nd ed., 3 vols. (La Haye: Leers, 1701).

more and more importance. This principle was first systematically implemented by Antoine Furetière and also applied by Samuel Johnson.

In this respect, Adelung's *Wörterbuch* thus became more similar to other European dictionaries. However, a direct impact from French and Italian dictionaries on Adelung is not very plausible. Rather, it was probably through Johnson that these principles became part of the German lexicographical tradition since Adelung admired and imitated Johnson's dictionary.

IS: The Brothers Grimm are an extraordinary pair of ethnographers interested in language, mythology, and folklore. What is their status in Germany today?

VH: The frontside of the old German 1,000-mark banknote, which was in use until the introduction of the Euro in 2002, depicted the Brothers Grimm. On the backside of the note, there was a picture of the frontispiece of *DWB*, an excerpt from Jacob Grimm's entry *Freiheit* (freedom) in his handwriting, and a view of the State Library in Berlin where the Prussian Academy of Sciences was located. At the margin of the backside, there was a small illustration of one of the Grimm's most famous fairy tales, "The Star Money."

The image program of the banknote is revealing: Apparently, by focusing on the dictionary rather than on the fairy tales, the designers of the banknote intended to tell us something about the unknown sides of the Grimms: "There is much more to the Grimms than only fairy tales." But as far as I can see, this effort has not changed anything in the public image of the Brothers Grimm – a ten- or twenty-mark banknote would have done a better job than the 1,000-mark note which was never part of the daily life of ordinary people. Despite this and many other attempts to familiarize a broader audience with different aspects of their work and their personalities, the Grimms are mainly known as the creators of the fairy tales still today.

At least, the fact that a digitized version of *DWB* is now available on the internet is helpful in this respect. But here again, many people still have difficulties to understand the dictionary and the information it provides. A common mistake is found in utterances such as "the Brothers Grimm wrote about the word *Grund* in their dictionary." No one seems to known that only three-and-a-half volumes out of thirty-two were compiled by the Grimms themselves (the article *Grund* dates from 1931). But there is some hope as there is a wonderful museum in Kassel which is dedicated entirely to the Grimms' life and works, and it has a special focus on their dictionary. The museum (*Grimmwelt*) is one of the most popular in Germany, so I am optimistic that things will change.

IS: *DWB*, I understand, was left unfinished. What happened with the dictionary after the Brothers Grimm died?

VH: The Grimm Brothers did not take any precautions in order to ensure the continuation of their work after their death – although they were already in their fifties when they started working on the dictionary. When Jacob Grimm died in 1863 (Wilhelm had already passed away in 1859), they left behind a torso of three-and-a-half dictionary volumes reaching from *A* to *Frucht* (fruit) and a lot of unsolved problems.

It took nearly 100 years and twenty-eight additional dictionary volumes until Z was reached. After the completion of the first edition of *DWB* in 1960, lexicographers in Göttingen and (East) Berlin embarked on a second edition in nine volumes (*DWB2*), one of the few scientific enterprises where both German states worked together in spite of the Iron Curtain. *DWB2* was a complete revision of the most outdated alphabet section from A to F, and it was finished in 2018.

IS: What a fascinating story, Volker.

VH: I had the honor of being chief editor of the Göttingen part of *DWB2*. Working on a dictionary of German that was rooted in the nineteenth century on the one side and that had to meet the standards of contemporary lexicography was quite an experience. The question remains however why *DWB2* has not gone beyond F. The simple answer: after nearly sixty years of work on only six letters, there was no one who wanted to fund more volumes of *DWB2*. Instead, the Göttingen team embarked on a new project in the Grimmian tradition: *Wortgeschichte digital*.

IS: How do you explain the delay?

VH: There are several reasons why it took so long until *DWB* was finished (the first edition of the *Oxford English Dictionary*, in comparison, was published in a time span of only forty years). I just mention the lack of centralization and organization, a deficient inherited by the Brothers Grimm themselves, who saw no need for professional structures beyond their (rather loose) brotherly collaboration. Whoever wants to learn more about the time after the Grimms' death should read Alan Kirkness' wonderful documentation of the dictionary history.[17]

IS: Can you reflect on the legacy of Daniel Sanders and his *Wörterbuch der deutschen Sprache* (1860–65)?[18]

VH: Daniel Sanders conceived his *Wörterbuch der deutschen Sprache* as a direct alternative to Grimm's *DWB*, against which he had heavily polemicized in 1852. Rather than presenting a monumental historical record of German, Sanders wanted to compile a smaller dictionary for the practical needs of contemporary language users. So, with the three volumes of his *Wörterbuch der deutschen Sprache*, Sanders filled a void left by *DWB*, which was a work for philologists rather than ordinary people.

Today, much can be learned from Sanders' dictionary: clear entry structure, fine definitions, a very systematic way of unfolding the polysemy of words, a balanced selection of original quotations, and most importantly the intention of mirroring the language as it is, without ideological bias (which is not completely absent from some entries of *DWB*). Even the most obvious flaw of Sanders' dictionary is a virtue in disguise: he decided to arrange the lemmata in nested word family entries rather than presenting them in strict alphabetical order. Therefore, on the one hand, looking up individual words in Sanders is sometimes difficult. But on the other hand, the arrangement of the lemma inventory according to morphological principles is highly progressive. Thereby, semantic connections between members of a word family can become apparent. With this

---

[17] Alan Kirkness, "Behind the Scenes of Grimms' German Dictionary (1838–1863): A Survey of Original Source Materials," in *Märchen, Mythen und Moderne: 200 Jahre Kinder- und Hausmärchen der Brüder Grimm*, Vol. 2, ed. Claudia Brinker-von der Heyde, Holger Ehrhardt, Hans-Heino Ewers, and Annekatrin Inder (Frankfurt am Main: Lang, 2015), 1063–82.

[18] Daniel Sanders, *Wörterbuch der deutschen Sprache: Mit Belegen von Luther bis auf die Gegenwart*, 3 vols. (Leipzig: Wigand, 1860–65).

macrostructure, Sanders somehow anticipated modern word family dictionaries such as Gerhard Augst's *Wortfamilienwörterbuch* (2009).[19] And after all, Sanders' *Wörterbuch* holds a crucial lesson for every lexicographer: a good dictionary should be finished in time (and preferably in your own lifetime)! Whereas *DWB* needed more than a century, Sanders managed to prepare, compile, and publish his three volumes within two decades. As a result, his A is not very different from his Z, which is one explanation for the enormous success of his dictionary.

IS: Most of what you've chronicled is connected with monolingual dictionaries.

VH: Compiling monolingual dictionaries of German is my job (and I cannot think of a better one), but I sometimes ask myself of what use it is to explain German to German-speaking people. It always comforts me, however, that monolingual dictionaries get an enormous number of clicks on the internet. Monolingual dictionaries must be of some use to a lot of people, native speakers as well as learners of German.

IS: Can you elaborate on this use?

VH: I fear, I am not an expert on user studies. So, I do not know what users out there really do with our monolingual dictionaries. I have a faint idea, though, how *Wortgeschichte digital*, the dictionary I am currently working on, is used. At the present stage of our work, we are focusing on the vocabulary of politics and society, dealing with words such as *Staat* (state), *Volk* (people), or *Bürger* (citizen). The lemmata which are looked up most frequently are not those essential words which I mentioned.

The audience is much more interested in words with a strong image component or a stimulating story behind them. *Otto Normalverbraucher* (John Doe) and *Vitamin B* (old boy network) are examples of words which users seem to prefer. I am completely happy with this, because it shows that our purpose – to write interesting and informative word histories in our dictionary – is reached. And my hope is that people, when looking up *Vitamin B* in the dictionary, come across entries like *Staat* or *Bürger* which have a word history certainly no less intriguing.

IS: Who consults the *Digitales Wörterbuch der deutschen Sprache (DWDS)*?[20]

VH: According to recent research into the use of *DWDS*, a monolingual online dictionary of German, people consulting the dictionary especially focus on the sense section of an entry rather than on the sections where spelling or grammar are dealt with. This insight is very reassuring for me, too, because normally most of a lexicographer's work is invested in describing the meaning of words. This effort thus seems not to be useless; on the contrary, good sense definitions are apparently what users are looking for.

IS: I want to talk about bilingual dictionaries.

VH: I have worked on monolingual dictionaries only. Therefore, I cannot say anything substantial about bilingual lexicography. I just admire those who master two languages to such a perfection that they are able to compile a dictionary, and

---

[19] Gerhard Augst, *Wortfamilienwörterbuch der deutschen Gegenwartssprache: Studienausgabe* (Tübingen: Niemeyer, 2009).
[20] www.dwds.de

I specifically admire lexicographers who excel both in monolingual and bilingual lexicography. Daniel Sanders is one of those rare masters who were able to set standards in both fields.

As a maker of monolingual dictionaries of German, I permanently use bilingual dictionaries, and my admiration for those works is growing every time I look up something in them. Without reliable information about other languages, especially when it comes to donor languages of loanwords in German, I would be lost. And as I have a strong personal interest in lexical typology, I frequently use bilingual dictionaries for getting a first impression of the similarities and differences of corresponding words – just look up for instance English *culture*, French *culture*, and German *Kultur* in a bilingual and then perhaps in a monolingual dictionary. The insights will be thrilling.

IS: I'm fascinated by the universe of online dictionaries.

VH: It is a truism to say that all future dictionaries will be online dictionaries. As a lexicographer, I am happy with that because of the many advantages online dictionaries have not only for users but also for dictionary makers. But there are some problems coming with the shift from printed to online lexicography. I can easily go to my university library and consult, say, the *Vocabolario degli Accademici della Crusca* in an edition from 1686. I just have to put on gloves. Will it be as simple for anyone in 300 years to look up things in *Wortgeschichte digital*, the dictionary I am currently working on? I hope there will be some technical solution for the problem of long-term storage of digital data during my lifetime. For the time being, I keep thinking about a printed version or at least a PDF version of my online-dictionary – which would be absurd since many crucial features of the online dictionary would be lost.

IS: Earlier you said you couldn't think of a better job than compiling dictionaries. I agree: the job is superb. I have worked for the *Oxford English Dictionary* and have compiled a dictionary of Spanglish. How did you come to be a lexicographer?

VH: What has led me to lexicography was my fascination with historical semantics. While working on my PhD in linguistics (it was about semantic change in perception verbs), I had to consult a vast number of dictionaries of older Germanic languages, which was always fun and my favorite study. Immediately after finishing my PhD, I got the chance to work at the Göttingen office of *DWB2*. It was the ideal job for me. I could do what I liked most, working with words, identifying the nuances of their meaning, and tracing their history. This fascination has grown ever since.

IS: What does the job entail?

VH: First of all, the job entails reading and sorting hundreds and thousands of quotation slips. This takes days and sometimes weeks for a single word. And you need a large desk to create piles (do not open the window unless you have put something heavy on them). Then, you have to write definitions and to find an arrangement for all the senses and subsenses in the article. In the digital age, the work is strikingly similar.

Instead of sifting through paper slips, you work with large lists of quotations on the screen, using search filters and other useful tools. The computer system of our project is certainly one of the most advanced lexicographical tools which

	exist.[21] The only thing which I miss, however, is the large desk for my quotation slips. This way of sorting things with your own fingers remains unrivaled.
IS:	Our conversation has been in English, in which you seem to be at ease. How many languages do you speak?
VH:	In my youth, I lived in Belgium for a couple of years. I speak Dutch and French (both have become a bit rusty). At the moment, I am working on my Italian.
IS:	In your knowledge, what is the difference between German lexicography and that of other standardized European languages, say French, Spanish, Portuguese, and Italian?
VH:	First of all, I believe that the lexicography of European languages has more in common than one might think, and the differences are rather minor. If I am thinking of something that is specific for German lexicography, however, it is perhaps the lexicography of loanwords (*Fremdwörter*). German, it is often said, is the only language which has a special kind of dictionaries dedicated exclusively to words of foreign origin. There is, for example, a special *Duden* volume dealing with lexical borrowings, and there is the magnificent *Deutsches Fremdwörterbuch*, a multivolume dictionary in the tradition of Grimm's *DWB* recording the history of loanwords, especially those of Latin and Greek origin.[22] This kind of dictionary is perhaps unthinkable for the Romance languages you mentioned – pace the wonderful French *Dictionnaire des anglicismes* by Rey-Debove and similar examples.[23]
	What is perhaps unique, too, is a lexicographical landscape of regional dictionaries covering nearly the whole language area. As early as in 1913, it was decided to systematically compile large dictionaries for each of the greater dialect regions in Germany. Many of these dictionaries are finished and can be consulted online, but a few are still in progress.
IS:	What are the regions?
VH:	The linguistic landscape of German is traditionally divided into large dialect regions such as Bavarian, Alemannic, Franconian, etc. Our dialect dictionaries do not necessarily match these traditional dialectological subdivisions. There is a dictionary of Rhenish (*Rheinisches Wörterbuch*), for example, but there is no such thing as a "Rhenish" dialect.[24] This mismatch goes back to some far-reaching decisions which were taken at the beginning of the twentieth century.
	As I mentioned, at the beginning of the twentieth century it was decided to make dictionaries of federal states rather than dictionaries of dialects. In consequence, the Rhenish dictionary was about all the dialects spoken in the Rhine Province, the westernmost province of Prussia. Another example is the dictionary of Lower Saxony, the state where I live: there is no Lower-Saxonian

---

[21] *Zettel's Traum*, available on Github, https://github.com/WortgeschichteDigital/ZettelsTraum.

[22] *Duden – Das Fremdwörterbuch*, 12th ed., ed. Dudenredaktion (Berlin: Dudenverlag, 2020); Hans Schulz and Otto Basler, *Deutsches Fremdwörterbuch*, Weitergeführt im Institut für deutsche Sprache unter der Leitung von Alan Kirkness, 7 vols. (Berlin: De Gruyter, 1913–88).

[23] Josette Rey-Debove, *Dictionnaire des anglicismes: les mots anglais et américains en français*, 2nd ed. (Paris: Robert, 1990).

[24] Josef Müller, *Rheinisches Wörterbuch*, 9 vols. (Bonn: Klopp, 1928–71).

dialect, the dictionary rather includes two different dialect regions, namely "Eastphalian" and "Westphalian."

Compiling dictionaries of states rather than dialects may seem odd, but it is perfectly reasonable. In a country like Germany which has a strong federal tradition, only the states are able to fund and to organize the dictionary work. And it is reasonable, too, because the usual dialectological subdivisions are based on phonological and morphological criteria rather than on dialect words.

IS: In terms of methodology, what is the difference between compiling a regional and a national dictionary?

VH: Regional dictionaries are normally based on questionnaires where dialect speakers answer questions. National dictionaries, by contrast, are mainly based on written sources. So, when you work on a regional dictionary, there is much fieldwork to do, whereas compiling a national dictionary is mainly desk work.

IS: For the purpose of compiling dictionaries, is it harder to recruit regional lexicographers vis-à-vis national ones?

VH: It is hard to recruit lexicographers for standard language dictionaries, and it is even harder to find people who are willing and able to work on dialect dictionaries. Interestingly, many dialect lexicographers have never had dialectology training in a narrow sense, at least to my knowledge – nevertheless, they became excellent dialect lexicographers. The most obvious reason for this dire situation is that the number of departments where dialectology is taught is apparently shrinking. This holds particularly for Low German (spoken in North Germany). In South Germany, as well as in Austria and Switzerland, the situation seems to be slightly better, since there, dialects are more widely spoken and held in higher esteem, both in daily life and academic research.

IS: Does language change at the same speed at the regional and national levels?

VH: At the regional levels, language change is much faster. But the regional dictionaries cannot hold pace with this change. They have to work on thousands of questionnaires, some of them dating back to the first half of the twentieth century. So, these dictionaries are mostly occupied with documenting dialects which no longer exist as such.

IS: This lexicographic abundance is enviable.

VH: There is another typical feature coming to my mind: Germany has a strong tradition of philological/historical dictionary-making. We have several etymological dictionaries of high quality next to each other (notably *Kluge*, *Pfeifer*, and *Duden Herkunftswörterbuch*), and there are excellent multivolume dictionaries for each period of our language history.[25] This philological tradition has brought forth many historical dictionaries for other European and even non-European languages which are compiled by German researchers. I will just mention the dictionary of Old French by Adolf Tobler and Erhard Lommatzsch, the *Lessico*

---

[25] Friedrich Kluge, *Etymologisches Wörterbuch der deutschen Sprache*, 25th ed., ed. Elmar Seebold (Berlin: De Gruyter, 2011); Wolfgang Pfeifer, *Etymologisches Wörterbuch des Deutschen*, digitized und revised version in *Digitales Wörterbuch der deutschen Sprache* (1993), www.dwds.de; *Duden – Das Herkunftswörterbuch: Etymologie der deutschen Sprache*, 6th ed., ed. Dudenredaktion (Berlin: Dudenverlag, 2020).

Etimologico Italiano, or the *Altuigurisches Wörterbuch*, a dictionary of Uyghur, an Old Turkic language from China.²⁶

IS: This strong tradition surely spills over into other dimensions of German culture, right? Crosswords, for instance? Or verbal humor?

VH: At first sight, I do not see where this philological tradition of lexicography has left any visible traces in German culture (certainly not in humor since Germans do not know such thing as humor!). But perhaps I am too much part of this culture, so I cannot see those traces. Crosswords and Scrabble however are as popular in Germany as they are in the English-speaking world. In 2015, the *Duden* has even published a special dictionary edition for Scrabble players.²⁷ And there certainly is a general fascination for words.

There are books, for example, where the most beautiful, funny, or odd words from the 320,000 lemmata of Grimm's *DWB* are selected for the use of a broader audience. Apparently, these books sell well, especially as a gift for Christmas. And there is, of course, Günter Grass' (2010) novel *Grimms Wörter* – a novel about the Grimm Brothers and their dictionary used as a background to tell something both about the authors autobiography and German history from the nineteenth century onwards.²⁸ So, the more I am thinking about possible traces of lexicography and philology in German culture, the more I find. We lexicographers should take much more advantage of this general interest in words!

IS: There is a rich tradition of lexicography, online and printed. Are you optimistic that this tradition will be continued? In what direction will German lexicography develop?

VH: I am definitely optimistic, since the need for good dictionaries will always be there. The language is constantly evolving and this asks for constant and reliable documentation. So, the work is there, and if we as professional lexicographers won't do it, others will try to take over. As for academic lexicography, I think we have to work more closely together, to coordinate our efforts in a better way, especially in order to overcome the technical challenges of online lexicography in times of dwindling resources. Coordination is not easy in a country with federal political structure and for a language community as ours with its strong regional differences. At a time long before German unification, Jacob Grimm once asked the rhetorical question what Germans had in common if not their language and literature ("*Was haben wir denn gemeinsames als unsere sprache und literatur?*"). We are in a different situation of course, but still today language is a strong bond across all kind of differences. If people say "language," they mean "words," and that is where lexicographers come in.

---

[26] Adolph Tobler and Erhard Lommatzsch, *Altfranzösisches Wörterbuch*, 12 vols. (Wiesbaden: Steiner, 1925–2008); *Lessico Etimologico Italiano* (Wiesbaden: Reichert, 1979–2023), https://online.lei-digitale.it/; *Altuigurisches Wörterbuch: Sprachmaterial der vorislamischen türkischen Texte aus Zentralasien*, ed. Akademie der Wissenschaften zu Göttingen, 9 vols. (Stuttgart: Steiner, 1979–2024).
[27] *Duden – Scrabble-Wörterbuch*, ed. Dudenredaktion (Mannheim: Dudenverlag, 2008).
[28] Günter Grass, *Grimms Wörter: Eine Liebeserklärung* (Göttingen: Steidl, 2010).

Suggested Readings

Adelung, Johann Christoph. *Grammatisch-kritisches Wörterbuch der Hochdeutschen Mundart: Mit beständiger Vergleichung der übrigen Mundarten, besonders aber der Oberdeutschen*. 2nd enlarged and improved ed. 4 vols. Leipzig: Breitkopf, 1793–1801. Reprint, Hildesheim et al.: Olms, 1990.

Deutsches Wörterbuch von Jacob Grimm und Wilhelm Grimm. 16 vols. [1–32]. Leipzig: Hirzel, 1854–1971. www.woerterbuchnetz.de/DWB1

Deutsches Wörterbuch von Jacob Grimm und Wilhelm Grimm. Revised ed. 9 vols. Edited by Berlin-Brandenburgischen Akademie der Wissenschaften (formerly Akademie der Wissenschaften der DDR) and Akademie der Wissenschaften zu Göttingen. Leipzig: Hirzel, 1960–2018. www.dwds.de/d/wb-2dwb, https://www.woerterbuchnetz.de/DWB2

Diehl, Gerhard, and Volker Harm, eds. *Historische Lexikographie des Deutschen: Perspektiven eines Forschungsfeldes im digitalen Zeitalter*. Lexicographica Series Maior Vol. 161. Berlin: De Gruyter, 2022.

Digitales Wörterbuch der deutschen Sprache [DWDS]. www.dwds.de

Duden. *Deutsches Universalwörterbuch: Das Große Bedeutungswörterbuch*. 10th ed. Berlin: Dudenverlag, 2023. www.duden.de/woerterbuch

Grass, Günter. *Grimms Wörter: Eine Liebeserklärung*. Göttingen: Steidl, 2010.

Harm, Volker. "Between Science and Romanticism: The Deutsches Wörterbuch of the Brothers Grimm." In *The Whole World in a Book. Dictionaries in the Nineteenth Century*, edited by Sarah Ogilvie and Gabriella Safran. New York: Oxford University Press, 2020, 73–92.

Harm, Volker. "Beyond the 'Grimm': German Historical Lexicography after Deutsches Wörterbuch." In *Broadening Perspectives in the History of Dictionaries and Word Studies*, edited by Hans Van de Velde and Fredric T. Dolezal. Newcastle upon Tyne: Cambridge Scholars, 2021, 117–34.

Harm, Volker. "*Wortgeschichte digital*: A Historical Dictionary of German on the Internet." *Dictionaries: Journal of the Dictionary Society of North America* 44, no. 1 (2023): 105–20.

Haß, Ulrike. *Daniel Sanders: Aufgeklärte Lexikographie im 19. Jahrhundert*. Tübingen: Niemeyer, 1995.

Haß, Ulrike, ed. *Große Lexika und Wörterbücher Europas: Europäische Enzyklopädien und Wörterbücher in historischen Porträts*. Berlin: De Gruyter, 2012.

Haß-Zumkehr, Ulrike. *Deutsche Wörterbücher: Brennpunkte der Sprach- und Kulturgeschichte*. Berlin: De Gruyter, 2001.

Kämper, Heidrun, Annette Klosa and Oda Vietze, eds. *Aufklärer, Sprachgelehrter, Didaktiker: Johann Christoph Adelung (1732–1806)*. Tübingen: Narr, 2008.

Kirkness, Alan. "Behind the Scenes of Grimms' German Dictionary (1838–1863): A Survey of Original Source Materials." In *Märchen, Mythen und Moderne: 200 Jahre Kinder- und Hausmärchen der Brüder Grimm*, Vol. 2, edited by Claudia Brinker-von der Heyde, Holger Ehrhardt, Hans-Heino Ewers, and Annekatrin Inder, 1063–82. Frankfurt am Main: Lang, 2015.

Kirkness, Alan. "Es leben die Riesenschildkröten! Plädoyer für die wissenschaftlich-historische Lexikographie des Deutschen." *Lexicographica* 32 (2016): 17–137.

Kirkness, Alan. *Geschichte des Grimmschen Wörterbuchs 1863 bis 1908*. 2 vols. Stuttgart: Hirzel, 2020.

Kluge, Friedrich. *Etymologisches Wörterbuch der deutschen Sprache*. 25th revised and expanded ed. Edited by Elmar Seebold. Berlin: De Gruyter, 2011.

Mittelhochdeutsches Wörterbuch. Vol. 1. Edited on behalf of Akademie der Wissenschaften und der Literatur Mainz and Akademie der Wissenschaften zu Göttingen by Kurt Gärtner, Klaus Grubmüller, Jens Haustein, und Karl Stackmann. Stuttgart: Hirzel, 2006.

Müller, Peter O. *Deutsche Lexikographie des 16. Jahrhunderts: Konzeptionen und Funktionen frühneuzeitlicher Wörterbücher*. Tübingen: Niemeyer, 2001.

Pfeifer, Wolfgang. *Etymologisches Wörterbuch des Deutschen*. Digitized and revised version in *Digitalen Wörterbuch der deutschen Sprache*, 1993. www.dwds.de/d/wb-etymwb

Rheinisches Wörterbuch. Digitized version in *Wörterbuchnetz*, Trier Center for Digital Humanities, Version 01/23. https://woerterbuchnetz.de

Sanders, Daniel. *Wörterbuch der deutschen Sprache: Mit Belegen von Luther bis auf die Gegenwart*. 3 vols. Leipzig: Wigand, 1860–65.

Wörterbuchnetz. Trier Center for Digital Humanities. https://woerterbuchnetz.de

Wortgeschichte digital. www.zdl.org/wb/wortgeschichten/

4 Chinese

Haoran Tong

To appreciate how Chinese dictionaries came to be, one has to understand the evolution of the Chinese language's writing system. Chinese dictionary-making has long been a continuous yet differentiated effort for scholars to reimagine and re-narrate the history of Chinese character-making and also to provide a road map for the recreation and expansion of Chinese language. From exegesis to calligraphic and phonetic standardization, each dictionary-maker proposed a unique model of organizing the Chinese language, providing some limited rationale that connects phonetic, morphemic, and structural elements between characters and, subsequently, words and idioms. This exploration is inevitably a product of ideological and cultural-political forces. From the "write same character" mandate that facilitated the birth of the Qin dynasty to the Chinese latinization reforms in the twentieth century, dictionaries were pushed to the center of a political understanding of ethnic and ideological unity in the Chinese-speaking sphere.

***

ILAN STAVANS: Let's talk about how Chinese dictionaries came to be. To my understanding, the prototypes of Chinese dictionaries came to life a lot earlier than some other languages. Is this true, and why is this the case?

HAORAN TONG: Every dictionary entails a distinct historiography of the language. As such, the inception of dictionary and dictionary-making culture has inextricable ties to the context in which the language was developed. To have a dictionary in the most rudimentary form, a language needs to marry meaning-making with writing and speaking. While many languages in the ancient world were spoken, a vast majority did not have sophisticated writing systems to document, preserve, and proliferate the meanings, therefore missing "dictionaries" that could be discovered by later generations.

Chinese was a different story. The earliest historical linguistic evidence of the spoken Chinese language dates back approximately 4,500 years, and examples of the writing system that would become written archaic Chinese are attested in a body of inscriptions made on bronze vessels and oracle bones (*jiaguwen* 甲骨文) during the late Shang dynasty (c. 1250–1050 BCE), with the very oldest dated to c. 1200 BCE. The signs to record the speech form of the Chinese language – now called "Chinese characters" – were gradually developed to replace "knot-tying," an ancient practice to record significant events in life.

While some of the earliest character inscriptions on oracle bones were pictographic of concrete subjects in nature, such as the sun, the moon, and the swine, by the time of the Western Zhou dynasty, it was evident that they represented more than drawings. The strokes were simplified, the forms were conventionalized, and patterns of character arrangement started to appear. Not all characters meant what they depicted. As simplification and conventionalization continued on divergent paths in different regions, some characters became divorced from the original meanings they were subscribed to. The messiness of character evolution and the urge for a standardized language system provided the impetus for dictionary creation.

IS: Let's dwell on character evolution for a second. What particular aspects of the Chinese language informed the difference in the generative processes of a dictionary? Chinese operates as a logographic system but no longer ideographies. Does that make word collection and compilation challenging?

HT: I'm not in a position to say that Chinese dictionary-making is more or less challenging than other languages, but the evolution of the Chinese writing system certainly made the word compilation process different. For alphabetic languages, their individual symbols represent sounds directly and lack any inherent meaning; but for logographic languages such as Chinese, characters should constitute meanings as well as phonetic information occasionally. This logographic construction marked the important distinction among *wen* 文 (pattern), *zi* 字 (character) and *ci* 词 (word).

Wen denotes characters composed of a single graphic, self-explanatory visual element, while *zi* refers to an organic composite of more than one element. Most *wen* and *zi* are monosyllabic and originally corresponded to only one pronunciation (while it has long been the case that one pronunciation corresponds to many *wen* and *zi*). In classical Chinese, most *wen* or *zi* could qualify as a *ci* on their own due to their interdependence in signifying meanings. In contemporary Chinese, though, multicharacter words became more common as each character was already overloaded with multiple attached meanings over centuries. Chinese dictionaries, ancient or contemporary, need to perform a basic yet complicated task of explaining the *ci* out of *zi* – interpreting meaning out of characters.

With simplification, conventionalization, and abstraction as the main themes for Chinese characters' change over time, it is not surprising to see a disconnect between a character's ancient and contemporary forms, therefore distinct meanings. The evolution of Chinese characters was primarily captured by the change of writing style: from *jiaguwen*'s square, delicate structures of many strokes to *dazhuan* 大篆 (large seal script), a style of calligraphy with complicated strokes current in the Shang and Zhou dynasties (c.1600–256 BCE), to *xiaozhuan* 小篆 (small seal script), which simplified its predecessor with "fewer-stroke seal characters" in the Qin dynasty (221–206 BCE), to *lishu* 隶书 (clerical script), whose rectilinearity radically deformed most of *xiaozhuan*'s strokes in the Han dynasty (206 BCE – 220 CE), to more mature, semi-cursive *kaishu* 楷书 (regular script) in the Tang dynasty (618–907) and onwards. Overall, the change made Chinese characters easier to write on paper but harder to interpret at first glance.

In this process, accuracy of pictograms gave way to convenience as more sophisticated meanings needed to be represented in the writing system. More and more composite characters were developed, most notably, through ideographic and pictophonetic formations. Both are composites of *wen*: the former merely designates a new meaning to their composite, while the latter has one indicating meaning and the other indicating sound. Ideographic constructions usually invoke creative metaphors and synecdoches; they represent complex relationship between simple, picturable subjects. Take *hua* 化 (change) as an example.

IS: How does a character represent such an abstract concept of change, which later formed the word "chemistry"?

HT: Well, 化 was literally two distinct profiles of a person – one standing upright, another upside down. Each character user may endogenize a different interpretation of this character, albeit memorizing its meaning: 化 could be used as a yin-yang kind of dichotomy or a generative process from life to death.

To make things more complicated, these two formations were often accompanied by phonetic loans and mutually explanatory formations. Characters, after all, are symbols recording commonly understood spoken language, so phonetic proximity between words could correlate with morphemic proximity between characters. For example, the oracle script for *mo* 莫 is ideographic – the sun is hidden in the grasses, meaning "sunset." However, this character was later extended to signify negation in a word (e.g. *mo wen* 莫问 meaning "don't ask"). It remained a puzzle to scholars how the character changed its meaning so drastically, but since it was conventionalized already, a variant of its oracle script, *mu* 暮, was deployed to inherit 莫's original meaning of sunset hours. Another example involves the swapped meanings between *lai* 来 (come) and *mai* 麦 (wheat).

Ironically, the oracle script of 来 was actually a pictogram of wheat, and that of 麦 was a composite between wheat and a foot pointing toward the earth, signifying the direction in which a farmer harvests the crop, i.e. "come" or "arrive." Perhaps because 来 involved fewer strokes, people gradually mapped it to a more popular meaning. These two examples are only a tiny fraction of the "many-to-many" matching problems in Chinese characters, where multiple characters could denote one meaning, correspond to one sound, and vice versa.

IS: Was clarifying the abstraction, simplification, and sometimes distortion of words part of the intent to create Chinese dictionaries?

HT: Definitely, on the surface, every dictionary was produced to clarify and standardize the meanings of words. But more precisely, every dictionary-making involves some form of translation. For some languages whose first dictionaries were bilingual, a dictionary translates one language into another. For Chinese, the vast majority of early dictionaries are monolingual, in which case, a dictionary translates the archaic to the vernacular, the past to the present.

Chinese dictionaries could serve as literacy textbooks, exegeses of classics, and/or encyclopedias of "everything between heaven and earth." The earliest prototype of a dictionary, *Shi Zhou pian* 史籀篇 (title roughly translated to

"Historian Zhou's reading primer"), was widely accepted as the first character textbooks of fifteen volumes created to teach children from royal families. Character writing was a noble subject because it enabled the children to appreciate the blossomed literary works and philosophical debates during the Spring and Autumn period, and the Warring States period after that. Some scholars accept that Historian Zhou, by the order from Emperor Xuan of the Zhou dynasty, compiled this book for the royal family.

Others like acclaimed literary historian Wang Guowei 王国维 argued that it resembled the writing style of Qin people during the Warring States. While no copy of the primer is available today, we could infer from Qin scholars' notes that the characters taught were a mix of frequently used words for daily communication and newly created words, all written in *dazhuan*. Only the most common variant of each character was selected. As the most authoritative textbook at the time, it is plausible to suggest that the author was likely tasked to standardize and normalize writing while collecting new characters. Later, when Qin's victory put an end to the Warring States, Ying Zheng 嬴政, the first emperor, sought standardization of the writing system as a political priority to building a unified China. By his order, the first government standardization of the characters took place, carried out by the statesman Li Si 李斯. An important project was the compilation of character textbooks following the style of *Shi Zhou pian* but replacing its scripts with *xiaozhuan*, the official writing script of the empire.

IS: How about the exegesis of classics? What is the representative dictionary?

HT: During the pre-Qin period, the proliferation of classical literature played a significant role in shaping Chinese culture. However, over time, the characters themselves underwent changes in both form and meaning, rendering many characters and their pronunciations unintelligible. This was particularly true for the more scholarly and remote classics. *The Five Confucian Classics*, which include *The Book of Changes*, *The Book of Ancient Texts*, *The Book of Songs*, *The Book of Rites*, and *The Spring and Autumn*, were codified as textbooks for later generations of scholars.[1] As a result, the explanation and interpretation of characters in these classics became an important and urgent task. The interpreting of characters and expressions in ancient books is known as exegesis (*xungu* 训诂: 训 as explicating difficult words in common language, 诂 as interpreting ancient words in contemporary language).

IS: Which is the first Chinese dictionary?

HT: The earliest dictionary in the Chinese language, *Erya* 尔雅, was the first comprehensive work of exegetic studies conducted on a systematic basis and the first thesaurus dictionary of an encyclopedic nature.[2] Believed to be compiled by Confucius and his disciples, it mainly aimed to explain the meaning of ancient texts and a great variety of object names. It implemented what Confucian scholars would call *zhengming* 正名 (literally, "rectifying the name"), the virtue of aligning the content with the form, the intrinsic quality with extrinsic

---

[1] Michael Nylan, *The Five "Confucian" Classics* (New Haven, CT: Yale University Press, 2014).
[2] A digitized version of *Erya* can be found at https://ctext.org/er-ya. A good English reference is: W. South Coblin, "Erh ya 爾雅," in *Early Chinese Texts: A Bibliographical Guide*, ed. Michael Loewe (Berkeley: Institute of East Asian Studies, University of California, 1993), 94–99.

perception of things. The received text contains 2,094 entries, covering about 4,300 words, and a total of 13,113 characters. It is divided into nineteen sections, the first of which is subdivided into two parts.

The title of each chapter combines *shi* 释 (explain and elucidate) with a term describing the words under definition. Seven chapters (4, 8, 9, 10, 12, 18, and 19) are organized into taxonomies. For instance, chapter 4 defines terms for: paternal clan (*zongzu* 宗族), maternal relatives (*mudang* 母黨), wife's relatives (*qidang* 妻黨), and marriage (*hunyin* 婚姻). The text is divided between the first three heterogeneous chapters defining abstract words and the last sixteen semantically arranged chapters defining concrete words.

The last seven – concerning grasses, trees, insects and reptiles, fish, birds, wild animals, and domestic animals – describe more than 590 kinds of flora and fauna. It is quite a notable document of natural history and historical biogeography. Entries for common terms are defined by grouping synonyms or near-synonyms and explaining them in terms of a more commonly used word, with additional explanations if one of the words has multiple meanings. Entries for specialized terms are defined by grouping related words and giving them a description, explanation, classification, or comparison.

Erya enjoyed a remarkable position in Chinese dictionaries because it was later named a Confucian classic along with the many texts it sought to elucidate. Generations of Confucian students since the Han dynasty would continually recite, expound upon, and update its character entries and word descriptions. This iterative process not only preserved *Erya* but also fostered a dictionary-making culture among aspiring scholars.

IS: It is remarkable that the first Chinese dictionary organized characters and their associated words by common themes, not their shapes or sounds. How did future lexicographers iterate on or improve this method of arranging Chinese characters?

HT: Although *Erya*'s method of organizing characters by themes was intuitive for the audience at the time of writing, it is not the most convenient or stable method for future generations. The script styles would change, the meanings would be modified, and the themes would no longer hold over time. Limited lists of synonyms loosely organized by semantic categories made it difficult to look up characters, let alone compare characters with similar forms and sounds.

In the Eastern Han dynasty, a Confucian scholar Xu Shen 许慎 vastly improved the character-arrangement method and compiled the monumental dictionary *Shuowen jiezi* 说文解字 (literally, "explaining patterns and analyzing characters").[3] Xu Shen was an expert in exegesis of Confucian texts and a believer in *zhengming* doctrine. Concerned by a faction of Confucian scholars who proposed to read Confucian texts "by how the texts could fit the current trend," Xu deemed it essential for proper governments to adopt what resembles an originalist and textualist interpretation of Confucian works: since social disorder is often caused by a conflicting interpretation of different concepts,

---

[3] Xu Shen 许慎 and Tang Kejing 汤可敬, *Shuowen jiezi* 说文解字 (Beijing: Zhonghua shuju, 2018).

Confucius noted, a society demands a standard set of definitions of words and their attached principles in which rulers could impose laws that confuse no one.

Xu pioneered the analysis of the characters' morphic structures and proposed a theory behind connecting structures to meanings. He was the first to substantially engage in the principle of organization by sections with shared components now called "radicals." Rather than organizing words by their thematic-semantic proximity to each other, Xu delved into the "Six Categories" (*liu shu* 六书) of Chinese character-making: self-explanatory, pictographic, pictophonetic, ideographic, mutually explanatory, and phonetic loans.

He postulated that characters with similar components would relate to each other by that component. For example, almost all characters describing variants of bodies of water would share a "water component," abstracted as 氵 nowadays. The character "water" itself – a pictographic building block of all water-related characters – would serve as a headword under which all related characters would be defined, sourced, and explained. The non-water component of each character in this radical section would be highlighted in the definition part, whether it signaled the pronunciation or modified water in any substantial way.

From previous dictionaries and classical texts, Xu compiled the 9,353 characters into 540 radical types. Under each radical, characters in emperors' names were prioritized, followed by words that "suggested virtues," then those that "suggested vice." While Xu did not intentionally instill moral teachings in dictionary-making, his very motivation to "rectify the names" manifested itself in character organizations.

IS: This model of arranging characters seems influential, and it seems that Xu Shen had achieved something groundbreaking here.

HT: Xu had a demonstrable ambition to create both a historiography of and a future pathway for Chinese characters. In the dictionary's preface, Xu spent passages narrating a romanticized history of Chinese characters, revering Cangjie 仓颉 as the "god of Chinese characters" and reflecting on how some key characters became the source of civilization. In the postface of *Shuowen jiezi*, he explained: "Now, as for writing systems and their offspring characters, these are the root of the classics, the origin of kingly government, what former men used to hand down to posterity, and what later men use to remember antiquity."

Xu sought to construct a rationale for how all Chinese characters in his time could be traced back to their prototypes in ancient times; hence, what was written in antiquity by Confucius and his disciples could still be relevant and poignant to later generations. A sense of historical responsibility in preserving and rectifying the meanings behind the words was evident in him, as he hoped his dictionary could facilitate the creation of more characters. A powerful metaphor Confucian disciples used could not have illustrated it better: "a grown person gives birth to another, who, in turn, would also create more lives."

And he certainly cemented his legacy in ensuring the meaningful continuity of Chinese. This model of organizing Chinese characters, while imperfect, informs the generative processes of future characters. It ensures that most characters could be interpretable, at least partially, by looking at their shape and sound jointly. A rather notable example is the Chinese names of chemical elements. *Yang* 氧 (oxygen) is a pictophonetic combination of *qi* 气 (air), which denotes that oxygen is most typically seen in its gaseous form, and *yang* 羊 (sheep), which denotes its pronunciation.

This pronunciation closely resembles that of an existing character, *yang* 养 (nurture), which also memorializes the important role oxygen plays in nurturing living creatures on Earth. In the Chinese version of the periodic ttable, it doesn't take much effort for a Chinese reader to distinguish between metallic and nonmetallic elements, for the former consists of the metal radical (钅), and the latter, the stone radical (石).

IS: Xu's definition of each character was still quite limited, wasn't it? For example, he only explicated characters based on their apparent connections in radicals and largely brushed over characters with shared radicals but completely different etymologies. Phonetic notations were also constrained to referencing a word of similar sound. In future iterations of dictionaries, how did lexicographers denote Chinese phonetics in a more systematic way?

HT: Documenting pronunciations was quite challenging for lexicographers. In Xu's time, the most convenient way to document pronunciation of a character was by assigning it a more common homophone. It wasn't until the Sui dynasty (600 CE) that a workable, standardized system was applied in a dictionary through and through. *Qieyun* 切韵, written by Lu Fayan 陆法言, was the first comprehensive rhyming reference book in Chinese.[4]

It adopted a phonetic notation system called *fanqie* 反切 (literally, "reverse cut"), which indicates the pronunciation of a monosyllabic character by using two other characters, one with the same initial consonant as the desired syllable and one with the same rest of the syllable. For example, the character 東 [tuŋ], described by the formula 德紅反, is given as the onset [t] of 德 [tək] with the final [uŋ] of 紅 [ɣuŋ], with the same tone as 紅. In terms of tone organization, the dictionary divided a total of 12,158 characters into five volumes, two for the many words of the "level" tone, and one volume for each of the other three tones.

The entries were divided into 193 final rhyme groups (each named by its first character, called the *yunmu* 韻目 (rhyme eye). Each rhyme group was subdivided into homophone groups, *xiaoyun* 小韻 (small rhyme). The first entry in each homophone group gives the pronunciation as a *fanqie* formula. In some sense, one can observe *Qieyun*'s organization as a phonetic inflection of *Shuowen jiezi*'s.

Fanqie became especially powerful in the Tang and Song dynasties when it became an authoritative source of rhymes for the flourishing classical poetry. Mastery of rhymes was a key ingredient in a successful poem and, potentially, a successful literati's career in public office through prose-based empirical examination. *Fanqie* was produced in various *Qieyun* revisions and redactions and, as pronunciation changed, reused in the subsequent dynasties. Even the two dominant phonetic notations used today – *bopomofo*, developed in the Republic of

---

[4] For a translation and explanation, see François Bottéro, "The Qièyùn Manuscripts from Dūnhuáng," in *Studies in Chinese Manuscripts: From the Warring States Period to the 20th Century*, ed. Imre Galambos (Budapest: Eötvös Loránd University, 2013), 33–48; S. Robert Ramsey, *The Languages of China* (Princeton, NJ: Princeton University Press, 1987).

China, and *pinyin*, developed in the People's Republic – are essentially offspring of *fanqie*, only in a simpler and computer-friendlier form.

IS: What and whose pronunciation is being featured in *Qieyun* and subsequent dictionaries?

HT: There's of course a prescriptive aspect in dictionary-making: the selection of character, pronunciation, definition, and example all involve inclusion and exclusion, normalization and peripheralization. For Chinese characters, most dictionaries took a default style of calligraphy and occasionally listed alternative ways of writing as *yitizi* 异体字 (variants). For pronunciation, inclusion of alternative sounds was rarer.

Not to say that only one sound corresponds to one Chinese character, nor does it suggest the lack of intent to record the alternatives. It was technically and logistically very difficult. To record dialects, the lexicographers had to travel to different places and record different sounds; if no character corresponded precisely to a dialect's pronunciation, another character had to be invented to store it. This iterative process costs time and money. Usually, the dictionary-makers recorded their own dialect as the default pronunciation.

Qieyun, for example, featured Lu Fayan's dialect most predominantly, making contemporary scholars skeptical of whether it "truly represented Chang'an [the capital city] pronunciation in the Tang dynasty."[5] But some dictionary-makers – mostly exegetic scholars – stated explicitly that their work did not record but instruct "how characters should be pronounced when reading the classics." This way they were trying to recover the archaic pronunciations from their own pronunciations and, in turn, created a hybrid of the two.

Noteworthy, still, dictionaries that specialized in collecting dialects of the same character were quite common throughout Chinese dictionary-making history. They were not popular, since they provided no reference to the "official" pronunciation which scholars and would-be officials needed to acquire in a centralized bureaucratic system. But they existed for a cultural-political purpose: the central government needed to understand, reorganize, and reconcile regional differences to better implement policies at the ground level.

Dialect survey has been an officially sponsored practice since the Zhou dynasties. The first dialect dictionary known today was *Fangyan* 方言, compiled by Yang Xiong 扬雄 (53 BCE – 19 CE), a poet and philosopher in the Western Han dynasty.[6] This is perhaps the earliest comprehensive dialect dictionary on record around the world. In a letter to his friend, Yang stated that the emperor "wanted to know keenly the local dialects, and by knowing local language, know local customs, therefore strengthening the connection between central government and local areas without the hassle of traveling in a carriage."[7]

---

[5] Jerry Norman, *Chinese* (Cambridge: Cambridge University Press, 1988), 24–25.

[6] Full title: *You xuan shizhe juedai yu shi bie guo fangyan* 輶轩使者绝代语释别国方言 [Local expressions of other countries in times immemorial explained by the Light-Carriage Messenger]. The digitized text can be found at https://ctext.org/wiki.pl?if=gb&res=888918&remap=gb, and a good English reference is: Gina Anne Tam, *Dialect and Nationalism in China, 1860–1960* (Cambridge: Cambridge University Press, 2020).

[7] See Shiyi Xu, *Hanyu yuwen cishu fazhanshi* 汉语语文辞书发展史 [History of the development of Chinese dictionaries] (Shanghai: Shanghai cishu chubanshe, 2016), middle sect., ch. 2.3.

Yang spent almost twenty-seven years investigating and collecting dialect vocabularies and their pronunciations. He interviewed students from all regions who would come to the capital for official examinations, soldiers who were relieved from garrisons, and officials traveling from one local post to another. The result, a fifteen-volume monolith, recorded not only how the same meaning was manifested in different characters but also how regional uses differed slightly in the cultural meanings they implied out of the same character.

In Volume 2, he listed the different conveyances of anger across different regions: "冯、䑛、苛: 怒也。楚曰冯, 小怒曰䑛, 陈谓之苛" (冯, 䑛, and 苛 mean 怒 "anger," which is 冯 in Chu State, 䑛 in the region of Xiaonu, and 苛 in Chen State).[8] In some other places, he offered detailed descriptions and speculated on how regional differences originated:

> In both Qin and Jin, the bigness of objects is called 假 or 夏, and the bigness of a man is called 奘 or 壮.

On the northern boundary of Yan and the overlapping area between Qi and Chu, it is called 京 or 将. These words are all from ancient sources but still in current use. They resulted from lack of communication between states. They may be similar to current characters but were treated as being colloquial in old books. (They had their own meanings, which were not known to later generations, hence the need to define and explain them.)[9]

IS: You mentioned the unique role for state agencies to collect dialects. What is the state's role in creating dictionaries? More broadly, who creates dictionaries? Who uses them?

HT: Who gets to create dictionaries closely mirrors how concentrated power is to shape culture. As such, it is not surprising to see an "officialization" of dictionary-makers, both on an individual level and across time. On an individual level, dictionary-makers are often poets and scholars as officials or officials-to-be. In some sense, since the preservation of Chinese characters was believed to be a state function, dictionary-makers got absorbed by the state spontaneously. Those with enough resources and talents to compile a dictionary would most likely undergo elite education, which almost always advocated for the Confucian value of "merited scholars should serve the country."

By "across time," I mean that such officialization goes hand in hand with the increasing level of regulation and discipline of thought in dynastic China and perhaps beyond. By rectification of name, Confucianism placed heavy emphasis on the influence language had over thought, and thus social harmony and political order. Unification of language and harmonization of thought contributed directly to the stability of political regimes and its lasting legacy in Chinese civilization.

This explains why some of the earliest and most prominent lexicographers in China like Xu Shen were Confucian scholars who, through making dictionaries, brought particular ideological visions of Confucius to reality. With the banishment of all other thoughts and reverence to Confucianism only in the Han

---

[8] See *Fangyan*, ch. 2, line 42, https://ctext.org/wiki.pl?if=gb&chapter=335931.
[9] *Fangyan*, ch. 1, line 12, https://ctext.org/wiki.pl?if=gb&chapter=509684.

dynasty, this phenomenon transpired to reinforce imperial authority through promoting Confucianism.

Dictionaries themselves became classic texts to be studied by students vying for official positions through imperial examinations. The proof of legitimacy of the entire literati class and its affiliation with the imperial system was a historically continuous lineage of such thought through evolving, yet always standardized, Chinese language. Dictionaries were built to not only witness and revere history but also to re-narrate and restore cultural legitimacy, especially after the transition of power from one dynasty to another.

It is thus not surprising that, with a stronger central government in late imperial China (Ming and Qing dynasties), dictionary-making became more than a state project. Compilation of classics, documentation of classics in history, and collecting the increasingly complicated Chinese expressions became a testament to state power while also serving a pragmatic role of reinforcing control. After all, "writing the same character," starting from a policy instrument, has been long regarded as the very source of Chinese civilization, where differences across diverse regions could be bridged and even superseded by writing the same character and interpreting the same set of classical literature.

Official education institutions such as the imperial college (Guozijian 国子监), along with official academics in culture and language agencies, bore high expectations from the supreme ruler. Wise emperors in ancient times paid much attention to and participated in the compilation of dictionaries and used the compilation of dictionaries to standardize the language of the whole society, forming a system of imperial edicts and official promulgation.

字汇 *Zihui*, the most groundbreaking dictionary since *Shuowen jiezi*, was compiled in the Ming dynasty.[10] Mei Yingzuo 梅膺祚, a scholar and student of the imperial college, vastly simplified *Shuowen*'s 540 radicals down to 214 based on the regular script instead of the seal script. Most dictionaries inherited the list of radicals thereafter. This is often considered the most compact form of indexing Chinese characters: even simplified Chinese, conventionalized in the 1950s, dropped only thirteen of its radicals. Another Mei innovation was the radical-stroke sorting method, which groups characters by their primary radical, such as the "women" radical in "mother," and then orders them by the number of pen strokes within the radical. This sorting method is pretty much what contemporary dictionaries employ.

IS: Did this approach reach a climax?

HT: The epitome of the state-made dictionary in imperial China is the *Kangxi Dictionary* (*Kangxi zidian* 康熙字典). The compilation of character dictionaries and classified (encyclopedic) dictionaries were the important components of official learning and culture in the Qing dynasty. Part of the Qing court's historical legitimacy rested on how a Manchurian-dominant ruling class reconciled with the language, culture, and customs of the Han majority.

Dictionary-making demonstrated the political and ideological intent of such reconciliation: the Qing court was capable of rescuing and promoting the Chinese

---

[10] A digitized version can be found here: https://ctext.org/wiki.pl?if=gb&res=562550. Norman, *Chinese*, 171–72, provides a brief description.

language from a state of "disorder and waste" in the late Ming. Indeed, many resources were dedicated to the collection, compilation, and printing of this "all-encompassing" multilith. A team of Hanlin Academy (Hanlinyuan 翰林院) scholars, headed by Zhang Yushu 张玉书 and Chen Tingjing 陈廷敬 initially, thoroughly reviewed the classics and their commentaries and put together 47,035-character entries, 1,995 graphical variants, different meanings, voluminous citations, and pronunciation labels within a mere six years (from 1710 to 1716).

The Kangxi emperor named this work *zidian* 字典 (model of characters) – the Chinese name for character dictionary still used today – and commended it on both its "beauty and completeness" so as to be valued as an "unchanging norm."[11]

A product of economic, political, and cultural centralization, the *Kangxi Dictionary* symbolized extensive imperial authority: to discipline the language and users; to cleanse the variants and dissidents. As such, challenges and disputes over the collection and definition methods were rare and, if any, treated as a supreme offense. An official-scholar in Qianlong's reign, Wang Xihou 王锡侯 sought to correct the *Kangxi Dictionary*'s minor errors and improve character-indexing methods. Against the high tide of literary inquisition (prosecuting speech crime), he enraged Qianlong with his alternative dictionary which violated naming taboos of Qing emperors. His life – and dictionary – ended in a miserable execution.

IS: Does contemporary dictionary-making involve similar kinds of authorship and usership? Who drove classical/Middle Chinese into the modern/contemporary world? Did any dictionary facilitate, or else document, this process?

HT: By the Qing dynasty's collapse at the end of the nineteenth century, China underwent troubled transformations both politically and socioculturally. Worsened state finances meant that the Qing institution no longer had resources to regulate the language and update the dictionaries. This responsibility was spontaneously transferred to a group of progressive scholars with a new (but perhaps competing) agenda to reform the Chinese language, industry, and culture. In the somewhat dichotomized conception of many, traditional dictionaries were imprinted with an elitist Confucian birthmark that ought to be replaced by something more scientific, systematic, and democratic to guide the Chinese modernization process.

In this context, Chinese became an open field for radical experiments in all directions. One strand of scholarship recognized Chinese character's resilience, flexibility, and self-contained quality even while illustrating foreign and modern concepts in engineering or political theory. They pioneered in producing some of the first Chinese word dictionaries, which treated vernacular or translated multi-character words as a unit to be defined in lieu of the single-character words in classical Chinese. The intuition was simple but powerful: if two simple characters can express the same meaning as one complex character can, then why not reduce illiteracy by teaching everyone to write simple characters? In addition, they were also among the first scholars who attempted to assign each character a part of

---

[11] See Preface of *Kangxi Dictionary*, www.kangxizidian.com/.

speech, attempting to parallel Western philological and grammatical rules to Chinese. While imperfect, parts of speech clarified the role a character could play when in combination with other characters to form different words and significantly diminished the chances of conflation.

Another strand was pessimistic of Chinese's robustness to modernization, arguing that complex characters introduced high barriers to achieving literacy, advocating for a full-swing Latin-letter-based writing system that should replace all Chinese characters. Socialists postulated that since Confucianism was built on the evolution of dynastic Chinese dictionaries, discontinuing classical dictionaries remained the only promising way to cut ties with toxic Confucian ideologies. These scholars used dictionaries just as the pre-Qin scholars did: as textbooks to teach and preach their writing system reforms.

Overall, these reforms were nonuniform and chaotic, but they left some significant legacies in Chinese dictionary-making. Colloquial and vernacular Chinese words, definitions, and examples replaced the archaic styles in new dictionaries. The goal for dictionary-making changed from preparing the literati for imperial examinations to educating the masses on useful science concepts. Even though latinization, the most extreme progressive reform, ultimately gained little traction among Chinese users, it catalyzed the institutionalization of the *pinyin* denotation system widely used in today's Chinese dictionaries, where a character is transliterated through a romanized phonetic alphabet with tone markers useful for students already familiar with the Latin letters.

Some dictionary-making institutions also merged with printing companies and journalists' organizations. The Commercial Press (Shangwu yinshuguan 商务印书馆), the first modern publishing organization in China, established its dictionary department headed by Lu Erkui 陆尔奎, who earned acclaim as "the first modern Chinese lexicologist" after compiling several revolutionary "New Dictionaries" (*xinzidian* 新字典). In Lu's thought, dictionaries were "a tool for increasing productivity," not "a classic for regressive regurgitation."

Institutions that regulate Chinese language remain centralized today. After the founding of the Republic of China government, Cai Yuanpei 蔡元培, then the minister of education, chaired the Commission on the Unification of Pronunciation which decided the "standard sounds" associated with each character, selected ancillary phonetic symbols for Chinese teaching in schools, and mandated all teachers to speak solely in "standard sounds" in middle schools from 1918 onwards. In 1919, the *Guoyin Dictionary* (*Guoyin zidian* 国音字典) was published to codify the commission's decisions and lay the foundation for the modernization of dictionary phonetic notations.[12] Similarly, less than five years after the founding of the People's Republic, the National Press and Publication Administration (Xinwen chuban zongshu 新闻出版总署) spearheaded the creation of *Xinhua Dictionary* (*Xinhua zidian* 新华字典; *Xinhua* means "New China"), led by linguists and educators Wei Jiangong 魏建功 and Ye Shengtao 叶圣陶, in charge of using dictionaries as a central vehicle of promoting a "people-centered" campaign against illiteracy.

---

[12] "A Dictionary of National Pronunciation," www.zgbk.com/ecph/words?SiteID=1&ID=115530.

IS: The Language Institute in the Chinese Academy of Social Sciences (Zhongguo shehui kexueyuan yuyan yanjiusuo 中国社会科学院语言研究所) has been responsible for editing *Xinhua Dictionary* ever since, including implementing new national guidelines like *putonghua* 普通话 (modern standard Han speech) and simplified characters "at the ground level."[13] Over the seventy years and twelve editions, *Xinhua* has sold more than 600 million copies – a Guinness World Record for "most popular dictionary" and "best-selling book (regularly updated)" awarded in 2016 – and become part of the collective memory for Chinese people. I remember that the little *Xinhua* red pocket dictionary was part of a standard tool for instruction in elementary school, when word look-up assignments were frequent. The dictionary was purposefully made accessible for people of all ages and socioeconomic backgrounds: the *Xinhua* pocket dictionary costs roughly the same as half a kilogram of pork. Of course, now *Xinhua* also has an app to keep abreast of the times.

IS: This looks like a universal top-down approach to Chinese dictionaries.

HT: Dictionary-making is never a one-way process. And one doesn't need to purchase a dictionary to reshape its future. Now it is common to engage in frequent and fiery debates about whether popular online phrases should be included as entries in official dictionaries. How definitions came to be also stirred attention. Recently, the editorial board of *Xinhua Dictionary* was sued by two users for its "inappropriate definitions," such as citing "play with women" as an example under the character *wan* 玩 (play) and including the definition of *wo* 倭 as a colloquial but impolite name for the Japanese. In the digital age, most people in my generation only look up words online, and we are not overly concerned about pronouncing words in a different way or inventing a different character.

   Paper dictionary purchases are rather infrequent, barring "mandatory purchases" for schoolwork. Still, dictionaries are still valued today as the standard authoritative "carrier" of Chinese language, but we users view it not entirely as a handy reference book but also as a work of critique-worthy literature as well, not dissimilar to how Han people incorporated *Erya* into the classics.

IS: You and I have been talking mainly about monolingual dictionaries. Let's talk more about bilingual dictionaries. What are they? How did they come to be?

HT: Every dictionary involves some form of translation. For Chinese dictionaries, the initial translation took place in a closed system: between its past form and present form. Bilingual dictionaries were usually products of cross-cultural contacts and, in the Chinese context, originated from the preachings of Buddhism in the Tang dynasty.

   Groups of Chinese monks made pilgrimages to India to study Sanskrit and translate sutras into Chinese. Since the two languages are very different in both sounds and shapes, Chinese monks compiled glossaries of Buddhist terms such as the names of Bodhisattvas and transliterated them using Chinese characters and variants. One of the oldest surviving Chinese reference guides for Buddhist technical terminologies, *Yiqiejing yinyi* 一切经音义 by Xuanying 玄应, is regarded as the prototype of a bilingual Chinese dictionary, as it defines many hard Sanskrit words and their usage in Chinese.[14]

---

[13] See Preface for *Xinhua Dictionary*, 11th ed.
[14] Xuanying 玄应, *Yiqiejing yinyi* 一切经音义 ([China]: Haishan xianguan, 1849).

The Sanskrit-Chinese exchange profoundly influenced the evolution of Chinese. Buddhism's prominence in the Tang and Song dynasties prompted the creation and repurposing of many Chinese words, many of which were rarely seen multisyllabic words, such as *shijie* 世界 (now meaning "the world") and *guoqu* 过去 ("the past" or "passing"). To record the sounds of Sanskrit consonants properly, monks had to invent a self-contained method to match Sanskrit sounds that did not previously correspond to any Chinese character, indirectly bringing the *fanqie* phonetic notation method to light.

Bilingual dictionaries between Chinese and languages of now-called ethnic minorities and neighboring cultures rose to the stage also in the Tang and Song dynasties. Surviving dictionaries included Sino-Japanese, -Goguryeo, -Tibetan, -Uyghur, -Vietnamese, -Tangut, -Mongolian, etc. Since the Yuan dynasty, official diplomatic and translation institutions such as Siyiguan 四译馆 have formalized state-sponsored multilingual dictionaries.

In the Qing dynasty, ethnic harmony was a political priority, and Manchurian-Chinese-Mongolian-Tibetan-Uyghur pentaglot dictionaries (*wuti qing wenjian* 五体清文鉴) detailed cultural customs, social norms, and regional agricultural produce in all territorial frontiers.

IS: How about the first Chinese-English dictionary?

HT: Bilingual dictionaries between Chinese and European languages originated in religious preachings by European missionaries in the Ming dynasty. Matteo Ricci, a Jesuit missionary who landed in Canton and started his Christian mission in 1582, learned Chinese widely and thoroughly. He received Emperor Wanli's recognition for a creative combination of Christian teachings and Confucian principles, which allowed him to further collect linguistic elements locally.

He was credited as the creator of the first version of Chinese romanization system based on the alphabets of the Portuguese and Italian languages and the Chinese tone indication system, all exemplified in his *Dizionario portoghese-cinese* (Portuguese-Chinese Dictionary).[15] In the seventeenth century, the Polish Jesuit Michał Boym (1612–59) compiled a Chinese-Latin and a Chinese–French dictionary, which were printed between 1667 and 1670 in the popular magazine *China Illustrata*.[16]

The first Chinese-English dictionary was compiled by Robert Morrison, a Protestant missionary who arrived in Canton in 1802.[17] Modeled after the *Kangxi Dictionary*, it contained an earnest effort to translate different meanings of the same Chinese character – a handy reference for other missionaries as well as young Chinese scholars aspiring to a Western education. From 1871 to the turn of the century, multiple Chinese-English dictionaries blossomed, each covering a different Chinese dialect. It is surprising from the Chinese native speaker's point

---

[15] See Gregory James and Bronson Ming-Cheung So, "A Cultural Introduction to the First Portuguese-Chinese Dictionary: Matteo Ricci and Michele Ruggieri's 'Dizionario portoghese-cinese (c.1583)," conference paper, 2003, https://repository.hkust.edu.hk/ir/Record/1783.1-13247.

[16] See David E. Mungello, *Curious Land: Jesuit Accommodation and the Origins of Sinology* (Honolulu: University of Hawai'i Press, 1989), 139.

[17] See Mungello, *Curious Land*, 139.

IS: of view that Chinese-English dictionaries (compiled by English speakers) often focus on a holistic representation of pronunciations across dialects, not characters. As such, the dictionary-makers helped improve the documentation method of Chinese phonetics.

IS: Talk to me about Herbert A. Giles. Jorge Luis Borges writes about him in one of his essays.[18]

HT: In the hope of finding "precise rhymes" while translating classical Chinese texts to English, Giles built onto his Cambridge sinologist colleague Thomas Francis Wade's work to invent the widely adopted Beijing-dialect-based Wade-Giles romanization system in his authoritative canon, *A Chinese-English Dictionary*.[19] Giles' rigor was reflected in 13,848 character entries; five Chinese dialects and Korean, Japanese, and Vietnamese pronunciations; and almost encyclopedic summaries of the Chinese official ranking system, family names, topographies, calendar system, etc. Wade-Giles is still ubiquitously used in Taiwan.

Some of the most purchased Chinese-English dictionaries today (English entries with Chinese definitions) are published by Oxford and Collins, in collaboration with The Commercial Press. It is safe to say that bilingual dictionaries make monolingual dictionaries more organized, as the former provides an outsider's view of how a dictionary could help foreigners by organizing the words most effectively.

IS: Where do you see Chinese dictionaries in the future?

HT: What I've narrated is only a montage of dictionary-making culture in China. Perhaps, Chinese dictionary-making could enjoy new opportunities in the digital world, with so many more language learners (both of native heritage and not) and much more decentralized ways of creating and popularizing new characters, meanings, and idioms online. The boundary of what constitutes "legitimate" Chinese is also blurring, as the mainland, Hong Kong, and Taiwan all speak one Chinese but with distinct regional characteristics. Following a winding history of Chinese diaspora, perhaps the new frontier of Chinese dictionaries (and lexicography in general) is to reflect on what Chinese has been shaped and where Chinese could be to encompass a more diverse set of Chinese-identifying and Chinese-speaking peoples, all while ensuring the crucial continuity from the distant past.

Suggested Readings

Chen Tingjing 陈廷敬, Zhang Yushu 张玉书, Wang Hongyuan 王宏源, and Feng Zheng 冯蒸. *Kangxi zidian* 康熙字典 [Kangxi dictionary]: hytung unicode database revision. Beijing: Shehui kexue wenxian chubanshe, 2008.

Coblin, W. South. "Erh ya" 爾雅. In *Early Chinese Texts: A Bibliographical Guide*, edited by Michael Loewe, 94–99. Berkeley: Institute of East Asian Studies, University of California, 1993.

---

[18] Jorge Luis Borges, "The Wall and the Books," trans. Eliot Weinberger, in *Selected Non-Fictions*, ed. Eliot Weinberger (New York: Viking, 1999), 344–46.

[19] Herbert Allen Giles, *A Chinese-English Dictionary*, 2nd ed. (Shanghai: Kelly & Walsh, 1912).

Creamer, Thomas B. I. "Lexicography and the History of the Chinese Language." In *History, Languages, and Lexicographers*, edited by Ladislav Zgusta, 105–36. Berlin: Max Niemeyer, 1992.

Giles, Herbert Allen. *A Chinese-English Dictionary*. 2nd ed. Shanghai: Kelly & Walsh, 1912.

Heinrich, Patrick. "Language Modernization in the Chinese Character Cultural Sphere: China, Japan, Korea and Vietnam." In *The Cambridge Handbook of Language Standardization*, edited by Wendy Ayres-Bennett and John Bellamy, 576–96. Cambridge Handbooks in Language and Linguistics. Cambridge: Cambridge University Press, 2021.

Jiang Lihong. *A General Theory of Ancient Chinese*. Singapore: Springer, 2023.

Kuzuoğlu, Uluğ. "Codebooks for the Mind: Dictionary Index Reforms in Republican China, 1912–1937." *Information and Culture: A Journal of History* 53, no. 3 (2018): 337–66. muse.jhu.edu/article/707833

Liang, Sihua. *Language Attitudes and Identities in Multilingual China: A Linguistic Ethnography*. Cham: Springer, 2015.

Nienhauser, William H., Jr. "Diction, Dictionaries, and the Translation of Classical Chinese Poetry." *T'oung Pao* 64, no. 1/3 (1978): 47–109.

O'Neill, Timothy Michael. *Ideography and Chinese Language Theory: A History*. Berlin: De Gruyter, 2016.

Packard, Jerome L. *A Social View on the Chinese Language*. New York: Peter Lang, 2021.

Shen Zhongwei. *A Phonological History of Chinese*. Cambridge: Cambridge University Press, 2020.

Watters, Thomas. *Essays on the Chinese Language*. Shanghai: Presbyterian Mission Press, 1889.

Wuti Qing wenjian = A five language glossary = Wu-t'i ch'ing wen chien 五体清文鉴. Beijing: Gugong bowuguan/Palace Museum, 2001.

Xinhua Dictionary. Wanyouzhidian Digital Media Technology (Beijing) Co. Apple App Store, 2020. https://apps.apple.com/us/app/xinhua-dictionary/id1570086935

Xu Shen 许慎 and Tang Kejing 汤可敬. *Shuowen jiezi* 说文解字 [Explaining patterns and analyzing characters]. Beijing: Zhonghua shuju, 2018.

Xuanying 玄应. *Yiqiejing yinyi* 一切经音义 [Pronunciation and meaning in all the sutras]. [China]: Haishan xianguan, 1849.

Yong, Heming, and Jing Peng. *Chinese Lexicography: A History from 1046 BC to AD 1911*. Oxford: Oxford University Press, 2008.

Yong Heming, Peng Jing, and Zhang Xiangming. *Chinese Lexicography in the Twentieth Century*. New York: Peter Lang, 2023.

Zhang Shilu 张世禄. *Zhongguo yinyunxue shi* 中国音韵学史 [History of Chinese phonetics]. Changsha: Commercial Press, 1938.

Zhou, Minglang. *Language Ideology and Order in Rising China*. Singapore: Palgrave Macmillan, 2019.

5 Hybrid Languages

Ilan Stavans and Margaret E. Boyle

How many new languages are born every year? How does their birth come about? And how many of them, and at what point, ever reach the catharsis of having a dictionary of their own? This conversation explores the concept of "hybrid" languages (i.e. languages in contact) through the prism of code-switching, border zones, English language learning (ELL), and second-language acquisition. Engaging with both linguistic landscapes and language heritage, it applies the concept to historical cases where hybrid languages have become full-fledged standardized languages, creoles, and others. It focuses on the development of Spanglish by Ilan Stavans, analyzing the changes in this language from 1846 to the present. The authors discuss the relationships between language and identity and how structures of languages reflect and challenge social, cultural and political beliefs. The conversation also explores immigration patterns and linguistic change, considering how and when hybrid languages move with their speakers. It also comments on lexicographic work in African American vernacular English, Yinglish, Franglais, and Portuñol, among others hybrid tongues.

***

MARGARET E. BOYLE: It's a joy to talk about hybrid and mixed languages with you – someone whose life story is so deeply engaged with movement across languages and geographies: Spanish, English, Yiddish, Hebrew. In 2020, in the journal *Dictionaries*, you published an article about your process editing the dictionary of Spanglish.[1] In it, you called yourself "a lay lexicographer," but to me you are much more. Can you offer a working definition of hybrid and mixed languages in relationship to what we think of as language standardization?

ILAN STAVANS: The terms "hybrid," "mixed," and "intertwined" are synonyms. Or else, they are preferred by different scholars. My own choice

---

[1] Ilan Stavans, "A Lay Lexicographer: On Codifying the Dictionary of Spanglish," *Dictionaries: Journal of the Dictionary Society of North America* 41, no. 2 (2020): 197–212.

is "hybrid." A phenomenon resulting from diglossia, a hybrid language is the offspring coming about from the effects of code-switching, that is, the back and forth between two distinct, standardized languages. Just as a mule is a hybrid of a horse and a donkey, a hybrid language emerges when a group of speakers negotiating two languages bring about a third one that is a mix. I come from Mexico, known for its mestizo culture, which is an in-between of indigenous and Spanish elements. I should say that among a small group of linguists, hybrid languages don't actually exist because they pose a challenge to the comparative method.

MB: There's a kind of messiness to all of this in-betweenness, especially as we think about the processes of language standardization or more traditional understandings of dictionaries as kinds of containers. But the messiness you describe also feels truer to the realities of diaspora. What does it mean to circumscribe the limits of a hybrid language through a dictionary?

IS: Language is by definition chaotic. It is also absolutely free. Life in a structured society imposes limits on everything, including how we arrange our words, the order that syntax brings along, the effort at standardization. An alphabet, for languages based around words and not pictograms for instance, is a technique to organize language. Why start with the letter *a* and not with the letter *p*? In other words, is there logic in our alphabetical arrangements? The answer is no. But logic isn't the only approach; chance is another, which of course has its own logic. There is a beautiful legend in the Talmud in which the Hebrew letters go before God prior to the creation of the world in order to fight for the rightful place in the alphabet.

The dictionary, which uses the alphabet as its order, is another tool to organize language. Whenever a dictionary emerges in the development of a hybrid language, the reasons have to do with consolidation: chance no longer rules the language; a logical coherence is now applied. In my mind, all this is part of the dialectical tension between civilization and barbarism.

MB: Beautiful – we can increasingly see more popular discourse engaged with playful, and sometime subversive, interruption of these organizational tools. I am also very interested in how we communicate these ideas to children. In 2022, for example, Ellen Heck's gorgeous *A Is for Bee: An Alphabet Book in Translation* included seventy-two languages to disrupt the monolingualism of the English alphabet book.[2] I know through Yonder, the children's division of Restless Books, you are also interested in many of these questions.

IS: Just as I believe that translators are activists, I'm convinced editors – and, obviously, publishers – have the tools at their disposal to change attitudes. That is what education is about: an endeavor, never static, to read our environment in ways that are coherent with our inner understanding of the self.

---

[2] Ellen Heck, *A Is for Bee: An Alphabet Book in Translation* (Hoboken, NJ: Levine Querido, 2022).

Launched in 2013, Restless Books, an independent nonprofit publisher, along with Yonder, is in the business of changing the diet of English-language readers. It brings out outstanding books written in other languages (fiction, nonfiction, memoir, poetry, theater) in translation, for adults and children, and it also reintroduces the literary classics to underserved audiences. In total, it has brought out 200 titles in translation from fifty-five different countries. The objective, as you rightly point out, is to question our conception of monolingualism. The United States might be the richest and most powerful nation in the world, but, unfortunately, it is also among the most provincial when it comes to other cultures. This also means other alphabets and other languages. One of the most recent books is *The People's Tongue: Americans and the English Language* (2023), exploring how American English has changed over 450 years as well as the way it coexists with other languages, like Spanish, Chinese, Vietnamese, Tagalog, and Arabic.[3]

MB: Yes, I so appreciate how that anthology is engaged with the realities of linguistic change for English. The volume brings together unexpected genres – poetry, letters, song lyrics, legislation, and tweets – all circling around a seemingly infinite range of expressiveness and mutation over time within a single language. How did the process of building the anthology shape your own experiences as a consultant for the Oxford English Dictionary?

IS: Earlier in my career, I concentrated on Spanglish as a hybrid language. The topic felt natural to me: I'm a Mexican immigrant to the United States. I arrived with a rudimentary knowledge of English. What struck me in those early days – I settled in New York City in the early 1990s – was the jazzy, creative code-switching between Spanish and English. It reminded me of Yiddish, which, along with Spanish, was one of my *mame loshn*, my mother tongues. Only recently have I felt the urge, or maybe the permission, to expand my view. The development of English fascinates me. How did American English become what it is today? What have been the forces behind that change? I'm not a traditional linguist. In fact, I never studied linguistics in a classroom. I have been attracted to the social, political, economic, and cultural dimensions of language change in a spontaneous, nonacademic way.

Indeed, I believe one of the misfortunes of linguistics is the esoteric jargon it employs, which distances the debates from the general audience. To me discussions about language should be accessible to everyone because everyone is involved in language formation. *The People's Tongue* is an anthology designed for all readers. As you mention, it is made of an array of common responses to linguistic change by those who are at the forefront: poets, translators, lexicographers, politicians, playwrights, writers, teachers, and so on. The overall message is that American English, unlike other languages, has less policing. For instance, there is no equivalent of the Académie Française in the United States. And bearing in mind the dispute between *Merriam-*

---

[3] *The People's Tongue: Americans and the English Language*, ed. Ilan Stavans (Amherst, MA: Restless Books, 2023).

Hybrid Languages 61

Webster and the *American Heritage Dictionary*, our dictionaries are generally descriptive rather than prescriptive. This means that there is no higher authority legislating the language; the decision of what is accepted and what isn't is left to us all.

MB: Let's talk about the environment and people that sustain hybrid and mixed languages. How would you describe the hybrid environments that produce these kinds of language innovations? What role does code-switching play? And how do you see power dynamics coming into play in the shaping of these language features?

IS: Depending not only on demographics but on historical, political, and social circumstances, immigrants, refugees, and exiles, as well as clusters of people existing in frontier territories might produce hybrid languages. From an abundance of examples, let me list a few: Bolze (French and Swiss German), Chinglish (Chinese and English), Dao (Chinese and Tibetan), Franglais (French and English), Hybriya (Hebrew and Arabic), Jopara (Guaraní and Spanish), Lomavren (Armenian and Indo-Aryan), Petuh (Danish and German), Phillipine Hybrid Hokkien (Philippine Hokkien, Tagalog, and English), Portuñol (Portuguese and Spanish), Spanglish (Spanish and English), and Yiddish (Hebrew and German). The force shaping hybrid languages might be colonialism, but circumstances are more complex. Border cultures are diglossic. Relatively isolated communities might develop a mestizo language.

MB: We share ties to Yiddish language via Mexico, historically spoken by Ashkenazi Jews. This is a hybrid language that was nearly evaporated by the Holocaust, and in most recent decades we see efforts to revitalize and protect the language and culture, in the United States for example via initiatives like the Yiddish Book Center. Can you talk more about your own work in relationship to the language, both past and forward looking?

IS: I'm the grandchild of Yiddish-speaking immigrants to Mexico, and the generation of my parents remained loyal to the language. Depending on the environment, we spoke Yiddish or Spanish. There were around 30,000 Jews in Mexico City when I was growing up in the 1970s. I attended Di Alte Yiddishe Schule. As time has gone by, Yiddish is used now by a very small number of Mexican Jews, mostly in their sixties and older.

I didn't feel the attachment to Yiddish I now nurture during my upbringing. In fact, I saw it as an imposition. I remember telling my parents that it was a mistake for them to have taught it to me because there were more practical languages to learn: French, German, English, and so on. It wasn't until I myself became an immigrant, leaving Mexico and, after a long search for a place to settle, relocated to New York, that I realized what Yiddish meant to me. Not that the practical side has changed. Depending on the source one trusts, there are between 150,000 and 250,000 Yiddish speakers in the world – although recently I saw a statistic, in my opinion inflated, suggesting there are close to 1 million. The vast majority are ultraorthodox in New York and Israel. For me, Yiddish is a springboard through which to understand how historical events impact language. In *How Yiddish Changed America and How America*

Changes Yiddish,[4] I have explored the culture it fostered in the Americas and its chances of survival.

MB: How essential are dictionaries of Yiddish or other immigrant languages to the project of preservation? What do you see as the relationship between dictionaries and translation? Can the translator work without the dictionary? Do dictionaries impact translation? How do dictionaries contain memories of immigrant itineraries?

IS: A series of superb, incisive questions. Dictionaries are more than compendiums of words; they are mirrors through which a language measures its own profile. Every time a dictionary is published anywhere in the word, it is a referendum about the vitality of that language: how it appreciates its past, the way it embraces the present, and how it looks at its future. In the case of hybrid languages and of languages under threat, these aspects are all the more important: a newly minted dictionary, in those cases, is a salvo, a survival mechanism, and a memorandum of understanding.

The case of Yiddish is intriguing, and, for the reasons I explained before, very close to my heart. The vast majority of Yiddish lexicons have been bilingual: Yiddish-Hebrew, Yiddish-Russian, Yiddish-German, Yiddish-English, and so on. It isn't difficult to find out why: Yiddish speakers, like most hybrid-language speakers, are at least bilingual, if not multilingual. That multilingualism is the cause behind the emergence of the hybrid language. But it doesn't die when the hybrid language is fully formed. This also means that hybrid-language speakers are often engaging in translation in order to communicate, and that translation is intimately linked to the code-switching mechanisms allowing the hybrid language to flourish.

The dictionary is the translator's best friend – and, on occasion, their worst foe. Most translators have more than one nearby. I, for instance, have an entire collection. Needless to say, in the internet age, the dictionary isn't an autonomous entity: it is inside your laptop, phone, tablet, or whatever other gadgets you're using. Either way, translators consult dictionaries the way lawyers look at legal codes and doctors the medical manual. At some point, as a translator, lawyer, or doctor you internalize those documents, which doesn't mean you no longer consult them. That's why the updating of dictionaries is essential: translators must find in them not a stilted, out-of-fashion language but a living one. In that sense, dictionaries have a considerable impact on translation, and on speech in general: they are the scripture that validates our lingo.

A *living* dictionary is regularly infused with new words. In a nation like the United States, and in any modern nation, immigrants, a major feature of contemporary life in the twenty-first century, are a word-making machine. Those words come from foreign languages but are also the result of code-switching. Take *hangiar* in Spanglish: it comes from hanging out but it follows a Spanish verb conjugation. Or *shlep* and *mafioso*, which come from Yiddish and Italian but are now integral to American English. If we studied closely how *Merriam-Webster*

---

[4] Ilan Stavans, *How Yiddish Changed America and How America Changes Yiddish* (Brooklyn: Restless Books, 2020).

has grown over the last 100 years, we would recognize how many immigrant words have trickled, confidently and consistently, into the national language.

MB: Of course, you have a tremendous body of work on the life of Spanglish, as in your book *Spanglish: The Making of a New American Language*,[5] as well as your numerous translations and OpEds on the language. Can you talk more about dictionaries of Spanglish before *Spanglish* and what you imagine for the future as we see an increasing prominence of Spanish and Spanglish within popular culture in the United States.

IS: When I began studying Spanglish, I was the target of consistent attacks by the language purists, both in Spanish and in English. Rather than deter me, that antagonism inspired me. Philology, to matter, must take an activist stand. It is a misrepresentation to believe that lexicographers passively study the language. It is the opposite: their analysis helps shape the course of things. My objective in *Spanglish* was to legitimate this hybrid tongue in the public sphere. My idol was Antonio de Nebrija, a fifteenth-century University of Salamanca grammarian of Jewish descent – his family is described as Converso, meaning at one point it converted to Christianity – known for publishing early, canonical works on Spanish as a national language.

In 1492, at a time when Latin was seen as the language of knowledge in an emergent Spain, he encouraged readers, and Queen Isabel la Católica, to embrace *el español* as the language of the powerful empire coalescing at that time. Nebrija was a witness, as well as a participant, in enormous changes taking place in his epoch: the Reconquista by the Christians of Muslim parts of the Iberian Peninsula, the "discovery" of new lands across the Atlantic Ocean, and the expulsion of Jews and Muslims from the newly formed Spanish nation. Our period is quite similar: lots of debate on immigration, the appearance of new cultural and linguistic modes of communication, and the sense that technology and travel accelerate the speed with which language acquires its shape.

MB: Absolutely: Nebrija's view that language has always been the companion of empire is behind that unification and building of Spanish empire as linked to forced persecutions and conversions in the name of "blood purity." If we see Nebrija policing the borders of the Spanish language as a tool of religious and racial discrimination, we can also delve into English-only movements within the United States context and ways nationalism is practiced in relation to language today.

IS: The "language police" is a mechanism intrinsic to every language, it is how it defines its own authority, its boundaries, what is accepted and what is considered improper. Today we talk of colonialism as a legacy of erasure of other cultural norms. And rightly so, but neofascist and woke jargons are also a language police.

MB: Can you talk about the relationship between *Don Quixote* and Spanglish? You have done a translation of the first chapter of *Quixote* as part of *Spanglish* as well as the 2018 graphic novel adaptation published in two editions: English and

---

[5] Ilan Stavans, *Spanglish: The Making of a New American Language* (New York: Harper Collins, 2002).

Spanglish, with illustrations by Roberto Weil.[6] As you know well, Cervantes was preoccupied with the stability of language and translation in various ways throughout the book. Do you see any parallels between your playful translations into Spanglish and the subplot of the novel about the palimpsest attributed to the Moorish historian Cide Hamete Benegeli, that is, the statement that Don Quixote itself was written first in Arabic and only later translated – by a *morisco aljamiado*, an Iberian-born moor with a questionable knowledge of Arabic?

IS: As you say, *Spanglish: The Making of a New American Language* includes a dictionary with about 6,000 *voces*, along with a translation of the first chapter of Cervantes' *Don Quixote*. Collecting the *voces* was a painstaking process lasting many years. It benefited from the support of dozens of colleagues, friends, and people I didn't know who kindly sent Spanglish words they harvested in their local communities: Houston, Miami, Los Angeles, El Paso, Chicago, New York.

For a *voz* to be include, it needed to be recorded in at least three unrelated locations, having the same meaning. Since at times the spelling differed, one of the strategies of the lexicon was to standardize spelling. For instance, the terms *liquiar* (to leak), *roofa* (roof), *la carpeta* (the carpet), *parquiar* (to park), *soquetes* (socks), *vacunar* (to vacuum), and *la migra* (immigration authorities). These terms come from English but become Spanglish as a result of code-switching. The team behind the Spanglish dictionary identified them in various contexts, verifying that the meaning was the same. On a few occasions, we were even able to trace the exact first time when a word was uttered.

The fact that Cervantes' novel is obsessed with translation was to me an inspiration to embark on my Spanglish translation. Plus, as you might remember, just as Cervantes was completing the second part of his novel, in 1613, another author by the name of Fernández de Avellaneda, whose true identity we don't know, published a spurious second part.[7] He did it to capitalize on the enormous success of Cervantes' first part. Naturally, Cervantes was furious, so he quickly completed his own second part. In it, he ridicules Fernández de Avellaneda, calling him inept. Ironically, several years ago I got an email from a friend in Spain who is a Cervantes scholar. In it, he mentioned that someone else has published another Spanglish translation of the *Quixote* and wondered if I was behind "the new Fernández de Avellaneda."

MB: Something I really appreciate about this translation is the way you are making Cervantes more accessible to new audiences. And, of course, the hope that this will prompt bilingual readers to dive back into Cervantes' original, not linguistically pure because it's from the sixteenth century, but rather because Cervantes is also intentionally playing with language throughout the text. *Don Quixote* is constantly mixing linguistic forms and is steeped in nostalgia for the multilingual, heroic literary world of chivalric texts, from *Orlando furioso* to *Amadís de*

---

[6] Miguel de Cervantes, *Don Quixote of La Mancha*, English and Spanglish editions, adapted by Ilan Stavans, illustrated by Roberto Weil (Philadelphia: Pennsylvania State University Press, 2018).

[7] *Segundo tomo del ingenioso hidalgo Don Quijote de la Mancha, que contiene su tercera salida: y es la quinta parte de sus aventuras, compuesto por el licenciado Alonso Fernández de Avellaneda, natural de la villa de Tordesillas* (Tarragona, 1614).

Gaula. How do you see this movement between past and present in your translation practice or in hybrid languages?

IS: Indeed, Cervantes is a magician of linguistic registers. This is clear from the beginning, as we are introduced to the hidalgo, whose last name oscillates between Quijada, Quesada, Quijana, and, finally, Alonso Quijano el Bueno. Among other things, this multiplicity hints at the layered Spanish of Conversos in early seventeenth-century Spain. Likewise, already in the second paragraph of Part I, Chapter 1, the narrator ridicules the style of old chivalry novels in the belabored, archaic sentence "*La razón de la sinrazón que a mi razón se hace, de tal manera mi razón enflaquece, que con razón me quejo de la vuestra fermosura*" (John Ormbsy's English-language translation (1885): "the reason of the unreason with which my reason is afflicted so weakens my reason that with reason I murmur at your beauty.")[8] My Spanglish translation plays with similar rhetorical devices, at times sticking closer to old Iberian Spanish while still embracing code-switching and in others invoking jargons, dialects, and other variances of the Hispanic world in the twenty-first century.

MB: Can we talk more about hybrid languages and the movement toward dictionaries?

IS: Probably the place to start is by acknowledging that words that are essential to hybrid languages are regularly absorbed into standardized dictionaries. For instance, the *Diccionario de la lengua española*, although allergic to Spanglish, includes a definition of "Espanglish," as well as scores of anglicisms, for instance básquetbol, chat, copyright, show, and tour, to name only a few.[9] *Diccionario Clave* is far more receptive to anglicisms, including terms a Spanish-speaker might not recognize, such as anti-bab for birth control.[10] My work as a consultant of the *Oxford English Dictionary* focuses on Hispanic terms in English, including botana, elote, migra, orale, and pinche.

In regards to Franglais, there are all kinds of humorous books, from Yves Larouche-Claire's *Évitez le franglais, parlez français* (2004) to Miles Kington's *Let's Parler Franglais* (2004).[11] To my knowledge, there is no such thing as a dictionary of this hybrid between French and English. On the other hand, I know of several anthologies of stories, poems, essays, lyrics, and other material in Portuñol, as well as manuals such as Patricia Varela González's *¿Hablas español o portuñol?*[12]

Leo Rosten published a dictionary called *The Joys of Yinglish*.[13] But the most expansive field in the constellation of hybrid languages is African American vernacular English. My friend Henry Louis Gates, Jr. is editing a new dictionary on this topic for Oxford University Press.

MB: As we think about the diaspora of Spanish and Spanglish speakers across the US, let's consider varieties within the language and how you would approach

---

[8] Miguel de Cervantes, *Don Quixote of La Mancha*, trans. John Ormbsy, 400th anniversary ed., introduction by Ilan Stavans (Brooklyn: Restless Books, 2015), 4.
[9] https://dle.rae.es/
[10] *Diccionario Clave de uso del español actual* (Madrid: Ediciones SM, 2008).
[11] Yves Larouche-Claire, *Évitez le franglais, parlez français* (Paris: Albin Michel, 2004); Miles Kington, *Let's Parler Franglais* (Suffolk: Robson Books, 2004).
[12] Patricia Varela González, *¿Hablas español o portuñol?* (Sao Paulo: LTC Grupo Gen, 2014).
[13] Leo Rosten, *The Joys of Yinglish* (New York: Plume, 1990).

representation without dictionaries of the language (Cubonics, Dominicanish, Mexican-American Spanglish, Nuyorican, etc.)

IS: Truth is, there is no such thing as Spanglish, at least not in a monolithic, homogenized fashion. Just as there are varieties of Spanish all over the world – it is, as you know, the fourth most popular language – there are different types of Spanglish. The ones you mentioned are among the most important. There is also the Spanglish of the immigrant generation, the immigrant children, the third generation, and so on. Over time, lexicographic efforts have been made to record each of these varieties. In my collection, I have dictionaries of Cubonics, Nuyorican, Texas Spanglish, etc. Representation is dependent on the effort by the group to study its own language. American Spanish, unlike the Spanishes of other parts (Colombia, Costa Rica, Chile, Paraguay) is multinational in nature. The differences of Spanglishes emerge from these national backgrounds.

MB: You have had very public debates with the Real Academia Española (RAE) about the status of Spanish language. What is it about Spanglish that you think elicits such a range of feelings, attachments, even hostility? Could you imagine an academy that would protect the status of Spanglish in the United States?

IS: The RAE strikes me as a byproduct of the Cro-Magnon age: a public institution with little public support. Happily, I have been persona non grata to them, so the feeling is mutual. What would an efficient RAE do in a utopian world? Understand more dynamically why language changes, which would stop the RAE from making undemocratic efforts. To me, whenever they announce a change in the language, the dictum feels Napoleonic.

For all those reasons, I don't believe Spanglish should ever have a similar academy. The proof is in the pudding: English doesn't have one, so why create a dinosaur if such a species has been extinct for millions of years? Without such an academy, a language is able to flourish more freely and independently. It boils down to the role of government in people's lives: Do we really want someone in Madrid or Washington telling us what to say?

By the way, I see the role of the public intellectual as an articulator of common thought. I don't expect anyone at the RAE or elsewhere to agree with me. My purpose is to make people think. It's an easy job: think openly and for the common good, even when you're in a minority.

MB: Your book *Dictionary Days: A Defining Passion* provides a kind of origin story for your personal relationship to the history of lexicography.[14] How has your relationship to dictionaries and hybrid languages changed since the publication of that book?

IS: As you say, *Dictionary Days* is an autobiography. But it did something for me I didn't expect: it set a path forward. Fiona McRae, editor-in-chief at Graywolf Press, invited me to turn a short lecture I delivered in Ann Arbor, Michigan, titled "Ink, Inc.," into a short book. That short book compelled me to delve deeper into my passion for dictionaries, to the point where I no longer think of it as another area of interest but as a way of life. In other words, my relationship with dictionaries intensified after *Dictionary Days* was published: my collection expanded, I found myself lecturing on this theme more often, and I was inspired

---

[14] Ilan Stavans, *Dictionary Days: A Defining Passion* (Minneapolis, MN: Graywolf, 2008).

to look at dictionaries from multiple perspectives. One day, I would like to compile a dictionary of lost words in multiple languages.

MB: In your article "A Lay Lexicographer," you describe yourself as an amateur even with your abundant writing about the lives of dictionaries and Spanglish. What about inexpert or nonprofessional approaches to this topic is most inspiring to you?

IS: Without false modesty, in the same sense that Nebrija and Samuel Johnson were: lovers of language, eager to understand how it functions.

MB: Behind this desire to understand how language functions, we also find abundant evidence for creative engagement and world-making through language. Could you talk in more detail about the inventive possibilities of hybrid language and the kinds of artistic languages created in fictional worlds, both in text and on screen. Here are a few famous examples: J.R.R. Tolkien's Quenya and Sindarin for *The Lord of the Rings*, Klingon for *Star Trek*, and Na'vi for *Avatar*.

IS: They are called "constructed" languages. Tolkien, a medievalist at Oxford and the translator of a mediocre rendition of *Beowulf*, is said to have written the whole Middle Earth saga in order to populate speakers of the various invented languages he had concocted.[15] Eugene Roddenberry, the creator of Star Trek, refers to Klingon in the first episode, "The Trouble with Tribbles," although audiences didn't hear a full sentence until a motion picture based on the TV show was released in 1979. A Native American language specialist, Mark Okrand, eventually put it together. And Na'vi was created by Paul Frommer, a professor at USC Marshall School of Business, at the request of James Cameron.

Although these languages are fanciful concoctions (again: aren't all languages that way?), there are worldwide fans who have taught themselves Quenya, Klingon, and Na'vi, proof that the human need to communicate has no limit.

MB: Some describe hybrid languages in terms of contact or interference. We've spoken quite a bit about the relationships between Spanish and English in the United States, but it would be helpful to talk about alternate examples: Portuñol, emerging as a result of the geographic contact along the Spanish-Portuguese border and the Brazilian border; of Franglais, on the border of England and France. In terms of language interference for bilingual s-peakers, the hybrid form can be seen as evidence in proficiency.

IS: Those two are important examples. Spending time in those hybrid areas, it is astonishing to witness the fluidity of speakers. But Franglais, for instance, is vigorous in countless other places. In France per se, radio, TV, and music frequently use English words, a fact that aggravates Francophone purists. Charles Aznavour's lovely song "For Me, For Me, Formidable," about a French speaker declaring his love to an English girl, always comes to mind. In Quebec, Canada, Franglais is for some a disgrace and for others an expression of true coexistence, which is the same emotion one experiences in Barcelona

---

[15] J. R. R. Tolkien, *Beowulf: A Translation and Commentary* (New York: Houghton Mifflin, 2014).

when hearing Spanish and Catalan intertwined. And Cameroon, with its English and French populations, also experiences this kind of interference. I have read poems in Franglais, just as I have in Portuñol. Speakers of these hybrid tongues feel a sense of liberation when they use them, since they are jazzy (i.e. nonstructured).

MB: How do you respond to the idea of hybrid languages as bad slang? In Franglais, we see speakers refer to *le week-end*. Or in Spanglish, you might eat *lonche* in the *marketa*. I am also curious how you see social media reframing alliances with these languages and identities, considering for example the #nosabokid phenomenon.

IS: Social media accelerated the development of a language. Whereas in the past it would take years for a new word to be disseminated in the linguistic ecosystem, Facebook, Twitter, Instagram, and other platforms accelerate that speed exponentially. Take the example of Spanish: it developed in the twelfth century but it wasn't until three centuries later, in 1492, when it consolidated its political, social, economic, and linguistic status. In contrast, the first time the word Spanglish was used was in the 1970s. A few decades later, thanks to social media, it became widespread, not only in the United States but in numerous parts of the Spanish-speaking world. This couldn't have happened were it not for TV, radio, movies, and, as I said, social media, the latter being the most democratic of any media format.

MB: As you say, there is so much about this contemporary moment that allows us to engage deeply with language innovation. But these innovations have long histories that are worth bringing into conversation as well. Can we think more about for example the fall of the Roman Empire and the birth of Romance languages from Latin?

IS: The Romance languages were born when the Roman empire fractured into pieces. Latin isn't spoken today in France, Portugal, Italy, Spain, Romania, and so on; instead, each of these areas developed its own language. French, Portuguese, Italian, Spanish, and Romanian were at some point hybrid languages. It's appealing to me to think of the possibility of the English-speaking world today (England and its commonwealth, the United States, Australia, New Zealand, etc.) breaking apart into sublinguistic regions. This is unlikely to happen, as it is unlikely that the Spanish-speaking world will break into linguistically distinct regions. The reason is that the historical conditions are dramatically different. Spanglish is indeed a breakaway reality. As such, it deserves all our scholarly attention.

MB: Can we talk more about Esperanto, today the most widely spoken constructed language in the world? L. L. Zamenhof created it in the 1880s to support the creation of a universal second language that would promote understanding, publishing the *Fundamento de Esperanto* in 1905.[16] How do you understand the relative success of Esperanto, and what we can learn from native speakers of the language?

---

[16] L. L. Zamenhof, *Fundamento de Esperanto: Gramatiko, Ezercaro, Universala Vortaro* (Paris: Hachette, 1905).

Hybrid Languages 69

IS: I love Esperanto. Zamenhof was a Yiddish speaker who believed the globe needed a new language in order to foster authentic international peace and cooperation. Yiddish was the lingua franca of Eastern European Jews; Zamenhof was inspired by its capacity to travel across borders.

Esperanto is what could be described as a "lab" language: a creation founded by a single individual but enhanced by thousands of others over time, not in situ but as an abstraction. It is also called an "auxiliary" language, a language that serves as a common ground for speakers who don't have a common first tongue. Like Yiddish but unlike the majority of standardized languages, it doesn't have an address (i.e. a territory), although it is included in the educational systems of China and Hungary, and there are numerous Esperanto speakers in Neutral Moresnet, between Belgium and Germany. It has also been repressed in various places and times, such as Stalinist Russia, Nazi Germany, and Franco's Spain.

The lessons of Esperanto are many: new languages are always popping up. What they need is a raison d'être: an ideology, a territorial claim, a religious justification, and so on.

MB: Back to Spanglish, we talked some about the support provided by social media in terms of identifying with the language. How do you understand the popular notoriety of the language through Hollywood? Why did it take until 2021 for *Encanto* to be released by Disney? What does it mean for Jennifer López to sing the national anthem in Spanish? Why not a century ago?

IS: Hollywood is both a trendsetter and a trend follower. The Spanglish of the children's movie *Encanto* is a reflection on the vitality of this form of communication on the streets, in kitchens, and in classrooms. Likewise, *Encanto* and other similar artifacts – say Steven Spielberg's version of *West Side Story* – validate this hybrid language, grading it political capital.

Why Spanglish now? Because Latinos in the US are a powerhouse, all 65 million of them. And because it is estimated that by 2060 Spanish will be spoken by 111 million people in the US, which is twice the current population of Colombia. A century ago, even fifty years ago, there was no such thing as a Latino. It is worth asking, as a nod to Nebrija: Is Spanglish the new companion of empire?

MB: What do you speculate about the future of Spanglish? What are your hopes for the language?

IS: I think the future of Spanglish has arrived. I hope we never have the equivalent of the Real Academia Española.

MB: Where do you see new hybrid languages emerging right now? What are the common strategies of these languages? What do these trends and deviations tell you about the possibilities for the future?

IS: Hybrid languages emerge wherever civilizations clash. This happens in border areas and wherever immigrants arrive in solid numbers. It is a natural reaction to cultural tension. We often lament the death of aboriginal languages – and we should, since their disappearance entails the death of an entire human structure: its customs, its memory. As I mentioned when talking about Esperanto, in contrast we seldom celebrate the emergence of fresh new languages, foolishly thinking that the creation of a new linguistic code is impossible. It isn't, though:

neither impossible nor improbable. New languages are born all the time, just as established languages change in order to survive.

Suggested Readings

Archive of the Indigenous Languages of Latin America (AILLA). University of Textas at Austin. https://ailla.utexas.org/about/

Cervantes, Miguel de. *Don Quixote of La Mancha.* English and Spanglish editions. Adapted by Ilan Stavans, illustrated by Roberto Weil. Philadelphia: Pennsylvania State University Press, 2018.

de León-Portilla, Ascención H. "Nebrija y el inicio de la lingüística mesoamericana." *Anuario de Letras, Lingüística y Filología* 31 (1993): 205–23.

Fuller, Janet M., and Jennifer Leeman. *Speaking Spanish in the US: The Sociopolitics of Language.* Vol. 16. Bristol: Multilingual Matters, 2020.

Gates, Henry Louis, Jr. *The Black Box: Writing the Race.* Hoboken, NJ: Penguin, 2024.

Hecht, Shasta. "Franglais." *The Oval* 16, no. 1 (2023): article 8.

Heck, Ellen. *A Is for Bee: An Alphabet Book in Translation.* Hoboken, NJ: Levine Querido, 2022.

Kent, David B. "Speaking in Tongues: Chinglish, Japlish and Konglish." *KOTESOL Proceedings PAC2, 1999 The Second Pan Asian Conference,* 1999.

Li, David C. S. "Between English and Esperanto: What Does It Take to Be a World Language?" *International Journal of the Sociology of Language* 164 (2003): 33–63.

Lipski, John. "Too Close for Comfort? The Genesis of 'Portuñol/Portunhol.'" *Selected Proceedings of the 8th Hispanic Linguistics Symposium.* Somerville, MA: Cascadilla Proceedings Project, 2006.

Lipski, John. "Spanish, English, or Spanglish? Truth and Consequences of US Latino Bilingualism." In *Spanish and Empire,* edited by Nelsy Echavez-Solano and Kenya C. Dworkin y Mendez, 197–218. Nashville: Vanderbilt University Press, 2007.

Lozano, Rosina. *American Language: The History of Spanish in the United States.* Berkeley: University of California Press, 2018.

Rosten, Leo. *The Joys of Yinglish.* New York: Plume, 1990.

Saint Exúpery, Antonie de. *El Little Príncipe.* Translated into Spanglish by Ilan Stavans. Neckarsteinach: Edition Tintenfass, 2017.

Stamper, Kory. *Word by Word: The Secret Life of Dictionaries.* New York: Vintage, 2018.

Stavans, Ilan. *Spanglish: The Making of a New American Language.* New York: Harper Collins, 2002.

Stavans, Ilan. *Dictionary Days: A Defining Passion.* Minneapolis, MN: Graywolf, 2008.

Stavans, Ilan. "A Lay Lexicographer: On Codifying the Dictionary of Spanglish." *Dictionaries: Journal of the Dictionary Society of North America,* 41, no. 2 (2020): 197–212.

Stavans, Ilan. *How Yiddish Changed America and How America Changes Yiddish.* Amherst, MA: Restless Books, 2020.

Stavans, Ilan, and Margaret Boyle. "How Dictionaries Define Us: Margaret Boyle and Ilan Stavans in Conversation." Los Angeles Review of Books, 2022. https://lareviewofbooks.org/article/how-dictionaries-define-us-margaret-boyle-and-ilan-stavans-in-conversation/

Varela González, Patricia. *¿Hablas español o portuñol?* Sao Paulo: LTC Grupo Gen, 2014.

Weinreich, Max. *History of the Yiddish language*. Vol. 1. New Haven, CT: Yale University Press, 2008.

6   English

Peter Gilliver

At the end of the first quarter of the twenty-first century, about 400 million people are native English speakers. With those for whom English is a second language, the number reaches far above: between 1.5 billion and 2 billion. Linguist David Crystal believes the ratio of non-native to native English speakers is three to one. Needless to say, English is a challenging language, especially when it comes to spelling – in James Joyce's words, it is "the most ingenious torture ever devised for sins committed in previous lives." This conversation concentrates on the *Oxford English Dictionary* (*OED*) as a Platonic model not only within the English language but in countless other linguistic ecosystems. It looks at Samuel Johnson as the cathartic figure whose lexicographic work shaped modern English dictionaries. And it ponders the sprawling *OED* products and compares the enterprise to its American counterpart, *Merriam-Webster*. (Peter Sokolowski, a conversant in the dialogue on French that appears in the next chapter, is editor-at-large at Merriam.) In short, what follows might be called a creative exploration of – or a series of efflorescences from – the ways in which the pragmatic perspective of the practising lexicographer differs from the philosopher's ideal/idealistic perspective.

***

ILAN STAVANS: The *OED* is the mother ship of lexicons. As an immigrant with limited means, I remember coming across with trepidation the two-volume edition that came in a box with a small drawer containing a magnifying glass. I bought myself a copy after I saved a bit of money. Looking up a word was simultaneously arduous and thrilling: arduous because the font was so small, you had the impression you were involved in an archeological quest; and thrilling because the lexicon invariably gave you the impression it was "total," meaning it had done everything in its power not to leave anything out, although, of course, this is impossible. You have been with the *OED* since 1987. I want to start with your family. Both your parents were linguists. Might you describe the role that studying, defining, and cataloging words played in your childhood household?

PETER GILLIVER: Yes, we were a very "language-minded" family: there were often discussions about language and usage (mainly English but also occasionally German – I spent my childhood in Germany, where my father worked for the British Army as a language lecturer, and my mother taught English classes in local German schools).

I can trace my interest in words as individual entities to, firstly, the family's enjoyment of the TV panel game *Call My Bluff* – a version of the "Dictionary Game" in which celebrities tried to guess the meaning of obscure words picked from the pages of the *OED* – and, secondly, a school dictionary (I've never been able to track down which one) which I found strangely readable. (I seem to have a particular memory of the word *chalazion*; what such a rare word for a pimple was doing in a small children's dictionary I can't imagine, but it stuck in my mind.)

Perhaps this laid the groundwork for the "feel for words" which I think makes a good lexicographer; but I credit the "watering" of that "ground" to Mr. Emberton, one of my teachers at boarding school. I certainly took to Latin (which was his subject), but he also spotted – and fed – my interest in English words and wordplay. (I learned how to tackle the *Times* crossword at his elbow, something for which I remain eternally grateful to him.)

Also, at boarding school I did something which I think a fair number of language-minded children do: in collaboration with my best friend at school – a remarkable boy who had begun to learn ancient Egyptian in his early teens (and who has gone on to become a very distinguished Egyptologist) – I devised a language of my own, which involved compiling a dictionary of it. This may have been partly inspired, as I know it is for many people, by the invented languages to be found in J. R. R. Tolkien's books, of which I (and he) was an admirer; certainly I'm not the only *OED* lexicographer who had a go at doing this.

Which is a bit of a hotchpotch of strands of influence; but I do think that some of those things contributed to my being a lexicographer.

IS: I like your use of parenthetical phrases, which dictionaries, of course, are precluded from doing. Anyway, in numerous cases in this volume, being aware of dictionaries in other languages has left a mark on lexicographers. Do you speak other languages? Do they serve as a "contrast" in the way you look at the development of English?

PG: I have a basic-to-decent knowledge of French and German, and Latin, and I can stagger by, on a tourist level, in one or two other Romance languages. I don't have a solid familiarity with dictionaries of any language other than English. So, no, dictionaries of other languages haven't had a significant influence on my relationship with the lexicography – or the history – of English. By the way, I don't know what you mean about dictionaries not parenthesizing: in my book, a lexicographer should feel free to use whatever means may be necessary to describe the lexicon.

IS: Sometimes in the dead of night, in a bout of insomnia, I like to imagine how languages came to be. I think of Jorge Luis Borges' story "Tlön, Uqbar, *Orbis Tertius*" (1940), about a fictional country where, like the materialist world in which we live, everything exists in ideal form.[1] Borges tells us that in Tlön's

---

[1] Jorge Luis Borges, "Tlön, Uqbar, *Orbis Tertius*," in *Collected Fictions*, trans. Andrew Hurley (New York: Viking, 1999), 68–81.

Ursprache there are no nouns; instead, there are impersonal verbs, modified by monosyllabic prefixes with an adverbial value. For instance, he argues that there is no word for "moon," but there is a verb which in English would be "to moon" or "to moonate." 'The moon rose above the "river,"' he says, "is *hlor u fang axaxaxas mlo*, or literally: 'upward behind the onstreaming it mooned.'"[2] Anyway, I enjoy imagining the dictionaries used in Tlön and wonder at what time they appeared in the development of the nation's language.

Like French, Portuguese, and Spanish, among others, English is an imperial language. Is the appearance of an authoritative dictionary at a precise moment in the history of a language a statement about its maturity?

PG: Well now, this isn't an interesting question I've ever given much thought to. (Another parenthesis: I've never read anything by Borges, but it strikes me as bizarre that he should envisage an ideal language as being one without nouns.) I'm afraid I will do what lexicographers do: query the word "authoritative." The way in which the *OED* is authoritative – namely as an exhaustively documented historical record of the development of English lexis – is a very different kind of "authoritativeness" from what many of today's readers look for in a dictionary: namely authoritative *assertion* about what is "correct" or "valid" in a language.

When I put it like that, I find myself wondering whether it's actually not *maturity* in a language that is most conducive to the creation of authoritative texts (in the latter sense) about it, so much as *insecurity* about the state – and the status – of a language. It's not hard to find, in writing about English in the seventeenth and eighteenth centuries, expressions of concern about linguistic disorder and decline, and – often in the same sources – advocacy of dictionaries as performing a welcome standardizing function.

And it's my impression that many of the dictionaries that appeared in this period were a response, sometimes explicitly so, to this expression of a need for regulation/standardization. Johnson's dictionary was, surely, one of these, certainly in its genesis (I'm thinking of Lord Chesterfield's acclamation of Johnson as a fit "dictator" to establish that "lawful standard of our language" that he has long felt the lack of.)[3]

But your question does suggest another, related question: How can we explain the appearance of particular dictionaries at particular points in time? I'm not enough of a Johnson scholar to be able to say just why Johnson's dictionary appeared when it did, but could it perhaps be argued that its appearance – as the most masterfully "authoritative" response to his contemporaries' desire for regulation/standardization – owes everything to Johnson being the man he was?

When it comes to the *OED*, on which I feel better qualified to comment, I think it's pretty clear that there was "something in the air" in mid nineteenth-century Europe, which gave rise to not one but several projects to compile dictionaries of particular languages that were unprecedentedly historical in their approach: the Grimm brothers' *Deutsches Wörterbuch* project, the

---

[2] Borges, "Tlön, Uqbar, *Orbis Tertius*," 77.
[3] Samuel Johnson, *A Dictionary of the English Language* (London: printed by W. Strahan for J. and P. Knapton et al., 1755); [Lord Chesterfield], letter published in *The World* No. 100, November 28, 1754.

Woordenboek der Nederlandsche Taal, and the *New English Dictionary on Historical Principles*, which we know better as the *OED*. When I wrote about this in my history of the *OED*, I argued that one of the "things in the air" was the Romantic conception of a language as the embodiment of a nation's identity;[4] I think the lexicographers of the time were moved to give this conception expression through what has come to be called the "historical principle" – the idea that (in the words of Franz Passow, who had done this for ancient Greek a few years earlier) a dictionary should tell "the life history of each individual word."[5]

Passow could hope to do this single-handedly for a language like ancient Greek, with its limited corpus; for modern languages the collection of the evidence from which these "life histories" could be told was a task too big for one individual, but one which could have the grand appeal of a "national" project. I put "national" in quotation marks because in the case of English the appeal reached beyond one nation to all corners of the English-speaking world – since that is the language which the *New English Dictionary* aspired to document. And today's *OED* lexicographers are continuing that work.

IS: Passow's lexicographic work, because it dealt with a limited corpus, was sharply focused. His *Vermischte Schriften* (1843) is a fascinating exploration of his method and affinities.[6] He had an impact on James Murray. Anyway, Samuel Johnson's *A Dictionary of the English Language*, to my mind, is the most astonishing of lexicons ever produced in any tongue. That a single man put it together almost alone is, in and of itself, a feat to reckon with. What have dictionaries lost in the process of becoming efforts done by committee?

PG: Johnson's achievement is certainly prodigious (though I'm glad, for the sake of his assistants, that you put in that "almost"). I think it could be argued that Noah Webster's achievement in compiling his 1828 dictionary "almost single-handedly" is also pretty impressive.[7] And who else is there? Charles Richardson, compiler of another two-volume English dictionary in 1835–37?[8] And I'm sure there are comparable figures in the lexicography of other languages (I find Émile Littré's four-volume work pretty amazing, for example).[9] But the size of the task of compiling a comprehensive dictionary – of English or any language with a comparably rich history – has now grown far beyond what a single individual could hope to achieve in a lifetime.

To be honest, I can't help seeing the development from one-person dictionaries to team efforts more in terms of gains than losses: quite apart from the

---

[4] Peter Gilliver, *The Making of the Oxford English Dictionary* (Oxford: Oxford University Press, 2016).
[5] Franz Passow, *Johann Gottlob Schneiders Handwörterbuch der griechischen Sprache: Nach der dritten Ausgabe des grössern Griechischdeutschen Wörterbuchs ... ausgearbeitet*, 2nd ed., Vol. 1: A–K. (Leipzig: F. C. W. Vogel, 1826), p. xvi (translation my own).
[6] Franz Passow, *Vermischte Schriften* (Leipzig: F. A. Brockhaus, 1843).
[7] Noah Webster, *An American Dictionary of the English Language* (New York: Sherman Converse, 1828).
[8] Charles Richardson, *A New Dictionary of the English Language* (London: William Pickering, 1835–37).
[9] Émile Littré, *Dictionnaire de la langue française* (Paris: Hachette, 1863–72).

simple fact that the person-hours – or person-centuries – required to compile a dictionary like the *OED* make a collective approach essential; having a team means that you can be sure of having at your disposal more of the different kinds of expertise that the work needs. Yes, of course a dictionary that hasn't been compiled by an individual may well be, well, less individual, less obviously showing the stamp of one person – though there are still all sorts of ways in which the guiding hand of a chief editor like James Murray can still be discerned in the *OED*'s character and policy and style (keen as he always was to stress its collective nature and to acknowledge the part played by his staff).

And indeed, if you know where to look, you can still find later English dictionaries compiled by an individual whose character strongly shines through its pages. Of course, there are works like Ambrose Bierce's *Devil's Dictionary*, but of course that's not a dictionary in the usual sense;[10] I was thinking more of H. C. Wyld's *Universal Dictionary of the English Language* (1932), whose definitions are sometimes almost Johnsonianly idiosyncratic (like the famous *bun* "small round sweet spongy cake with convex top and too few currants").[11]

IS: I frequently go to the definition in the *OED* of "God": "A superhuman person regarded as having power over nature and human fortunes; a deity (use in the singular usually refers to a being regarded as male (cf. *goddess* n.), but in the plural frequently used to refer to male and female beings collectively). Chiefly applied to the divinities of polytheistic systems; when applied to the Supreme Being of monotheistic belief, this sense becomes more or less modified." And it goes on, of course. I find troublesome countless aspects of this definition. For starters, "a superhuman person"? Anyway, what is the longest entry in the *OED*? Is there a house limit for length?

PG: Well, it depends what you mean by "longest" (what a predictable response from a lexicographer). If we're talking bytes, then at the moment it's the entry for the verb *run*. (An entry which I happen to have first-hand experience of: I spent nine months revising it. In fact, I was only one part of the revision process, and others were working on it before and after me.) "At the moment" is a key qualifier here, though: the revision of the dictionary is ongoing, and every unrevised entry – which may have been originally written a century ago or more – becomes quite a bit larger when it's revised.

This may be because an old word has acquired new meanings; but even a word which has remained semantically unchanged still needs – unless it's become obsolete – to have the documentation of its existence extended, with additional quotations bringing the illustration of its history down to the present (or down to when it ceased to be used). So it's possible that one of the bigger unrevised entries will overtake *run* when it's revised. One obvious candidate is that for *set* (verb), which occupied more printed pages than any other entry in the first edition of the dictionary, longer than *run*.

However, I think this is unlikely: *set* feels to me like a verb whose time has passed – it's not as common as it was, and it's been less "active" in the last

---

[10] Ambrose Bierce, *The Devil's Dictionary* (New York: Walter Neale, 1911).
[11] H. C. Wyld, *The Universal Dictionary of the English Language* (London: Amalgamated Press, 1932).

century (in the sense of throwing off new meanings and new uses) than *run*. So, yes, the entry will expand when it's revised, mainly because the paragraph of quotations that accompanies the definition of every current sense of *set* will get longer, but I don't think it will overtake *run*. Or *take* or *go* – these being the next two largest entries by bytes. Both are also revised entries for verbs. These "big verbs" certainly feel like the most challenging entries in the *OED*, in terms of stamina!

It's worth saying, though, that for a lexicographer the "size" of an entry may be better gauged by a different yardstick: not the number of bytes but the number of *components* into which it's divided. (These are how we measure out our progress on the *OED*; our quarterly and annual targets are set in terms of the number of components we get through.)

We normally call these components "senses," but this is sometimes a misnomer: in the case of a verb like *run*, yes, each of the subsenses of the word constitutes one unit of work – and each of the subsenses of the various phrasal verbs that it forms (*to run down*, *to run up*, etc) – but in the case of a noun like *sea*, the entry will contain not only the simple noun itself (in all its senses and subsenses) but huge numbers of compounds like *sea air* and *sea bed*, each of which requires to be separately documented. (The more important of these compounds, like *seagull* and *seaman*, are "promoted" to become separate entries in their own right, but there are hundreds of less important compounds that remain as sublemmas in the parent entry.)

In fact, measured in terms of number of components, the entry for *sea* (noun) is the second largest in the *OED* even though it hasn't yet been revised: it has 749 components. (The highest-scoring verb entry is *run* with 607.) The biggest of all, by this yardstick, is one that might surprise you: the entry for the combining form *over-*, which currently has 859 components, starting with the sublemmas *over-billow* and *over-branch* (verbs) and ending with the adjectives *over-ocean* and *over-shoulder*.

You might wonder to what extent formations like these are really worth documenting in their own right. So do we: sometimes it seems better to record the fact that a word, or a word-element, is productive of a particular kind of formation than to attempt the hopeless task of recording and illustrating every such formation.

That's the only way with something like the prefix *un-*, for example – which can be prefixed to just about every word in English to form another word. Working out how to deal with words beginning with *un-* in a historically appropriate manner without making the U volume of the dictionary outweigh the rest of the alphabet caused the editors of the first edition no end of headaches, and revising them for the third edition was also a challenge. The entries for *un-* (there are two) are big, but they could be much bigger if we'd dealt with the material differently. Neither of them make it into the top forty entries by either yardstick (bytes or components).

And no, there is no house limit on the length of an *OED* entry: if we're aiming to give a sufficiently full and fully documented account of the history of a word, it has to take as long as it takes. Which is not to say that we don't strive for concision, even though the constraints on physical extent that the compilers of the first edition laboured under – constraints imposed by the cost to the publisher of every inch, every millimetre of printed text – don't apply in the same way in an electronically issued dictionary: there is still the fact that the human reader needs to be able to cope with the entry, and this becomes more and more of a challenge the more "mental space" it takes up. So, no longer than necessary.

Oh, and as for "the" *OED* definition of "God": that of course is the current definition (of sense 1a), which is significantly different from that given in the first edition. Comparison of the two versions, and what the differences tell us about a whole range of things, may, as they say, be left as an exercise for the reader.

IS: Do you know if English, over its extended history, has produced more dictionaries, by which I mean more varieties, than other languages?

PG: I'm pretty sure there are more recognized regional varieties of English than of any other language; and certainly specific dictionaries for many of them have been published – more, I would guess, than for any other language. If I was trying to find a different answer to your question I suppose I might say that Latin gave rise to many regional "varieties" which went on to become distinct languages, and that if we count up all the dictionaries of all the Romance languages we might be able to beat the total for English; but (a) I'm not even sure about that and (b) I know that wasn't the question you were asking!

IS: It strikes me as meaningful that the *OED* is an academic endeavor based in the United Kingdom whereas *Merriam-Webster* is a commercial enterprise produced in America.

PG: I'm not quite sure where to go with this. Do you know the British expression "horses for courses"? Or "apples and oranges"? Some of the most important other dictionaries of English that are most like the *OED* – in being compiled on historical principles, with entries containing quotations illustrating each word's history – have in fact emerged, or are emerging, from North American academic institutions: the *Dictionary of American English*, compiled in four volumes under the auspices of the University of Chicago (1938–44); the *Middle English Dictionary*, done by the University of Michigan (1952–2001, revision ongoing); and the *Dictionary of Old English*, by the University of Toronto, still in progress.[12]

In some ways, I would argue that the closest British counterpart to *Merriam-Webster*'s "unabridged" is the *Shorter Oxford English Dictionary*: originally published in two volumes (like Noah Webster's original and several later editions), with some historical focus but only a sprinkling of quotations.[13] When Oxford University Press (OUP) was first approached about the possibility of publishing the Philological Society's proposed big historical dictionary, in

---

[12] William A. Craigie and James R. Hulbert, *A Dictionary of American English on Historical Principles* (Chicago: University of Chicago Press, 1938–44); Hans Kurath et al., *Middle English Dictionary* (Ann Arbor: University of Michigan Press, 1954–2001); Angus Cameron et al., *Dictionary of Old English* (Toronto: Centre for Medieval Studies, University of Toronto, 1986–).

[13] William Little, H. W. Fowler, Jessie Coulson, and C. T. Onions, *The Shorter Oxford English Dictionary on Historical Principles* (Oxford: Clarendon Press, 1933).

English

1877, they were blandished with the claim that they would be investing in "what promises to be a very safe and remunerative [undertaking]."

This of course proved not to be the case – the first edition of the *OED* was to cost OUP hundreds of thousands of pounds, and the Press's investment in the ongoing revision programme now runs into millions – but even after OUP reconciled itself to this, it was recognized from very early on that shorter abridgements of the dictionary *could* be profitable. And this was to prove to be the case: I believe the *Concise Oxford Dictionary* was a runaway commercial success from its first publication in 1911, and by the 1970s, sales of the *Concise* and other smaller dictionaries were bringing in millions of pounds a year.[14]

IS: Profit – this makes me think of the internet as today's default habitat of dictionaries. What I mean is that many more users seek words online than in a physical copy of the dictionary. Is the age of the printed dictionary coming to an end?

PG: I'm sure it must be the case that many, many fewer print dictionaries are sold now than was the case even a few years ago. And it's hard to see how the ready accessibility over the internet, mainly for free, of information that once was only available in a print dictionary is going to go away. Which implies that, yes, the age of the print dictionary must be passing. That being said, dictionaries have always served many different purposes ... and the question I would ask is, out of all of the different purposes which a dictionary can serve, are *all* of them now served better by online dictionaries than by print ones?

I don't know enough about the state of dictionary publishing to answer that – I'm a lexicographer, not a dictionary publisher – but my guess would be that there may be some use cases that are still well enough met by a print dictionary for it still to be commercially worthwhile to produce one. Most likely in contexts where access to the internet is most constrained.

IS: How has lexicography changed since you became a lexicographer?

PG: On the one hand, enormously; on the other, very little. When I started work on the *OED*, our lexicography was pretty well entirely paper-based, and almost all aspects of the work would have been recognizable to James Murray and the other compilers of the first edition. The evidence to be considered when drafting a dictionary entry for a new word or meaning – and I started as a new words editor – was all in the form of 6-inch-by-4-inch slips of paper, mostly handwritten; it's true that we supplemented the quotations that had been collected by the dictionary's paid and volunteer readers by checking in some computer-generated concordances of particular texts, but we did so by writing out more quotations on more slips.

The end result was a bundle of slips: a chronologically ordered selection of quotations illustrating the word, topped by a "top slip" bearing my draft definition, pronunciation, etymology, etc. Exactly what Murray or his assistants would have produced (although our bundles would then go off to be keyed into a database, rather than being typeset by compositors). There was no computer on my desk. There was a computer in the basement, hooked up to a modem, by

---

[14] H. W. and F. G. Fowler, *The Concise Oxford Dictionary of Current English* (Oxford: Clarendon Press, 1911).

means of which we could get "on-line" (it was hyphenated in those days) to some of the early searchable databases of text; but any database searches would be printed out and added to the bundle of slips.

Until the start of the 2020s, I would have said that on almost every *OED* lexicographer's desk there would still be some of those same paper slips; but they are rarer now (the inaccessibility of our paper files during the worst days of the pandemic probably contributed to that decline). The evidence we set about assessing when working out what needs to be said about a word is now almost entirely electronic; and we have access to more of that evidence, and more sophisticated access to it, than our predecessors could have dreamed of.

Not only can we summon up, with just a few keystrokes, every instance of a word to be found in any of dozens of databases of historical and contemporary text – from corpora of Middle and Early Modern English to X/Twitter, focusing on particular regions of the English-speaking world more or less at will – but we can also analyze the behavior of the word within these domains, using powerful text-crunching software that can tell us things like the most common objects of a particular verb, or the most typical nouns to which a particular adjective may be applied.

Instead of merely wondering whether a word or meaning may have originated in, say, the southern United States – perhaps prompted by the fact that that's where the earliest quotation slips come from – and maybe sending a library researcher on an almost-hopeless search for earlier examples in particular printed sources, a few searches of newspaper databases can take us almost to the smoking gun: yes, that word can first be found in Texas in the 1840s. Or it first came into general use among Freemasons in the late eighteenth century. Or among Australian speedway enthusiasts in the 1990s.

Often (though not always!) we can get closer to giving a definitive answer to the question "where does that word come from?" than we ever could before these amazing resources became available. This wealth of information can be a double-edged sword, though: I often liken it to having developed a far too acute sense of hearing – the "noise," in various senses of the word, can be deafening.

And anyway: though the *tools* may have changed, what we are *doing* with them hasn't. The lexicographers of the first edition of the *OED* – and, indeed, earlier lexicographers like Johnson – would recognize and understand the process as, essentially, the same as what they were doing: surveying the available data about how a word has been used, over time, and distilling this data into as accurate and comprehensive a historical account as we can manage. Analysis of the evidence, synthesis of that analysis. Because that's the right way to do lexicography. My kind of lexicography, anyway. That's what I meant by "very little has changed."

IS: Let's talk about the global aspect of English lexicography, especially its colonial endeavors. Personally, I'm intrigued by, and have worked on, how American English has matured over more than four centuries.

PG: So how long has English lexicography had a global aspect? Of course, there have been dictionaries dealing specifically with the English of regions other than the language's home country for quite a while, probably since very soon after those other varieties had become recognizable as distinct; but were there any dictionaries before the *OED* which aimed to cover – with whatever degree of comprehensiveness – multiple varieties of English within a single text?

I don't know of any. As early as 1860, in the *Canones Lexicographici*, an early statement of editorial policy for the *OED* (or, rather, of the "New English Dictionary" which would eventually become known as the *OED*), it was stated that "Americanisms and Colonialisms [...] shall be admitted on the same terms as our own words."[15] Of course, the very language used here makes it clear that the compilers had a very clear view of where the "centre" of the English language lay; and this combination of global *scope* with a Britocentric *perspective* was to persist until, I think, the last decade or so of the twentieth century.

Though James Murray, for one, was pretty inclusive in his approach, certainly by the standards of his time. Here he is in 1911:

Does [the English language] include the English of Great Britain and the English of America, the English of Australia, and of South Africa, and of those most *assertive* Englishmen, the Englishmen of India, who live in *bungalows*, hunt in *jungles*, wear *terai* hats or *puggaries* and *pyjamas*, write chits instead of letters and eat *kedgeree* and *chutni*? Yes! *In its most comprehensive sense, and* as an object of historical study, it includes all these; they are all forms of English.[16]

Amen to that.

Which is not to say that each variety of English doesn't have a distinct and vigorous identity of its own. I'm not quite sure what you mean, though, by "matured." Sure, the English that was first taken to North America over four centuries ago has had a long time to *evolve*. I suppose the thing that caused it to evolve in such a way as to become recognizably distinct from the kind of English the colonists left behind was *isolation*: that's what gives rise to speciation, isn't it? And the development of language feels a lot like biological speciation to me.

Certainly it's fascinating to explore – though this is absolutely not something on which I can claim any particular knowledge – the different things that have contributed to the identity of a variety like American English (by which I'm guessing you mean specifically US English?): the English that the earliest settlers brought with them – supplemented by all of the varieties brought by subsequent waves of immigrants – and subjected to influence from so many other languages with which those speakers have come into contact.

I know you have a particular interest in the interplay of Spanish and English, which must surely be an important influence on American English; I find myself often struck by what appear to be signs of the influence of German, such as the tendency to form compounds on the uninflected stem of a verb (e.g. *wait list*) rather than on the verbal noun (*waiting list*).

I do wonder, though, whether the era of divergence is coming to an end. If I'm right about isolation being a key factor in the divergence of one speech

---

[15] *Canones lexicographici: or rules to be observed in editing the New English Dictionary of the Philological Society, prepared by a Committee of the Society ... at two meetings, held Dec. 12, 1859 and Jan. 16, 1860, and revised by the Society at three meetings, held April 12 and 26, and May 12, 1860* (London: Philological Society, 1860), 4.

[16] J. A. H. Murray, unpublished lecture, quoted in Sarah Ogilvie, *Words of the World* (Cambridge: Cambridge University Press, 2013), 60.

community from another, well, surely it is now no longer possible for a community of speakers of a language to be as isolated from their co-linguists as the English speakers of North America (or Australia, or South Africa, or wherever) were before instantaneous international communication became universal.

I've noticed signs of *con*vergence between British and American English: whereas it used to be the case (within my recollection) that Brits said *railway station* and *aeroplane* and Americans said *train station* and *airplane*, now I'm far more likely to hear the latter pair, particularly *train station*. Though I'm sure there's no prospect of a complete homogenization of all varieties of English any time soon.

Suggested Readings

Cowie, A. P., ed. *The Oxford History of English Lexicography*. Oxford: Clarendon Press, 2009.

Durkin, Philip, ed. *The Oxford Handbook of Lexicography*. Oxford: Oxford University Press, 2016.

Gilliver, Peter. *The Making of the Oxford English Dictionary*. Oxford: Oxford University Press, 2016.

Green, Jonathon. *Chasing the Sun: Dictionary-Makers and the Dictionaries They Made*. London: Jonathan Cape, 1996.

Green, Jonathon. *Green's Dictionary of Slang* (online). greensdictofslang.com

Martin, Peter. *The Dictionary Wars: The American Fight over the English Language*. Princeton, NJ: Princeton University Press, 2019.

McMorris, Jenny. *The Warden of English: The Life of H. W. Fowler*. Oxford: Oxford University Press, 2001.

Mugglestone, Lynda, ed. *Lexicography and the OED: Pioneers in the Untrodden Forest*. Oxford: Oxford University Press, 2000.

Murray, K. M. Elisabeth. *Caught in the Web of Words: James Murray and the Oxford English Dictionary*. New Haven, CT: Yale University Press, 1977.

Ogilvie, Sarah, ed. *The Cambridge Companion to English Dictionaries*. Cambridge: Cambridge University Press, 2020.

Oxford Dictionaries Premium. https://premium.oxforddictionaries.com/english/

Proffitt, Michael, et al. *Oxford English Dictionary*. www.oed.com

Shea, Ammon. *Reading the OED: One Man, One Year, 21,730 Pages*. New York: Perigee, 2008.

Simpson, John. *The Word Detective: A Life in Words from Serendipity to Selfie*. London: Little, Brown, 2016.

Stamper, Kory. *Word by Word: The Secret Life of Dictionaries*. New York: Pantheon, 2018.

Winchester, Simon. *The Surgeon of Crowthorne*. London: Viking, 1998. Published in the US as *The Professor and the Madman*.

7 French

Marie-Hélène Drivaud and Peter Sokolowski

A total of twenty-nine countries have French as their official language – from Niger to Belgium to Burundi. The expanse of nations is called la Francophonie. In the eighteenth century, French became the language of European diplomacy. In the twenty-first, there are close to 450 million Francophone speakers worldwide. Yet France is the matrix, the center of gravity. This conversation ponders the tradition of French dictionaries, showcasing the way the Enlightenment prompted a reawakening of lexicographic endeavors. It discusses the creation of the Académie française and concentrates on the role *Le Robert*, arguably the anchoring dictionary in France, and its approach to the French language.[1] It also discusses bilingual dictionaries and various regional dictionaries, as well as creole dictionaries. The portions in this exchange by Marie-Hélène Drivaud were translated from French by Hipólito Slomianski.

***

ILAN STAVANS: The Académie française was incorporated in 1635 by Cardinal Richelieu, although he started it the year prior. It was formed as an attempt to standardize *le français classique*, what today is called *le français moderne*. Dictionaries in French have had a major impact on the standardizing of the language. Peter, let me start with you, a lover of French language.

PETER SOKOLOWSKI: As always, a joy to be in conversation, Ilan. My first project at Merriam-Webster was a French-English bilingual dictionary which was a great introduction to the world of dictionaries and the research that goes into them.

In terms of the history of French dictionaries, we have to start in Italy. The spirit of the Renaissance expressed itself as a tension between the past and the present. This was plainly true for art and architecture, which we can see with our own eyes, but it's also true for language. Unlike these other arts, we don't have sculpture or

---

[1] *Le Grand Robert de la langue française* (Paris: Le Robert), https://grandrobert.lerobert.com/.

buildings to look at when we consider the evolution and presentation of language; partly this is because language is the water in which we swim when describing ideas, which makes the changes over time hard to notice in our daily lives. This is why the dictionaries of the past are the edifices we need to inspect.

Just as there were ancient examples to follow for elegance and proportion in the visual arts, the earliest French dictionaries looked to Latin as their ideal for what they viewed as a perfection of rhetoric, grammar, and literature. It's important to remember that this was a time when people considered the past to be superior to the present. Today, our post-Enlightenment spirit requires the promise of progress, but in the sixteenth century, the motive was to emulate the past. That's what the "rebirth" was all about. The French took inspiration from what they saw in Renaissance Italy, and the parallel with architecture is more apt than you might think: the first-ever grammar of a Romance language was written by the famous Florentine architect Leon Battista Alberti in the mid 1400s, a work that argued that the Tuscan vernacular could be analyzed as a "regular" language just as Latin could. It was an assertion that Italian could also be a literary language.

Alberti could point to the then-recent examples of Petrarch, Dante, and Boccaccio for the literary use of Italian. In the century that followed, a canon of French vernacular literature was being established by Ronsard, Rabelais, and Marguerite de Navarre. The French were paying attention to language in royal and bureaucratic use as well, and in 1539 François I signed into law the *Ordonnance de Villers-Cotterêts*, which established French as the language for laws and contracts – a law still in effect today. A decade later the poet Joachim Du Bellay published his *Défense et illustration de la langue française,* a manifesto on the validity of French as a literary language, and he cited not just Latin models but Italian forms for emulation.

IS: I love these references to other languages, since the perception of French speakers is that they roll their eyes at foreigners. Mark Twain, *The Innocents Abroad* (1867), talks of how in Paris he couldn't insert a word from English in his exchanges – until he finally gave up. "We did not succeed in making those idiots understand their own language," he jokes. When did the first French dictionary appear?

PS: This emulation of what was happening in Italy became increasingly literal and concrete. First, the French printer and lexicographer Robert Estienne made a new Latin dictionary, which began as a revision of Ambrogio Calepino's celebrated 1502 *Dictionarium*. Working in northern Italy, Calepino, known in Latin as Calepinus, in French as Calepin, and in English as Calepine, created the bestselling Latin dictionary of the sixteenth century. The fact that such an influential work was entitled *Dictionarium* was itself influential, since this kind of reference book about words was new enough that it hadn't yet settled into a category of publishing. He looked to classical texts for his words and examples rather than the Latin lingua franca of medieval Europe, which made his work an assertion of the new importance of old standards.

Calepino's dictionary became so well-known that the word *calepin* became a generic synonym of *dictionnaire* in France. In his essay "Of Experience," written in the 1580s, Montaigne describes the exasperation of someone who constantly challenges the meanings of words in conversation by saying that such an exchange will "drive the respondent to the end of his Calepin."[2] The use of *calepin* broadened over time to refer to a collection of notes, words, and quotations, and it is still in active use today meaning "notebook" in French.

IS: Was Calepino embraced in other parts of Europe?

PS: Very much so. Lexicographers across Europe translated his definitions and created bilingual and polyglot lexicons out of his dictionary, works that continued in new editions until the late eighteenth century. They kept adding translations until there were entries in eleven languages in some editions. Estienne's initial Latin dictionary of 1531, the *Latinae linguae Thesaurus,* notably used some French to clarify definitions. It wasn't a full-fledged bilingual dictionary, but it was the important first step. He then made a second work by translating all the definitions to create a Latin-French dictionary, published in 1538.[3]

Estienne's next move had commercial motives as much as intellectual ones. He flipped the order of entries and their translations to make a list of French headwords, a relatively easy way to create an entirely new work destined for advanced students of Latin. Using French, rather than Latin, as the alphabetical list of headwords for the first time, this book, known as the *Dictionnaire francoislatin* was proof of the increasing status of French.[4] Appropriately enough, it also has the distinction of being the first time *Dictionnaire* was used as the title of a book in French, showing the influence of Calepino. Since the *Ordonnance de Villers-Cotterêts* dates from the same year, we can safely consider 1539 as an important starting point for French-language dictionaries.

His two bilingual dictionaries nevertheless required a high level of literacy, so Estienne innovated once again, this time by creating smaller student versions of each. He had now made an entire series of language books, with intended users ranging from the child learner to the intermediate reader to the advanced scholar. This was not just the work of a lexicographer; it was the work of a printer and publisher who had assessed the needs of the marketplace.

IS: In the spirit of the Reformation.

PS: Indeed, Ilan. Dictionaries don't develop in a vacuum, and understanding the circumstances of Estienne's work connects us with the cultural and commercial realities of his time. When someone is the "first" to achieve something that is later considered to be notable, we have a natural tendency to assume that the achievement was itself the goal, like the first person to walk on the moon or the first to climb Mount Everest. But it takes nothing away from Estienne's innovation as the first to create a dictionary of French words to say that his *Dictionnaire francoislatin* was also the consequence of the intersection of the intellectual movements and debates of the Renaissance and the Reformation.

His deep scholarly interest in the accuracy of translations from Greek and Hebrew led him to check and revise the translations made by Jerome that were established as the Vulgate, and ultimately to publishing a French-language

---

[2] Montaigne, "Oeuvres Completes," ed. Albert Thibaudet and Maurice Rat (Paris: Bibliotheque de la Pleiade, Gallimard, 1962), 1046.
[3] John Considine, *Dictionaries in Early Modern Europe: Lexicography and the Making of Heritage* (Cambridge: Cambridge University Press, 2008), 41–44.
[4] Considine, *Dictionaries in Early Modern Europe,* 44.

version of the Bible.[5] He made a major contribution to biblical studies with his system of separation of the Bible further from chapters into numbered verses – the system we still use today. These activities placed him squarely in an emerging Protestant tradition in the years leading up to the French wars of religion, and he was later forced to flee Catholic France and settle in Geneva, where he would become the publisher of many of Calvin's writings.

IS: You're talking now about the Bible as an engine in the development of lexicography.

PS: A key tenet of Protestant thought has always been that the Bible should be read, understood, and interpreted by individuals, an idea that opposed the hierarchical authority of the Catholic Church. This meant, above all, the availability of translations for non-scholars. Translation was the philosophical engine of both the Renaissance and the Reformation. Estienne used French in the *Thesaurus* to clarify the more difficult technical and idiomatic Latin phrases – more as explanations than as literal translations. These were expanded to make the fully bilingual *Dictionarium Latino-Gallicum*.[6]

Estienne would come full circle to make one final dictionary in 1553, an edition of Calepino's Latin dictionary.[7] He had abandoned his initial revision of Calepino some twenty-five years earlier in order to write his large *Thesaurus*, but in the intervening years other unscrupulous publishers had been selling versions of his work, titling them with the safely generic name of Calepino. In the days before intellectual property rights and copyright protection, there was little Estienne could do but fight fire with fire: if dictionaries under Calepino's name were still selling well, he would sell them also.

IS: How did French dictionaries evolve after Estienne?

PS: The tradition of French-language lexicography was continued after Estienne's death with a new version of his French-Latin bilingual dictionary made by Jean Nicot, published in 1606.[8] Not yet a true monolingual dictionary, Nicot's was a bit of a transitional hybrid: some definitions were given in French; some equivalents were given in Latin; and some entries provided extensive encyclopedic information. The title had also changed, from *Dictionnaire françoislatin* to *Thresor de la langue françoyse*, an indication of both the implicit strength of Estienne's title of *Thesaurus* (treasury) for a large and scholarly dictionary and the continued instability of the name given to an alphabetical reference book containing a (mostly) alphabetical account of the meanings of words.

IS: Now to the Académie française.

PS In Italy by this time, a new and official gathering of linguistic experts had begun meeting in Florence. Called the Accademia della Crusca, the group was formed in 1583 under the protection of Duke Cosimo I de' Medici. It was to be

---

[5] Elizabeth Armstrong, *Robert Estienne Royal Printer: An Historical Study of the Elder Stephanus* (Cambridge: Cambridge University Press, 1954), 72, 228.

[6] Considine, *Dictionaries in Early Modern Europe*, 44.

[7] Martine Furno, "Les dictionnaires de Robert Estienne: Sens et finalités d'une oeuvre lexicographique," in *Voces*, 10–11 (Salamanca: Ediciones Universidad de Salamanca, 1999–2000), 11–27.

[8] Terence Russon Wooldridge, *Les débuts de la lexicographie française: Estienne, Nicot et le Thresor de la langue françoyse (1606)* (Toronto: University of Toronto Press, 1977), 17.

the second great linguistic phenomenon to be copied by the French. This academy was given the task of creating the first true dictionary of Italian, published in 1612 as *Vocabolario degli Accademici della Crusca*.[9] The seal and symbol of the Accademia is the grain mill or sifter, making their mission a metaphor: *crusca* is the word for "bran," which is sifted and separated from the flour. They saw their task as one of purification of the language – the English idiom is "separate the wheat from the chaff" – which was precisely the intention of Cardinal Richelieu for the founding of the Académie française in 1635.

Their stated mission wasn't just the "purification" but the "perfecting" of the French language, and creating a dictionary would be their goal. As in Italy for Italian, in France there was anxiety about the status of French as a serious and literary language. The renewal of interest in ancient texts during the fifteenth and sixteenth centuries that had made classical Latin the model of perfection now instilled a desire to establish French as its literary equal. The question of what constitutes a "perfect," functioning, and artistic language is one that can be debated forever – and that's more or less what took place next.

IS: An academy to make perfect a language that is by definition imperfect. Other similar institutions, for instance the Real Academia Española in Madrid, published their own dictionary. This is a strategy to exercise linguistic control.

PS: Precisely. The project began in 1639 with high hopes. However, progress proved to be disappointingly slow, since the academicians would debate the wording for each definition in their meetings while attempting to find consensus through argument and opinion. This had the effect of paralyzing progress, and enlightened suggestions for streamlining the work went unheeded. Some of the efforts made to instill discipline seem comical, such as the issuing of tokens redeemable for cash to individual members who would deign to assemble for two whole hours per week. Group debate is the most inefficient possible method for editing a dictionary.

The inefficiency of this process was underscored by two private dictionary projects that took place while the Académie debated, both of which successfully produced very good dictionaries. The lexicographers Pierre Richelet and Antoine Furetière looked to their contemporaries rather than the ancients for linguistic standards and included the language of the ideal enlightened gentleman, or *honnête homme*, as well as the highly mannered but precise language of *préciosité*. They incorporated a broader vocabulary than the limited and "purified" one in the task set for itself by the Académie.

Both works earned their authors unique distinctions.

Richelet's *Dictionnaire françois* (1680) was the first true monolingual dictionary of French, given that Nicot's *Thresor* still used Latin translations in many entries.[10] It was also the first European monolingual dictionary to be published as two large volumes – the same way that later dictionaries by Samuel Johnson and Noah Webster would be presented. And Louis XIV let it

---

[9] John Considine, *Academy Dictionaries 1600–1800* (Cambridge: Cambridge University Press, 2014), 9.
[10] Considine, *Academy*, 41.

IS: be known that he preferred Furetière's dictionary to the Académie's once theirs was finally published in 1694 – a deep insult to their labors.[11] Perhaps mercifully, none of the original members of the Académie was alive to hear this news. It had taken nearly sixty years to complete the project.

IS: It smells of "officialness."

PS: Right, and because the Académie had a royal privilege, or exclusive right, for the publication of a dictionary "to polish and perfect the French language," the works of Richelet and Furetière were printed outside of France in 1680 and 1690, respectively. These contraband publications predictably led to drama and scandal, including the burning of many copies of Richelet's dictionary and Furetière's expulsion as a member of the Académie.

IS: Nothing better than competition to improve a product.

PS: Very true. In a concrete manifestation of the difference between the forward-looking independent dictionary-makers and the backward-looking Académie, both Richelet and Furetière organized their headwords in alphabetical order, but the Académie used the nested semi-etymological ordering in the tradition of Calepino, Estienne, and Nicot. Etymologically related terms were defined at the base or root word. This meant that, for example, *désarmer* and *gendarme* can be found at *armer* rather than alphabetically in the letters *D* and *G*; to find definitions of *construction* and *destruction* one had to know to find them at the entry for *structure*; *lecture* and *lecteur* were at the verb *lire*; and *amant* and *amour* were found at *aimer*.

There has always been an enormous gap between the perceived authority of the Académie and their actual influence. Since the days of Richelet and Furetière, other commercial dictionaries have served as the standard references for the French public, from the more literary Littré to the more encyclopedic Larousse to the more descriptive Robert.[12] References to the Académie in the English-speaking press often make them out to be a kind of Supreme Court of Language, which mandates the use of certain words and makes other words – notably anglicisms – illegal, and otherwise makes consequential decisions about the French language. The reality is quite otherwise; the Académie serves as a career-capping honor for its members and brings focus on the importance of linguistic matters for a culture that cares deeply about the French language, but its attempts to create a normative and prescriptive dictionary provide an example of the futility of trying to govern a language as if it were policy: although languages certainly do follow rules, they don't follow orders.

IS: I turn now to Marie-Hélène. Your whole career is in Dictionnaires Le Robert, a cultural force in France. How did *Le Robert* come to be?

MARIE-HÉLÈNE DRIVAUD: The birth of Robert begins in the mid 1940s in Algeria, then a French colony, with a young man destined for a brilliant political future, with nothing predisposing him to lexicography. Paul Robert, a law

---

[11] Considine, *Academy*, 55.
[12] É. Littré, *Dictionnaire de la langue française* (Paris: Hachette, 1863–72, supplement 1877); *Larousse du XX e siècle*, ed. Paul Augé (Paris: Larousse, 1928–33); *Le Grand Robert de la langue française* (Paris: Le Robert) https://grandrobert.lerobert.com/.

student, became a lawyer at the bar of Algiers. Continuing his studies, he wrote academic papers, including a thesis on political economy focusing on citrus cultivation. He needed a book to find the right word based on an idea or concept. Not finding such a book, he decided to create the dictionary that met his expectations – as crazy as it may sound! To embark on this venture, he needed money. He asked for his share of the inheritance from his father, a wealthy orange planter in Mitidja, a fertile region of Algeria.

His family tried to reason with him and dissuade him, but determined, he didn't give up on his project and launched a subscription among his acquaintances in North Africa. He enlisted volunteers to help with his endeavor before hiring collaborators – Alain Rey being the first, followed by Josette Debove and Henri Cottez. The first installment of the dictionary, crowned in 1950 with the Saintour Prize awarded by the French Academy, received encouragement from numerous figures in the literary and political world. The Société du nouveau Littré (SNL), founded in 1951, benefited from its illustrious predecessor. The small team traveled from Algiers to Casablanca before settling in Paris in 1955. The sixth and final volume of the *Dictionnaire alphabétique et analogique de la langue française*, which would become *Le Grand Robert*, was completed in 1964. The idea of offering a condensed version in a single volume quickly emerged. This became *Le Petit Robert*, published in 1967. It became a standard dictionary for the public.

IS: What were the dictionaries that Paul Robert modeled his after ?

MHD: I'm not an expert on the genesis of *Le Grand Robert*, but Paul Robert aimed to create a work that allowed one to move from an idea to a word. If you consult the article on *cheval* (horse) in *Le Grand Robert*, you'll find all the vocabulary related to this animal, including the names of the colors of its coat, its gaits, its anatomy, etc. *Le Grand Robert* follows in the tradition of language dictionaries (as opposed to encyclopedic dictionaries), from the Académie to Littré, aiming to be rooted in its time and offering contemporary citations, which Littré did not have the courage to do, stopping at the beginning of the nineteenth century and "forgetting" Balzac, Flaubert, Stendhal, and others. It adopts Littré's classification of meanings in a historical and logical order.

IS: What is the process of selecting words for inclusion in *Le Grand Robert*? What kind of debate takes place internally?

MHD: The update of *Le Grand Robert* typically occurs after that of *Le Petit Robert*. It includes the same choices, expanded with rarer and more specialized words. The citations are much longer, the etymological notes more detailed, and the remarks are frequent and comprehensive.

IS: What is the approach of *Le Grand Robert* to anglicisms?

MHD: It's the same approach as in *Le Petit Robert*. When an anglicism is commonly used by a large part of the population, it is included in the works. The etymology indicates its origin, the definition is preceded by the label "ANGLIC" (sometimes followed by "criticized"), and the official recommendation, if it exists, is mentioned. This position may be shocking to our Quebecois friends, but it seems difficult for us not to address an anglicism that appears on the front page of all French newspapers! I'm thinking specifically of the integration of *big data*, a term that regularly appeared on the front page of *Le Monde* and sparked lively debates in Canada.

IS: I'm interested in spelling changes. How does *Le Grand Robert* standardize French spelling?

MHD: The spelling reform, approved in 1990, struggles to gain acceptance in France. Some regularizations of anomalies are fairly well accepted, while modifications affecting the circumflex accent are widely rejected. The dictionary, supposed to reflect usage, is in a precarious position as long as this usage is not widespread.

IS: Is the world of dictionary-makers in France still dominated by men? And has it been diversified in terms of lexicographers from other ethnic, cultural, and geographic groups?

MHD: When I started at Dictionnaires Le Robert in the late 1980s, the French lexicographical scene was animated by two prominent female figures: Josette Rey-Debove at Le Robert and Claude Kannas at Larousse. When we observed the high number of women in the dictionary sector, Josette Rey-Debove used to explain this imbalanced situation by citing the modest salaries and the patience required for this profession – qualities she deemed incompatible with men, according to her. The fact is that in their partnership, it was Alain Rey who had media notoriety.

Being a native French speaker is an essential requirement to be a lexicographer at Le Robert, which inevitably limits the diversity of collaborators. We have correspondents in several regions of the French-speaking world who shed light on connotations and sociocultural aspects challenging for a foreigner to grasp – information we need to refine our descriptions.

IS: In what way has the internet revamped lexicography in France? Is it the same as everywhere else, almost displacing actual books?

MHD: It's challenging to cover this topic in just a few lines! The internet and digital technology have profoundly changed our way of working. Digital composition makes the annual update process much easier. No longer do we need to search the page for the three or four lines needed to integrate a new word. This tedious manual search used to lead to subtle modifications of the text to remove a few characters, interventions that were cleverly commented on by metalexicographers, which used to amuse us because it was simply about gaining a line! Today, the machine takes care of balancing the white spaces on the page and easily creates room.

The internet has simplified the constant research we conduct. No need to get up to consult the *Trésor de la langue française* (TLF) in the proofreaders' office.[13] No need to go down to the library to check a quote or look for an edition of the *Dictionnaire de l'Académie française*. Google Images helps us describe an unknown object, and YouTube videos inform us about the most common way to pronounce a loanword. Each word treated in *Le Petit Robert* includes its date of appearance in French. This dating process used to involve trial and error and approximations. Easy and quick access to massive corpora of

---

[13] *Trésor de la langue française* (Paris: Centre national de la recherche scientifique/Gallimard, 1971–94).

carefully written texts (press; theses; Gallica, the digital library of the Bibliothèque nationale de France, etc.) has radically changed the practice of dating.

The internet facilitates connecting with the competent person who can provide the information we have been searching for in vain. Identifying the person who created the variety of strawberry named *gariguette* at the Institut de la recherche agronomique (INRA) and questioning them about the origin of this name that intrigued us was very simple. We quickly found the specialist in the Hindi language at the Institut national des langues et civilisations orientales (INALCO) to enlighten us on the etymology of the word *basmati*. We had previously queried major brands that market rice, without success.

Le Robert was a pioneer in transitioning from paper to digital. *Le Grand Robert* was offered in the form of a CD-ROM in 1989, when home computer equipment was still very modest. This disk, extremely expensive and with fairly limited search capabilities, was the first milestone in a range that would develop rapidly. The digital version of *Le Petit Robert* assists us in our daily work of enrichment and improvement through the quick and fruitful explorations it allows. This move from an idea to a word, a characteristic of all Le Robert dictionaries, naturally lent itself to the digital revolution. Paper cross-references flourished into hypertext links, prompting an exciting journey through the dense contents of the dictionary.

IS: Back to you, Peter Sokolowski. What is the difference, in your view, between Le Robert and Larousse?

PS: The tradition of Larousse dictionaries is of enormous importance in French culture. *Le Petit Larousse* is far and away the bestselling dictionary of the twentieth century. Building from the nineteenth-century traditions of large, multi-volume dictionaries and encyclopedias, *Le Petit Larousse* was designed to be the household answer book when it was first published in 1905. It contained both a dictionary of the French language and a section, nearly as large, for proper names, giving short articles on historic people, places, and events. *Le Petit Robert* is a much more detailed descriptive and synchronic dictionary, with more etymological information and a wider coverage of vocabulary. It's fair to say that *Le Petit Robert* is the dictionary oriented for students and writers and editors while *Le Petit Larousse* is intended for nonspecialists. They are distinct and important parallel traditions.

IS: I am interested in the role of French dictionaries as communicating vessels between France and la Francophonie. Does Le Robert regularly include words from more than two dozen French-speaking countries? I assume many of these nations, some more than others, have their own native dictionaries, as is the case in the Spanish-speaking Americas.

PS: I know that *Le Petit Robert* absolutely does enter terms from la Francophonie. Their sources are the publications from different countries such as newspapers and books. It's very hard to be everything to everyone, and many students from the Francophone countries come to France for advanced degrees just as professional writers and editors look to France for example and authority in linguistic matters, so the exchange of vocabulary flows in both directions.

IS: How do French dictionaries cover slang?

PS: *Le Petit Robert* treats informal language much as the Merriam-Webster dictionaries do, usually indicating its status with a label like *familier* (informal) and by adding an example or two to show the context and usage. For example, the verb *kifer*, meaning "to like" or "to appreciate," is illustrated with the sentence "*Sa musique me fait kifer*" (I really love their music).

Suggested Readings

Cellard, J., with A. Rey. *Dictionnaire du français non conventionnel.* [1980.] Paris: Hachette, 1991.
Considine, John. *Dictionaries in Early Modern Europe.* Cambridge: Cambridge University Press, 2008.
Dictionnaire de l'Académie française. Paris, 1694.
Dictionnaire de l'Académie française, 9th ed., online, 1992. http://atilf.atilf.fr/academie9.htm
Dictionnaire historique de la langue française, 9th ed., edited by Alain Rey. Paris: Le Robert, 2016.
Dictionnaire québécois d'aujourd'hui. Saint-Laurent: Dicorobert, 1992.
Diderot, D., with J. Le Rond d'Alembert. *L'Encyclopédie ou Dictionnaire raisonné des sciences, des arts et des métiers.* Paris: Chez Briasson, David, Le Breton, Durand, 1751–72.
Dubois, J., with C. Dubois. *Introduction à la lexicographie: le dictionnaire.* Paris: Larousse, 1971.
Francard, M., et al. *Dictionnaire des belgicismes.* Brussels: De Boeck Duculot.
FranceTerme, 2010. http://franceterme.culture.fr
Furetière, A. *Dictionnaire universel*, edited by A. Rey (1978), Paris, Le Robert, 1690.
Furno, Martine. "Le mariage de Calepin et du Thesaurus sous l'olivier de Robert Estienne, à Genève en 1553." *Bibliothèque d'Humanisme et Renaissance* 63 (2001): 511–32.
Furno, Martine. "Les dictionnaires de Robert Estienne: Sens et finalités d'une œuvre lexicographique." *Voces* 10–11 (2000): 11–27.
Grand Dictionnaire encyclopédique Larousse. Paris: Larousse, 1985.
Grevisse, M. *Le Bon Usage: Grammaire française*, 13th ed., reformulated by André Goosse. Louvain-la-Neuve, Paris: Duculot, 1993.
Hanse, J., with D. Blampain. *Nouveau dictionnaire des difficultés du français moderne.* 4th ed. Brussels: De Boeck-Duculot, 2000.
Larousse du XX e siècle, edited by Paul Augé. Paris: Larousse, 1928–33.
Le Grand Robert de la langue française. Paris: Le Robert. https://grandrobert.lerobert.com/
Le Grand Robert de la langue française: Dictionnaire alphabétique et analogique de la langue française. 2nd ed. Paris: Le Robert, 1985.
Le Petit Larousse illustré. Paris: Larousse, 2023.
Le Petit Robert: Dictionnaire alphabétique et analogique de la langue française, new ed. of *Petit Robert de Paul Robert*, edited by Alain Rey and Josette Rey-Debove. Paris: Le Robert, 2023.
Le Petit Robert des enfants. Paris: Le Robert, 1988.
Le Robert Benjamin. Paris: Le Robert, 1997.

Le Robert Collège. Paris: Le Robert, 1997.
Le Robert illustré. Paris: Le Robert, 2023.
Le Robert Junior illustré. Paris: Le Robert, 1993.
Littré, É. *Dictionnaire de la langue française*. Paris: Hachette, 1863–72. Supplément, 1877.
Office québécois de la langue française. La Banque de dépannage linguistique. www.oqlf.gouv.qc.ca/ressources/bdl.html
Office québécois de la langue française. Le Grand Dictionnaire terminologique. www.granddictionnaire.com
Quemada, B. *Les dictionnaires du français moderne 1539–1863*. Paris: Didier, 1967.
Richelet, P. *Dictionnaire françois*. [1680.] Geneva: Slatkine, 1970.
Thibault, A., with P. Knecht. *Dictionnaire suisse romand: Particularités lexicales du français contemporain*. [1997.] Geneva: Zoé, 2004
Trésor de la langue française. Paris: Centre national de la recherche scientifique/Gallimard, 1971–94.

8   Italian

Carla Marello and Claudio Marazzini

Dante Alighieri inaugurated a tradition in Europe of embracing the vernacular, in his case Florentine, which he considered more noble than Latin, in the name of the inherent rights of natural speech. It might be said that, with *De vulgari eloquentia* (1305), a fresh approach to words came about among the intelligentsia, a move that opened the door to embracing a varied, polymorphous vocabulary. Furthermore, Dante used the people's language to address mundane and lofty affairs, somehow giving Italians permission to connect the earthly and the heavenly. This conversation, translated from Italian by Giuseppina Cortese, starts with a couple of sixteenth-century lexicographic examples, Francesco Del Bailo's *Fabrica del mondo*, and Stefano Montemerlo's *Frasi toscane* (1566), and encompasses the tradition of Italian dictionaries such as the *Vocabolario degli Accademici della Crusca* published by Italy's Accademia della Crusca, and Nicola Zingarelli's popular *Vocabolario della lingua italiana*, published for the first time in 1917.[1] It also reflects on the role the Accademia has had in the development of the Italian language and on the role of bilingual dictionaries.

***

ILAN STAVANS: Prior to the *Vocabolario degli Accademici della Crusca*, published in 1612, which stands as the first full-fledged dictionary of the Italian languages, what types of efforts were there around lexicography?

CLAUDIO MARAZZINI: It should be said that already in the sixteenth century Italian lexicography had been producing excellent records. Two of these works deserve to be mentioned, namely the *Fabrica del mondo* (1548), authored by Francesco Del Bailo from Ferrara, who bore

---

[1] Francesco Alunno (Francesco Del Bailo), *Fabrica del mondo* (Venice: Nicolò de Bascarini, 1548); Gio. Stefano da Montemerlo, *Delle phrasi toscane libri XII* (Venice: Camillo et Francesco Franceschini Fratelli, 1566); Accademia della Crusca, *Vocabolario degli Accademici della Crusca* (Venice: Giovanni Alberti, 1612); Nicola Zingarelli, *Vocabolario della lingua italiana* (Milan: Bietti & Reggiani, 1917).

the nom de plume of Alunno, and the *Frasi toscane* (1566), by Stefano Montemerlo from Tortona, now in Piedmont but then part of the Duchy of Milan. Before the *Crusca* was published in 1612, the *Memoriale della lingua* had been printed in Venice by Giacomo Pergamini from Fossombrone, in the region of Marche.[2] This was the earliest vocabulary providing true definitions for many, although not all, of its lemmatized words.

None of these dictionaries bears the word "vocabulary" or "dictionary" on its title page; rather, their titles are very attractive inventions showing their function as writing aids which offer suggestions not alien to mnemotechnics and rhetoric. The *Fabrica del mondo* was not a vocabulary organized in alphabetical order but a lexical collection – a methodical one, divided into ten thematic categories within which it was possible to trace the words. Likewise, Montemerlo devised a methodical order for his *Frasi toscane*. A certain amount of effort is required of today's readers to comprehend the architecture of works so distant from our modern vocabularies and yet in their own way, if you like, even more original, with a proclivity for a kind of encyclopaedic yearning for a key that would sort out meanings by groups and a zest for semantic couplings rich with profound meaning, like modern analogic dictionaries.

From this point of view, the 1612 *Crusca* is "modern," much closer to our current concept of dictionary, a dictionary less prone to fantasizing and more mechanical (what is there that is more mechanical than the alphabetical order?). The architecture of the *Crusca* is doubtless more systematic and the title finally reads "vocabulary," even though it does not yet in any way specify that the matter at hand is the Italian language, not even the language of Tuscany. The authors merely stated in the frontispiece that it actually was the *Vocabolario degli Accademici della Crusca*, and that was considered to suffice.

CARLA MARELLO: Bilingual lexicography was present in Italy, but in the form of Latin-vernacular glossaries showing dialectal features, in relation to the place in which a manuscript version is copied.

Even the first example of a printed bilingual dictionary of Italian belongs to the family of Venetian-Bavarian works known as *Introito e porta* (1477) and *Solenissimo vochabulista* (1479), Venetian being a northern vernacular understood in the whole territory ruled by the Republic of Venice and Bavaria being the southern part of Germany from where most merchants came.[3] They are more similar to modern travel guides; they do not contain grammatical or etymological information and words are arranged

---

[2] Giacomo Pergamini, *Memoriale della lingua* (Venice: Gio Battista Ciotti, 1602).
[3] *Introito e porta de quele che voleno imparare e comprender todescho a latino cioe taliano* (Adam von Rottweil, 1477); *Solenissimo vochabulista* (Bologna, 1479).

according to travelers' needs (i.e. food, lodging, and stables for horses, etc.).

Mirroring the major commercial and cultural exchanges of the period in 1558, there were editions in Greek, Latin, Flemish, French, Spanish, Italian, English, and German. The presence of Greek and Latin, which by the way are also the languages in which efforts to provide meaning discriminations are made in *Vocabolario degli Accademici della Crusca*, can be explained as a common ground for people who might make sure of a translation into modern languages by checking its Latin or Greek corresponding translation. Another bestseller of the sixteenth century is Ambrogio Calepio's *Dictionarium Latinum* (1502).[4] Commonly known as Calepino (the Latin form of his name), Calepio was a Bergamo humanist and his work, originally only in Latin, rapidly became a multilingual reference tool: in 1550, it appeared for the first time with Italian translations.[5]

IS: The *Vocabolario* appeared just a year after Sebastián de Covarrubias' *Tesoro de la lengua castellana o española* (1611) in Spanish.[6] What were the historical forces in Europe making it possible for ambitious dictionaries of this type to materialize?

MARAZZINI: That such consultation tools should come into existence is certainly part of the larger process whereby stable cultural roots further strengthened Europe's great languages, which grew firmly established in the very regions where Latin had long held the lion's share as the main instrument of culture. However, the circumstances leading to the Spanish vocabulary probably have more to do with the rise and success of a national monarchy, something which by the way had already occurred with Nebrija's Castilian grammar, the first grammar of a European language to appear in print.[7]

In Spain, this national feature – a political feature – can be seen in the dedications to the various monarchs (e.g. the case of Covarrubias addressing King Philip III).[8] In Italy, it simply wasn't there, for political and administrative unity were completely lacking, and so the Italian language was utterly detached from any unifying political and bureaucratic power. The vocabulary was an eminently literary tool; the language of the *Crusca* thus represents a sort of inspiring ideal for the writing process, first of all in the service of the Republic of Letters.

IS: In the fourteenth century, Dante, whose work has been close to my heart for decades, had been instrumental in choosing the vernacular instead of

---

[4] Ambrogio Calepino, *Dictionarium latinum* (Rhegium Lingobardum, 1502).
[5] Ambrogio Calepino, *Dictionarium latinum* (Venezia, Paolo Manuzio e Johannes Gryphius, 1550).
[6] Sebastián de Covarrubias Orozco, *Tesoro de la lengua castellana* (Madrid: Luis Sanchez, 1611).
[7] Antonio de Nebrija, *Gramática de la lengua castellana* (Salamanca: Juan de Porras, 1492).
[8] Covarrubias, *Tesoro de la lengua castellana*.

Latin. *De vulgari eloquentia* is the best linguistics book of the Middle Ages.[9]

MARAZZINI: This is the Italian miracle, most definitely. Dante – the *fiorentinissimo* – in spite of his deep attachment to the native milieu, was sentenced to exile, and consequently his works had to be circulated in his whereabouts, hence the north of Italy.

He chose to write a poem in the vernacular instead of Latin, and some of his readers, even among his admirers, were perplexed. But he had not nourished any doubt: the theory of his *De vulgari eloquentia* proves his persuasion and absolute trust in the potentialities of the vernacular. This trust was not shared by Petrarch, who in fact penned his poem on Africa in Latin, with the result that this poem is only known to specialists.[10] No common reader would go near it now.

Dante's early readers and admirers, then, were people of northern Italy who in their daily life spoke their own vernacular, quite different from the Florentine vernacular and from the language of the *Commedia* (*The Divine Comedy*), the most important poem of the fourteenth century, from which the Italian language proceeds. Dante, sent to exile from Florence, his city, died in Ravenna, after visiting many northern Italy courts. The original manuscript of *Commedia* was not preserved, and the oldest manuscripts we have were written in northern Italy. This is why the so-called β branch of the fourteenth-century codes of the *Commedia* is so intriguing, for it witnesses Dante's rapport with the north of the country and the diffusion of the text from north to south. It is a marvelous, I believe a fascinating, testimony of the reactions of his early readers, alien to the Tuscan vernacular and yet passionate readers of the poem, whose immediate success led to massive circulation.

These were the circumstances that caused the copyists to introduce errors, which in the β branch are often "northernisms," such as *meggio* for *mezzo* (middle), from the very first line in the Urbino Code ("*Nel meggio del cammidi nostra vita*"), or *oleggio* for *lezzo* in the sense of "smell," or the other *megio* in the Riccardiano-Braidense Code, next to *legio* for the already mentioned *lezzo*.

Obviously, modern philologists who produce critical editions of Dante do not let into their text the phonetic blasphemy of these poor northern readers who were inadvertently forced to damage Dante's Tuscan vernacular, thus spoiling the poem which they truly loved and admired. But the philological apparatus also helps to literally savor the historic and cultural meaning of errors, which

---

[9] *De vulgari eloquentia* written between 1304 and 1307, editio princeps by Jacopo Corbinelli Paris in 1577.
[10] Written between 1338 and 1343; editio princeps Venezia, 1501.

IS: are to be amended and yet at the same time do show something of the relationship between works and their readers.

IS: I want to stay with Dante. I just spent a few days in Florence, following his path. In retrospect, his embrace of the vernacular is a benchmark not only in Italian but in world history. I have spent years studying Spanglish, the mix of English and Spanish, which in itself is a form of vernacular. Can you go further in explaining that revolutionary act? Were there any precedents in the written form? What was it in Dante's character that allowed for such an embrace?

MARAZZINI: Definitely. Even before Dante there existed a written language, in Florence and also in Bologna. It was an Italian vernacular, adopted for various purposes, ranging from poetry and treatises to translation, rhetorical oratory and epistolography (consider Guido Faba and his didactic writing models).[11]

However, Dante's innovation lies in the power and richness of what he wrote, surpassing any precedent. Thus, the philosophical prose of the *Convivio* and the narrative prose of the *Vita nova* (1294) came about. Above all, the idea was born of a poem capable of addressing heaven and earth, everyday life and eternity, ultimate destiny and chronicles. This, of course, is *The Divine Comedy* (1308–21). Without this power of description and imagination, the new language, Italian, could not have so suddenly gained such great added value. Let's not forget that Dante's operation on the vernacular was not accidental. The treatise *De vulgari eloquentia* shows how he had in mind a grand project for the promotion of the new language.

IS: It might be appropriate to continue on the subject. The vernacular remains a presence in every language where there is a tension between the authoritative and the popular spheres. I was just in Rome, Florence, and Sicily. What is the role, or roles, of the vernacular in Italian today, in different parts of Italy?

MARELLO: The many Italo-Romance vernacular varieties, called *dialetti* in the Italian linguistic literature, that contribute to the linguistic landscape of present-day Italy show different degrees of vitality and endangerment. Florentine and other Tuscan varieties, and Romanesco, the variety spoken in Rome, are perceived by their speakers as closer to standard Italian, and thanks to their use in fiction (television, movies) they are better understood by Italians in other Italian regions. In fact, their structural distance from Italian is smaller. Sardinian and Friulian are often considered to be autonomous Romance languages, separate from Italian.

The vast majority of the Italian population (85.3 percent to 95.5 percent) state that they speak Italian today, although one third of the population declare that they still alternate Italian and a

---

[11] Faba (1190–1243) wrote *Doctrina ad inveniendas, incipiendas et formandas materias* in 1237.

	vernacular variety in informal situations.[12] Among the generations born between 1950 and 1970, Italian has begun to represent the actual mother tongue in one of its many regional varieties. Vernacular is still used frequently amongst people with lower levels of education; elderly people speak vernacular more than younger people. Those living in small towns and villages use the vernacular more. Gender does not seem to correlate with the use of Italian or vernacular. The influence of vernacular is clear in regional varieties of Italian, with mostly lexical and phonetic features. Italianization of the vernaculars is growing.
IS:	Unlike Covarrubias' *Tesoro*, the *Vocabolario* was made collectively and anonymously, meaning it doesn't have a single author, although I understand it was edited by Bastiano de' Rossi, who was also in charge of the second edition in 1623.[13] What kind of lexicographer was de' Rossi?
MARAZZINI:	It's hard to say what one would identify as the peculiar features of Bastiano de' Rossi. As suggested in your question, the editorial board of the Crusca was set up as a society of "peers" who took their decisions together, without revealing the outstanding personalities.

When Bastiano de' Rossi was sent to Venice to closely monitor the printing process of the *Vocabolario* in 1612, he was given precise, even strict, instructions. He was forbidden to prompt any modifications whatsoever; should any problem rise at the last minute, in the course of the typographic composition, he was to eliminate the problematic parts, rather than making any changes himself in extremis. |
| IS: | The publication of *Grande dizionario della lingua italiana* (1861) by Giuseppe Pomba in Turin represented a major step forward in Italian lexicography. |
| MARAZZINI: | It certainly did. In any case, with the Tommaseo–Bellini – a dictionary which preserves the names of its authors even though they both died before their work was entirely accomplished – we make a huge chronological step into a historic age which is quite far from the centuries we were discussing earlier.[14]

The Kingdom of Italy had come into existence, and a modern political state it was, like France and Spain. The dictionary now represented the language of the new nation. Pomba's dictionary no longer was the result of contributions by outstanding intellectuals working on their own or in academies. Rather, it was the product of a modern publishing industry, the Unione Tipografico-Editrice in Turin, owned by the Pomba family. |

---

[12] Censimento permanente della popolazione 2024.
[13] Bastiano de' Rossi, Accademia della Crusca, *Vocabolario degli Accademici della Crusca* (Venice: Jacopo Sarzina, 1623).
[14] Niccolò Tommaseo, with Bernardo Bellini, *Dizionario della lingua italiana* (Turin: Giuseppe Pomba, 1861).

MARELLO: Italian publishers did not encourage a similar step forward in bilingual lexicography since in Italy there was not a lucrative market for foreign-language teaching and learning, while in Europe Italian was still part of the educated upper classes. The authors of bilingual dictionaries were teachers of Italian outside Italy or Italian exiles who had escaped for religious and political reasons.

Worthy of mention is Annibale Antonini's *Dictionnaire italien, latin et françois*, first published in Paris in 1735,[15] which was later integrated by Alberti di Villanuova with encyclopaedic information inspired by the Enlightenment and appeared as *Dizionario francese-italiano* (1772), first published in Marseille.[16] For English, the most successful bilingual dictionary of the eighteenth century was Giuseppe Baretti's *A Dictionary of the English and Italian Languages* (1760).[17] It answered a market demand because, at the time of the Grand Tour, wealthy English travelers liked to learn Italian and to approach Italian literature. And we must not forget that business with the Middle East was still carried out in an Italian-based lingua franca.

IS: I want to focus on the *GDLI*, known as "Battaglia" after its creator, Salvatore Battaglia.

MARAZZINI: The *Grande dizionario della lingua italiana* (*GDLI*) "Battaglia,"[18] named after its first director, the philologist and literary critic Salvatore Battaglia, would never have seen the light of day without the Tommaseo–Bellini *Dizionario della lingua italiana*, though it must be acknowledged that most of the work done in Turin is due to others, notably Giorgio Bàrberi Squarotti.

The immense *GDLI* is thus the last great vocabulary compiled by a literary scholar, not by a linguist; in this sense, it will remain a unique and unrepeatable monument of its own kind, offering an extremely rich documentation of twentieth-century literary Italian.

MARELLO: A remarkable contribution to *GDLI* was given by Edoardo Sanguineti. A poet, writer, and omnivorous reader, he opened the search for lexicographic sources to journals, newspapers, and even the internet. He was editor in chief of the two supplementary volumes to *GDLI* which appeared in 2004 and 2009 respectively. In these volumes, neologisms and borrowings received more attention, thus paving the way for a dictionary devoted to the history of each Italian word, definitely a non-negligible feature in the evolution of any modern language.

---

[15] Annibale Antonini, *Dictionnaire italien, latin et françois* (Paris: Vincent, 1735).
[16] Francesco Alberti di Villanova, *Dizionario francese-italiano* (Marseille, 1772).
[17] Giuseppe Baretti, *A Dictionary of the English and Italian Languages* (London: C. Hitch and L. Hawes et al., 1760).
[18] Salvatore Battaglia and Giorgio Bàrberi Squarotti, *Grande dizionario della lingua italiana* (Turin: Unione Tipografico-Editrice Torinese (UTET), 1961–2002).

IS:	Let's talk about the *Tesoro della lingua italiana delle origini* (*TLIO*).[19]
MARAZZINI:	During the difficult time of the Fascist regime, the task of producing the national vocabulary had been assigned to the Accademia d'Italia. The *TLIO* originated when the reestablished Crusca again decided to aim for a large modern historical vocabulary, and to meet the challenge via the aid of the electronic tools which were coming into usage, though in a pioneering fashion. For practical reasons, it was decided to limit the new opus to the ancient language only, from its origins to the death of Giovanni Boccaccio. That certainly wasn't the whole of Italian vocabulary, but it was the initial part, an approach coherent with the tradition of the *Crusca*.
The actual implementation of the project was then passed on into the hands of the Consiglio Nazionale delle Ricerche (CNR). The CNR worked on the *TLIO* using the instruments of the Crusca, and the team of editors settled in the Medicean mansion in Castello, occupying half of it by virtue of a regularly renewed agreement. The *TLIO* is a "treasure" of the language in the Italian sense of the word *tesoro*, meaning a complete collection of the materials instead of the selection usually done by lexicographers. The ancient language documented by *TLIO* in fact constitutes a closed corpus whose limits can be defined a priori, something that would be unfeasible for the modern age, where materials are available in such massive quantities that they cannot be globally handled. The experience of *TLIO* has also stimulated lexicographers to devise new and specific instruments, such as the *Vocabolario dantesco* now underway at the Accademia della Crusca.[20]
IS:	In Spain and France, their respective academies, the Académie française and the Real Academia Española, have as their mission to safeguard – maybe even legislate on – the national language, yet a considerable segment of the population finds these institutions pedantic and out of step. What is the perception of the Accademia della Crusca?
MARAZZINI:	Unlike the French and the Spanish academies, which began precisely as imitations of the Florentine Accademia but were right from the start in the service of national states, the Crusca has no legislative nor public authority assigned to it in the political arena. The Crusca provides counsel and formulates opinions. This limitation can be seen as an advantage, for language users quite correctly enjoy freedom to choose. However, the Crusca deploys remarkable prestige, its authority being appreciated also by the large majority of Italians with little competence in language

---

[19] *Tesoro della lingua italiana delle origini* (1964), http://tlio.ovi.cnr.it/TLIO/.
[20] *Vocabolario dantesco* (2015), www.vocabolariodantesco.it/.

matters. We can see this routinely in everyday matters and also in the media, from print and television to public and private radio, and of course the internet.

Disputes quite obviously arise, and conceivably so, since the language touches on and involves the sphere of identity and is thus a delicate, deeply felt issue. It so happens that the Crusca is charged with being old and affected by pedantry precisely by those whose attitudes are not approved by it. This happened in the course of the polemic about the lavish overuse of English in university teaching, and it happened again when the Crusca firmly condemned the use of asterisks and of schwa as (inadequate) instruments devised to advocate gender rights through language measures presumed to be libertarian and supportive. But this is part of the current linguistic debate, a sort of modern "questione della lingua." I would say that these disputes prove the vitality of the Accademia della Crusca.

MARELLO: The vitality of the Accademia della Crusca is witnessed by its online site, which boasts a section devoted to linguistic guidance – more than 1,350 answers to questions from Italophones and foreign speakers who ask about any aspect of the Italian language and very often about the acceptability of English borrowings. Academicians and guidance staff always try to support their answers (sort of mini-essays) with reliable dictionaries and grammars, specialist literature derived from sociolinguistic fieldwork, and from the internet.

The Accademia also hosts the INCIPIT Group, a monitoring center run by Italian and Swiss scholars founded in 2015 (Italian is one of the official languages in Switzerland). The task of INCIPIT is to provide public administrators and legislators with Italian alternatives to borrowings, if any, so as to avoid the spread of borrowings in common usage and mass communication.

IS: Why do you think English doesn't have an equivalent academy? Would Italian have developed the way it did without the Accademia della Crusca?

MARAZZINI: The history of Romance languages is different from that of Germanic languages, including English. The major language academies are the Crusca in Florence, the oldest one, started in 1583 and to this day quite active, the Académie française (started in 1635), and the Real Academia Española (started in 1713). The Crusca began as an expression of the Florentine culture, developing an especially close relationship with the literature in the Tuscan, or rather in the Florentine, vernacular, which was the genuine starting nucleus of the literature which became "Italian" – suffice it to think of Dante, whom we mentioned earlier.

In Florence, the veneration for Dante and his primacy remained constant, from Boccaccio onward, even when Dante was no longer the dominant author because of new cultural favorites, as was the case in the seventeenth and eighteenth centuries. The Crusca has taken on various positions over the centuries, which at times proved unsuccessful, as is the case of the negative judgment expressed on an important Italian writer like Torquato Tasso, author of *La Gerusalemme liberata*, the greatest poem in Italian in the second half of the sixteenth century.[21] However, for better or worse, the Crusca has been the cornerstone for the language history of Italy.

Think of the spelling of Italian, which has limited its etymological and paraetymological "h," unlike other languages where it proved much more resistant. Italian spelling has been dictated by the choices of the Crusca, which were oriented in a modern direction. Further, the Crusca has been instrumental in keeping Italian close to its origin, that is the works of fourteenth century authors, so that the language of these writers is still close to modern Italian, even though this proximity is beginning to crumble. Some will see in this proximity – still surviving – a lack of modernity, whereas others may see in it a strong imprint of tradition, nearly a miracle of stability. It all depends on viewpoints, obviously.

IS: Can the Philological Society of London be considered an equivalent academy?

MARELLO: In 1857, they called for a new English Dictionary; in 1879, the society made an agreement with Oxford University Press (OUP) and James A. H. Murray: the resulting *Oxford English Dictionary* is regarded as the accepted authority on the English language. I in turn would like to ask: might the English language have developed differently without learner's dictionaries such as those by OUP, Longman, Macmillan, just to mention the most successful? It can be safely said that before the internet, English publishing houses most active in the field of teaching English as a second or foreign language played and still try to play a normative role.

IS: I'm not sure, Carla. In any case, I would like to ask you both to map your own intellectual journey. How did you develop your passion for words?

MARELLO: I started higher education during the era of generative grammar, but I was not satisfied with the Chomskyan approach, so I studied text linguistics in Germany with Janos Sandor Petőfi. He and my Italian mentor, Professor Bice Mortara Garavelli, led me to study semantics and pragmatics. The move from semantics to dictionaries was encouraged by Giovanni Nencioni, at that time in Scuola Normale di Pisa and president of Accademia della Crusca, who

---

[21] Some printed versions not controlled by the author appeared before the 1581 version approved by Tasso, edited by Febo Bonnà and printed in Ferrara by Baldini.

helped me with a scholarship to develop my survey of Italian non-alphabetical dictionaries in the nineteenth century.

These dictionaries were tools aiming both to cover lexical fields rarely present in literary texts and to teach Italian to people who spoke an Italian vernacular different from Tuscan. Through a thesaural, pragmatic arrangement of words, they tried to avoid the use of bilingual dictionaries coupling a vernacular word with its Italian translation.[22] Since then, I kept investigating semantic relations among words and ways to represent them properly and effectively in monolingual dictionaries. My second book – about bilingual lexicography with Italian – represented a further shift toward metalexicographic studies: from love for words to love for representation of words in dictionaries.[23]

IS: And you, Claudio. How did you become so fond of words?

MARAZZINI: Although my family was petit bourgeois, my father was an art collector and had put together a fine library, with many ancient books covering a wide range of topics. Culture was always there in our home, in other words. My mother was an elementary school teacher, always paying close attention to the proper use of language, or at least what she considered as such. Writing, nourished by good readings, has always come easily and naturally to me. Then, at university, I encountered structuralism and linguistics, which provided me with additional analytical tools. However, I don't think I love words more than material objects. On the contrary, I believe words are only useful when they serve actual things.

IS: In the development of late twentieth-century historical dictionaries, there is often the moment when definitions were no longer validated with written quotes (novels, poems, speeches, etc.). Instead, popular culture became an equally important source in etymological history. What is the case in Italian?

MARELLO: Etymology in Italian dictionaries is still based on written records. The large presence of "Netspeak," *parlato digitato* (punched-in speech) on the internet, and also of transcribed oral corpora helped lexicographers (more and more linguists rather than literature scholars) pay greater attention to spoken Italian, exploiting oral sources in order to give better examples for discourse markers, phatic expressions (such as Italian *beh, allora, dunque* at the start of the dialogic move, similar to English *well, let's see*), short forms (such as *raga* for *ragazzo/i*, *clima* for *climatizzatore*), and morphological adaptations of loanwords (such as *chattare* from *to chat*).

---

[22] See Carla Marello, *Lessico ed educazione popolare: Dizionari metodici italiani dell' '800* (Rome: Armando, 1980).
[23] Carla Marello, *Dizionari bilingui: Con schede sui dizionari italiani per francese, inglese, spagnolo, tedesco* (Bologna: Zanichelli, 1989).

IS: Carla, you mentioned the vigor of the Accademia's online site. Dictionaries, in recent decades, have moved from the printed page to the screen. This reinvention makes them more democratic but, also, more ephemeral. How do you explain the difference of usage among generations? Is it a stereotype to suggest that older people are reverential toward the history of a language and younger people feel less constrained by it?

MARELLO: I think that it has always been like that: older people, above all women with a good level of education, are more conservative, while younger people's use of Italian is innovative, Italianizing foreign (mainly English) words, adopting vernacular words and making them pan-Italian. What can be observed is the shorter span between changes in productive and receptive individual lexical assets.

Linguists used to say there was a remarkable lexical change every forty years. Now we can say it tends to occur every fifteen to twenty years because everybody has more opportunity to write, to read, to catch new words or a new usage of an already existing word and adopt it.

Suggested Readings

Alberti di Villanova, Francesco. *Dizionario francese-italiano*. Marseille, 1772.
Alunno, Francesco (Del Bailo, Francesco). *Fabrica del mondo*. Venice: Nicolò de Bascarini, 1548.
Antonini, Annibale. *Dictionnaire italien, latin et françois*. Paris: Vincent, 1735.
Baretti, Giuseppe. *A Dictionary of the English and Italian Languages*. London: C. Hitch and L. Hawes et al., 1760.
Battaglia, Salvatore, and Giorgio Bàrberi Squarotti. *Grande dizionario della lingua italiana*. Turin: Unione Tipografico-Editrice Torinese (UTET), 1961–2002.
Berruto, Gaetano. "The Languages and Dialects of Italy." In *Manual of Romance Sociolinguistics*, edited by Wendy Ayres-Bennett and Janice Carruthers, 494–525. Berlin: De Gruyter, 2018.
Calepino, Ambrogio. *Dictionarium latinum*. Rhegium Lingobardum, 1502; four-languages ed. (Hebrew, Greek, Latin, and Italian), Venice: Peter Liechtenstein, 1509.
De Mauro, Tullio. *Grande dizionario italiano dell'uso*. Turin: Unione Tipografico-Editrice Torinese (UTET), 1999.
Marazzini, Claudio. *La lingua italiana: Profilo storico*. Bologna: il Mulino, 2002.
Marazzini, Claudio. *L'ordine delle parole: Storia di vocabolari italiani*. Bologna: il Mulino, 2009.
Marello, Carla. *Lessico ed educazione popolare: Dizionari metodici italiani dell' '800*. Rome: Armando, 1980.
Marello, Carla. *Dizionari bilingui: Con schede sui dizionari italiani per francese, inglese, spagnolo, tedesco*. Bologna: Zanichelli, 1989.
Pergamini, Giacomo. *Memoriale della lingua*. Venice: Gio Battista Ciotti, 1602.

Rossebastiano Bart Alda. *Antichi vocabolari plurilingui d'uso popolare: La tradizione del Solennissimo vochabuolista*. Alessandria: Edizioni dell'Orso, 1984.
Tesoro della lingua italiana delle origini. 1964. http://tlio.ovi.cnr.it/TLIO/
Tommaseo, Niccolò, with Bernardo Bellini. *Dizionario della lingua italiana*. Turin: Giuseppe Pomba, 1861–65.
Vocabolario dantesco. 2015. www.vocabolariodantesco.it/

9 Arabic

Hassan Hamzé

The Arabic lexicographic tradition is very ancient. Its principles were developed in the eighth century. Any linguistic change was considered a corruption compared to classical Arabic, *faṣīḥ* (literally, pure). With the shock of modernity, partly due to Napoleon's campaign in Egypt and Syria (1798–1801), the situation became untenable. Neologisms that circulated in oral varieties and specialized works began to appear timidly in general dictionaries toward the end of the nineteenth century. However, it was only in the second half of the last century that the vocabulary of so-called Modern Arabic was fully incorporated into the dictionary. The *Kitāb al-ʿAyn* by al-Ḫalīl b. Aḥmad al-Farāhīdī (d. 170 AH/786 CE) founded the Arabic lexicographic tradition.[1] This conversation focuses on its structure, the conditions under which it emerged, and how it shaped other Arabic dictionaries. It begins with a reflection on the Arabic dictionaries of orientalists before addressing ancient and modern bilingual dictionaries. This exchange was translated from French to English by Hipólito Slomianski.

***

ILAN STAVANS: I want to start – perhaps controversially – with orientalists dictionaries in the Arab world. My definition of "orientalism" is the representation of Arabia, especially the Middle East, based on stereotypes that came about as a result of colonialism.

HASSAN HAMZÉ: The first lexicographical works involving orientalists were bilingual dictionaries between Arabic and Latin during the medieval period. These dictionaries emerged in Spain, a meeting point between Arabic and the West. Initially motivated by religious considerations for evangelization, these bilingual dictionaries did not focus on classical Arabic but rather on the dialectal variations in Andalusia.

---

[1] al-Ḫalīl b. Aḥmad al-Farāhīdī, *Kitāb al-ʿAyn*, ed. Mahdī Maḫzūmī and Ibrāhīm as-Sāmurrā'ī (Beirut: Dār wa Maktabat al-Hilāl, n.d.).

The earliest mention is of an Arabic-Latin dictionary by an unknown author around the twelfth century, followed by another Arabic-Latin and Latin-Arabic dictionary by an unknown author in the thirteenth century.[2] In 1505, Pedro de Alcalá published a dictionary titled *Vocabulista aravigo en letro castellana*.[3] This monk released his dictionary a few years after the fall of Granada (1492) and directed it toward the clergy responsible for converting Arabic speakers to Christianity. To achieve this, he used the two "vulgar languages" present: the Arabic of Granada and Castilian. It wasn't until 1970 that Federico Corriente published his *Diccionario español-árabe* focusing on Spanish and classical Arabic.[4]

In 1653, the Dutchman Golius published his Arabic-Latin dictionary in Leiden.[5] This dictionary, focusing on literary Arabic, is based on *Ṣiḥāḥ* d'al-Jawharī (d. around 400/1010).[6] However, it also draws inspiration from other Arabic dictionaries, notably al-Fayrūzābādī's *Qāmūs* (d. 817/1415),[7] which had a significant influence not only among Arabic scholars divided between supporters and opponents but also beyond these circles. The German Georg Wilhelm Friedrich Freytag, a professor of oriental languages at Bonn and a student of the famous Sylvester de Sacy, published his *Lexicon Arabico-Latinum* between 1830 and 1837, building upon and correcting Golius' work.[8]

During the nineteenth century, bilingual dictionaries proliferated, with varied target languages. Interest in Latin as a scholarly language waned in Europe, giving way to current languages. Following Latin and Castilian, English and French began to attract authors.

The *Arabic-English Lexicon* by Edward Lane, published between 1863 and 1893, is the first dictionary between Arabic and English.[9] It draws inspiration from Ibn Manẓūr's *Lisān al-ʿarab* (d. 711/1311) and az-Zabīdī's *Tāj al-ʿarūs* (d. 1205/1790),[10] with attention to the numerous criticisms made by Arabic authors of al-Fayrūzābādī's *Qāmūs*.

For French, there was a French-Arabic lexicon by J. F. Ruphy in 1802 aimed at those "destined for Levant Commerce."[11] The first general French-Arabic

---

[2] Abd al-ʿAzīz Al-Ḥamīd, *Aʿmāl al-mustašriqīn al-ʿarabiyya fī l-muʿjam l-ʿarabī*, Vol. 1 (Riyadh: al-Imam Muhammad Ibn Saud Islamic University, 2012), 173.
[3] Pedro de Alcalá, *Vocabulista aravigo en letro castellana* (Granada: Iuan varela de salama[n]ca, 1505; Alicante: Biblioteca Virtual Miguel de Cervantes, 2003).
[4] Federico Corriente, *Diccionario español-árabe*, 2nd ed. (Madrid: Instituto Hispano-Arabe de Cultura, 1980).
[5] Golius Jacobus, *Lexicon Arabico-Latinum* (Leiden: Typis Bonaventurae and Abrahami Elseviriorum, 1653).
[6] al-Jawharī, *Aṣ-Ṣiḥāḥ tāj al-luġat wa ṣiḥāḥ al-ʿarabiyyat*, 2nd ed., ed. Aḥmad ʿAbd al-Ġafūr ʿAṭṭār (Beirut: Dār al-ʿilm li l-malāyīn, 1979).
[7] al-Fayrūzābādī, *Al-Qāmūs al-muḥīṭ* (Cairo: al-Bābī al-ḥalabī, 1952).
[8] Georg Wilhelm Friedrich Freytag, *Lexicon Arabico-Latinum* (Halle an der Saale: Schwetschke et filium, 1830).
[9] Edward William Lane, *An Arabic-English Lexicon Derived from the Most Copious Eastern Sources*, repr. from the London ed. (1st ed., 1863–93; Beirut: Librairie du Liban, 1997).
[10] Ibn Manẓūr, *Lisān al-ʿarab* (Beirut: Dār Sādir, 1968); az-Zabīdī, *Tāj al-ʿarūs min jawāhir al-Qāmūs* (Cairo: al-Maṭbaʿat al-ḥayriyyat, 1906).
[11] J. F. Ruphy, *Dictionnaire abrégé françois-arabe* (Paris: Imprimerie de la république, An X [1802 v. st.]).

dictionary by Ellious Bochtor, not an orientalist but an Egyptian interpreter with the French army in Egypt, was completed in 1821 and later published by A. Caussin de Perceval in 1829.[12] A. Kazimirski's Arabic-French dictionary, published in 1860, is still appreciated for translating ancient Arabic texts.[13]

Two notable dictionaries in Arabic lexicography must be mentioned. First, the Dutch scholar Reinhart Dozy published a supplement to Arabic dictionaries in 1882, focusing on formal or conceptual neologisms not recognized by Arabic lexicographers.[14] Second, German scholar August Fischer (d. 1949) undertook a comprehensive project for a historical Arabic dictionary at the Arabic Academy of Cairo (Majmaʿ al-luġa al-ʿarabiyya, al-Qāhira), emphasizing literary aspects with a historical focus up to the first centuries.[15]

IS: I understand that traditional Arabic dictionaries rotate around families of words more than words themselves.

HH: Since *Kitāb al-ʿAyn* by al-Ḫalīl (d. 170/786), the general language dictionary has been organized according to roots. This organization seems to suggest that the Arabic dictionary was primarily a dictionary of word families. Words are often defined in relation to other words of the same root.

The classification of roots was a major concern in organizing the macrostructure of the dictionary. Evidently, the classification of words into families was not on the agenda. Faced with the explicit interest in the Arabic lexicographical tradition in the classification of roots and the diversity of methods used for this classification, there is complete silence regarding the classification of words presented haphazardly under the root, often through a sort of association of ideas. To search for a word, one must read the entire article dedicated to the root. It can be at the beginning of the article, in the middle, at the end, or not there at all.[16] The time spent on research varies significantly, depending on the size of the article and the graphical means employed, especially in modern dictionaries.

This classification has gained popularity. It has been followed as is in *Muʿjam al-luġa al-ʿarabiyyat al-muʿāṣira* by Aḥmad M. ʿUmar (2008), with variations in the order of augmented verbs in *al-Muʿjam al-ʿarabī al-ʾasāsī* by ALECSO (1999), and with a grouping of derivatives under the corresponding verbal form in *al-Munjid fī al-luġa al-ʿarabiyya al-muʿāṣira* (2000), a grouping already initiated in *al-ʿUbāb az-zāhir* by aṣ-Ṣaġānī.[17]

---

[12] Ellious Bochtor, *Dictionnaire français-arabe*, rev. and aug. A. Caussin de Perceval (Paris: Chez Firmin Didot père et fils, Libraires, 1828–29).

[13] A. De Biberstein Kazimirski, *Dictionnaire arabe-français* (Paris, Maisonneuve et Cie, 1860).

[14] Reinhart Dozy, *Supplément aux Dictionnaires Arabes* (Beirut: Librairie du Liban, rep. of the original edition, Leiden: E. J. Brill, 1881).

[15] August Fischer, *Al-Muʿjam al-luġawī at-tārīḫī*, Pt. 1 (Cairo: Majmaʿ al-luġa al-ʿarabiyya, 1967).

[16] Hassan Hamzé, "Ḥurūf az-ziyāda wa tartīb al-afʿāl fī al-muʿjam al-ʿarabī," *Revue de la Lexicologie* 30 (2014): 55–58.

[17] ʿUmar Aḥmad Muḫtār, *Muʿjam al-luġa al-ʿarabiyya al-muʿāṣira* (Cairo: ʿĀlam al-kutub, 2008); Al-Munaẓẓama al-ʿarabiyya li t-tarbiya wa ṯ-ṯaqāfa wa l-ʿulūm, *Al-Muʿjam al-ʿarabī al-ʾasāsī* (Larousse, 1999); *Al-Munjid fī al-luġa al-ʿarabiyya al-muʿāṣira* (Beirut: Dār al-Masriq, 2000); aṣ-Ṣaġānī, *Al-ʿUbāb az-zāhir wa l-lubāb al-fāḫir*, ed. Muḥammad Ḥasan Āl yāsīn (Baghdad: Dār ar-Rašīd, 1977–87).

IS: In modern times, the classification of words within the root has undergone a change worth noting with the dictionary of the Arabic Academy of Cairo, *al-Wasīṭ*, published in 1960, and *al-Kabīr*, which is still ongoing.[18] Verbs are classified first, starting with the bare form of the verb, followed by augmented forms with one, two, or three augmentations, and then verbs with more than three radical consonants. Other parts of speech are then presented in alphabetical order.

IS: When does a dictionary of words per se appear in Arabic?

HH: It wasn't until the mid twentieth century that a dictionary of individual words emerged, competing with the family dictionary without ever managing to replace it. With the developments of electronic dictionaries today, the question may no longer be relevant.

The resistance to the classification by roots is not surprising. A classification by words would distort the Arabic lexicon due to a fundamental property of Arabic morphology based on internal inflection, unlike agglutinative languages such as English and French. This judgment is not that of a purist attached to the old ways but an observation. A comparison of the arrangement of words from the same family in two alphabetical dictionaries in Arabic and French, for example, helps to measure the drawbacks of alphabetical classification of words in Arabic.

If we set aside prefixal derivation and certain transformations, the words, or at least most words, from the same family in an agglutinative language generally form a continuous graphic sequence, as shown in the uninterrupted sequence in the French dictionary *Le Petit Robert*.[19]

The alphabetical classification of words in Arabic raises formidable difficulties. The ease of alphabetical classification of words in Arabic is only a projection from European dictionaries, whether this classification is based on the spelling of words or their phonetic form, especially due to the uncertainty about the status of short vowels and the status of the famous *alif*: consonant (ʿ) or long vowel (ā), not to mention the thorny problem of broken plurals and the numerous variants of the same word.

It is understandable, therefore, why the alphabetical classification of words has never been followed in tradition and why it faces challenges to this day, although it is gaining ground among the younger generation and is becoming prevalent in school dictionaries.

The authors of word dictionaries justify their choice, which is a thinly veiled imitation of the European dictionary, by citing the presence in the tradition of word dictionaries such as *at-taʿrīfāt* by al-Jurjānī (d. 816/1413), *al-Kulliyyāt* by al-Kafawī (d. 1093/1682?), and *Kaššāf iṣṭilāḥāt al-ʿulūm wa l-funūn* by at-Tahānawī (d. 1158/1745).[20] This argument confuses the general language

---

[18] Majmaʿ al-luġa al-ʿarabiyya (Arabic Academy of Cairo), *Al-Muʿjam al-wasīṭ*, 5th ed (Cairo, 2021).

[19] *Le Petit Robert: Dictionnaire alphabétique et analogique de la langue française*, new ed. of Petit Robert de Paul Robert, ed. Alain Rey and Josette Rey-Debove (Paris: Le Robert, 2023).

[20] Alī b. Muḥammad Al-Jurjānī, *Kitāb at-taʿrīfāt* (Beirut: Librairie du Liban, 1978); Ayyūb b. Mūsā Al-Kafawī, *Al-Kulliyyāt*, 2nd ed. (Beirut: Muʾassasat ar-Risāla, 1998); Muḥammad Alī At-Tahānawī, *Kaššāf ʿiṣṭilāḥāt al-funūn wa l-ʿulūm* (Beirut: Librairie du Liban Publishers, 1996).

dictionary with the specialized terminological dictionary. The two types of dictionaries operate on entirely different logics. The object of study is not the same. On one side are word families with a common root and kinship ties between the meanings of words. On the other side are families of terms without regard to form. The connection between terms in the family is not formal; it is conceptual.

IS: This brings me to my next question, which reaches further back in history. In the spirit of lexicographic exploration, I want to know about how the discipline of lexicography began in the Arab world.

HH: Arabic occupies a very unique position in the history of global lexicography. Partly due to the early and keen interest of intellectuals in compiling a "sum" of lexical elements of the language, but mostly due to the perspective these intellectuals had on the Arabic language.

Toward the end of the first century CE and the beginning of the second, Arab-Muslim society witnessed extraordinary development on all fronts. Politically, it had already become an empire stretching from the Atlantic Ocean to the Caucasus and India. The political expansion inevitably triggered an unprecedented Arabization movement. Culturally, it was a vibrant society that inherited and developed the scientific movements of Persian, Indian, and especially Greek cultures for centuries before passing them on to the European Renaissance.

The inception of Arabic lexicography seems to be linked to the needs of this environment, providing a response to the challenges posed by the ġarīb (raria), especially in the Quranic text. Its development can only be understood in relation to other linguistic and religious disciplines of the time. The work that truly establishes the Arabic lexicographical tradition appears toward the end of the eighth century, along with other foundational works in grammar and jurisprudence.

IS: I'm interested in the term ġarīb.

HH: Several small books with the title Ġarīb al-Qur'ān emerged before the ninth century, attributed to figures such as Ibn ʿAbbās (d. 68/687), Zayd b. ʿAlī (d. 122/740), Abān b. Rabāḥ (d. 141/759), al-Kisāʾī (d. 189/805), and as-Sadūsī (d. 174/791 or 195/811), among others.[21] In these books of interest, the focus is on explaining certain words from the Qur'ān – words that are uncommon or whose meaning may not be readily understood by everyone.

During the same period, in the eighth century, Arabic-language scholars ventured into the desert to meet Bedouins, collecting linguistic data directly from their mouths. The Bedouins were considered to speak a pure form of Arabic, having not mixed with non-Arabs. Some Bedouins even traveled to the cities to meet scholars, sometimes as a means of earning a living.

The ġarīb is no longer solely connected to the needs of the Quranic text. Alongside ġarīb al-Qur'ān, other vocabularies began to emerge. Predecessors of al-Ḫalīl b. Aḥmad, the author of the first true Arabic dictionary, were credited with small books that compiled rare words on specific topics. For example, Kitāb al-Ḥašarāt, in French Livre des petites bêtes, or Book of Small Creatures,

---

[21] Lost works. See Ḥusayn Naṣṣār, al-Muʿjam al-ʿarabī, Vol. 1 (Dar Misr, n.d.), 33–34.

by Abū Hayra al-Aʿrābī (early eighth century), who also wrote another book, *Kitāb aṣ-ṣifāt*, *Livre des attributs* in French, or *The Book of Attributes*. Other examples include the *Books of Nawādir* or *Rarities* by Abū ʿAmr b. al-ʿAlāʾ (d. 154/771) and *Kitāb al-ḫayl*, *Livre des chevaux* or *Book of Horses*, by Abū Mālik ʿAmr b. Kirkira (second/eighth century), who also had a book on humans called *ḫalq al-insān*.[22]

The beginning of Arabic lexicography was likely with these small books of *ġarīb* and small lexicons that compile vocabulary related to a specific subject, especially what is rare and little known. Apparently, this work started as a utilitarian task, a simple tool intended for specific services.

In later periods, more extensive thematic vocabularies specific to certain subjects or fields appeared, such as *Kitāb an-nabāt* (The book of plants) by Abū Ḥanīfa ad-Dīnawarī (d. 282/895) and *al-Ġarīb al-muṣannaf* (The rare vocabulary classified into classes) by Abū ʿUbayd al-Qāsim b. Sallām (d. 224/838).[23] These thematic dictionaries were termed in tradition as *maʿājim al-mawḍūʿāt* or *maʿājim mubawwaba*, contrasting with dictionaries focusing on phonetic forms (*maʿājim al-alfāẓ* or *maʿājim mujannasa*).

Unfortunately, very little remains of these early vocabularies from the period before the appearance of the first true dictionary, al-Ḫalīl's *Kitāb al-ʿAyn* (d. 170 or 175/786 or 791), which laid the foundation for the Arabic lexicographical tradition.

IS: Let's talk about the first dictionary of the Arabic language *Kitab al- ʿAyn* (كتاب العين), by al-Ḫalīl b. Aḥmad al-Farāhīdī, in the eighth century. What were the circumstances of its conception? Prior to al-Ḫalīl, are there any vestiges of lexicography imagining a possible lexicon, anything for instance in the *Qurʾan*, in the spirit of Psalm 119?

HH: The project of the book, as it emerges from its introduction and structure, appears to aim at three closely linked objectives: The first objective is to outline the theoretical limits of the system that generates the vocabulary of Arabic. To delineate these limits, al-Ḫalīl employs a permutation of radical consonants, allowing for all mathematically possible combinations in theory.

The second objective is to build a general dictionary. Al-Ḫalīl's dictionary, as conceived, is a project that, unlike previous works, does not target specific topics or thematic vocabulary. It aims, as stated in its introduction, to encompass the Arabic vocabulary (*kalām al-ʿarab*), whether clear (*wāḍiḥ*) because it is familiar and frequent, or unclear (*ġarīb*) because it is rare. This implies that it will include, at least in part, the vocabulary found in onomasiological dictionaries (*mubawwab*). Thus, the dictionary can meet the needs of the cultivated person as well as the ordinary individual without a deep knowledge of Arabic, without excluding those learning Arabic, especially among converted peoples.

The third objective is to distinguish what is pure Arabic from what is not. Describing Arabic vocabulary in terms of phonetics and morphology allows for the identification of borrowed elements. In this description, al-Ḫalīl observes

---

[22] Lost works. See Ḥusayn Naṣṣār, *al-Muʿjam al-ʿarabī*, Vol. 1 (Dar Misr, n.d.).
[23] Abū Ḥanīfa Dīnawarī, *Kitāb an-nabāt* (Wiesbaden: Frantz Stayner, 1974); Abū ʿUbayd al-Qāsim b. Sallām, *Al-ġarīb al-muṣannaf* (Saudi Arabia: Maktabat al-Bāz, 1997).

Arabic

that an Arabic root cannot have more than five consonants. Any additional consonant is, therefore, an augmentation (*zā'ida ʿalā l-bināʾ wa laysat min aṣl al-kalima*). If it is not an augmentation, the word is inevitably foreign.

IS: What is the organization of *Kitāb al-ʿAyn*?

HH: The *Kitāb al-ʿAyn* is classified based on exclusively consonantal roots. The twenty-nine letters of the Arabic alphabet are divided between twenty-five "healthy letters" (*ḥarf ṣaḥīḥ*), in contrast to the four "sick letters" (*ḥarf muʿtall*) that undergo transformations during inflection and are grouped in a single chapter at the end of the work. Each chapter of the dictionary corresponding to a healthy letter is divided into several subchapters based on the number of root consonants: two, three, four, or five letters. The triliteral, which is the essential part of the system, is further divided into a healthy triliteral and a sick triliteral that includes one or two sick letters.

Within each chapter, entries are obtained by permuting the consonants of the root, starting with the farthest consonant that constitutes the head of the chapter. To look up a word in the dictionary, one must follow this order: identify the root, the farthest consonant in that root, the number of root consonants, the nature of the radicals, and whether they contain one or two "sick" letters before proceeding to the permutations attested in usage. Words with all "sick" letters – their number is extremely limited – are grouped in the twenty-sixth chapter at the end of the dictionary.

In this way, the volume of the chapters decreases. The first chapter alone occupies nearly a third of the dictionary. The last ones are extremely limited, as their contents are exhausted gradually by the preceding consonants that are farther back along the vocal tract.

IS: What was its foreign influence?

HH: To answer this question, one must return to the general organization of *Kitāb al-ʿAyn*. This organizational structure should be relied upon to identify any potential connections with other lexicographical traditions or to deny any foreign influence in the conception of this dictionary. The organization is highly complex and clearly demonstrates a very close relationship with the morphology specific to Arabic, making it incompatible with other languages such as Greek or Sanskrit.

First, it's essential to note that this is not just a dictionary of words but rather a dictionary of word families. The organization revolves around families, not individual words. The division into subchapters based on the number of root consonants that may permute – biconsonantal, triconsonantal, quadriconsonantal, quinquiconsonantal – is unique to Arabic and cannot correspond to non-Semitic languages. Similarly, the distinction made between "healthy letters" and "sick letters" that may undergo transformations is also specific to Arabic. The decision not to start the dictionary with the letter *alif*, which is the first letter of the Arabic alphabet, follows this logic, aligning the organization with Arabic morphology.

The only aspect that could be considered in connection with foreign influence is the phonetic classification of roots. Based on available information, the hypothesis of Indian influence on this point remains unverifiable. Moreover, this type of phonetic classification cannot be a mere imitation. It indeed corresponds to one of the author's objectives, which is to distinguish pure Arabic from non-Arabic elements. The differentiation between Arabic and foreign words, the status of quadriconsonantal or quinquiconsonantal words, and the justification for excluding part of the Arabic vocabulary are all linked to phonetic considerations.

The phonetic classification adopted by al-Halīl has continued to captivate certain minds. At least four major dictionaries have followed this classification: al-Qālī (d. 356/967) in his *al-Bāri'*, al-Azharī (d. 370/981) in his *Tahdīb al-luġa*, aṣ-Ṣāḥib b. Abbād (d. 385/995) in his *al-Muḥīṭ*, and finally Ibn Sīda (d. 458/1066) in his *al-Muḥkam*.[24]

However, this classification was soon challenged by alphabetical sorting based on writing. Shortly after al-Halīl, another dictionary, the *Kitāb al-Jīm* by aš-Šaybānī (d. 206/821), adopted alphabetical sorting based on the first consonant of the root.[25]

IS: When did this approach change?

HH: With al-Jawharī (d. around 400/1010) in the *Ṣiḥāḥ*, the roots are classified in alphabetical order, but reversed: it's the last radical consonant that forms the basis of the classification, not the first. A dual objective is aimed for: on one side, avoiding the first radical consonant subject to changes; and on the other, providing poets and prose writers with a work that allows them to choose the rhymes and assonances they need. Contrary to what is widespread and announced by the author himself, it is al-Bandanījī (d. 284/897), benefiting from Ibn as-Sikkīt (d. 244/858), who should be considered the pioneer of reverse classification, even if he only took into account the last consonant of the root.[26]

This classification has achieved great success among lexicographers. It has been followed until modern times: *al-'Ubāb az-zāhir* by aṣ-Ṣaġānī (d. 650/1252), *Lisān al-'arab* by Ibn Manẓūr (d. 711/1311), *al-Qāmūs al-muḥīṭ* by al-Fayrūzābādī (d. 817/1415), and *Tāj al-'arūs* by az-Zabīdī (d. 1205/1790). This success is all the more surprising as the "normal" alphabetical classification based on the actual order of consonants was well known since *Asās al-balāġa* by az-Zamakšarī (d. 538/1144), not to mention *Maqāyīs al-luġa* by Ibn Fāris (d. 395/1005) and *al-Jamhara* by Ibn Durayd (d. 321/933) who followed this order with some variations.[27]

IS: How about bilingual dictionaries?

HH: The general bilingual dictionary took a long time to appear in the Arabic tradition. The great admiration that Arab scholars had for their language, often considered a language of divine institution, diverted them from other languages, even though many of them were of foreign origin.

---

[24] Abū Alī Al-Qālī, *Al-Bāri' fī al-luġa* (Baghdad, 1975); Al-Azharī, *Tahdīb al-luġa* (Cairo: ad-Dār al-misriyya, n.d.); Aṣ-Ṣāḥib b. Abbād, *Al-Muḥīṭ fī al-luġa* (Baghdad: Maṭba'at al-ma'ārif, 1975); Ibn Sīda, *Al-Muḥkam wa l-muḥīṭ al-'a'ẓam* (Beirut: Dār al-kutub al-'ilmiyya, 2000).

[25] Abū 'Amr Aš-Šaybānī, *Kitāb al-Jīm* (Cairo, 1974).

[26] Al-Bandanījī, *At-taqfiya fī al-luġa* (Baghdad: Mataba'at al-'ānī, 1976); Ibn as-Sikkīt, *'Iṣlāḥ al-manṭiq* (Cairo: Dār al-ma'ārif, 1956).

[27] Az-Zamahšarī, *Asās al-balāġa* (Beirut: Dār Ṣādir, 1965); Ibn Fāris, *Maqāyīs al-luġa* (Cairo: Dār 'Ihyā' al-kutub al-'arabiyya, 1946–52); Ibn Durayd, *Jamharat al-luġa* (Beirut: Dār al-'ilm li l-malāyīn, 1987–88).

However, with the significant rise of translation during the Abbasid era, particularly from the time of Caliph al-Ma'mūn (d. 218/833) who founded Bayt al-Ḥikma (House of Wisdom), it was difficult for the specialized bilingual dictionary not to emerge in one form or another. For instance, Discorides' *De materia medica* was translated from Greek, first by Uṣṭufān b. Bāsīl (d. 3rd/9th century), and later revised by Ḥunayn b. Isḥāq (d. 260/873),[28] and Galen's *Simple Medicines* was also translated by the same Ḥunayn b. Isḥāq.[29]

The first general bilingual dictionary in the tradition emerges two centuries after specialized dictionaries. Unsurprisingly, it does not involve Arabic and Greek. It begins with languages within the same circle of Arab-Islamic civilization: Persian and Turkish. A Turkish-Arabic lexicon by Kashghari (d. 11th century) titled *Diwān luġat at-turk* is created, followed by an Arabic-Persian dictionary by Zamaẖšarī (d. 1144) called *Muqaddimat al-adab*.[30]

Outside this circle, Latin takes the lead in the medieval period. It is only after the Renaissance that dictionaries between Arabic, French, and English start emerging. The need for general bilingual dictionaries between Arabic and European languages becomes apparent, and this movement intensifies in the twentieth century. English-Arabic or French-Arabic dictionaries multiply, as do dictionaries in the other direction, such as Hans Wehr's Arabic-English dictionary: *A Dictionary of Modern Written Arabic* and the Arabic-French dictionary, *as-Sabīl*, by Daniel Reig.[31]

IS: That's fascinating. I suspect bilingual dictionaries in the Arab world might therefore be seen as a tool of globalization.?

HH: In modern times, there is a significant interest in bilingual dictionaries crafted from European languages that have become languages of knowledge, notably English and French. This applies to general dictionaries as well as specialized ones. A pioneer in this field is the dictionary developed by Muḥammad b. ʿUmar at-tūnusī (d. 1857): *aš-Šudūr ad-dahabiyyat fī al-alfāẓ aṭ-ṭibbiyyat*.[32] This dictionary originally started as a translation of an eight-volume French encyclopedia titled *Dictionnaire des dictionnaires de médecine français et étrangers, ou traité complet de médecine et de chirurgie pratiques* (Dictionary of French and foreign medical dictionaries, or Complete treatise on practical medicine and surgery), published between 1840 and 1842.[33] The Arabic dictionary author compiled and revised the translated Arabic terms and added Arabic terms extracted from ancient Arabic medical works and general dictionaries such as al-Jawharī's *Ṣiḥāḥ* and

---

[28] Lost works. See Ibn Abī ʿUṣaybiʿat, *ʿUyūn al-'anbā' fī ṭabaqāt al-'aṭibbā'*, Vol. 1 (Cairo, 1882), 199; Ibn an-Nadīm, *kitāb al-Fihrist* (Leipzig, 1872), 298.

[29] See Ibrahim Ben Mrad, *Al-Muʿjam al-ʿilmī al-ʿarabī al-muhtass* (Beirut: Dār al-Garb al-'isgāmī, 1993), 42.

[30] Maḥmūd Al-Kāšġarī, *Kitāb diwān luġāt at-turk* (Turkey: Dār al-Ḥilāfa, 1915); Az-Zamaẖšarī, *Kitāb muqaddimat al-'adab* (Ṣaḥḥāf, 1843).

[31] Hans Wehr, *A Dictionary of Modern Written Arabic* (Beirut: Librairie du Liban, 1980); Daniel Reig, *As-Sabīl, Dictionnaire arabe-français, français-arabe* (Paris: Larousse, 1983).

[32] Muḥammad b. ʿUmar At-Tūnusī, *Kitāb aš-šudūr ad-dahabiyya fī al-muṣṭalaḥāt aṭ-ṭibbiyya* (Cairo: Maṭbaʿat al-Muqtaṭaf, 1914).

[33] François-Antoine-Hippolyte Fabre, *Dictionnaire des dictionnaires de médecine français et étrangers* (Paris : Germer-Baillière, 1840–42).

al-Fayrūzābādī's *Qāmūs*. The final product, dedicated to the National Library of Paris in 1851, is presented as the *Dictionnaire des termes anciens et modernes des sciences médicales, naturelles et vétérinaires* (Dictionary of ancient and modern terms in medical, natural, and veterinary sciences).

In modern times, bilingual dictionaries cover a wide range of disciplines. They target not only scientific disciplines but also the fields of humanities and social sciences. In most cases, these aren't dictionaries in the strict sense found in the market, but bilingual or trilingual lexicons – simple lists without definitions, examples, or citations – providing Arabic equivalents proposed by their authors for foreign scientific or technical terms. The ALECSO Arabization Coordination Bureau has published dozens of these trilingual lexicons in English, French, and Arabic under common titles such as *Unified Dictionary of Linguistic Terms/ Pharmacy Terms/ Information Terms/ Archaeology Terms/ Human Sciences Terms*, etc.

A noteworthy aspect of these dictionaries, as well as bilingual or trilingual lexicons into Arabic, is their role in neologism creation in Arabic: the formation of new terms or the validation and recognition of already coined neologisms. Notable examples include the significant number of neologisms coined in Mounir Baalbaki's English-Arabic dictionary *al-Mawrid* and J. Abdel-Nour and S. Idriss' French-Arabic dictionary *al-Manhal*.[34] The latter indicates 1,140 neologisms marked with an asterisk, demonstrating substantial results.

Contrary to expectations, it is the bilingual, not the monolingual, Arabic dictionary that meets new needs and suggests neologisms. The monolingual dictionary often lags behind and eventually follows, representing a reversal of roles. A striking example of this role reversal is found in the monolingual *al-Munjid fī al-luġa al-ʿarabiyya al-muʿāṣira*, which declares in its introduction that a significant portion of its entries has been selected from two bilingual dictionaries, French-Arabic and English-Arabic. It explicitly states that the concerns of the educated Arab are the same as those of the educated Westerner in a world moving toward globalization.[35]

IS: To approach the topic from another angle, I would like to explain how Modern Standardized Arabic (MSA) shaped Arabic dictionaries.

HH: Modern Arabic dictionaries, starting with *Muḥīṭ al-muḥīṭ* by Buṭrus al-Bustānī (d. 1883),[36] *Aqrab al-Mawārid* by Saʿīd aš-Šartūnī (d. 1912), and the famous *al-Munjid* by Louis Maʿlūf published in 1908, remained closely tied to ancient dictionaries. The latter explicitly states in his introduction that he did everything possible to preserve the original terms of the Ancients, but he removed anything that was morally offensive: terms whose knowledge has no interest and whose omission does no harm.

---

[34] Mounir Baalbaki, *Al-Mawrid, A Modern English-Arabic Dictionary* (Beirut, Dār al-ʿilm li l-malāyīn, 1967); Jabbour Abdel-Nour and Souheil Idriss, *Al-Manhal, Dictionnaire français-arabe*, 7th ed. (Beirut: Dār al-ʿilm li l-malāyīn, 1983).

[35] *Al-Munjid fī al-luga al-ʿarabiyya al-muʿāṣira*, 1.

[36] Buṭrus al-Bustānī, *Muḥīṭ al-muḥīṭ* (Beirut: Librairie du Liban, 1987); Saʿīd Aš-Šartūnī, *Aqrab al-mawārid fī fuṣaḥ al-ʿarabiyya wa š-šawārid* (Qom, 1983); Louis Maclūf, *Al-Munjid* (Beirut, Dār al-Mašriq, al-Maṭbacat al-kātūlīkiyyat, 1908).

It was not until the publication of *al-Wasīṭ*, the dictionary of the Arabic Academy of Cairo in 1960, that new terms and, especially, new meanings for old words began to appear, albeit rather moderately. The preface of the dictionary is very eloquent: The lexicographers (Bustānī, Šartūnī, Maʿlūf) tried to open up to the vocabulary of the twentieth century. But "they did not dare." To do so, it says, required "more authority and stronger linguistic arguments."[37] As a result, Modern Arabic remained practically outside the dictionary.

However, it was impossible for Modern Arabic to remain outside the dictionary. Its very timid presence in *al-Wasīṭ* began to assert itself toward the beginning of our century. This is reflected in the effort to include the vocabulary of modernity, reduce the obsolete, allocate more space to contemporary examples and quotations, and adopt Modern Arabic in definitions. Moreover, dictionaries dedicated to Modern Arabic have emerged, even though they struggled to have a truly representative corpus of Modern Arabic, which remains problematic to define.

IS: Finally, on a personal note I want to know how you became interested in Arabic dictionaries, and how wide a reach does the discipline have in the Arabic world?

HH: In my university studies, I focused on linguistics, particularly Arabic grammar and its terminology. There was perhaps a turning point when I concluded several cooperation agreements within the framework of the Joint Committee for University Cooperation (CMCU) and the Lexicology, Terminology, Translation (LTT) network with academics in Tunisia, Lebanon, Jordan, and Senegal. I published the work of our teams in several books: *The Literal and Figurative Meaning in the Bilingual Dictionary, Examples and Citations in the Work of Arab Grammarians and Lexicographers, The Status of Scientific and Technical Terms in the General Dictionary*, as well as in several special issues of the *Lexicology Review of Tunis* directed by Ibrahim Ben Mrad, head of the Tunisian team.[38]

Since then, my participation in the historical Arabic dictionary project in Doha as vice president of its scientific council has only intensified this orientation. The last element, finally, is my teaching in the Linguistics and Arabic Lexicography Program, which I directed for six years at the Doha Institute for Graduate Studies. The dictionary inevitably became the center of my research.

Training in this discipline is very recent in the Arab world. The Linguistics and Arabic Lexicography Program at the Doha Institute for Graduate Studies is, to my knowledge, unique. There are, here and there, at the bachelor's or master's level, departments of linguistics in Arab universities. This is not the case for lexicography. It is usually just a course, rarely more, in lexicology or lexicography that can be found in the departments of Arabic or foreign languages of these universities. The situation may change in the coming years. Fingers crossed.

---

[37] Majmaʿ al-luġa al-ʿarabiyya, *Al-Muʿjam al-wasīṭ*, 27.
[38] Hassan Hamzé, Bassam Baraké, and Ibrahim Ben Mrad, eds., *Le sens propre et le sens figuré dans le dictionnaire bilingue français-arabe* (Tripoli: Dar al-Mouna, 2007); Hassan Hamzé and Bassam Baraké, eds., *L'exemple et la citation dans l'œuvre des grammairiens et des lexicographes arabes* (Beirut: Dar wa maktabat al-Hilal, 2010); Hassan Hamzé, ed., *Le terme scientifique et technique dans le dictionnaire général* (Beirut: Dar wa maktabat al-Hilal, 2013); *Revue de la Lexicologie*, no. 20 (2004), no. 24 (2008), no. 27 (2011), no. 36–38 (2020–22).

Suggested Readings

Abū ʿUbayd. *Al-Ġarīb al-muṣannaf*, edited by Ṣafwān Dāwūdī. Damascus-Beirut: Dār al-Fayḥāʾ, 2005.
Majmac al-luġa al-carabiyya, al-Qāhira. *Al-Muʿjam al-wasīṭ*, 5th ed. Cairo, 2021.
Baalbaki, Ramzi. *At-Turāt al-muʿjamī al-ʿarabī min al-qarn at-tānī ḥattā al-qarn at-tānī ʿašar li l-hijra*, translated from English by Ramzi Baalbaki. Beirut: Arab Center for Research and Policy Studies, 2020.
Ben Mrad, Ibrahim. *Al-Muʿjam al-ʿilmī al-ʿarabī al-muhtaṣṣ, ḥattā muntaṣaf al-qarn al-ḥādī cašar li l-hijra*. Beirut: Dār al-Ġarb al-islāmī, 1993.
Bochtor, Ellious. *Dictionnaire français-arabe*, revised and augmented by A. Caussin de Perceval. Paris: Chez Firmin Didot père et fils, Libraires, 1828–29.
al-Bustānī, Buṭrus. *Muḥīṭ al-muḥīṭ*. Beirut: Librairie du Liban, 1987.
Dozy, Reinhart. *Supplément aux dictionnaires arabes*. Beirut: Librairie du Liban, 1991; original edition, Leiden: E. J. Brill, 1881.
Dubois, Jean, and Claude Dubois. *Introduction à la lexicographie, le dictionnaire*. Paris: Larousse, 1971.
al-Fayrūzābādī. *Al-Qāmūs al-muḥīṭ*. Cairo: al-Bābī al-ḥalabī, 1952.
al-Ḫalīl b. Aḥmad al-Farāhīdī. *Kitāb al-ʿAyn*, edited by Mahdī Maḫzūmī and Ibrāhīm as-Sāmurrāʾī. Beirut: Dār wa Maktabat al-Hilāl, n.d.
Hamzaoui, Mohamed Rachad. *Al-Muʿjam al-ʿarabī: Iškālāt wa muqārabāt*. Tunis: Fondation Nationale, 1990.
Hamzé, Hassan, dir. *Al-Maʿājim at-tārīhiyyat, muqāranāt wa muqārabāt*. Beirut: Arab Center for Research and Policy Studies, 2023.
Hamzé, Hassan. "Ḥurūf az-ziyāda wa tartīb al-afʿāl fī al-muʿjam al-ʿarabī." *Revue de la lexicologie* 30 (2014): 55–88.
Hamzé, Hassan. "Les niveaux de langue dans le dictionnaire français-arabe," in *Le sens propre et le sens figuré dans le dictionnaire bilingue français-arabe*, edited by Hamzé Hassan, Bassam Baraké, and Ibrahim Ben Mrad, 119–40. Tripoli: Dar al-Mouna, 2007.
al-Hawārizmī, Muḥammad b. Aḥmad b. Yūsuf. *Mafātīḥ al-ʿulūm*. Cairo: Idārat at-ṭibāʿat al-munīriyyat, 1924.
Haywood, John A. *Arabic Lexicography: Its History, and Its Place in the General History of Lexicography*, 2nd ed. Leiden: E. J. Brill, 1965.
al-Humayd, Abdulaziz. *Aʿmāl al-mustašriqīn al-ʿarabiyya fī al-muʿjam al-ʿarabī*. Saudi Arabia: Jāmiʿat al-ʾimām Muḥammad bin Saʿūd al-ʾislāmiyya, 2012.
Ibn Manẓūr. *Lisān al-ʿarab*. Beirut: Dār Ṣādir, 1968.
Ibn Sīda. *Al-Muḥaṣṣaṣ*. Beirut: Dār al-kutub al-cilmiyyat, n.d.
Ibn Sīda. *Al-Muḥkam wa al-muḥīṭ al-aʿẓam*, edited by Abdelhamīd Hindāwī. Beirut: Dār al-kutub al-ʿilmiyyat, 2000.
al-Jawharī. *Aṣ-Ṣiḥāḥ tāj al-luġat wa ṣiḥāḥ al-ʿarabiyyat*, 2nd ed., edited by Aḥmad ʿAbd al-Ġafūr ʿAṭṭār. Beirut: Dār al-ʿilm li l-malāyīn, 1979.
Lane, Edward William. *An Arabic-English Lexicon Derived from the Most Copious Eastern Sources*. Beirut: Librairie du Liban, 1997; repr. from the 1st ed., London, 1863–93.
Nassār, Ḥusayn. *Al-Muʿjam al-ʿarabī, našʾatuhu wa taṭawwuruhu*, 4th ed. Cairo: Maktabat Miṣr, 1988.
aṣ-Ṣaġānī. *Al-ʿUbāb az-zāhir wa l-lubāb al-fāḫir*, edited by Muḥammad Ḥasan Āl yāsīn. Baghdad: Dār ar-Rašīd, 1977–87.
az-Zabīdī. *Tāj al-ʿarūs min jawāhir al-Qāmūs*. Cairo: al-Maṭbaʿat al-ḫayriyyat, 1906.

10 Hebrew

Ruvik Rosenthal

Hebrew was the language of the Davidic kingdom. Considerable portions of the Bible are written in it. But after the destruction of the Second Temple in 70 CE, it ceased to be a national language used within the boundaries of a territory at that point under Greek occupation and became the tongue of the Jewish diaspora. As such, it was used, over a period of centuries, for rabbinical learning. Things changed with the nationalist fervor in Europe in the second half of the nineteenth century, when Hebrew was used by Zionists as a tool for the creation of a Jewish homeland. Since then, the revival (I call it "resurrection," which has theological undertones, in my book *Resurrecting Hebrew* [2008])[1] is both miraculous and mundane. Miraculous because it brought the language back from a state of fossilization; and mundane because it has made it like any other national language: pedestrian, even vulgar. This conversation meditates on the distinction between biblical and Modern Hebrew, focusing on the revival of the latter as part of the Zionist project in the last third of the nineteenth century and up until the creation of Israel as a Jewish state in 1948. It discusses the work of Eliezer ben Yehuda, whose efforts to compile the first modern dictionary were left unfinished at the time of his death.

***

ILAN STAVANS: Being such a young nation in the modern sense of the term (of course, Israel is one of the oldest nations as well), the fact that its resurgence involved the modernization of biblical Hebrew places dictionaries at the center of Israel's life. While my focus in this conversation is dictionaries of Modern Hebrew, from Eliezer ben Yehuda to the twenty-first century, I want to start way before, in biblical, Talmudic, and other early forms of the language. What efforts were there in biblical times to standardize words, to catalogue and preserve them?

RUVIK ROSENTHAL: Words and speech have a theological importance in the Jewish tradition, as the world was created according to it by the words of God. Nevertheless, the writers and editors of the Bible hardly

---

[1] Ilan Stavans, *Resurrecting Hebrew* (New York: Schocken Books, 2008).

paid attention to the language in general and to Hebrew (named "Yehudit") as an object of research, but rather as a natural means of communication or as a component of national identity. We can find hints to such interest in some acrostics like chapter 119 in Psalms, which indicate that they referred to the alphabetic order and preserved it. The concept of any kind of a dictionary, as well as grammatical system, emerged much later.

IS: Psalm 119 is indeed a superb example of the centrality of words in the biblical covenant. Time and again, the psalmist repeats that through the divine word moral rectitude is achieved, connecting language with ethics, as in verse 105 (King James Version), "Thy word is a lamp unto my feet, and a light unto my path." Judaism is clearly a logocentric religion. Plus, as you say, the use of acrostics is an endorsement of linguistic order, though, of course, the alphabet is as arbitrary in its organization as any other model.

RR: We must differentiate between speech communication and the language as an object, or metalinguistic utterances. God and humans speak all along the Bible, but rarely refer to language as such.

IS: What insights might we draw from that narrative strategy?

RR: I don't refer to it as a "strategy" but as an outcome of the inner sources that created the Bible, which were based on strong emotions like love, fear, jealousy, and faith, rather than on systematic arguments. The language was used to express these emotions, as well as uncriticized myth and chronicles. So, the whole concept of a metalinguistic approach that is the base of a lexicographic work is not relevant here.

IS: Has that logocentrism become central in diasporic Jewish life?

RR: Thoughts, ideas, interpretation – literacy was the backbone of the Jewish culture all along the years of Diaspora. I would say that the holy scripts and Hebrew language preserved the Jews more than the Jews preserved the holy scripts and Hebrew.

IS: Let's talk about the period of the Sages (Leshon Hahamim). How was lexicography conceived?

RR: The Sages, 200 BCE to 600 CE, created fundamental scripts that preserved, enriched, and interpreted the Jewish culture and religion: Mishna, Talmud, Midrash, and the early Piyyut. Though the concept of a dictionary emerged later, in the early medieval era, some earlier elements can be found in these monumental scripts. The Sages referred to letters as a category in language, like in the famous Midrash Ha-Otiyot (Midrash of letters) of Rabbi Akiva, which relates also to the alphabetic order. The Sages referred to words of uncertain meaning and tried to define them. The different branches of the Masorah traditions needed a precise understanding of pronunciation and meaning of every word in the Bible. These various issues created an infrastructure toward the medieval Hebrew lexicography.

IS: Saadia Gaon's *Egron* (tenth century) isn't a dictionary in the modern sense in that it doesn't define words, but it provides alphabetically organized word lists for the purposes of *paytanim*, that is, versification.[2] Might it be considered a lexicographic forerunner?

---

[2] Saadia Gaon, *Sefer Ha-Egron* [The book of collection], scientific ed., ed. Nehemia Aloni (Jerusalem: Hebrew Language Academy, 1969).

RR: By no means is Saadia Gaon's *Egron* the first Hebrew lexicon. It is not a comprehensive dictionary that includes all the words in use at that era, and it lacks many components which we meet in later medieval dictionaries, or modern dictionaries, though in the second edition he added Arabic translations. Nevertheless, it is the first known attempt to describe the Hebrew language by a list of words in a systematic order. A dictionary has various components, not all of them are used in every dictionary: entries, definitions, origins, etc. Saadia focused on the entries and referred especially to poetry, but by this he established the concept of a dictionary as a part of Hebrew studies. His work relates to his contribution to Hebrew grammar, which was also part of his work in his book *Tsahut Ha-Lashon* (Clarity of the language).

IS: During Saadia Gaon's life, in Babylonia the Jewish intelligentsia communicated in Arabic. How did he negotiate the various languages in his life? And what is the tenor of *Tsahut Ha-Lashon?*

RR: Saadia Gaon spoke in what we call today "Jewish Arabic" and wrote most of his works in Arabic. As I mentioned, he also added Arabic to his *Egron*. His grammatical work was influenced by work in the field of Arabic grammar. In many ways it resembles the mutual influence of Jewish and Arabic scholars in Spain centuries later. The *Egron* is organized in two separate sections. The first lists the entries in alphabetic order of the first letter, so it serves the acrostics; the second lists the entries in alphabetic order of the closing syllables, so it serves the rhymes.

IS: There is a famous lexicological dispute between Ibn Saruk and Dunash Ben Labrat. I was recently reflecting on it when translating the work of medieval Hebrew poets like Samuel Hanagid, Salomon ibn Gabirol, and Yehuda Halevi.

RR: Menachem Ibn Saruk (920–70) created his lexicographic work *Machbarot Menachem* (Menachem's notebooks). He based his work on the Semitic roots system. For each root he added various words, derived from the defined root. Ibn Saruk based his work on the concept of two-consonants root theory, or even one-consonant root. The three-consonants root was constructed some decades later. Ibn Saruk believed that the Jewish linguistic tradition must rely only on the biblical *peshat* (literal meaning) and not on the Sages' interpretation, a belief he shared with the banned Karaite tradition. The poet and linguist Dunash Ben Labrat (920–90) wrote a "book of answers," criticizing Ibn Saruk's linguistic approach and findings, as well as his Karaite attitude. As a result, Ibn Saruk was banned and deported, but his work is a fundamental contribution to lexicographic work in the following generations.

IS: The eleventh century was quite productive in Hebrew lexicography. Can you tell us more about it?

RR: Hebrew lexicography flourished in this century. Yonah ibn-Janah wrote his important work *Kitab al-usul* (The book of roots).[3] It was the first lexicon that adopted the three-consonants root theory, devised by Ibn-Janah's master, Yehudah ibn Hayyuj. His work was written in Arabic and was translated into Hebrew in the twelfth century by Yehudah ibn Tibon. David ben Abraham

---

[3] Yonah Ibn-Janah, *Sefer Ha-Shorashim/Kitab al-usul* [The book of roots] (Berlin: Hevrat Mekitzey Nirdamim, 1893).

al-Fasi (d. 1026) worked in Morocco and Jerusalem parallel to the Jewish scholars in Spain. He created his dictionary *Kitāb Jāmiʿ al-Alfāz* (The book of Abraham al-Fasi).[4] He was a Karaite believer, but he didn't share Ibn Saruk's bad fortune. Like Ibn Saruk he based his work on the roots system. As we'll show later the roots system became the leading theory in modern lexicography, though some other systems challenged it. Another dictionary was written during the eleventh century by Natan Me-Romy [Natan from Rome] – *Ha-Aruch* (The edited/The arranged).[5] This dictionary focused on difficult words of the Sages' scripts. The dictionary is based on various components of the language, which later became typical of Modern Hebrew dictionaries: meaning of the entry (or "definition"), original appearance in the Sages scripts (or "origin"), and some linguistic comments.

IS: Did the leading Medieval interpreters (*parshanim*) contribute to Hebrew lexicography?

RR: The leading figures in this category, Rashi, Ibn Ezra, and others, provided an important contribution to lexicography in the semantic aspect, though they didn't create dictionaries. Later, in the thirteenth century, Rabbi David Qimhi (Radaq) created his *Sefer Ha-Shorashim* (The book of roots).[6] It was based mainly on the work of Ibn Janah, translated into Latin, and had a decisive influence on the Christian scholars who later worked in the field of biblical lexicography.

IS: A branch of Kabbalah is linked to the power of letters. For instance, *Sefer Yetzirah*, whose historical origin is the subject of scholarly debate, emphasizes the role of the Hebrew letters in the creation of the universe. Might there be a connection with lexicography?

RR: *Sefer Yetzirah* refers to some elements in the alphabet, like pronunciation, form, words that are initiated by a specific letter, etc. From these elements and others, the book derives insights about the universe, the creation, God, etc., based on mystical traditions. It may seem that the growing interest in the structure of the Israeli lexicon – from letters to words – has some influence on the book, but it was orally created earlier in Saadia Gaon times. I can hardly see any influence of the book on Hebrew lexicography, which maintains linguistic knowledge and theories in a strict system, opposing the mystical approach of *Sefer Yetzirah*.

IS: The Haskalah, the Jewish Enlightenment, which emerged as a defined ideological worldview during the 1770s and ended with the rise of Jewish emancipation in the early 1880s, opened new paths of knowledge connected with secular, rational, and scientific thinking. What kinds of dictionaries resulted from it?

RR: Beside a rich corpus of poetry, fiction, nonfiction, and newspapers, some Jewish scholars in the Haskalah era published dictionaries. The dictionaries

---

[4] David ben Abraham al-Fasi, *Kitāb Jāmiʿ al-Alfāz* [The book of Abraham al-Fasi] (New Haven, CT: Yale University Press, 1936).

[5] Natan Me-Romy, *Ha-Aruch* [The edited/The arranged]. Venice: Daniel Bombirgi Press, 1539.

[6] Rabbi David (Radaq) Qimhi, *Sefer Ha-Shorashim* [The book of roots] (Berlin: Rephael Hirsh Bizental Press, 1847).

focused on separate layers of Hebrew. We may say that the first dictionary in this period is *Otsar Ha-Shorashim* (Roots' treasure) by Yehuda Leib Ben Zeev, published in 1808 and focused on biblical roots. It was followed by a German-Hebrew dictionary and served the need of the maskilim from eastern Europe to study German. In 1858, Joseph Schönhak published his work *Sefer Ha-Mashbir*, focusing on the Sages scripts.[7] Another important dictionary of the period is *Ha-Otzar* (The treasure) by Shemuel Yosef Finn, which covers the Hebrew lexicon of the Bible, Talmudic literature, and later Hebrew writings, including Piyyut literature. It also provides translations into Russian and German.

In 1880 Yehoshua Steinberg published a biblical dictionary – *Mishpat Ha-Urim* (Lights judgment), followed by Russian and German translations. The writer Mendale Mocher Sefarim is considered as the mediator of the Haskalah literature from Yiddish and archaic Hebrew toward Modern Hebrew. His monumental book *Sefer Toldot Ha-Teva* (The history of nature) is an encyclopedic dictionary of animals of various kinds.[8] In 1884 Shelomo Mandelkern published his first edition of the biblical concordance, completed in 1896.[9] His work is pioneering and iconic and serves scholars up to these days. These dictionaries and others show the deep connection and the rich knowledge of the holy scripts held by the Haskalah scholars and their attempts to adapt this knowledge to the modern era.

IS: In the nineteenth century, there was a current in German lexicography devoted to biblical lexicography. I'm thinking, for instance, of Christian Hebraist Wilhelm Gesenius' *Hebräisch-deutsches Handwörterbuch* (1810–12).[10]

RR: Gesenius' dictionary, focusing on biblical Hebrew, is an outcome of the growing interest in comparative Semitic languages in the nineteenth century, especially by German scholars. Another important biblical dictionary was written by Ludwig Köhler and Walter Baumgartner (1953), compiled on scientific philological principles. In 1876 Jacob Levi published his dictionary of Talmud and the Midrashic literature.[11] Some decades later Marcus Jastrow published a dictionary of the Midrashic literature.[12] As we can see, each scholar focused on one of the Hebrew layers and didn't try to bring a

---

[7] Joseph Schönhak, *Sefer Ha-Mashbir* [The book of the mediator] (Warsaw: Abraham Zuckermann, 1888).
[8] Mendale Mocher Sefarim, *Sefer Toldot Ha-Teva* [The history of nature], 3 vols. (Leipzig: 1861–72).
[9] Shelomo Mandelkern, *Concordanzia La-Tanach* [Biblical concordance] (1884–96) (Tel Aviv: Shoken, 1955).
[10] Wilhem Gesenius, *Hebräisch-deutsches Handwörterbuch über die Schriften des Alten Testaments mit Einschluß der geographischen Nahmen und der chaldäischen Wörter beym Daniel und Esra* [The Hebrew-German hand dictionary on the Old Testament scriptures including geographical names and Chaldean words, with Daniel and Ezra] (Leipzig: Friedrich Christian Wilhelm Vogel, 1810).
[11] Jacob Levi, *Neuhebräisches und Chaldäisches Wörterbuch über die Talmudim und Midraschim* (Leipzig: Brockhaus, 1879).
[12] Marcus Jastrow, *A Dictionary of the Targumim, the Talmud Babli and Yerushalmi, and the Midrashic Literature* (London: Luzac and Co., 1903).

comprehensive dictionary that includes the complete corpus of Hebrew lexical entries.

IS: Eliezer ben Yehuda (1858–1922) is the father of Modern Hebrew. In my book *Resurrecting Hebrew*, I explore his quest to revive an ancient language in the context of nineteenth- and twentieth-century political movements. He was involved in his revival from an ancient language into a means of communication of the emerging state of Israel as a twentieth-century nation. Among other tasks – and arguably the most significant – Ben Yehuda spent his life composing a monumental lexicon, but he left it unfinished. Apparently, the last word he was writing as he died was *nefesh*, soul.

RR: Ben Yehuda is the iconic founder of Modern Hebrew, known as "the reviver of the Hebrew language." In his lifetime and until today there is a dispute concerning his importance. The facts show that he gained his reputation justifiably, in various actions, projects, and decisions he took during his active life in Israel. One of them, and in my opinion the most important, is *Hamilon Ha-Gadol* (The big dictionary), which contains seventeen volumes.[13] The dictionary includes about 22,000 entries which reflect the vocabulary of those years. He included in the dictionary about 200 of his own neologisms, marked by a chain sign.

Indeed, Ben Yehuda didn't finish the dictionary, but his successors worked under the principles he established and with the materials he gathered. His dictionary changed the path of Hebrew lexicography in almost every aspect. It combined in one dictionary the various layers of Hebrew: biblical, Sages, medieval, and Modern Hebrew. It is a dictionary of words and lemmas, though the roots are included as independent entries, followed by the verbs derived from them. His dictionary was the first comprehensive historic dictionary. He read broadly in Jewish intellectual history and cited his findings in the dictionary. By this he also consisted in his dictionary the linguistic principle of "use," the semantic shifts of each lexeme across generations. These principles have been adopted by his successors and shaped the world of Hebrew lexicography up to these days.

IS: What was Ben Yehuda's criteria for inventing neologisms?

RR: Ben Yehuda wrote specific instructions for inventing neologisms, published in the introduction of his dictionary. He based them on the Semitic root-pattern system. He suggested the phases needed to create a neologism. First: find a word in the Hebrew scripts and check if you can provide it with a modern meaning; for example, in its single appearance in the Bible, *ekdach* (today: pistol) means a gem. If not, find an adequate root and an adequate pattern and combine them to form a neologism; for example, take the root NGB, which contains the meaning of dryness, and the pattern *maktelet* to create the combined neologism *maggevet* – a towel. Some patterns relate to a semantic field, like *katol* for colors, so the denominative root VRD (derived from *vered*, a rose) creates the color *varod*, pink. So, root+pattern is the basic system. Another system is the base+suffix model; for example, *milla* (word) + the suffix *-on* creates the neologism *millon* – a dictionary. In Modern

---

[13] Eliezer ben Yehuda, *Hamilon Ha-Gadol* [The big dictionary]. 17 vols (Tel Aviv: La'am, 1948).

	Hebrew, almost all neologisms are based on these principles, while in classic Hebrew thousands of words are not part of the root+pattern system.
IS:	How did Ben Yehuda's politics affect his lexicography and vice versa?
RR:	Ben Yehuda was a devoted Zionist. He believed that reviving Hebrew is crucial to the young Zionist movement, thus a comprehensive dictionary is necessary to fulfill it. His declared linguistic vision was that Hebrew should be based only on pure Hebrew words. In his dictionary he avoided foreign loanwords which were used by Hebrew speakers or writers. He also tried to create neologisms for interlingual words like university or democracy, but his partners rejected his suggestions.
IS:	I find it moving that when Ben Yehuda died, as the legend goes, he was working on his dictionary and on the definition of the word *nefesh* – soul. How different is twenty-first-century Israeli Hebrew from the one Ben Yehuda codified?
RR:	The main and expected outcome of the revival of Hebrew is that it went into a vivid ongoing path of changes. This dynamic process was defined by the linguist Haim Rosen (1922–99) as *ivrit israelit* – Israeli Hebrew. The phenomena of Israeli Hebrew are wide and refer to every aspect of the language: phonology, syntax, morphology, vocabulary, and discourse. Still, the basic grammatical rules and the Semitic characteristics of classic Hebrew are the firm base of Israeli Hebrew.
IS:	What can you tell us about the dictionary of Yehuda Gur?
RR:	Yehuda Leib Grozovski (1862–1950), known as Yehuda Gur, published his dictionary *Millon Ivri* (Hebrew dictionary) in 1938,[14] sixteen years after the death of Ben Yehuda. Gur followed Ben Yehuda's principles, though the historic origins he cited have fewer examples and shorter references. As Ben Yehuda's dictionary was large and scholarly oriented, there was a need for a popular dictionary, and Gur provided it successfully. Gur also added to many entries a list of idioms and phrases which include the relevant word, influenced by leading dictionaries in other languages. Idioms and phrases became a component of subsequent dictionaries, which were published after the declaration of the state of Israel.
IS:	Avraham Rozenshteyn (1906–84), aka Avraham Even-Shoshan, the Belarusian-born Hebrew lexicographer, compiled the *HaMilon HeHadash* (The new dictionary) (1946–58).[15] People call it the "Even-Shoshan." It is fully vowelized.
RR:	Even-Shoshan's dictionary is the iconic dictionary of Modern Hebrew. He arranged a comprehensive organizing system. The verbs refer to roots and are divided by verbal stems (*binyanim*). In his dictionaries, he includes loanwords and neologisms. He declared in his dictionary that his mission is to follow "the living Hebrew." He also added etymological data, idioms and phrases, and quotations from classic and Modern Hebrew. Even-Shoshan and his successors updated the dictionary, and in the 2003 edition they added

---

[14] Yehuda Gur, *Millon Ivri* [Hebrew dictionary] (Tel Aviv: Devir, 1938).
[15] Avraham Even-Shoshan, *Ha-Milon He-Hadash* [The new dictionary] (Jerusalem: Kiryat-Sefer, 1948).

	many slang entries. Some lexicographers like Eitan Avneon, Reuven Alkalay, Shoshana Bahat, Yaacov Choueka, and Maya Fruchtman published comprehensive dictionaries but did not challenge the iconic status of Even-Shoshan's dictionary.
IS:	Did Even-Shoshan pay tribute to Ben Yehuda?
RR:	Not in public. In his introduction he thanks some linguists who advised him. He also emphasizes the differences between his dictionary and former dictionaries, hinting to Ben Yehuda's dictionary.
IS:	Are all Hebrew dictionaries today the product of commercial enterprises? I think, as a point of comparison, of the *Oxford English Dictionary*, which is made by an academic institution.
RR:	Almost all the Israeli dictionaries are not related to an academic institute but were published by a commercial publishing house. Nevertheless, the creators are professionals, expert in the Hebrew language and its academic aspects.
IS:	How are the other dictionaries you mentioned different from Even-Shoshan's dictionary?
RR:	The main dilemma of the Hebrew dictionaries is the verb entries. There are four systems concerning this issue. First, the root system, used by Even-Shoshan (e.g. under the root-entry *GBR*, the user finds different verb-stem subentries: *gavar*, *higbir*, *hitgabber*, and others). This system, used also by Ben Yehuda, seems to be the best in grammatical consideration, though it is sometimes hard to know the right root to look for. The second system is third-person past tense (e.g. *gavar* and *higbir* are independent entries, stated in different letter-sections (G and H)). The third system is first-person present tense (*ho-ve*) (e.g. *gover*, *magbir* as independent entries). The fourth system is the infinitive construct (e.g. *ligbor*, *lehagbir*, stated in the letter-section L). I prefer the second system, as it is closer to the intuitive search of a nonprofessional Hebrew speaker.
IS:	How about the difference between prescriptive and descriptive dictionaries? Where do the lexicons we've been talking about fall?
RR:	In principle a dictionary is a descriptive product. Its task is to tell the user everything about the language as it is. The dilemma lies in the tension between standard, norms, and speech. Many words are considered as normative words but for some reasons didn't get the regulative stamp of the academy of Hebrew; for example, *mizron* (a mattress, non-standard but normative) versus *mizran* (standard). Some dictionaries label *mizron* as speech oriented. Most of the dictionaries label slang and jargon, and in the past even added "vulgar" or "obscene" when appropriate. Some dictionaries totally ignore these lexemes.
IS:	One of the most important developments in lexicography and a byproduct of the Enlightenment as well are bilingual dictionaries. Their mission is to create a bridge across cultures and linguistic ecosystems. Bilingual Hebrew dictionaries in Russian, English, Spanish, French, Italian, and other languages are ubiquitous. Which of them have broken new ground in lexicographic terms?
RR:	It is hard to say. As you mentioned almost every language is presented in a Hebrew bilingual dictionary, including Jewish languages like Yiddish or

IS: Jewish-Moroccan. They are quite basic and include only simple entries without details, for example, "*mizran* ... mattress," and vice versa. A fabulous Yiddish-Hebrew dictionary adds idioms and phrases all along the book. I refer to Alexander Harkavy's dictionary, published in 1925.[16]

IS: How about Arabic-Hebrew dictionaries?

RR: There are some dictionaries in this field. The classic one is Ayalon-Shin'ar's dictionary. Menachem Milson recently published a Modern Arabic-Hebrew dictionary. A unique lexicographic work had been done by the Israeli French Catholic monk Yochanan Elichay, in the field of the Palestinian Arabic dialect.[17]

IS: What can you tell me about dictionaries that focus on a specific field of the language, like idioms and phrases, slang, etc.?

RR: The lexicographic activity in Israel is astonishing. Besides comprehensive and shortened Hebrew-Hebrew dictionaries, almost every field of Israeli life was followed by a dictionary. I'll mention some examples. In 1934, Aharon Mazia and Shaul Tshernichovsky published a comprehensive dictionary for medical terms, including thousands of neologisms.[18] In 1972, Dan Ben Amotz and Netiva Ben Yehuda published an amazing slang dictionary.[19] In 2005, it was followed by a comprehensive slang dictionary, created by me.[20]

In 1987, Ernest Klein created a comprehensive etymological dictionary of the Hebrew language.[21] Twelve years later, the linguist Uzi Ornan published "the dictionary of the forgotten words."[22] It includes thousands of words used during the Hebrew-revival decades (1880–1920) and since abandoned. In 1991, Baruch Sarel and Rimmona Gerson published a visual topic-oriented dictionary.[23] In 2009, I published a comprehensive idioms and phrases dictionary, including etymological and linguistic data.[24] The interest of the Israeli speakers and hence the market in dictionaries is impressive.

IS: Talk about the place that the Academy of the Hebrew Language plays in Israeli culture.

RR: The Academy of the Hebrew Language was founded under a parliament law in 1953 and followed the voluntary activity of the committee of language

---

[16] Alexander Harkavy, *Yiddish-Hebrew Dictionary* (New York: published by the author, 1925).

[17] Yochanan Elichay, *The Olive Tree Dictionary: A Transliterated Dictionary of Conversational Eastern Arabic* (Jerusalem: Minerva, 2004).

[18] Aharon Mazia, *Sefer Ha-Munachim Lirefu'ah Ulemada'ey Ha-Teva* [Dictionary of medical and allied sciences], ed. Shaul Tshernichovsky (Jerusalem: Margalit, 1934).

[19] Dan Ben Amotz and Netiva Ben Yehuda, *Milon Olami Le-Ivrit Meduberet* [An awesome dictionary of spoken Hebrew] (Tel Aviv: Zemora, Bitan, 1972).

[20] Ruvik Rosenthal, *Milon Ha-Sleng Ha-Makif* [Comprehensive slang dictionary] (Ben Shemen: Keter, 2005).

[21] Ernest Klein, *A Comprehensive Etymological Dictionary of the Hebrew Language* (Jerusalem: Carta and the University of Haifa, 1987).

[22] Uzi Ornan, *Milon Ha-Milim Ha-Ovdot* [Dictionary of the forgotten words] (Tel Aviv: Shoken, 1996).

[23] Baruch Sarel and Rimmona Gerson, *Visual Dictionary, English-Hebrew, Hebrew-English* (Jerusalem: Carta, 1991).

[24] Ruvik Rosenthal, *Milon Ha-Tzerufim* [Dictionary of idioms and phrases] (Ben Shemen: Keter, 2009).

	(*va'ad ha'lashon*) that Ben Yehuda founded sixty years earlier. Officially it regulates the language in the public sphere, states grammatical regulations when necessary, and answers public questions. People treat the academy as an authority but also used to complain about some of its activities and decisions, claiming it is detached from the living language. In the last decades, the academy opened itself to the public, especially through social media, and that raised its popularity.
IS:	Is the academy involved in making dictionaries?
RR:	Absolutely. One of its main activities is creating professional dictionaries in various fields, made by committees of experts, and they include many neologisms. Up to these days, the website of the academy includes 220 professional dictionaries; some examples: archeology (1942), insurance (1960), artificial intelligence (2017), mass media (2013), this last was created by a committee that was initiated and led by me.[25] Besides these dictionaries, a "committee of words for general use" suggested hundreds of neologisms, arranged in forty dictionaries. Some years ago, the academy published a wide-ranging product: "the historic dictionary," which follows the use of Hebrew lemmas along 3,000 years of Hebrew written culture.
IS:	How different is Haredi Hebrew, if there is such a variant, from standard Israeli Hebrew?
RR:	Haredi Hebrew is a sociolect, mostly strange to a non-Haredi ear. It is based on Israeli Hebrew, though some of its uses are in the Ashkenazi accent (e.g. *shidech* (matchmaking), *oyved* (a devoted observant)). Most of the Haredi sociolect includes words and phrases that serve their unique way of life, beliefs, and regulations. Yiddish is today quite rare in the everyday use of the Haredi people, except for some extreme communities.
IS:	How about Arab Hebrew?
RR:	Most of the Israeli-Arab citizens study and understand Hebrew. Its use changes according to geography and occupation. The noteworthy phenomenon is what I call "Arabic Hebrew," a hybrid use of the two languages along a free discourse. This unique phenomenon widens, especially by more educated Arabs who engage in the general Israeli public institutes and economy.
IS:	Over the years, I have focused on hybrid languages, such as Spanglish. Is Arabic Hebrew written in Arabic or in Hebrew? Or is there a fusion script?
RR:	The hybrid language I mentioned is spoken but not written, except sometimes in the social websites.
IS:	In the case of Spanglish, a new syntax is emerging. There is already a Spanglish-English dictionary. Corporations use Spanglish for marketing purposes. There are children's books in Spanglish, music, telenovelas, poetry, translations of literary classics like *Don Quixote* and *Alice in Wonderland*. How developed is Arabic Hebrew?
RR:	There is a book about it, initiated and edited by me, written by Abed Rachman Mar'i. It is called *Walla Bseder* – a hybrid Israeli expression.[26] It includes a comprehensive dictionary of Hebrew words used in this hybrid language.

---

[25] https://hebrew-academy.org.il/
[26] Abed Rachman Mar'i, *Walla Bseder* (Ben Shemen: Keter, 2013).

IS: I'm interested in lexicographers as people. Is the field in Israel diverse? For instance, does it have an equal number of men and women? Are Ashkenazim, Sephardim, and Mizrahi involved in the endeavor? How about Haredi and Arabs?

RR: Most of the lexicographers are educated scholars, not necessarily linguists, who have the passion to create a dictionary, quite exhausting work. It seems that most of the lexicographers are Ashkenazi males. In the large scale, Arabs and Haredi do not get involved in this effort, except in some professional dictionaries.

IS: You've published some dictionaries, as you mentioned before. What can you tell me about the experience of creating a dictionary?

RR: As you may know I published books in various genres. Creating a dictionary does not resemble any other genre. It demands the hard work of collecting data and arranging it. The lexicographer is not expected to be creative but rather meticulous and accurate. The work needs passion and diligence. What drives you is the imagined book standing on your shelves and in the shops. That is why there are so many writers in Israel but so few lexicographers.

IS What about online dictionaries. Is it expanding?

RR: Online dictionaries are a firm part of the dictionaries market today. Some printed dictionaries added an online edition parallel to the printed edition. There are two leading online comprehensive dictionaries: Rav-Millim,[27] published by the company Melingo, and Milog,[28] an independent enterprise created by Yotam Rosenthal, who happens to be my son. Both are very good. Milog is free of charge and based on ads, hence its use is enormous. Rav-Millim is a paid dictionary. One of its advantages is the English parallel words. Both dictionaries provide enrichments like synonyms, rhymes, grammar, etc.

IS: How has the frequent use of English in Israel changed Hebrew?

RR: Up to now, English influence has been quite marginal in grammar and syntax aspects. It is highly present in spoken vocabulary, in various jargons (high-tech, music, science), and in small talk.

IS: To conclude, let's go back to biblical Hebrew, which is alive and well. There was a strong tradition in the nineteenth century of these dictionaries, including concordances. This tradition continues today.

RR: The interest in the Bible, including biblical Hebrew is wide and rich, but not in the dictionaries field. I don't think more work in this aspect is needed anymore.

IS: Do you get a sense that Modern Hebrew, in its development, as a result of all sorts of factors (immigration, technology, popular culture, etc.), is moving further and further away from its biblical foundation?

RR: Not at all. I write a lot on Modern Hebrew, and up to these very days I find biblical traces in written and spoken Hebrew, in every linguistic aspect.

---

[27] *Rav-Millim*, online Hebrew dictionary (Tel Aviv: Melingo), www.ravmilim.co.il.
[28] Yotam Rosenthal (creator), *Milog*, online Hebrew dictionary, www.milog.co.il.

Suggested Readings

Al-Fasi, David ben Abraham. *Kitāb Jāmiʿ al-Alfāz* [The book of Abraham al-Fasi]. New Haven, CT: Yale University Press, 1936. Arabic; Hebrew; English.
Avneon, Eitan. *Milon Sapir* [Sapir dictionary]. Tel Aviv: It'av, 2002. Hebrew.
Ayalon, David, and Pesach Shin'ar. *Milon Aravy-Ivry* [Arabic-Hebrew dictionary]. 1st ed. Jerusalem: Magnes, 1947. Arabic; Hebrew.
Ben Amotz, Dan, and Netiva Ben Yehuda. *Milon Olami Le-Ivrit Meduberet* [An awesome dictionary of spoken Hebrew]. Tel Aviv: Zemora, Bitan, 1972. Hebrew.
Ben Yehuda, Eliezer. *Hamilon Ha-Gadol* [The big dictionary]. 17 vols. Tel Aviv: La'am, 1948. Hebrew.
Ben Zeev, Yehuda Leib. *Otsar Ha-Shorashim* [Roots' treasure]. Vienna: Y. Knapfelmacher und Söhne, 1862. German; Hebrew.
Elichay, Yochanan. *The Olive Tree Dictionary: A Transliterated Dictionary of Conversational Eastern Arabic*. Jerusalem: Minerva, 2004. Arabic; English.
Even-Shoshan, Avraham. *Ha-Milon He-Hadash* [The new dictionary], 1st ed. Jerusalem: Kiryat-Sefer, 1948. Hebrew.
Gesenius, Wilhem. *Hebräisch-deutsches Handwörterbuch über die Schriften des Alten Testaments mit Einschluß der geographischen Nahmen und der chaldäischen Wörter beym Daniel und Esra* [The Hebrew-German hand dictionary on the Old Testament scriptures including geographical names and Chaldean words, with Daniel and Ezra]. Leipzig: Friedrich Christian Wilhelm Vogel, 1810. German; Hebrew.
Gur, Yehuda. *Millon Ivri* [Hebrew dictionary]. Tel Aviv: Devir, 1938. Hebrew.
Harkavy, Alexander. *Yiddish-Hebrew Dictionary*. New York: published by the author, 1925. Yiddish; English; Hebrew.
Ibn Saruk, Menachem. *Machberet Menachem* [Menachem's notebooks]. London: Hevrat Me'orerey Yeshenim, 1854. Hebrew.
Ibn-Janah, Yonah. *Sefer Ha-Shorashim/Kitab al-usul* [The book of roots]. Berlin: Hevrat Mekitzey Nirdamim, 1893. Arabic; Hebrew.
Jastrow, Marcus. *A Dictionary of the Targumim, the Talmud Babli and Yerushalmi, and the Midrashic Literature*. London: Luzac and Co., 1903. English; Hebrew.
Klein, Ernest. *A Comprehensive Etymological Dictionary of the Hebrew Language*. Jerusalem: Carta and the University of Haifa, 1987. Hebrew; English.
Levi, Jacob. *Neuhebräisches und Chaldäisches Wörterbuch über die Talmudim und Midraschim*. Leipzig: Brockhaus, 1879. German; Hebrew.
Mandelkern, Shelomo. *Concordanzia La-Tanach* [Biblical concordance] (1884–96). Tel Aviv: Shoken, 1955. Hebrew.
Mar'i, Abed al-Rahman. *Walla Bseder: Portrait of the Israeli Arabic*. Ben Shemen: Keter, 2013. Hebrew.
Mazia, Aharon. *Sefer Ha-Munachim Lirefu'ah Ulemada'ey Ha-Teva* [Dictionary of medical and allied sciences], edited by Shaul Tshernichovsky. Jerusalem: Margalit, 1934. Hebrew; English; Latin.
Natan Me-Romy. *Ha-Aruch* [The edited/The arranged]. Venice: Daniel Bombirgi Press, 1539. Hebrew.
Ornan, Uzi. *Milon Ha-Milim Ha-Ovdot* [Dictionary of the forgotten words]. Tel Aviv: Shoken, 1996. Hebrew.

Qimhi, Rabbi David (Radaq). *Sefer Ha-Shorashim* [The book of roots]. Berlin: Rephael Hirsh Bizental Press, 1847. Hebrew.
Rav-Millim. Online Hebrew dictionary. Tel Aviv: Melingo. www.ravmilim.co.il. Hebrew.
Rosen, Haim. *Ha-Ivrit Shelanu* [Our Hebrew]. Tel Aviv: Am Oved, 1957. Hebrew.
Rosenthal, Ruvik. *Medabrim Bisefat Ha-Tanach* [Speaking the biblical language; English title: *Old Language, New Language*]. Ben Shemen: Keter, 2018. Hebrew.
Rosenthal, Ruvik. *Milon Ha-Sleng Ha-Makif* [Comprehensive slang dictionary]. Ben Shemen: Keter, 2005. Hebrew.
Rosenthal, Ruvik. *Milon Ha-Tzerufim* [Dictionary of idioms and phrases]. Ben Shemen: Ketter, 2009. Hebrew.
Rosenthal, Yotam (creator). *Milog*. Online Hebrew Dictionary. www.milog.co.il. Hebrew.
Saadia Gaon. *Sefer Ha-Egron* [The book of collection]. Scientific edition, edited by Nehemia Aloni. Jerusalem: Hebrew Language Academy, 1969. Hebrew; Arabic.
Schönhak, Joseph. *Sefer Ha-Mashbir* [The book of the mediator]. N. Shriftgiser Press, 1858. Hebrew.
Steinberg, Yehoshua. *Mishpat Ha-Urim* [Lights judgment]. Ram Widow and Brothers, 1896. Hebrew; Russian.

11 Indigenous Languages

Mark Turin

It is estimated that there were approximately 15 million speakers of over 2,000 Indigenous languages in the entire Western Hemisphere when Christopher Columbus arrived in 1492. Specifically, about 300 Indigenous languages are estimated to have been actively spoken in what is now the United States, of which around 175 remain. Needless to say, there are Indigenous languages everywhere on the globe. Mark Turin leads the *Relational Lexicography* project, which brings together online some 700 dictionaries of North American Indigenous languages and associated technologies. In addition, Turin directs both the World Oral Literature Project, an urgent global initiative to document and make accessible endangered oral literatures before they disappear without record, as well as the Digital Himalaya Project, which he cofounded in 2000, a platform to make multimedia resources from the Himalayan region widely available online. This conversation discusses the meaning of the word "indigenous" and reflects on the effort at preserving Indigenous languages worldwide. Dictionaries are one tool in that effort. Other themes covered include Indigenous lexicography, language revitalization, research ethics, and collaboration.

***

ILAN STAVANS: It is best to start with a definition. What makes a language "indigenous"? The scope seems to me infuriatingly ambiguous. For instance, how do these languages differ from all others? According to *Merriam-Webster*, "indigenous," as an adjective, refers to someone or something "having originated in and being produced, growing, living, or occurring naturally in a particular region or environment," that is, innate or inborn. The vast majority of languages fall into that category: they emerge from a place, regardless of how we define the word *place*.

MARK TURIN: I'm glad you're starting with this important question, Ilan. The *Oxford English Dictionary* notes that the earliest known use of the word *indigenous* dates to the mid 1600s, suggests that the earliest written evidence for the term *indigenous* was 1632, in the writing of

M. Stanhope. In other words, "indigenous" – increasingly written with a capital I (more about which below) – is an idea that's been with us for some time. All terms like this – and we might think of identity, ethnicity, and race in the same breath – exist in a particular sociocultural context and can be best understood as relational (as in, the relationships between things often being more salient than the things themselves). I would suggest that if all languages are Indigenous, then in effect no single language is Indigenous.

IS: Yes, the definition is preposterous.

MT: Mainstream dictionaries all point to a common, underlying principle: communities and the languages they speak are not simply "Indigenous" but rather Indigenous to a place. Indigeneity is thus locational, geographic, and spatial. While English could be said to be indigenous to England, as the language spread across the world through its speakers utilizing the vehicles of imperialism, colonialism, and globalized capital, English came to settle and take root in new places, in locations that it was not originally from or spoken in.

I now live and work in Canada, a country internationally celebrated for its federal commitment to bilingualism. By the monolingual standards of the Anglosphere, Canada is often uplifted for committing resources and legislation to supporting two languages – English and French. Yet the curious, even perverse, reality is that neither of these two federally assisted and recognized languages are actually from Canada – both came from Europe with migrants who first traded and then settled here – and both are arguably not in need of much assistance. What role and visibility is given to the original, autochthonous languages from the lands that have come to be known as Canada?

A key element in definitions of Indigeneity, whether of language, people or plants and animals, is that being Indigenous implies being somewhere first. The Canadian Constitution recognizes three groups of Aboriginal (another vexed word) peoples: First Nations (formerly known by the ever-shocking misnomer "Indian"), Inuit, and Métis. These three distinct peoples have unique histories, languages, cultural practices, and spiritual beliefs. Once again, if you and your community are the original and only inhabitants of a land, and no one else comes to settle there, then you don't need to assert your Indigeneity: you're simply living and being where you're from.

IS: A history of dislocation.

MT: Yes, it is only through migration, colonization, and its associated horrors that it became necessary for communities to articulate their sense of primacy and rights to land, resources, cultural practices, and the languages they spoke.

In this reading, Indigenous can be helpfully contrasted with "colonial," and Indigeneity thus speaks to the existence of a community, culture, and language system which had its own integrity prior to foreign contact with a dominant world power.

IS: Time is therefore a crucial coordinate.

MT: Colonial governments have been outright hostile to Indigenous cultures and languages by outlawing their practice and use, legislating against them, engaging in processes of forced assimilation and cultural destruction, and then – at the eleventh hour and only the "progressive" governments like Canada – informing Indigenous peoples that their languages have become critically endangered and fragile, and not fit for the modern world or in urgent need of support and programming. This is a kind of linguistic gaslighting: bringing something to pass and then blaming the victim. As a social and political response, language revitalization and reclamation seek to make space for Indigenous languages not [only to] survive but to thrive once again.

IS: This approach is a feature of the Enlightenment. The list of extinct languages is enormous. For example, Uto-Aztecan languages that have disappeared (I'm from Mexico) include Baciroa, Colotlan, Conicari, Tahue, Tecual, Tepanec, Teui, Toboso, Totorame. And Xixime. And in the Iberian Peninsula, some extinct languages are Auitanian, Gothic, Vandalic, Mozarabic, Judeo-Aragonese, Judeo-Catalan, Judeo-Poryguese, and Phoenician.

MT: Absolutely right. It's quite reasonable to point out that European settlement of the "New World" served to create the organizing framework for what it means to be Indigenous today.

At the highest level of abstraction, an Indigenous language is a language that originated in and from a specified place and which was not brought to that place from somewhere else, already fully formed.

IS: I would like you to reflect on the capitalization of the "I" in Indigenous.

MT: Increasingly, "Indigenous" is capitalized in relation to peoples and languages, with lowercase "indigenous" reserved for contexts in which the term doesn't apply to specific Indigenous people, such as flora and fauna.

IS: Is it truly possible to say how many Indigenous languages had already disappeared by 1492, as I have tried in the headnote to this conversation?

MT: Another wonderful question. Let's start with a simple acknowledgement that linguists, statisticians, and governments don't even agree on the number of languages that are spoken across our fragile planet. In some cases, estimates vary by hundreds. In this context, projecting backwards by 500 years is fraught with considerable complexity. Daniel Nettle, writing in the *Proceedings of the National Academy of Sciences*, suggests that the Americas were home to 157 language "stocks" totaling 1,219 languages, although Nettle does note this may be inflated due to some languages being counted twice.[1]

The older a continent is, the fewer linguistic stocks it contains yet the greater number of languages per stock exist. It is unlikely there was much language loss prior to European contact, given how young the continent was as compared to Africa, for example.

Distinguishing a language from a dialect is intricate and often political work, and even more so when there is little recorded and written history to work with. By way of example, a 1996 report from the Office of the Commissioner of Official Languages in Canada entitled *Our Two Official Languages Over Time* sites sources that suggest an estimated 450 languages and dialects were spoken in Canada at the time of contact with European settlers.[2] The inclusion of dialects in this total has likely resulted in the number being higher than those of other estimates.

---

[1] Daniel Nettle, "Linguistic diversity of the Americas can be reconciled with a recent colonization," *Proceedings of the National Academy of Sciences* 96, no. 6 (1999): 3325–29.
[2] Office of the Commissioner of Official Languages, *Our Two Official Languages Over Time* (Ottawa: Government of Canada, 1996).

IS: Are there any attempts at shaping a catalogue of words, oral or written, in Indigenous languages prior to the eighteenth century, which is when most standardised languages in Europe, Asia, and the Arab world embraced dictionaries as a common practice, although, obviously, scores of them have important lexicographic antecedents?

MT: The written documentation of linguistic data relating to the Indigenous languages spoken in North America is generally associated with colonialism and the spread of religious missions charged with evangelical activity and governmental activity.

IS: What could be called "missionary linguists."

MT: Yes. For missionaries, it was essential to know Indigenous languages in order to facilitate the religious and ideological conversion of Indigenous people to Christian scripture. While some missionaries (and evangelical linguists) were genuinely interested in and committed to the deeper understanding of Indigenous languages, others simply saw such languages as convenient vehicles that could be harnessed for the transmission of Christian scripture.

Back to your initial question. Some of the works on Mexican Indigenous languages date back to the sixteenth century, such as the *Vocabulario de verbos nahuas* (1547) by Fray Andrés de Olmo; the *Vocabulario en lengua misteca* (1593) by Francisco de Alvarado; or *Arte de la lengua tarasca* (1714) by Diego Basalenque, all within the framework of religious missions. In Colombia, the recorded documentation of languages may have commenced with the work *Diccionario y gramática chibcha*, by an anonymous author. Neither date nor place of publication is recorded for it.

As colonization deepened and infrastructure was developed, the documentation of Indigenous languages in America, Africa, and Asia became prolific, gaining support from established publishers, like Brill in the Netherlands.

IS: I assume there is little that precedes these *Vocabularios*.

MT: While there are relatively few publications prior to the eighteenth century which explicitly refer to themselves as a dictionary or might by today's standards be considered to be even a modest word list, there are some notable exceptions.

The first vocabularies of Algonquian and Iroquoian languages come from the sixteenth century, with the first grammatical descriptions given in the early seventeenth century. Specific examples include: Jacques Cartier's account of Laurentian (Northern Iroquoian language formerly spoken along the St. Lawrence River) between 1534 and 1536; Thomas Harriot's written descriptions of Carolina Algonquian between 1585 and 1586; Paul Le Jeune's grammatical sketch of Montagnais (Cree dialect) in 1634; John Eliot's grammar of Massachusett in 1666; and Gabriel Sagard-Théodat's Huron grammatical description and phrase book *Dictionaire de la langue huronne* in 1632.

In the wonderful *Revitalization Lexicography: The Making of the New Tunica Dictionary* (2020), Patricia Anderson writes about the use of dictionaries in the early days of settler-colonialism to ensure military conquests, "culturally, politically, and spiritually."[3] Anderson includes several early dictionaries as examples: Alonso de Molina's Spanish–Nahuatl dictionary called *Vocabulario en lengua*

---

[3] Patricia Anderson, *Revitalization Lexicography: The Making of a New Tunica Dictionary* (Tucson: University of Arizona Press, 2020), 33.

castellana y mexicana (1571) and Père Delauney's *Dictionnaire français-kiswahili* (1885).

IS: When thinking of a dictionary, it is essential to reflect not only on what went in but what was left out as well. With missionary lexicography, the question acquires a particularly religious dimension.

MT: That's absolutely right. Until more recently, dictionary compilation and design have been dominated by the theories, practices, and tools that emerged from the needs of the world's largest, majority, written languages in ways that do not always adequately support the needs of dictionaries for under-resourced and Indigenous languages or the communities that speak them.

Likewise, and as we've discussed above, current practices for making dictionaries of under-resourced or Indigenous languages have been shaped, in part, by colonial, imperial, and evangelical motivations and perspectives. Many of the earliest dictionaries of Indigenous languages were compiled by missionaries in order to translate the Bible and make religious teachings available more broadly. The result of this complex legacy is that religious ideology has influenced how certain words were defined.

For example, a Cree dictionary, developed by missionaries from the Church of England in Canada, defined the word *wètikoo* as "devil," emphasizing the relation to Christian religion. More recent dictionaries developed with community interests in mind instead define the same word through a traditional story: *Windigo* "cannibal, giant man-eating monster." To this day, the faith-based organization SIL Global (formerly known as the Summer Institute of Linguistics International) is involved in dictionary projects of Indigenous languages in over 100 countries, working both in partnership with speech communities and for an external, religious calling at the same time.

Needless to say, every dictionary reflects the idiosyncrasies of the language that it documents, the goals of its compilers, and the community that it serves. In the case of missionary lexicography, the goals of the compilers are at least apparent and can be more easily interrogated.

IS: Let me ask you a question I've asked another contributor in this volume, Quechua poet and lexicographer Odi Gonzales. At what historical point do the "Indigenous" people take the reins of their own lexicography, and, along the way of their own dictionaries?

MT: I love this question! The simple answer is now, and also that this has already been happening for some time. Indigenous communities have long and uninterrupted traditions of harnessing emerging technologies to strengthen cultures and languages. Dictionaries are vital resources for language learning, particularly for Indigenous languages. For under-resourced, Indigenous communities, dictionaries also contain crucial historical, cultural, territorial, and dialectal information. When languages become endangered, dictionaries can become primary tools for their reclamation, and we're witnessing a rich and impressive explosion of Indigenous lexicography at this very moment.

IS: What is the process through which a language gets revitalized? I have worked on Nahuatl, but I would like to get the fuller picture.

MT: I have often described the three stages of language revitalization as "collect," "protect," and "connect." Improved access to language materials is essential for communities looking to revitalize and reclaim their ancestral languages. Independent scholar Linda Yamane describes her journey of trying to access her language through archival documentation, including dictionaries. Of the word lists she was able to find, Yamane writes, "They are obscure publications not readily available to the average person in the average library, but these are what made the beginning of my Rumsien language learning possible."[4]

IS: You've begun responding to a topic I was hoping to incorporate into our conversation. In standardized languages, online dictionaries have become essential. Most people today access dictionary definitions not on a physical book but on a screen. What is the status of online dictionaries of Indigenous languages?

MT: For five years, my research team and I have been working to develop an open-access Knowledgebase of 700 dictionaries of North American Indigenous languages together with a peer-reviewed analysis of the tools and technologies commonly used to build and compile dictionaries. The *Dictionaries Knowledgebase* is an extensive catalogue of what we believe to be every dictionary of an Indigenous language spoken in what is now Canada and the United States published between 1950 and the present day.[5] In January 2020, we began the dictionary scoping process using a combination of Glottolog, Wikipedia, advanced web searches, and library catalogues, locating over 700 dictionaries of more than 300 North American Indigenous languages including: print publications, e-books, archival scans, websites, and apps for mobile devices.

IS: And since we're in this terrain already, missionary lexicography was the exclusive domain of men. Are things different now?

MT: I truly hope that things are different now, and they certainly look to be, but we must be wary of resting on our laurels and assuming that the battle of inclusion is won. Some of the most important and comprehensive dictionaries of Indigenous languages have been spearheaded by women, and in some cases, Indigenous women.

Notable publications include the *Dictionary of Tlingit* (2009) by Keri Edwards, which provides information on the source of Tlingit language data in the Acknowledgments section, and includes consultant speakers, previously published Tlingit materials, and a manuscript from another author.[6] This dictionary cites, by name, four speakers as primary language consultants and three more who contributed example sentences and audio recordings. Each previously published resource along with the compilers are cited. Edwards also makes explicit that all entries in the dictionary identified as being from the interior Tlingit dialects derive from the 2001 *Interior Tlingit Noun Dictionary*.[7]

In addition, the *Online Tlingit Verb Dictionary* compiled by Keri Eggleston and *Iñupiatun Uqaluit Taniktun Sivuniŋit* (North Slope Iñupiaq to English dictionary) by Yuarcuun Technologies, an online version of Edna Ahgeak MacLean's *Iñupiatun Uqaluit Taniktun Sivuniŋit* (Iñupiaq to English dictionary),

---

[4] Linda Yamane, "New life for a lost language," in *The Green Book of Language Revitalization in Practice*, ed. Leanne Hinton and Ken Hale (Leiden: Brill, 2013), 430.
[5] https://knowledgebase.arts.ubc.ca
[6] Keri Edwards, *Dictionary of Tlingit* (Juneau: Sealaska Heritage Institute, 2009).
[7] Jeff Leer, Doug Hitch, and John Ritter, *Interior Tlingit Noun Dictionary* (Whitehorse: Yukon Native Language Center, 2001).

are compelling examples of brilliant dictionaries directed by female language workers.[8] The *Online Tlingit Verb Dictionary* uses a simple, predominantly textual, interface that can be navigated through clickable links. The Tlingit and English indexes are both scrollable word lists, with expandable verb paradigms included in the Tlingit section.

IS: You have also done research on the Indigenous languages of Northern South Asia.

MT: I grew up in the heart of London, with a Dutch mother and an Italian father, surrounded by people of other nationalities, languages, and cultures. Perhaps more importantly, I also grew up bilingual, speaking Dutch with my mother at home and English outside of the house, and at school. As a child, I remember being surprised that people could only speak one language – a state that linguists refer to as "monolingualism" – a single language for everything that they thought, did, hoped for, dreamed, and said. This curiosity about language and sense of wonder at linguistic plurality has stayed with me since childhood and guides me to this day.

For thirty years, I have worked in the Himalayas, in particular in Nepal, northern India, and a little in Bhutan. I first visited Nepal in 1991 to work as a volunteer English school teacher in the lower reaches of Mustang district and was immediately inspired by the complexity, beauty, and sophistication of the languages that I heard spoken around me.

Many of the most lasting professional and personally fulfilling relationships of my life have been with members of the Thangmi-speaking community who live in the central-eastern part of Nepal and number around 30,000. Thangmi is an under-documented and endangered language that is classified as part of the Tibeto-Burman language family. Major world languages – like English, Russian, Nepali, and so many others – are comprehensively documented: there are texts, dictionaries, school books, literature, poetry, and scientific publications in and about these languages. In most cases, these written documents stretch back hundreds or even thousands of years.

IS: Were you perceived as an impostor?

MT: To the contrary: I was welcomed as a guest. The Thangmi people were surprised that someone had come all the way from Europe to focus on their language. I often wonder how it was that I was offered such a generous reception when I arrived in 1996, and have, over time, come to understand this better. I believe that the reason that I was invited into the community with such warmth was that the Thangmi felt under-recognized and almost invisible to the state, and had therefore not received the associated benefits of being on the official and recognized "ethnic" map of the nation. Local cultural leaders and language activists hoped that my work on their language would help to set the record straight and make them visible, so that they could then access the benefits that came with being a minority community in the fast-modernizing nation of Nepal. The openhearted generosity with which I was met was matched only by the high expectations that people had for my work: they wanted their language written down and they wanted a dictionary, and they needed it to be comprehensive and

---

[8] http://ankn.uaf.edu/~tlingitverbs/; https://inupiaqonline.com.

representative. Elders in the community were just as exacting as my own formidable PhD supervisor and had a greater stake in my work being accurate and comprehensive.

IS: How long did it take you to learn Thangmi?

MT: Three years to a level sophisticated enough to tell a joke, and another year to be able to tell a joke that was actually funny.

Bilingual Thangmi-Nepali speakers were my first point of contact, and my early months in Dolakha (the home district of most Thangmi-speaking people, in central-eastern Nepal) were spent using (and improving) my existing Nepali language skills to ask increasingly complex questions on the lines of "In your language, how would you say 'that man over there is my mother's elder brother'?" – to which I might receive the weary and slightly irritated reply in Thangmi, "I told you already, he's not my mother's elder brother but my mother's elder sister's husband," often suffixed with a mutter under their breath "this English chap learns really slowly." But then, my progress really *was* slow. Learning a language means you become a child again.

IS: Describe an aspect of Thangmi for me.

MT: The Thangmi equivalents of the English verb "to be" have a range of different roots, contingent on the perceived state of permanence of being and whether the speaker has seen the event with their own eyes and thus verified the occurrence. In addition, motion verbs vary by angle of inclination, so that "to come up a hill" is completely different and unrelated to the verb stem for "to come down the mountain." It is inconceivable that a native speaker would confuse the two, showing just how deeply the local geography and mountainous topography are etched into the language. The Thangmi lexicon – or inventory of words – is profoundly different from that of English or Nepali.

For instance, while there are no Thangmi terms for "chair," "table," "left," or "right," there are specific verbs to mean "to be exhausted by sitting in the sun all day" and "to be infested with lice," as well as precise nouns to describe the edible parts of certain leaves or particularly chewy meat that gets stuck in one's teeth. In other words, the Thangmi language encodes those things that are culturally salient and meaningful to its speakers.

IS: Among your books is *A Grammar of Thangmi with an Ethnolinguistic Introduction to the Speakers and Their Culture.*[9] You also coauthored, with Bir Bahadur Thami, a *Nepali-Thami-English Dictionary* (2004).[10]

MT: That's right. For ten years, I worked with the community to document their language as best I could. Along the way, I produced a short, pocket-sized Nepali-Thangmi-English dictionary – really more of a word list – that was published locally for school teachers and other officials to try and learn a little of the language in the villages that they had been posted to. And I also produced a

---

[9] Mark Turin, *A Grammar of Thangmi with an Ethnolinguistic Introduction to the Speakers and Their Culture*, 2 vols., Vol. 5/6 of Brill's Tibetan Studies Library: Languages of the Greater Himalayan Region (Leiden: Brill, 2012).

[10] Mark Turin, with Bir Bahadur Thami, *Nepali-Thami-English Dictionary* (Kathmandu: Martin Chautari, 2004).

two-volume, 1,000-page grammar and a trilingual dictionary of Thangmi, along with many local stories and rituals in translation.

There are now many Thangmi-Nepali-English dictionaries, school books, and poems circulating in print, and countless recordings of songs and dances on YouTube. Thangmi is now online, in print and on air – occupying new digital spaces – as young Thangmi commit to relearning the language of their ancestors, and ever more government programs in Nepal support education in the mother tongue. For the last 5,000 years, the rise and fall of languages was intimately tied to the plow, sword, and book. In our digital age, the keyboard, screen, and web play a decisive role in shaping our future linguistic diversity.

IS: For the *Nepali-Thami-English Dictionary*, what was the criteria for including words?

MT: It was, as you can imagine, difficult to decide and involved lots of conversation and careful negotiation. Selecting vocabulary that was indisputably Thangmi (according to phonology and morphology) was relatively easy: body parts, kinship terminology, flora and fauna, and hundreds of verbs.

Beyond that, it became more complicated. Thangmi has absorbed many Nepali words and Indigenized them, sometimes to such a degree that they look and feel Thangmi. As a case in point, the Thangmi word for "shaman" or "ritual specialist" is *guru*, which is of Indo-European origin. When I noted that this word might have come to Thangmi via Nepali or another neighboring Indic language, my friends and language teachers in the community were quite displeased.

To the contrary, they said, the term was of Thangmi origin and had been borrowed from their language into Nepali and other languages. In short, deciding which words to include in a dictionary, as well as which writing system and alphabetical ordering to use, are politically sensitive matters that require much thoughtful discussion, much consultation with speakers, and careful navigation.

IS: How was the dictionary received? It has been two decades since its appearance. Is the dictionary "dead," meaning there are no second, third, and subsequent editions?

MT: The dictionary is anything but dead; in fact, it's in active development and growing, but more about that in a moment. Dr. Sheryl Lightfoot, a brilliant professor at the University of British Columbia and Anishinaabe intellectual, says that her grandmother noted that a good compromise is when all parties come away a little displeased. Bearing that in mind, I think our original dictionary was a good compromise. Following the publication of our short dictionary, there was an explosion of Indigenous lexicography in the community.

Until that point, Thangmi intellectuals and language workers were intimidated by the idea of publishing a dictionary and didn't want to be the first to test the waters. Seeing a rather modest word list of their language with an outsider's name on it rather catalyzed local cultural production, and there are now four other much more comprehensive and impressive dictionaries of the language in circulation, each compiled and produced by members of the community. This is exactly what I hoped would happen and has given me enormous satisfaction.

Related to this is the question of authorship, and I have grappled with the question of how to credit community members in my own work. In 2004, I was asked by research partners in Nepal to assume authorship, and thereby, responsibility, for the short, trilingual dictionary of Thangmi that we've discussed above.

As the first ever lexical compilation of this under-documented Tibeto-Burman language, the publication was expected to be politically inflammatory and polarizing.

Thangmi community researchers, with whom I had been collaboratively working since 1996, were at once eager to see the lexical collection in print and yet concerned about the potential of negative fallout and sociopolitical repercussions. Community members anticipated – quite rightly, it turned out – that in response to the publication, there would be much public discussion (at times quite heated) about which (head)words had been included, which orthography had been used, and which of the various regional variations and dialects had received most attention.

The emerging language authority proposed a compromise: I, the outside linguist, would assume primary authorship, while Bir Bahadur Thami – a highly respected Indigenous intellectual in his own right and my longtime research partner and language teacher – would be listed on the cover under the intentionally vague byline "with." This subdominant billing would both acknowledge Bir Bahadur's central involvement and investment in the project but also insulate him somewhat from the expected fallout. In cases like these, authorship and visibility are less about authority and more about responsibility. The protection that members of the Thangmi community desired was not intended to obscure their contributions and expertise but rather to establish chains of accountability and liability in the event of negative consequences.

IS: I want to know how it changed you as a scholar. Other lexicographers who are outsiders to the ecosystem where they harvest the material describe the effort as a theft. I myself produced a dictionary of Spanglish. The word "theft" isn't quite accurate; after all, every intellectual endeavor, from my viewpoint, is a usurpation. To me being a dictionary-maker is a bit like the biblical Noah, who is tasked to choose a pair of animals of every species to survive.

MT: I feel that there are two questions here, the first more internal and emotional, about inner transformation, and the other about the process of linguistic documentation with a particular focus on dictionaries. On the first topic, I can honestly say that my time working in collaborative partnership with members of the Thangmi community has been the greatest journey of my life, at both intellectual and emotional levels. I started the work thinking that I might help to document their beautiful language and came out, a decade later, as a language activist deeply committed to Indigenous sovereignty and language reclamation.

I was educated, schooled, and transformed by Thangmi intellectuals – elders and youth – who had (and have) a powerful vision for their language and invited me to participate in realizing their dreams. As to the second part of your question, I agree that much linguistic fieldwork has been (and even continues to be) acquisitive, with some linguists behaving like a mining company, looking for and then extracting verbs rather than diamonds. This kind of work – in which the outside linguist is in service to the language rather than the community – has been the norm for most of the history of the discipline and might be called colonial linguistics. The tide is starting to turn, thanks to the extraordinary efforts of Indigenous scholars both within and outside of the academy, and we're beginning to see more work that is *by* and *with* Indigenous communities rather than *on* or *for* (in a paternalistic way). There are also large collections of language data – recordings, publications and fieldnotes – in ethnographic museums, archives, and libraries around the world that communities have had trouble accessing until more recently.

Its perverse that these precious voices and recordings of ancestors are in London, Berlin, New York, or Ottawa and not in community archives, or local cultural centers and museums. Ethically engaged curators and archivists have been working hard to set this right and ensure that linguistic knowledge and cultural teachings are repatriated and returned to communities of origin. Increasingly, I am happy to say, there is less need for repatriation as collections are not being taken away from communities but rather archived and deposited locally. After all, you only need to repatriate something if it has been expatriated to begin with.

IS: In what way is a dictionary a tool, one among many, to preserve an endangered language?

MT: People enjoy dictionaries, and they love dictionaries of their own language. Both the physicality of a printed dictionary and its online form are exciting and important tools for communities looking to document, preserve, protect, and revitalize their languages. That old line attributed to Max Weinreich that a language is a dialect with an army, a navy, and a flag could be reimagined now to say that a language is a dialect with its own Unicode font, app, and a dictionary.

The affordances of newer digital media allow dictionaries to be much more than basic word lists, becoming interactive audio-visual resources with recordings of speakers, images, videos, and learning tools built around them. In fact, in some language-learning programs, the lesson plans and resources are all built around the central spine of a dictionary.

Suggested Readings

Alexander-Bakkerus, Astrid, Rebeca Fernández Rodríguez, Liesbeth Zack, and Otto Zwartjes, eds. "Missionary Linguistic Studies from Mesoamerica to Patagonia." In *Missionary Linguistic Studies from Mesoamerica to Patagonia*. Leiden: Brill, 2020.

Chelliah, Shobhana L., and Willem de Reuse. "Lexicography in Fieldwork." In *Handbook of Descriptive Linguistic Fieldwork*, 227–49. Dordrecht: Springer, 2010.

Dietrich, Wolf. "The Lexicography of Indigenous Languages in South America." In *International Handbook of Modern Lexis and Lexicography*, edited by Patrick Hanks and Gilles- Maurice de Schryver, 1–17. Berlin: Springer, 2014. https://doi.org/10.1007/978-3-642-45369-4_91-1

Fernández Rodríguez, Rebeca, and María Alejandra Regúnaga. "Patagonian Lexicography (Sixteenth–Eighteenth Centuries)." In *Missionary Linguistic Studies from Mesoamerica to Patagonia*, edited by Astrid Alexander-Bakkerus, Rebeca Fernández Rodríguez, Liesbeth Zack, and Otto Zwartjes, 236–59. Leiden: Brill, 2020. https://doi.org/10.1163/9789004427006_009

Frawley, William, Kenneth C. Hill, and Pamela Munro, eds. *Making Dictionaries: Preserving Indigenous Languages of the Americas*. Berkeley: University of California Press, 2002.

Garrett, Andrew. "Online Dictionaries for Language Revitalization." In *The Routledge Handbook of Language Revitalization*, edited by Leanne Hinton, Leena Huss, and Gerald Roche, 197–206. New York: Routledge, 2018.

Hernández, Esther. *Lexicografía hispano-amerindia 1550–1800: Catálogo descriptivo de los vocabularios del español y las lenguas indígenas americanas. Lingüística misionera 9*. Madrid: Iberoamericana, 2018. https://doi.org/10.31819/9783954877591

Hill, Deborah. "One Community's Post-Conflict Response to a Dictionary Project." *Language Documentation and Conservation* 6 (2012): 273–81.

Hinton, Leanne, and William F. Weigel. "A Dictionary for Whom? Tensions between Academic and Non-Academic Functions of Bilingual Dictionaries." In *Making Dictionaries: Preserving Indigenous Languages of the Americas*, edited by William Frawley, Kenneth C. Hill, and Pamela Munro, 155–70. Berkeley: University of California Press, 2002.

Mosel, Ulrike. "Lexicography in Endangered Language Communities." In *The Cambridge Handbook of Endangered Languages*, edited by Peter K. Austin and Julia Sallabank, 337–53. Cambridge Handbooks in Language and Linguistics. Cambridge: Cambridge University Press, 2011.

Rice, Keren, and Leslie Saxon. "Issues of Standardization and Community in Aboriginal Language Lexicography." In *Making Dictionaries: Preserving Indigenous Languages of the Americas*, edited by William Frawley, Kenneth C. Hill, and Pamela Munro, 125–54. Berkeley: University of California Press, 2002.

Rice, Sally "Lexicography." In *The Languages and Linguistics of Indigenous North America: A Comprehensive Guide*, edited by Carmen Dagostino, Marianne Mithun, and Keren Rice, 479–96. The World of Linguistics (WOL), 13.1. Berlin: De Gruyter Mouton, 2023.

Schreyer, Christine, and Mark Turin, eds. "Indigenous Lexicography (Special Issue)." *Dictionaries: Journal of the Dictionary Society of North America* 44, no. 2 (2023): 1–5. https://doi.org/10.1353/dic.2023.a915062

Sear, Victoria and Mark Turin. "Locating Criticality in the Lexicography of Historically Marginalized Languages." *History of Humanities* 6, no. 1 (2021): 237–59. https://doi.org/10.1086/713266

Trotter, Bailey, Christine Schreyer, and Mark Turin. "An Open-Access Toolkit for Collaborative, Community-Informed Dictionaries." *Dictionaries: Journal of the Dictionary Society of North America* 44, no. 2 (2023): 161–85.

Turin, Mark. "Indigenous Language Resurgence and the Living Earth Community." In *Living Earth Community: Multiple Ways of Being and Knowing*, edited by Sam Mickey, Mary Evelyn Tucker, and John Grim, 171–84. Cambridge: Open Book Publishers, 2020.

"Recognizing Authority and Respecting Expertise in Language Work." In *Rethinking Pseudonyms in Ethnography*, edited by Carole McGranahan and Erica Weiss, *American Ethnologist* website, December 13, 2021. https://americanethnologist.org/panel/pages/features/collections/rethinking-pseudonyms-in-ethnography/recognizing-authority-and-respecting-expertise-in-language-work/

Warner, Natasha, Lynnika Butler, and Quirina Luna-Costillas. "Making a Dictionary for Community Use in Language Revitalization: The Case of Mutsun." *International Journal of Lexicography* 19, no. 3 (2006): 257–85. https://doi.org/10.1093/ijl/ecl014

Wörterbücher / Dictionaries / Dictionnaires: Ein internationales Handbuch zur Lexikographie / An international encyclopedia of Lexicography / Encyclopédie internationale de lexicographie. Berlin: De Gruyter Mouton, 2008. https://doi.org/10.1515/9783110124217.3

Zwartjes, Otto, Ramón Arzápalo Marín, and Thomas C. Smith-Stark, eds. *Missionary Linguistics IV / Lingüística Misionera IV: Lexicography*. Studies in the History of the Language Sciences 114. Amsterdam: John Benjamins, 2009.

12   Irish

Seán Ua Súilleabháin

The Celts are a people with a stubborn approach to history. In *Fairy and Folktales of the Irish Peasantry* (1888), W. B. Yeats states that "the Celt, and his cromlechs, and his pillar-stones, these will not change much – indeed, it is doubtful if anybody at all changes at any time. In spite of hosts of deniers, and asserters, and wise-men, and professors, the majority still are averse to sitting down to dine thirteen at table, or being helped to salt, or walking under a ladder, of seeing a single magpie flirting his chequered tale."[1] Gaeilge, also known as Irish, which has its own government organization in charge of promoting it, Foras na Gaeilge, and a rich history of dictionaries, is used today in areas of Ireland collectively known as the Gaeltacht, as well as in the Irish diaspora. This conversation is an examination of the creation and impact of the *Dictionary of the Irish Language: Based Mainly on Old and Middle Irish Materials*, published by the Royal Irish Academy,[2] and the evolution of Irish dictionaries from the seventeenth century to the present, including historical, bilingual, and regional dictionaries.

***

ILAN STAVANS:	The earliest versions of dictionaries are often glossaries. And, in the case of Europe, bilingual dictionaries, with Latin as one of the grounding languages, emerge in order to explain ecclesiastical terms. That, I believe, is the case of Irish.
SEÁN UA SÚILLEABHÁIN:	We have Old Irish glosses, but these were generally just translations or explanations of Latin words or passages written by a native speaker of Old Irish usually in the eighth or ninth century (the Würzburg, Milan, and Turin glosses) but perhaps datable to the seventh century in the case of Trinity College Manuscript MS

---

[1] W. B. Yeats, *Fairy and Folktales of the Irish Peasantry* (London: Walter Scott, 1888), x.
[2] *Dictionary of the Irish Language: Based Mainly on Old and Middle Irish Materials* (Dublin: Royal Irish Academy, 1913–76; Compact ed., 1983; electronic ed., with corrections, 2014– (ongoing)), https://dil.ie.

55 ("Codex Usserianus Primus").[3] However, this work could not properly be classified as Irish lexicography. It was what enabled German speaking linguists to reconstruct Old Irish grammar but was no more than an Irish student's convenience while dealing with Latin texts.

The Irish were unusual in taking an interest in their vernacular at a very early period. They began to compile glossaries, which were an attempt to trace the origins of words, and thus to reveal the essence of the words, origin and meaning combined. The word *sanas*, "a whisper" or "secret knowledge," and *sanasán*, "a collection of recondite knowledge on words," were used. The origin of the word was expected to clarify its meaning and explain it. When lists of words, roughly in alphabetical order, appeared, the urge was to add to the list, so many glossaries have layers. The earliest Old Irish glossary is the oldest stratum of what is called O'Mulconry's Glossary (recently re-edited by Pádraic Moran of the National University of Ireland Galway).[4] This material may be dated to about 650 CE.

It attempts to derive Irish words from Hebrew, Latin, and Greek. The Old Irish *trena* (plural of *trían*, "a third") can mean "rites," "funeral" games. An attempt is made to derive it from Greek *threnos* θρῆνος, "wailing, lamenting," giving Latin *lamentatio* as an explanation and an erroneous Hebrew form *trena*. The most famous of these glossaries was ascribed to Cormac mac Cuileanáin (836–908), king of the province of Munster and possibly a bishop. A wonderful example from Cormac's glossary (*Sanas Cormaic*) is "Bás .i. bēo as .i. as tēit in bēo"; in English: "*Bás* (death), i.e. life out of it, life goes out of it."[5] While modern linguists may not be convinced by the etymology, this gloss provides a succinct and clear explanation of the word *bás* (death). Later glossaries were interested in explaining archaic and obscure words.

IS: How do you explain the early Irish interest in the vernacular?

SUAS: It is difficult to say at this remove. I suspect that a strong oral culture existed which survived until the twentieth century and that the Irish people were accustomed to discussing cultural matters, reciting poetry, etc. in their own language.

IS: In what way are Irish dictionaries of the so-called Middle Ages instruments of nationalism?

SUAS: Ireland and Gaelic Scotland were unified by a common language and culture down to the seventeenth century. However, political unity did not exist. Although high kings are mentioned in literature and pseudohistory, the only one who came close to dominating the country was probably Brian Boru in the tenth and eleventh centuries. The only dictionaries in the Middle Ages were glossaries. They were scholarly works and tools and I don't believe that

---

[3] Würtzburg, Milan, and Turin glosses published in Whitley Stokes and John Strachan, *Thesaurus Palaeohibernicus*, Vols. 1 and 2 (Cambridge: Cambridge University Press, 1901–3). For "Codex Usserainus Primus," see https://digitalcollections.tcd.ie/concern/works/kk91fn47w.

[4] Pádraic Moran, ed., *De Origine Scotticae Linguae* (Turnhout: Brepols, 2019).

[5] Kuno Meyer, ed., *Sanas Cormaic: An Old-Irish Glossary Compiled by Cormac úa Cuillennáin, King-Bishop of Cashel in the Tenth Century*, Anectoda from Irish Manuscripts, Vol. 4 (Halle: Max Neimeyer, 1912), 16.

IS: nationalism was an issue at that time. While any such achievement is culturally uniting, I don't believe we can speak about Irish nationalism before the sixteenth century.

IS: How have dictionaries reflected, maybe even pushed toward a broader maturity, the various stages of Irish: Old Irish, Middle Irish, and Early Modern Irish?

SUAS: As time went on scholars were anxious to give their works an archaic appearance and made use to some extent of archaic words found in glossaries. But since no complete dictionary of Irish existed until 1662, I don't believe that glossaries could have contributed much at any of these periods.

IS: By the eighteenth century, it is English, not Latin, that is the language that will serve as the bilingual counterpart in Irish dictionaries.

SUAS: In the seventeenth century the Irish Franciscans, whose scholarly and political headquarters was in Leuven in the Spanish Netherlands, were anxious to publish a complete Irish dictionary and an Irish grammar, along with a calendar of Irish saints, giving the lives of the Irish saints arranged by their feast days and also the history of Ireland arranged as annals. They wished to make clear that Ireland was a European nation with all the cultural trappings which could be expected. The first printed "dictionary" was O'Clery's (Ó Cléirigh's) glossary, published in Leuven in 1643: a list of archaic words with explanations in more recognizable Irish to assist younger scholars grappling with ancient manuscripts.[6]

A letter written by Fr. Thomas Sheeran, director of publications in the Irish Franciscan college in Leuven, speaks of an extensive dictionary compiled by Baothghalach Mac Aodhagáin (who died in 1654) which was almost finished but needed additional technical vocabulary.[7] This dictionary is now lost. It was almost certainly a Latin-Irish dictionary, since exhaustive dictionaries of the vernacular languages scarcely existed at the time. Most monolingual dictionaries confined themselves to obscure words. Copious dictionaries of Latin words had been produced with translations to a vernacular.

In 1662, Risdeard Pluincéad completed an extensive manuscript Latin-Irish dictionary, "Vocabularium Latinum et Hibernum: Foclóir Lainne agus Gaoidheilge," which is kept in Marsh's Library, Dublin (MS Z4.2.5). It contains some 34,500 headwords. It is largely based on the 1631 edition of Thomas Thomas's Latin-English *Dictionarium* but also drew on another Latin-English dictionary in the Rider-Holyoke series which has not been identified.[8] Pluincéad has been referred to as the "father of Irish lexicography" because his work was borrowed by the Welsh linguist, Edward Lhuyd, and used in the "Irish-English Dictionary" section of his *Archaeologia Britannica*,[9] the first Irish-English dictionary, and also in the "Comparative Vocabulary" section;

---

[6] Mícheál Ó Cléirigh, *Focloir no Sanasan Nua* (Leuven: Coláiste na mBráthar nÉireannach, 1643).
[7] Benignus Millett, *The Irish Franciscans 1651–1665* (Rome: Gregorian University Press, 1964), 490.
[8] [Thomas Thomas] Thomae Thomassii, *Dictionarivm summa fide ac diligentia accuratissime emendatum* ... (London: Ex officina Iohannis Legati, 1631).
[9] Edward Lhuyd, *Archaeologia Britannica, Giving some Account Additional to What Has Been Hitherto Publish'd, of the Languages, Histories and Customs of the Original Inhabitants of*

many of Pluincéad's words were copied from Lhuyd to nineteenth- and twentieth-century dictionaries. Pluincéad's dictionary remains unpublished. Some were miscopied since Lhuyd's knowledge of Irish, and that of his assistants, was limited, giving rise to ghost words.

A much neglected, extensive dictionary was compiled in the eighteenth century, "Dictionarium Latino-Anglo-Hibernicum" and is also in Marsh's Library (MS Z3.1.13). It was begun by Franciscan Francis Walsh and completed by Tadhg Ó Neachtain. It does not derive from Pluincéad's work. It was never published.

The manuscripts of these dictionaries may be consulted online via the Irish Script on Screen project by going to Marsh's Library.[10]

In 1732, Conchobhar Ó Beaglaoich, perhaps assisted by Aodh Buidhe Mac Cruitín, published *The English Irish Dictionary: An Foclóir Béarla Gaoidheilge*,[11] and the change from Latin and Irish to English and Irish was complete. This dictionary appears to be partially derived from an English dictionary or list of hard words,

In 1739, Tadhg Ó Neachtain completed a manuscript Irish-English dictionary, "Foclóir Gaeilbhéarlach."[12] This is very extensive and at times seems to pride itself on its completeness, adding strange adjectives to accompany nouns, for example.

In 1768, Bishop John O'Brien of Cloyne published *Focalóir Gaoidhilge-Sags-Bhéarla or an Irish-English Dictionary*.[13] It contains many common words and phrases.

Only bilingual Irish and English dictionaries appeared in the nineteenth century: a reprint of O'Brien's Irish-English dictionary, this time in Gaelic script, and several in the O'Reilly series beginning in 1817.[14] O'Reilly admitted when faced with criticism that he had not included common words from the spoken language and that he did not notice this omission until it was brought to his attention.

IS: Why was the nineteenth century limited to bilingual lexicons? Is there a cultural explanation?

SUAS: The simple fact is that it is much easier to translate a word than to define it. Monoglot Irish speakers were generally illiterate. Anyone who could read Irish

---

Great Britain: From Collections and Observations in Travels through Wales, Cornwal, Bas-Bretagne, Ireland and Scotland (Oxford: Printed at the Theater [sic] for the Author, 1707).

[10] Pluincéad: Irish Script on Screen, MS Z 4.2.5, www.isos.dias.ie/MARSH/MS_Z_4_2_5.html; Walsh and Ó Neachtain: Irish Script on Screen, MS Z 3.1.13, www.isos.dias.ie/MARSH/MS_Z_3_1_13.html

[11] Conchobhar Ó Beaglaoich, assisted by Aodh Buidhe Mac Cuirtín, *The English Irish Dictionary: An Foclóir Béarla Gaoidheilge* (Paris: Seamus Geurin, 1732).

[12] Tadhg Ó Neachtain, "Foclóir Gaeilbhéarlach" (Trinity College, Dublin, manuscript 1290 (H.I.16), 1739).

[13] John O'Brien, *Focalóir Gaoidhilge-Sags-Bhéarla or an Irish-English Dictionary* (Paris: Nicolas-Francis Valleyre, 1768).

[14] John O'Brien, *Focalóir Gaoidhilge-Sags-Bhéarla or, an Irish-English Dictionary*, 2nd ed., revised and corrected (Dublin: Hodges and Smith, 1832), Preface by Robert Daly; Edward O'Reilly, *An Irish-English Dictionary* (Dublin, 1817; various eds., finally including a supplement by John O'Donovan, 1864, 1877).

	could also read English. We have seen Cormac's definition of *bás* (death). To define "death" in a monolingual dictionary is quite challenging. It is much easier to give a translation.
IS:	Is it possible to describe the specific social strata to which all or many of these lexicographers belonged?
SUAS:	They were all learned, many of them priests, one a bishop, others laymen of a prosperous background. Peadar Ó Conaill (1755–1826) was a son of a prosperous farmer, traveled in Ireland and in Scotland, was supported by patronage, and taught school.
IS:	Talk to me about "Croidhe Cainnte Chiarraighe."[15]
SUAS:	In the course of the nineteenth century, Ireland had changed from being a predominantly Irish-speaking country to one mainly speaking English. A census was taken in 1901, and what we find is that a large majority of people born before 1840 spoke Irish, but most people born in the second half of the nineteenth century spoke only English. Especially toward the end of the nineteenth century, there was a strong cultural revival, and many people wished to learn Irish.

Naturally a dictionary which didn't include the normal words of the spoken language was of little use to these learners, useful as it might have been to native speakers dealing with abstruse manuscripts. The Irish Texts Society was anxious to produce a readers' Irish-English dictionary and came to an agreement with the major Irish lexicographer of the twentieth century, Fr. Patrick S. Dinneen, who set to work and produced an extremely useful dictionary for the society in 1904.[16] During the 1916 rebellion, the plates for this dictionary were destroyed and Dinneen compiled a much larger dictionary in 1927.[17] This was still the standard Irish dictionary when I was in school in the 1960s and 70s and remains extremely useful, especially for eighteenth-century texts and for the language of Munster Irish-speaking areas. Work was also proceeding on dialect dictionaries, one of the earliest being *Sean-Chaint na nDéise* (1906), containing several lists of words from County Waterford.[18] By the time Dinneen completed his larger dictionary, word lists had also appeared from West Kerry and County Clare. This work continued through the twentieth century.

Reverting to your question, although it is frequently referred to as "Croidhe Cainnte Chiarraighe," with lenition[19] (*h*) of the word *Ciarraighe* as in modern spoken Irish, the actual title is "Croidhe Cainnte Ciarraighe" without lenition as

---

[15] Seán a' Chóta Ó Caomhánaigh, "Croidhe Cainnte Ciarraighe." National Library of Ireland manuscripts G 601–29, 1935–42. Published online by Dr. Tracey Ní Mhaonaigh: http://forasnagaeilge.ie

[16] Patrick S. Dinneen, *Foclóir Gaedhilge agus Béarla: An Irish-English Dictionary* (Dublin: Irish Texts Society, 1904).

[17] Patrick S. Dinneen, *Foclóir Gaedhilge agus Béarla: An Irish-English Dictionary*, new ed., revised and greatly enlarged (Dublin: Irish Texts Society, 1927).

[18] Most Reverend Michael Sheehan, *Sean-Chaint na nDéise: The Idiom of Living Irish* (Dublin: M. H. Gill and Son, 1906).

[19] Lenition, now written as *h* after a consonant is often grammatical in Irish. It changes the pronunciation of the consonant.

it would appear in Early Modern Irish. The author, Seán an Chóta (1885–1947), who variously called himself "an Cóta" (the local word for "petticoat" or "kilt"), "Seán Óg Ó Caomhánaigh," and "Seán Mac Murchadha Caomhánach," was a native of Dunquin (Dún Chaoin). He was a brother to Muiris, better known as "Kruger," proprietor of the local hostelry. Another brother was Séamas Kavanagh, Professor of Celtic Languages and Philology in University College Cork. The surname is Ó Cíobháin (originally Ó Ciabháin – "descendant of the dark-haired one") in West Kerry, but this version was shunned by the brothers. Seán an Chóta spoke wonderful native Dunquin Irish, with a wide vocabulary and impeccable accuracy. He was asked by the Irish-Government Department of Education to produce a dictionary of his dialect of Irish which would be suitable as a secondary-school textbook and a contract was drawn up.

As the work submitted increased in bulk, it was decided to include the dictionary, once completed, in the category of general literature, rather than school textbooks. Had Seán an Chóta decided to reproduce his own Irish faithfully, the work would be a national treasure. It does contain a wealth of idiomatic West Kerry words and phrases. However, Seán an Chóta was a poseur. He wished to display his learning, and for this reason left "Ciarraighe" rather than "Ch-" in the title, using historical rather than contemporary grammar. He sought to give the impression that he belonged to suburbia rather than to an isolated rural parish. For example, while illustrating the phrase *ar deighilt* (separated, apart), he writes "*bíonn drúthlanna ar deighilt i gceanntaraibh leo féin*" (brothels are kept apart in their own districts), using the literary word *drúthlann* which is not found in West Kerry speech. Similarly, he uses *sgiath* (a shield) for "a tray" as no native word was used in his dialect. He also used the verbal particle *nach* rather than the Munster *ná*.

The government department feared that the work would become very extensive and expensive. The contract was modified. The dictionary was completed between 1935 and 1943 but was never published on paper. The tragedy is that much of the vocabulary it contains derives from Seán an Chóta's profound knowledge of his native language and that of his neighbours, but eighty years on, it is extremely difficult to discern whether an otherwise unattested phrase is genuine West-Kerry Irish or springs from the author's pretentions. What might have been the definitive dictionary of Corca Dhuibhne (West Kerry) Irish is ruined by dishonesty. The work has been edited and published online by Dr. Tracey Ní Mhaonaigh.

IS: I'm interested in the dialectical relationship between oral and written Irish. Earlier, you mentioned that dictionaries didn't pay attention to how people spoke. I would like you to go further into that dichotomy. Can Irish dictionaries be "liberated" from the tyranny of the written word?

SUAS: It isn't even the "written word," as the writers at the end of the nineteenth and the early twentieth centuries reflected local usage. Fr. Peter O'Leary (An tAthair Peadar Ua Laoghaire) from West Muskerry, County Cork, insisted on writing his native Irish as did writers from other parts of the country. In the 1940s it was decided to standardize the spelling of Irish and in the 1950s to standardize forms of words and grammar. Subsequent dictionaries (de

Bhaldraithe, Niall Ó Dónaill) refused to recognize dialects.[20] If I look up *car park* in my *Oxford Spanish Dictionary* (Spanish-English, English-Spanish), it sends me to *parking lot*, tells me that this is North American English, that it is called *estacionamiento* in American Spanish and *aparcamiento* in Spain. Both de Bhaldraithe's and Ó Dónaill's dictionaries refuse to recognize that differences exist among the types of Irish spoken in Munster, Connaught, and Ulster. The government services responsible for these dictionaries were committed to promoting standard Irish, which is unnatural and sounds childish to native speakers. Perhaps this could be reversed, but Google Translate Irish is becoming increasingly common.

IS: I am fascinated by *Dictionary of the Irish Language: Based Mainly on Old and Middle Irish Materials*, also called the *"DIL."*

SUAS: A scholarly dictionary of the Irish language was proposed in the middle of the nineteenth century, involving the scholars Eugene O'Curry and John O'Donovan, but both had passed away by 1862 and little progress had been made. O'Donovan did draw up his ideas on how the dictionary should proceed: older manuscripts should be excerpted, the meanings should be based on citations, no etymologies should be included except from within Irish and some loanwords. The School of Irish Learning was founded in 1903. In that same year the philanthropic Rev. Maxwell Close died, leaving the sum of £1,000 to assist with the publication of a scholarly Irish dictionary.

He stipulated that the money would not be forthcoming if some portion of the dictionary were not published within ten years. Several scholars took a hand, but it was left to Carl Marstrander of Denmark to produce the first fasciculus of the dictionary, *D* to *degóir*, just in time to preserve the funding. Marstrander was rebuked by other scholars for compiling too extensive a dictionary, and he soon withdrew from the School of Irish Learning. Marstrander's approach would now seem to be the correct one. The project was continued with fluctuations by part-time volunteers until the letter *B* was published in 1975, and *h* was added in 1976. A compact single volume edition with miniscule type appeared in 1983. A new digitized version was prepared between 2003 and 2007 under the direction of Prof. Gregory Toner, incorporating published corrections to some entries, preserving the page numbers and the line numbers of the printed editions. This version, sometimes referred to as eDIL, is searchable for Irish or English words, and is expanded and revised by an editorial team: unlike a dictionary published in book form, it is constantly being updated.

IS: Why doesn't the *DIL* include Modern Irish?

SUAS: In 1903, it was probably felt that Modern Irish was being catered for by the Irish Texts Society and scholars of spoken Irish. Modern Irish is not entirely excluded: it is "based mainly on Old and Middle Irish Materials." Some examples from bardic poetry (c. 1200–1650) are cited. Peadar Ó Conaill's

---

[20] Tomás de Bhaldraithe, *English Irish Dictionary* (Dublin: Oifig an tSoláthair, 1959); Niall Ó Dónaill, *Foclóir Gaeilge-Béarla* (Dublin: Oifig an tSoláthair, 1977).

extensive dictionary (c. 1826),[21] containing mostly modern material, was used to help elucidate obscure early vocabulary. As dialect dictionaries were produced it was felt that the modern language was adequately served and that attempting to include all phases of the language might only lead to confusion.

IS: What role does the Royal Irish Academy play in Ireland? Do people care about it?

SUAS: The Royal Irish Academy (RIA) took charge of the *Dictionary of the Irish Language* after the demise of the School of Irish Learning. The academy hosts academic lectures, produces many learned publications, houses the Modern Irish Dictionary (Foclóir Stairiúil na Gaeilge) project, which has produced Corpus na Gaeilge, an extremely useful lexicographical tool, giving examples in context of published Irish approximately from 1600 to the present or almost. The academy also hosts the Dictionary of Irish Biography and the Dictionary of Medieval Latin from Celtic Sources, to mention a small part of its work. Many are unaware of the work of the RIA, but it contributes greatly to Irish and Gaelic culture.

IS: Have Irish dictionaries been produced predominantly by men?

SUAS: Indeed, men entirely dominated the work prior to the twentieth century. After that, many fine women scholars worked on the Dictionary of the Irish Language. Women have also worked on the Department of Education dictionaries, several have produced dialect dictionaries, and there has been a strong female presence in the RIA Modern Irish Dictionary project.

IS: The internet has changed the way in which lexical meaning is disseminated. People in the twenty-first century want fast, easy access.

SUAS: Undoubtedly, eDIL and Corpus na Gaeilge have made life easier for scholars. What is disconcerting is the increasing, uncritical, and lazy use of Google Translate, which has greatly improved but still will foul a translation unless adequately supervised. The arrival of www.tearma.ie since 2015 (originally focal.ie), a list of technical terms, makes it easy to find how a technical term may be rendered in Irish but is often used as a dictionary by students, making their prose stilted and difficult. The Irish I have always heard for "carpenter" is *siúinéir*, a nativized borrowing from the English word *joiner*. However, tearma.ie gives *cearpantóir* (a word that is sometimes heard in Ulster) as the Irish for "carpenter" and *siúinéir* as the equivalent of "joiner." One can see how this would assist a lawyer drafting legislation, but to find *cearpantóir* in a short story written by a native of Kerry is disconcerting. The domination by civil servants in the devising and standardizing of vocabulary is making written Irish increasingly unnatural and gives rise to division between native speakers (and those who have carefully learned Irish from native sources) and officialese, which has the appearance of English translated word for word.

IS: Every lexicographic tradition has its heroes and villains. I'm interested in Tomás de Bhaldraithe.

---

[21] Peter O'Connell, "An Irish-English Dictionary" (British Library manuscript Egerton 83: autograph, highly corrected, difficult to read; Egerton 84–85: neat copy by John O'Donovan, c. 1826).

SUAS: Tomás de Bhaldraithe is hero for some, providing a modern English-Irish dictionary in 1959.[22] He also halted the dominance of Munster Irish in the first half of the twentieth century, giving increasing prominence to Western Irish, which was hailed by some but not very popular in Munster. In fairness, speakers and readers from both Ulster and Munster can easily understand Connemara Irish. De Bhaldraithe's dictionary is fairly scanty; his aim was to give Irish equivalents for English words, which can impoverish written and spoken Irish, making it a straight translation of English. As I wrote Munster Irish, I frequently found de Bhaldraithe's dictionary frustrating: I was not always happy with what I found in it and had to seek more elegant phraseology or more convincing Munster vocabulary elsewhere.

IS: How about the villains?

SUAS: Perhaps Google Translate could be considered, but compared to what it produced ten years ago it doesn't cause the same level of pain.

IS: What is your own journey with dictionaries?

SUAS: My mother was from the Gaeltacht of West Muskerry. Her sister, my aunt, suffered from Parkinson's disease and came to live with us from when I was six years of age. She had Dinneen's excellent dictionary and Lambert McKenna's English-Irish dictionary which cited sources and especially relied on three native speakers: Siobhán Ní Mhainín, a nun from near Ballyferriter in West Kerry; Póilín Bhreathnach from Ros Muc in Connemara; and Niall Ó Dónaill, a Donegal native speaker who later became a prominent lexicographer.[23] I remember her buying de Bhaldraithe's dictionary and expressing her disappointment with it. I have transcribed Pluincéad's seventeenth-century Latin-Irish dictionary and hope to publish it (possibly online) within the next few years. Increasingly I only use Dinneen and McKenna while writing in Modern Irish, and afterwards I refer to texts which I have digitized in order to find authentic usage from native speakers. For my scholarly work on historic texts, eDIL and Corpus na Gaeilge are extremely useful.

IS: How many languages do you speak? And could you describe your relationship with the Irish language?

SUAS: I only speak Irish, English, and Spanish. My wife is from Valladolid in Spain, and we converse in Spanish. As I said, my mother and aunt were Gaeltacht women. I find English extremely useful but feel an affection for Irish and for Spanish that I do not feel for English. I love to speak Irish with Gaeltacht people. Several of them have expressed astonishment when I told them that Irish was not my first language. I can read Latin. I don't have too much trouble understanding other Romance languages when written. I have some knowledge of ancient Greek but generally depend on my wife to explain it to me.

IS: Not too long ago, in a conversation with a diverse group of high-schoolers in Los Angeles, I was surprised when a majority told me they never used dictionaries, or almost never. This might simply be a feature of youth: its belief

---

[22] de Bhaldraithe, *English Irish Dictionary*.
[23] Láimhbheartach Mc Cionnaith, S. J., *Foclóir Béarla agus Gaedhilge: English-Irish Dictionary* (Dublin: Oifig Díolta Foillseacháin Rialtais, 1935).

that language belongs to them. Do you see a decline in the use of dictionaries in Ireland?

SUAS: I'm afraid so. Google Translate is the preferred tool. Also, young people are increasingly less curious. They are happy to read a text without understanding it or simply bypass the Irish text and have Google translate it into English.

The Irish have shown great interest in their own language from early times. This has given rise to dictionaries (or glossaries) produced from the seventh century to today. Many of the historical dictionaries are very useful to Irish language enthusiasts. I have spent hours discussing the meanings and correct usage of words, writing copious examples, with wonderful native speakers with little formal education but with keen intellect and academic rigour. These ladies and gentlemen have all passed away, but Gaeltacht people continue to discuss the intricacies of their language in kitchens, pubs, and on Raidió na Gaeltachta (the Irish language radio station).

Suggested Readings

An Bunachar Náisiúnta Téarmaíochta don Ghaeilge: The National Terminology Database for Irish, www.tearma.ie

Bhailis, Froinsias, and Tadhg Ó Neachtain. "Dictionarium Latino-Anglo-Hibernicum." Marsh's Library manuscript (Dublin) Z3.1.13. 1730.

Connellan, Thaddaeus. *An English-Irish Dictionary*. Dublin: Graisberry & Campbell, 1814.

de Bhaldraithe, Tomás. *English-Irish Dictionary*. Dublin: Oifig an tSoláthair, 1959.

de Vere Coneys, Thomas. *Foclóir Gaoidhilge-Sacs-b[h]éarla*. Dublin: Published for the Irish Society by Hodges and Smith, Grafton Street, 1849.

Dictionary of the Irish Language: Based Mainly on Old and Middle Irish Materials. Dublin: Royal Irish Academy, 1913–76. Compact ed., 1983. Electronic ed., with corrections, 2014– (ongoing). https://dil.ie/

Dinneen, Patrick S. *Foclóir Gaedhilge agus Béarla: An Irish-English Dictionary*. Dublin: Irish Texts Society, 1904.

Foclóir Gaedhilge agus Béarla: An Irish-English Dictionary. New ed., revised and greatly enlarged. Dublin: Irish Texts Society, 1927.

Foley, Daniel. *An English-Irish Dictionary*. Dublin: William Curry and Company Booksellers to the Queen, 9, Upper Sackville-Street, 1855.

Fournier d'Albe, Edmund E. *An English-Irish Dictionary and Phrase Book*. Dublin, 1903.

Historical Irish Corpus. 1600–1926. http://corpas.ria.ie

Lhuyd, Edward. *Archaeologia Britannica, Giving some Account Additional to What Has Been Hitherto Publish'd, of the Languages, Histories and Customs of the Original Inhabitants of Great Britain: From Collections and Observations in Travels through Wales, Cornwall, Bas-Bretagne, Ireland and Scotland*. Oxford: Printed at the Theater [sic] for the Author, 1707.

Mc Cionnaith, Láimhbheartach, S. J. *Foclóir Béarla agus Gaedhilge: English-Irish Dictionary*. Dublin: Oifig Díolta Foillseacháin Rialtais, 1935.

Ó Beaglaoich, Conchobhar, assisted by Aodh Buidhe Mac Cuirtín. *The English Irish Dictionary: An Foclóir Béarla Gaoidheilge*. Paris: Seamus Geurin, 1732.

O'Brien, John. *Focalóir Gaoidhilge-Sags-Bhéarla or an Irish-English Dictionary.* Paris: Nicolas-Francis Valleyre, 1768.

Ó Caomhánaigh, Seán a' Chóta. "Croidhe Cainnte Ciarraighe." National Library of Ireland manuscripts G 601-29, 1935–42. Published online by Dr. Tracey Ní Mhaonaigh: http://forasnagaeilge.ie

Ó Cléirigh, Mícheál. *Focloir no Sanasan Nua.* Leuven: Coláiste na mBráthar nÉireannach, 1643.

O'Connell, Peter. "An Irish-English Dictionary." British Library manuscript Egerton 83: autograph, highly corrected, difficult to read; Egerton 84–85: neat copy by John O'Donovan, c. 1826.

Ó Dónaill, Niall. *Foclóir Gaeilge-Béarla.* Dublin: Oifig an tSoláthair, 1977.

Ó Neachtain, Tadhg. "Foclóir Gaeilbhéarlach." Trinity College (Dublin) manuscript 1290 (H.I.16), 1739.

O'Neill-Lane, Timothy. *Larger English Irish Dictionary (Foclóir Béarla-Gaedhilge).* London: Constable, 1915.

O'Reilly, Edward. *An Irish-English Dictionary.* Dublin. 1817. Various editions, finally including a supplement by John O'Donovan, 1864, 1877.

Pluincéad, Risdeard "Vocabularium Latinum et Hibernum: Foclóir Laidne & Gaoidheilge." Marsh's Library (Dublin) manuscript, Z4.2.5, 1662.

Russell, Paul, Sharon Arbuthnot, Pádraic Moran. Early Irish Glossaries Database. www.asnc.cam.ac.uk/irishglossaries/

13 African Languages

Dion Nkomo and Paul Achille Mavoungou

Africa is one of the most linguistically diverse habitats on the planet. For example, Swahili or Kiswahili is spoken by between 160 and 200 million, Hausa by 77 million, Lingala by 60–65 million, Amharic by around 56 million, Yoruba by approximately 46 million native and second-language speakers, and Oromo by some 37.4 million. Other languages include Fula, Igbo, Xhosa, Somali, Zulu, and Wolof. This conversation explores the role of dictionaries in the shaping of national identities, looking at specific instances in Africa. It looks at instances of governments using language as either a unifying or a dividing force. It also reflects on how publishers have prioritized some of the continent's languages over others and the degree to which one might talk of an African "dictionary culture."

***

ILAN STAVANS: How many languages are spoken in Africa today? Which are the most popular in terms of numbers of speakers?

PAUL ACHILLE MAVOUNGOU: In linguistic terms, Africa is incredibly varied, with thousands of languages spoken. Depending on what definition of language and dialect one assumes, there are between 1,250 and 2,100 languages in Africa.

It is a well-attested fact that all languages change over time and space. Social change is one of the factors contributing to the inevitability of linguistic change. For example, older people complain about the falling standards of the language competence of the younger generation and often blame this on changes in social institutions like schools and broadcasting (radio and TV), as well as the history of both European and Arabo-Islamic hegemony in Africa.

Most African languages have a number of significant different dialects because when people speaking those languages move away from each other or become separated by, for instance, political or ecological barriers, their resultant lack of everyday communication can cause a change in terms of sound production, vocabulary, and grammar. Vocabulary is particularly susceptible

African Languages   157

to changes due to new ideas and objects that were introduced in Africa during the Arabo-Islamic invasion since the seventh century and the European colonization in the late nineteenth century.

Not surprisingly, names of plants and animals, names of new products, and religious and belief terms brought by explorers, missionaries, colonial administrators, and traders from Arabia, Europe, and America have undergone important alterations when entering the lexica of African languages. Data obtained from different sources show that a number of these borrowings are from Arabic, Portuguese/Spanish, Dutch, German, English, and French. Therefore, Arabic and European languages have contributed to the development of the vocabulary of African languages.

In terms of the numbers of speakers, it is said that of the 1 billion Africans (in 2009, the year with the most recent trustworthy figure), about 17 percent speak an Arabic dialect. About 10 percent speak Swahili or Kiswahili (a Bantu language with significant influences from Arabic), the lingua franca of Southeast Africa; about 5 percent speak a Berber dialect; and about 5 percent speak Hausa, a Chadic language originally from the northern regions of Nigeria and Niger as well as one of the largest languages in the Sahel.

IS: This diversity is astonishing. What are the political, social, and cultural implications of it?

PAM: The effects of this diversity are multifaceted and can be observed in various aspects of life across the continent. The political landscape is often shaped by these divisions, leading to challenges in nation-building and governance. Geopolitical factors often play a significant role in governance structures and decision-making in many African countries.

IS: Have there been, throughout history, efforts to make Africa linguistically homogeneous?

PAM: Yes, historically there have been such efforts in certain regions of Africa, often linked to colonial and postcolonial policies. These efforts were influenced by various factors, including administrative convenience, economic interests, and the imposition of cultural and political dominance.

During the colonial era, European powers implemented policies that often favoured the imposition of a single official language for administrative purposes. This policy aimed to streamline governance and facilitate communication between the colonial authorities and local populations. In many cases, this involved the promotion of the colonial language, such as English, French, Portuguese, or Spanish, at the expense of indigenous languages. Some postcolonial African nations, in their efforts to build a sense of national unity and identity, designated a particular indigenous language as the official language.

For example, Swahili has been promoted as a lingua franca in East Africa. In Northern Africa, Arabic is a dominant language in countries like Egypt, Sudan, Libya, Tunisia, Algeria, and Morocco. This was done with the intention of fostering linguistic homogeneity within the nation. However, this approach could also marginalize speakers of other languages within the country.

IS: Which was the first dictionary ever made in the continent? What were the factors behind its birth?

PAM: The first dictionary or lexicographic reference work ever made in Africa was compiled in the Atlantic Coast region of Central Africa, in the kingdom of Kongo. This lexicographic referential work is called *Vocabularium Latinum, Hispanicum, e Congense*.[1]

This vocabulary is the oldest surviving lexicographical source of Kikongo and, indeed, of any Bantu language. It dates back to 1652 and was handwritten by the Flemish Capuchin missionary Joris van Gheel, who certainly was not its sole author. This lexicographic reference work was indeed a useful aid for Christian evangelization. It also helped the Capuchin missionaries in their daily routine in order to communicate with the Bakongo.

Therefore, the purpose of earlier dictionaries was basically to serve as reference works for European explorers, traders, and colonial administrators in their daily routine. Moreover, dictionaries have served as a source for the compilation of pedagogic or teaching materials, such as the translation of the Bible (for evangelization purposes), grammar books, and syllabi to teach the inhabitants to read and write.

DION NKOMO: The *Vocabularium Latinum, Hispanicum, e Congense* illustrates the general history of dictionaries in African languages, particularly pertaining to their compilers, users, and purposes. Generally, the earliest dictionaries were compiled by external members of the African language communities for their own use in conducting their own activities with the communities. More examples can be found even in the African languages spoken in Southern Africa.

For example, in Xhosa, a South African language that celebrates 200 years of its existence in print in 2023, *A Kafir–English Dictionary* was compiled by Rev. Albert Kropf with a clearly stated purpose of supporting language learning needs of missionaries in the Eastern Cape where the Xhosa language is predominantly spoken. Even in the twentieth century, dictionaries in African languages were still being compiled to serve language learning needs of non-mother-tongue speakers of African languages, some of whom became linguists and teachers of these languages. Another example is James McLaren's *A Concise Kafir-English Dictionary* (1915) and *A Concise English-Kafir Dictionary* (1923), which were clearly linked to his Xhosa grammar book.[2]

The same applies to the *English-Zulu Dictionary* (1958) by Clement Doke and Bennedict Wallet Vilakazi.[3] It was also linked to Doke's work on Zulu grammar. What is important, though, is to note that these earliest dictionaries, which were compiled by non-mother-tongue speakers of African languages for their own use, laid firm foundations for African languages and some of them remain important lexicographic references even today.

---

[1] J. Van Gheel [religious name of Adriaen Willems; Fl. Joris van Gheel; Fr. Georges de Gheel; Lat. Georgius Gelensis], *Vocabularium Latinum, Hispanicum, e Congense: Ad Usum Missionariorû transmittendorû ad Regni Congo Missiones* (1652). Manuscript kept in the National Central Library of Rome: Fundo Minori 1896, MS Varia 274.

[2] James McLaren, *A Concise Kafir–English Dictionary* (London: Longmans, Green and Company, 1915); James McLaren, *A Concise English–Kafir Dictionary* (London: Longmans, Green and Company, 1923).

[3] Clement M. Doke and Bennedict Wallet Vilakazi, *Zulu–English Dictionary* (Johannesburg: Witwatersrand University Press, 1958).

African Languages 159

IS: I'm interested in the lexicographers behind these efforts. How did they come about shaping their endeavours? What were their models?

DN: The lexicographers who compiled pioneering lexicographic works in African languages were mainly explorers, missionaries, and colonial administrators, as indicated earlier. Their occupations, particularly the missionaries and colonial administrators, required that they interacted with local communities. They could not do this using their own languages. Pioneering lexicographic work was therefore inextricably linked with the development of the script in African languages (i.e. converting the languages which were hitherto only in oral forms to literary forms).

While missionaries were translating the Bible and other scriptural material into African languages, it was noted that dictionaries, grammars, and other language learning materials were needed to support the teaching and learning of the languages. The European settlers wanted to learn African languages to expedite their Christian and colonial missions. Learning the languages orally from Africans was neither effective nor sufficient. So, Africans, who were masters of their languages in oral forms, also needed to acquire literacy in the basic sense of the word to refer to reading and writing in their own languages.

For missionaries, the early bilingual dictionaries facilitated the coordination between African languages and those of the settlers in ways that expedited the teaching and learning of African languages. As indicated, the main target users of those dictionaries were the Europeans, not the speakers of African languages. The lexicographers themselves were clear on that. For example, Rev. Albert Kropf was motivated to compile *A Kafir-English Dictionary* to ensure that missionaries and European settlers who arrived in the Eastern Cape after him didn't experience the challenges associated with learning a language without reference materials.[4] McLaren expresses a similar motivation for his dictionaries, while the subtitle of M. E. Wealie's *Matebele and Malaka Vocabulary: Intended for the Use of Prospectors and Farmers in Mashonaland* (1903) clearly excludes the speakers of the Zimbabwean languages from its user profile.[5]

Although Africans were not part of the target users of the pioneer dictionaries in their languages, they contributed immensely in the dictionary-making processes. Linguistic research in African languages was still at infancy. Rev. Robert Godfrey, who revised Kropf's *Kafir-English Dictionary*, recounts how the Xhosa people helped with bird names and their descriptions. However, coming from societies with more established literary and lexicographic traditions, the compilers drew more from their own traditions when it came to lexicographic presentations and descriptions. This had implications on the orthographic, lexicographic, and even sociocultural representations of the languages and the lives of Africans.

The implications of European orthography on the orthography of African languages are complex and varied. European languages, particularly those of

---

[4] Albert Kropf, *A Kafir–English Dictionary*, 2nd ed. (Alice: Lovedale, 1915).
[5] M. E. Wealie, *Matebele and Malaka Vocabulary: Intended for the Use of Prospectors and Farmers in Mashonaland* (Cape Town: Murray and St. Leger, 1903).

former colonial powers, have had a significant impact on the written forms of many African languages. For example, European colonial powers often introduced the Latin alphabet to write African languages. This has led to the adoption of a writing system that may not perfectly match the phonetic and phonological characteristics of the African languages. In other words, African languages often have phonetic features that are not present in European languages.

This can lead to challenges in accurately representing the sounds of African languages using the Latin alphabet. Some sounds may not have direct equivalents in the European languages, leading to compromises and approximations. One of the major motivations for the production of *The Greater Dictionary of isiXhosa* was the recognition that the revised orthography of the language adopted in 1955 rendered Kropf's dictionary outdated.[6] The revised orthography of the language was approved in 1955. Dictionary work began in 1967. The dictionary was published in three parts. The first volume was published in 1989 and the final one which completed the dictionary was published in 2006.

IS: What kind of reception did these dictionaries get?

DN: Some pioneer dictionaries made landmark contributions in the development of African languages. They established lexicographic foundations and provided authoritative standards for language learning, and the production of educational and religious material in African languages. Their importance has outlived their era. For example, Michael Hannan's *Standard Shona Dictionary* remains the major bilingual dictionary in Shona, while the *Kafir-English Dictionary* remains an important tool for isiXhosa translators and compilers of new dictionaries.[7] However, these dictionaries had some shortcomings, especially in regards to the misrepresentation of African linguistic, cultural, and religious systems. The richness of African languages and their complexities is often lost, in part because of the lexicographers' own prejudices.

IS: I assume that, as in the case of Latin America (I am from Mexico), the tension between oral and written spheres in Africa remains tangible, including a vast segment of the population that is illiterate. Have there ever been efforts to create "oral" dictionaries of African languages?

DN: It is true that many speakers of African languages remain illiterate. As such, dictionaries are mainly produced for the school market. However, as noted earlier, the marginalization of African languages effectively undermines the value of African language dictionaries among the speakers of these languages. Those who can read barely recognize the value of dictionaries while those who cannot and may benefit from dictionaries are marginalized by the print medium.

Oral dictionaries that exploit digital affordances can bridge the gap.

Such a dictionary genre has emerged in African languages but its uptake has been low. An initiative to develop the so-called talking dictionaries was

---

[6] H. W. Pahl, et al., *The Greater Dictionary of (isi)Xhosa* (Pietermaritzburg: Nutrend, 1989–2006).

[7] M. Hannan, *Standard Shona Dictionary*, compiled for the Southern Rhodesia Native Affairs Department (London: Macmillan, 1959).

introduced in countries such as Nigeria and Zimbabwe by the Living Tongues Institute for Endangered Languages. Adopting some strategies of vernacular lexicography, linguists from the institute trained language speakers on the use of recorders and asked them to provide translation equivalents of selected English words, record them, and provide brief definitions.

IS: Can we discuss the availability, scope, and formats of dictionaries in African languages today?

PAM: Dictionaries for African languages vary widely in terms of availability, scope, and format. Indeed, bilingual dictionaries providing translations between African languages and other languages such as Arabic, Portuguese, Spanish, Dutch, German, English, and French are more common and widely available. These dictionaries play a crucial role in facilitating communication and language learning between speakers of different languages.

They are particularly valuable for language learners, translators, and individuals engaging in cross-cultural communication. The scope of dictionaries in African languages can vary based on factors such as the size of the linguistic community, linguistic diversity within the language, and the level of academic and community interest. Some dictionaries cover a broad range of vocabulary and include detailed linguistic information (e.g. dictionaries available for Hausa), while others may focus on specific dialects, domains, or usage contexts (especially African languages that are currently endangered). With regard to the format, dictionaries of African languages are available in various formats, including both printed dictionaries and online dictionaries. Traditional printed dictionaries are common, and they may be published by academic institutions, language associations, or commercial publishers. With the advancement of technology, there is an increasing trend toward online dictionaries. These may be freely accessible or subscription-based, and they can include interactive features, multimedia elements, and regular updates. Some dictionaries are even available as mobile apps, making language resources more accessible to users with smartphones and tablets.

IS: Yet I assume these dictionaries are seen as colonial tools?

PAM: To some extent, this has been the case regarding some dictionaries. Racial and ethnic undertones have been identified in some early dictionaries. The word *kafir* in the title of Kropf's historic dictionary, for instance, is a racist colonial and apartheid word that characterized isiXhosa speakers and Africans in general as uncivilized people.

In recent times, there has been a growing recognition of the need to empower local communities and reclaim linguistic and cultural heritage. This includes efforts to create dictionaries that reflect the perspectives and priorities of indigenous communities rather than perpetuating colonial legacies. Some language revitalization efforts involve communities in creating their dictionaries and language resources. This approach allows for the inclusion of local knowledge, cultural nuances, and a more community-centric representation in language documentation.

IS: This makes monolingual dictionaries all the more important.

PAM: Monolingual dictionaries do exist in African languages, namely *Duramazwi reChiShona* (Shona monolingual dictionary, 1996), *Isichazamazwi SesiNdebele* (Ndebele monolingual dictionary, 2001), and *Duramazwi Guru reChiShona* (advanced Shona monolingual dictionary, 2001), to list but a few.[8] They are valuable resources for language learners, researchers, and individuals interested in deepening their understanding of specific languages spoken on the continent. Moreover, one finds both online resources as well as printed dictionaries.

Quite surprisingly, a substantial number of such dictionaries is already available for a large number of languages with a relatively large number of users. It should however be mentioned that while online resources are becoming increasingly popular for European languages, a very few African language dictionaries are available online (Swahili, Yoruba, Hausa, Zulu, Igbo, Amharic, Wolof, Twi, Shona...). With the rise of digital language learning platforms, there is a growing trend of incorporating African languages into these systems. These platforms often include interactive dictionaries, lessons, and language resources.

Dictionaries for some lesser-known or endangered African languages may be limited due to factors such as a lack of resources, fewer speakers, and insufficient documentation efforts. Efforts to revitalize and document endangered languages are crucial for preserving linguistic diversity (for example the Taa Language (!XÓÕ) Online Dictionary for a Khoisan language spoken by a very small population in Botswana and Namibia).[9]

IS: Are these efforts done by commercial companies? In other words, are they always profit-driven? Do any of them come from government entities?

DN: African lexicography has been undermined by limited commercial viability of dictionaries in African languages. The generally low prestige of African languages and their restricted functional roles limit the motivation for the learning of African languages and the use of dictionaries associated with language learning. Even in instances where African languages have elevated functional status, dictionary culture is poor among speakers of African languages.

As a result, efforts to compile dictionaries of various types in African languages is met with poor interest from major commercial publishers who are profit-driven.

IS: What role do universities and research institutions play in all this?

DN: Academic institutions have certainly played an integral role in the development of African lexicography. Worthy of mention would be the Institute for Kiswahili Studies, previously the Institute for Kiswahili Research. The Centre for Kiswahili Lexicography and Grammar, which was established in 1930, is one of the major sections of the institute. Since the publication of *Kamusi ya Kiswahili: A Swahili-Swahili Dictionary* (1935), the institute has published numerous Kiswahili dictionaries.[10] Its lexicographic work has contributed to

---

[8] H. Chimhundu, ed., *Duramazwi reChiShona* (Harare: College Press, 1996); S. Hadebe, ed., *Isichazamazwi SesiNdebele* (Harare: College Press, 2001); H. Chimhundu, ed., *Duramazwi Guru reChiShona* (Harare: College Press, 2001).

[9] https://lughayangu.com/index.php/xoo#

[10] Frederick Johnson, *Kamusi ya Kiswahili: A Swahili-Swahili Dictionary* (London: Sheldon Press, 1935).

the standardization and development of Kiswahili as a major African language. Similar historic university projects existed in other African countries.

In South Africa, the Xhosa Dictionary Project, which was approved by the University of Fort Hare council in 1966, culminated in the publication of the *The Greater Dictionary of isiXhosa*, a tri-volume trilingual dictionary whose last volume was published in 2006. This dictionary, which features English and Afrikaans, remains the basis for later isiXhosa dictionaries compiled by the isiXhosa National Lexicography Unit. In Zimbabwe, the African Languages Research Institute also marked a lexicographic boom in Shona and Ndebele. However, another crucial role played by academic institutions such as Stellenbosch University and the University of Pretoria in South Africa in the twenty-first century was the introduction of formal academic training programs at master's and doctoral levels.

These programs asserted lexicography as a formal academic and professional discipline in Africa, drawing students from different parts of the continent, thereby producing trained theoretical and practical lexicographers. This ensured that dictionaries were being produced by qualified practitioners and guided by relevant theoretical models.

IS: Talk to me about the connection of dictionaries and nationalist currents in the African continent.

DN: Bilingual dictionaries pairing European languages and African languages dominated early lexicographic practice in African communities and continue to be the dominant type even today.

In African languages, which have a more recent literary tradition that was mainly established by European explorers and missionaries, the European languages provided the metalanguage. African languages were objects of lexicographical description, and the descriptions needed to be in the languages that the primary dictionary users could understand. Furthermore, in the colonial language policy context, the use of African languages was restricted to the domestic and less prestigious domains, while learning European languages such as English, French, or Portuguese was more rewarding for Africans. As such, for lexicography, producing monolingual dictionaries for the use of mother-tongue speakers of African languages was not a priority.

The monolingual dictionary genre emerges with the growing wave of linguistic patriotism when educated African scholars start to drive the advocacy for the development, promotion, teaching, and learning of African languages for use in high-status domains. For example, the first monolingual dictionary in Zulu was compiled by the first black vice-chancellor of the University of Zululand, the late Prof. Abraham Nkabinde, while National Lexicography Units were established with the primary mandate of producing comprehensive monolingual dictionaries in African languages which were elevated into official languages in the 1996 postapartheid constitution, alongside English and Afrikaans, which had hitherto enjoyed such a privileged status.

IS: In other words, does making a language "official" translate into a lexicographic boom?

DN: While this hasn't always been the case in Africa, it seems to have been true in South Africa. After the declaration of nine historically marginalized indigenous languages as official languages alongside English and Afrikaans, National

Lexicography Units were established for each official language. Lexicography was recognized as one of the practical measures of contributing to the corpus development of these official languages.

The National Lexicography Units were mandated with the production of comprehensive historical monolingual dictionaries that would assert the status of the official language, and it was decided that this important work would be funded under the Pan South African Language Board (PanSALB), which receives funding from the National Treasury. Coupled with the establishment of the Association for African Lexicography, known as AFRILEX, and the *Lexikos* journal as AFRILEX's official mouthpiece, this made South Africa the epicenter of African lexicography in the late 1990s and first decade of the twenty-first century. African lexicography even started to gain global visibility.

Thanks to the National Lexicography Units initiative, all the official languages now boast at least one bilingual dictionary and a monolingual dictionary, even though these products may be a far cry from the vision that inspired the establishment of the units. Previously, some languages such as Xitsonga and isiNdebele existed in the pre-lexicographic era (i.e. they had no single dictionary). However, the National Lexicography Units have been weakened by several factors, with funding being the most critical one. Nevertheless, although the elevation of a language into an official language does not necessarily translate into a lexicographic boom, the South African context illustrates the nexus between lexicography and language policy, as captured in publications such as Gouws (2007) and Nkomo (2018).[11]

IS: I have heard about Zimbabwe's African Languages Lexical Project, which I believe was a collaboration with Norwegian and Swedish universities.

DN: Yes, the African Languages Lexical (ALLEX) Project was a collaboration between the University of Zimbabwe, the University of Oslo, and the University of Gothenburg between 1992 and 2007 that led to the establishment of the African Languages Research Institute. It heralded a shift of emphasis from bilingual dictionaries compiled by non-mother-tongue speakers to monolingual dictionaries compiled by mother-tongue speakers of Zimbabwe's major languages, Shona and Ndebele. It produced *Duramazwi reChiShona*, *Isichazamazwi SesiNdebele*, and *Duramazwi Guru reChiShona*, as its flagship products.

With several bilingual dictionaries produced by missionaries already existing in those languages, the publication of the monolingual dictionaries in the two major Zimbabwean languages was historic, almost in the same way as Samuel Johnson's *Dictionary of the English Language*, the *Vocabolario degli Accademici* for Italian or the *Dictionnaire de l'Académie française* produced by the Académie française.[12] I am sure Paul can provide similar examples from Gabon.

---

[11] R. H. Gouws, "On the Development of Bilingual Dictionaries in South Africa: Aspects of Dictionary Culture and Government Policy," *International Journal of Lexicography* 20, no. 3 (2007): 313–27; D. Nkomo, "Dictionaries and Language Policy," in *The Routledge Handbook of Lexicography*, ed. P. A. Fuertes-Olivera, 152–65 (New York: Routledge, 2018).

[12] Samuel Johnson, *A Dictionary of the English Language* (London: J. and P. Knapton, 1755); Accademia della Crusca, *Vocabolario degli Accademici* (Florence: Accademia della Crusca, 1612); Académie française, *Dictionnaire de l'Académie française* (Paris: Académie française, 1867).

PAM: Yes, indeed. As far as Gabon is concerned, the Séminaire sur la Lexicographie Bantu held at the Centre International des Civilisations Bantu (CICIBA) in Libreville can be regarded as the beginning of modern day lexicographic training for Gabonese students and other persons interested in gaining insight into and practical experience of the planning, compilation, and management of a dictionary.

This seminar took place in 1997 at the invitation of Dr. V. Kukanda, director-general of CICIBA, and was attended by delegates from six African countries. Dr. F. J. Lombard and Dr. D. J. van Schalkwyk, at the time respectively senior coeditor and editor-in-chief of *Woordeboek van die Afrikaanse Taal* (WAT), conducted the lexicographic training in Libreville, Gabon.[13] In 1999, Gabonese students started to be trained in South Africa thanks to the agreement between the Bureau of the Woordeboek van die Afrikaanse Taal and the Groupe de Recherches en Langues et Cultures Orales.

They first completed training courses at the Bureau of the Woordeboek van die Afrikaanse Taal. Then they enrolled as postgraduate students in lexicography with Prof. R. H. Gouws from the Department of Afrikaans and Dutch at the University of Stellenbosch. Since 2003, there have been some developments in the field of lexicography in Gabon, such as the emergence of a new generation of Gabonese professional lexicographers. Lexicography is taught as a discipline at Omar Bongo University in particular, and upon completion of their degrees, students graduate each year from master's and PhD programs in lexicography and related fields.

So far and compared to the situation in South Africa, government bodies are not directly involved in dictionary production in Gabon. National Lexicography Units are not established yet, and mother-tongue education is not yet a reality in the country. However, since 2002 and quite surprisingly, a substantial number of bilingual dictionaries is already available, for a large number of languages, with a relatively large number of users. Gabonese lexicographers are spreading the "gospel" of lexicography in Central Africa. For example, both master's and PhD students in lexicography and related fields are offered lexicographic training each year in Marien Ngouabi University in Brazzaville, Congo.

IS: Let's talk about specialized lexicography, which, I understand, has also gained momentum in the continent, especially in South Africa, in response to the drive to ensure parity of use of official languages in the formal and powerful domains such as education and the judiciary.

PAM: Specialized lexicography has gained traction alongside terminology development in order to equip African languages for use in specialized academic and professional fields. While the National Lexicography Units in South Africa were meant to focus on general dictionaries, the Terminology Coordination Section in the Department of Sport, Arts, and Culture had to focus on terminology development, documentation, and publication as multilingual glossaries and dictionaries for schools, government departments, and other clientele.

---

[13] See Buro van die/Bureau of the Woordeboek van die Afrikaanse Taal 1997–1998, *Woordeboek van die Afrikaanse Taal* (Stellenbosch: Woordeboek van die Afrikaanse Taal, 1998), 5–6.

However, the National Lexicography Units, commercial publishers such as Oxford University Press, Cambridge University Press, Maskew Miller, and Longman, as well as universities, have also been compiling specialized dictionaries. As noted above, the specialized dictionary genre is hoping to support the needs of language speakers in different specialized fields. The African Languages Research Institute produced a few such dictionaries for fields such as linguistics, music, and health. However, one would suspect that specialized dictionaries played such a role to a greater effect in the promotion of Kiswahili in Tanzania in the light of the prominence given to specialized dictionaries on the website of the Institute for Kiswahili Studies.

IS: I find your depiction of Oxford and Cambridge as commercial publishers interesting, since strictly speaking they are academic presses, even though they function as commercial enterprises. At any rate, would you comment on the impact of technology on African language lexicography? In what way has it impacted the role of corpora and dictionary writing systems, as well as electronic dictionaries in African languages?

DN: There seemed to be excitement regarding the potential impact of technology on African language lexicography at the turn of the twenty-first century. As elsewhere in the world, the hope was that technology would expedite and enhance the accuracy of lexicographic processes such as explanation of meaning and selection of illustrative examples from corpora. There was great anticipation that dictionary projects would be completed quicker and that the overall quality and impact of dictionaries would improve significantly.

The ALLEX Project general-purpose dictionaries that we referred to above were corpus-aided. In South Africa, Prof. Danie Prinsloo of the University of Pretoria invested time in building corpora for all the official languages with hopes that the corpora would grow organically and become valuable resources for the National Lexicography Units. Similarly, Gilles-Maurice de Schryver invested in corpus work and the development of dictionary writing systems for African languages, with TshwaneLex (a software platform designed for creating and managing dictionaries) being his flagship accomplishment with David Joffe. However, the general scarcity of a variety of texts in African languages, which for a long time remained constrained to less formal oral communication, undermined the prospects of corpus-based lexicography. None of the African languages National Lexicography Units has a corpus for its work.

Even TswaneLex has not been optimized. It is clear that lexicography in African languages has some way to go before technology may be fully harnessed. African language lexicographers have some catch-up ground to cover before they can become active role players in e-lexicography. This includes improving the quality of print dictionaries and their use. There is hope that entities such as the South African Centre for Digital Language Resources (SADiLaR) will help make that game-changing breakthrough for lexicography in African languages.

IS: How about dictionaries in Afro-Asiatic languages?

PAM: The Afro-Asiatic language family is one of the major language families in the world, encompassing a wide range of languages spoken across North Africa, the Middle East, and parts of the Horn of Africa. This language family

African Languages 167

IS: includes several subgroups, such as Semitic (including Arabic and Hebrew), Cushitic, Berber, and Chadic (including Hausa).
IS: What are the key points highlighting the diversity of Hausa?
PAM: All languages change over time and space (the diachronic perspective and the geographic perspective). For instance, the geographic spread of Hausa across West Africa has resulted in the development of several dialects, each exhibiting variations in pronunciation, grammar, and vocabulary. Among these, the Hausa spoken in Kano State, Nigeria, is regarded as the standard dialect. This standard form not only serves as the norm for the written language but also acts as the principal dialect employed by radio and television announcers.

Differences in modern vocabulary between the Hausa spoken in Nigeria and that spoken in Niger can be attributed to their distinct colonial histories. The influence of colonial languages is evident, with the Nigerian variant of Hausa incorporating a significant number of English loanwords, while the version spoken in Niger features a greater influence of French borrowings. This linguistic divergence highlights the impact of historical and colonial factors on language development, leading to distinct variations in vocabulary and expressions within the broader Hausa language community. The standardization of the Kano State dialect and its prevalence in media further contribute to the shaping of linguistic norms within the Hausa-speaking region.

IS: Let's talk about dictionaries in Nilo-Saharan languages.
PAM: I shall start with some general considerations regarding the Nilo-Saharan language family. The Nilo-Saharan language family is a large and diverse group of languages spoken across a wide geographic area in North Africa and parts of East Africa. This language family includes a variety of languages with diverse linguistic features. Some of the major languages within the Nilo-Saharan group include: Kanuri, Nubian languages, Maasai, Kunama, Nuer, Dinka, Songhay, Teso, and Kanembu.

There is a variety of dictionaries available for different Nilo-Saharan languages. It's important to note that resources may vary in terms of scope, depth, and accessibility. Some dictionaries may focus on specific dialects or variations within a language. In addition to printed dictionaries (monolingual and multilingual lexicographic reference publications), online resources and language learning platforms do exist in major Nilo-Saharan languages such as Kanuri, Nuer, Dinka, etc.

In academic institutions, efforts are also made to revitalize and document endangered languages within the Nilo-Saharan language family, as was the case with the publication of *Ik Dictionary* by Bernd Heine.[14] Ik is an endangered language, and this study represents the first Ik-English/English-Ik dictionary. The grammar of Ik hasn't been satisfactorily described until this study.

IS: How about dictionaries in Niger-Congo languages?
PAM: We thought you'd never ask. Actually, we were waiting for you to ask us that! The Niger-Congo language family is one of the largest language families in the world, encompassing a vast number of languages spoken across West, Central, Southeast, and Southern Africa. Both printed dictionaries, digital

---

[14] Bernd Heine, *Ik Dictionary (Nilo-Saharan)* (Cologne: Rüdiger Köppe, 1999).

platforms, and online dictionaries are available in the Niger-Congo major languages: Swahili, Lingala, Yoruba, Igbo, Xhosa, Akan, Zulu, Wolof, Kikongo, Tswana, Sotho, Pedi, Ndebele, Tsonga, Swazi, Venda, and Fang.

All printed dictionaries in Niger-Congo languages help bridge the gap between these African languages and European languages (English, French, Portuguese, Spanish, German, and Dutch).

Monolingual dictionaries for Niger-Congo languages play a crucial role in documenting, preserving, and promoting these languages. They provide a comprehensive resource for speakers and learners, aiding in vocabulary expansion, understanding grammar, and preserving cultural nuances. While there might not be as many monolingual dictionaries for Niger-Congo languages compared to more widely spoken languages, in particular English, efforts have been made to compile dictionaries for various Niger-Congo languages. Finally, and as already said, comprehensive databases and resources for learners are being compiled for major Niger-Congo languages. They provide dynamic tools for ongoing language documentation. Here are a few examples:

The Kamusi Project is a nonprofit organization and digital initiative dedicated to building dictionaries and linguistic resources for languages around the world, with a particular focus on African languages. The term *kamusi* itself means "dictionary" in Swahili. The project aims to address the lack of comprehensive dictionaries for many languages, especially those spoken in Africa. It's worth noting that the Kamusi Project has evolved over the years, and its activities continue to contribute to the documentation and promotion of linguistic diversity. The project reflects the broader global effort to address the challenges faced by many languages in terms of documentation and preservation.

IS: What about creole languages?

PAM: Creole languages are stable natural languages that have developed from a mixture of different languages. They often emerge in communities where people with diverse linguistic backgrounds come into contact and need to communicate. Creole languages are characterized by a simplified grammar and vocabulary, and they typically emerge as a means of communication among people who do not share a common language.

Creole languages in Africa are mainly found in Cape Verde, Mauritius, and in São Tomé and Príncipe. In Cape Verde, a country located off the coast of West Africa, the linguistic landscape is shaped by a distinctive creole language known as Cape Verdean Creole or Kriolu (*Crioulo Cabo-verdiano*). Cape Verdean Creole is a significant part of the cultural identity and communication among the people of Cape Verde. As far as lexicographic products are concerned, the *Historical Dictionary of the Republic of Cape Verde* and the *Cape Verdean Dictionary* are of the utmost importance.[15] The fourth edition of the *Historical Dictionary of the Republic of Cape Verde* by Lobban and Khalil Saucier (1988) offers a comprehensive history of the country, linking the precolonial and colonial past with postcolonial events. The book entitled

---

[15] Richard A. Lobban and Paul Khalil Saucier, *Historical Dictionary of the Republic of Cape Verde* (Lanham, MD: Scarecrow Press, 2007); Manuel Da Luz Goncalves, *Cape Verdean Dictionary* (Boston, MA: Mili Mila, 2015).

Cape Verdean Dictionary by Manuel Da Luz Goncalves captures the authentic Cape Verdean culture, artifacts, and landscapes.

Mauritian Creole, also known as Morisyen, is spoken in Mauritius. It has influences from French, English, and various Indian languages. Lexicographic referential works regarding Morisyen include many translation dictionaries, such as *Morisyen-English-français/diksyoner kreol morisyen*, *Dictionnaire français-créole mauricien*, and *BABADADA, kreol morisien-Australian English, diksioner viziel*, as well as online resources such as the Mauritian Creole Pronunciation Dictionary by Forvo.[16]

In São Tomé and Príncipe, a small island nation in the Gulf of Guinea off the western equatorial coast of Central Africa, the primary language spoken is Portuguese. Portuguese is the official language and is used in government, education, and administration. However, there is also a local creole language known as Forro. Forro, sometimes spelled Forró, originated as a Portuguese-based creole and developed as a means of communication between Portuguese settlers, African slaves, and other groups during the colonial period.

As was the case for Morisyen, the Portuguese-lexified creole of São Tomé has given rise to a substantial number of bilingual dictionaries: *Dictionnaire étymologique des créoles portugais d'Afrique* and *Dicionário lexical Santome-Português* (2004), as well as *Dicionário livre santome/português*.[17]

IS: As we reach the conclusion of our conversation, I would like to contemplate what is known as "dictionary culture" (e.g. the way dictionaries affect daily life and vice versa). You have partially alluded to it earlier.

DN: The issue of dictionary culture represents a major challenge in African language communities, particularly when it comes to dictionaries in African languages. Speakers of African languages may appreciate the value of an English or French dictionary, believing that those dictionaries can empower them with respect to those languages that they acquire formally through school and need for both vertical and horizontal social mobility, but not so much with dictionaries in their languages. However, research indicates that societal dictionary culture is a challenge that needs to be addressed for the thankless efforts of African lexicographers to be appreciated and for their work to improve.[18] Lexicographers find it difficult to improve their work as they do not get sufficient feedback on the user-friendliness of their products which are

---

[16] Philip Baker and Vinesh Y. Hookoomsing, *Morisyen-English-français: Diksyoner kreol morisyen* (Paris: L'Harmattan, [1987] 2006); Karamchand Goswami Sewtohul, *Dictionnaire français-créole mauricien* (Mauritius: Pandit Ramlakhan Gossagne, 1997); Babadada, *BABADADA, kreol morisien-Australian English, diksioner viziel/Mauritian Creole-Australian English, Visual Dictionary* (Hamburg: Babadada, 2022); Forvo, Mauritian Creole Pronunciation Dictionary, https://forvo.com/languages/mfe/.

[17] Jean-Louis Rougé, *Dictionnair étymologique des créoles portugais d'Afrique* (Paris: Karthala, 2004); Gabriel Antunes de Araujo and Tjerk Hagemeijer, *Dicionário livre santome/português: Livlu-nglandji santome/putugêji* (São Paulo: Editora Hedra, 2013).

[18] See, for example, Rufus H. Gouws, Ulrich Heid, Wolfgang Schweickard, and Herbert E. Wiegand, eds. *Dictionaries: An International Encyclopedia of Lexicography* (Berlin: De Gruyter Mouton, 2013); and D. Nkomo, "Dictionary Culture in African Language Communities: Research, Development, Challenges and Prospects," *Lexicographica* 36 (2020): 11–37.

IS: not even integrated in everyday teaching and learning within African education systems. Dictionaries gather dust until they lose their shelf-life in bookshops and libraries. South African lexicographers have been trying to address this challenge through dictionary awareness campaigns for teachers and learners, as well as through the celebration of International Dictionary Day annually in October lately.

IS: What is the future of African lexicography? In general terms, is the young generation engaged with dictionaries the way previous ones have been?

PAM: The landscape of lexicography evolves over time due to various factors, including technological advancements, changes in educational approaches, and shifts in language use. The increasing use of technology and digital platforms may influence how dictionaries are accessed and used. Online dictionaries, mobile applications, and other digital resources could play a significant role in shaping the future of lexicography, making lexical information more accessible to the younger generation.

Indeed, the way people, especially the younger generation, engage with dictionaries has evolved over time. Traditional print dictionaries are not as commonly used today, thanks to the widespread availability of digital resources and the internet. The younger generation may not be as engaged with dictionaries in the traditional sense because changes in educational methods and curricula may impact their engagement with dictionaries. In the past two decades, in Gabon, South Africa, and elsewhere in Africa, dictionary-using skills are learned and taught from the first years of primary school.

With the advent of smartphones and the internet, young people have easy access to a plethora of online dictionaries and language resources. Online dictionaries provide quick definitions, pronunciation guides, and examples, making them more convenient for quick reference compared to flipping through pages of a print dictionary. Search engines like Google have become the go-to source for information. When young people encounter unfamiliar words, they often turn to search engines for instant definitions and context.

The search results often include dictionary entries along with other relevant information. Language learning apps and platforms often integrate dictionary features within their interfaces. These apps offer interactive and dynamic ways to learn new words, making the process more engaging and tailored to individual learning styles. The younger generation is often more drawn to multimedia content such as videos, podcasts, and interactive learning experiences. These formats provide a more engaging way to learn and understand language compared to traditional dictionary entries.

While the format of engagement may have changed, the need for understanding and expanding one's vocabulary remains crucial. Thus, training new generations of African lexicographers is a key aspect of the future of African lexicography.

Suggested Readings

Antunes de Araujo, Gabriel, and Tjerk Hagemeijer. *Dicionário livre santome/português: Livlu-nglandji santome/putugêji*. São Paulo: Editora Hedra, 2013.

Babadada. *BABADADA, kreol morisien-Australian English, diksioner viziel/Mauritian Creole-Australian English, Visual Dictionary*. Hamburg: Babadada, 2022.

Baker, Philip, and Vinesh Y. Hookoomsing. *Morisyen-English-français: Diksyoner kreol morisyen*. Paris: L'Harmattan, [1987] 2006.
Botha, Willem, and Etienne Botha. "Lexicographic Training at the Bureau of the Woordeboek van die Afrikaanse Taal." *Lexikos* 8, no. 1 (2012). https://doi.org/10.5788/8-1-958
Botha, Willem, Mavoungou Paul Achille, and Dion Nkomo, eds. *Festschrift RUFUS H. GOUWS*. Stellenbosch: SUN Press, 2013.
Buro van die Woordeboek van die Afrikaanse Taal 1997–1998. *Woordeboek van die Afrikaanse Taal*. Stellenbosch: Woordeboek van die Afrikaanse Taal, 1998.
Buro van die Woordeboek van die Afrikaanse Taal 1998–1999. *Woordeboek van die Afrikaanse Taal*. 1999. Stellenbosch: Woordeboek van die Afrikaanse Taal.
De Kind, Jasper, Gilles Maurice de Schryver, and Koen Bostoen. "Pushing Back the Origin of Bantu Lexicography: The Vocabularium Congense of 1652, 1928, 2012." *Lexikos* 22 (2012): 159–94.
De Schryver, Gilles Maurice. "Online Dictionaries on the Internet: An Overview for the African Languages." *Lexikos* 13 (2003): 1–20.
Forvo. Mauritian Creole Pronunciation Dictionary. https://forvo.com/languages/mfe/
Fuertes-Olivera, Pedro A., ed. *The Routledge Handbook of Lexicography*. London: Routledge, 2018.
Goncalves, Manuel Da Luz. *Cape Verdean Dictionary*. Boston, MA: Mili Mila, 2015.
Goswami Sewtohul, Karamchand. *Dictionnaire français-créole mauricien*. Mauritius: Pandit Ramlakhan Gossagne, 1997.
Gouws, Rufus H., Ulrich Heid, Wolfgang Schweickard, and Herbert E. Wiegand, eds. *Dictionaries: An International Encyclopedia of Lexicography*. Berlin: De Gruyter Mouton, 2013.
Heine, Bernd. *Ik Dictionary (Nilo-Saharan)*. Cologne: Rüdiger Köppe, 1999.
Heine, Bernd, and Derek Nurse. *African Languages: An Introduction*. Cambridge: Cambridge University Press, 2000.
Kaschula, Russell H., Pamela Maseko, and H. Ekkehard Wolff. *Multilingualism and Intercultural Communication: A South African Perspective*. Johannesburg: Wits University Press, 2017.
Koen, Bostoen, Ndonda Tshiyayi Odjas, and Gilles Maurice De Schryver. "On the Origin of the Royal Kongo Title Ngangula." *Africana Linguistica* 19 (2013): 53–83.
Lobban, Richard A., and Paul Khalil Saucier. *Historical Dictionary of the Republic of Cape Verde*. 4th ed. Lanham, MD: Scarecrow Press, 2007.
Major, Ayres Veríssimo/Ministério da Educação e Cultura. *Dicionário lexical santomé-português*. São Tomé: Dória Design, 2004.
Newman, Roxana Ma, and Paul Newman. "The Hausa Lexicographic Tradition." *Lexikos* 11, no. 1 (2001): 263–86.
Rougé, Jean-Louis. *Dictionnaire étymologique des créoles portugais d'Afrique*. Paris: Karthala, 2004.
Webb, Vic, and Kembo-Sure. *African Voices: An Introduction to the Languages and Linguistics of Africa*. Cape Town: Oxford University Press, 2000.

14 Nahuatl

John Sullivan

Nezahualcoyotl (1402–72), the warrior-philosopher-king who died fifty years before the arrival of Hernan Cortez and his Spanish soldiers to Tenochtitlan, in what is now Mexico City, used Nahuatl, the language of the Aztec Empire, to draft his poems about war, nature, and the afterlife. Through transcription into the Roman alphabet, these poems, a part of the largest corpus of older Indigenous language writing in America, have survived to this day. A spectrum of mutually intelligible Nahuatl variants are spoken today by approximately 1.5 million people in Mexico and by migrants in the United States. The Zacatecas Institute for Teaching and Research in Ethnology (IDIEZ), a Mexican nonprofit cofounded by John Sullivan in 2002 in association with the Universidad Autónoma de Zacatecas, provides scholarships to Indigenous Nahuatl-speaking college students and trains them to teach, conduct research, and carry out projects designed to revitalize their language and culture, in collaboration with "Western" scholars. This conversation explores the history of Nahuatl dictionaries, from the colonial period to the present.

***

ILAN STAVANS: How many Nahuatl speakers are there estimated to be today? What is the status of the contemporary Nahuatl they use?

JOHN SULLIVAN: According to the Mexican National Population and Housing Census of 2020, Nahuatl is spoken by around 1,650,000 people over the age of three.[1] However, the intergenerational transmission of the language is in rapid decline, and most speakers of Nahuatl also practice a bilingualism that is both unstable and transitional toward monolingualism in Spanish.

IS: What are the various types of classification of the language?

JS: At the time of the arrival of the Spaniards, there were many different variants of Nahuatl spoken in what is today Mexico and Central America. The Mexican National Institute of Indigenous

---

[1] Instituto Nacional de Estadística y Geografía, Censo de Población y Vivienda 2020, www.inegi.org.mx/programas/ccpv/2020/.

IS: Languages identifies thirty variants of Nahuatl spoken in the country today. There have been several attempts to propose a dialectological classification of Nahuatl variants, but none have attained general acceptance, and this is due in part to the fact that they do not consider both historical and modern data.

IS: How so?

JS: Comparing features of today's existing Nahuatl variants obviously allows a researcher to identify some criteria for classification. Limiting one's study to modern data is like trying to put together a jigsaw puzzle with less than half the pieces. We have 480 years of linguistic data for Nahuatl. Varietal features from the past can be identified, and their evolution can be traced to their present forms. Combining synchronic and diachronic perspectives would provide a stronger foundation for the classification of Nahuatl and its variants.

IS: Nahuatl was the default langue of the Aztec Empire. To what degree did it absorb elements of other Indigenous languages?

JS: As with all languages in contact, the different variants of Nahuatl have assimilated words and, to a lesser degree, grammatical structures and sounds from the other individual Indigenous languages that are in their geographical proximity. Nahuatl and Spanish have also borrowed words, morphemes, grammatical structures, and sounds from each other. People are familiar with common Nahuatl loans in Spanish, such as *chilli* and *tomatl*, for example; but the grammatical influence of Nahuatl on Spanish, especially in regions that have a high population of Nahuatl speakers, often goes unnoticed. In the Huasteca and other regions of Mexico, people say *dejé comido*, meaning "I ate before I left," which is a grammatical calque of a Nahuatl auxiliary verb construction.

IS: Have any of these borrowings, individually and in groups, been studied? Is there something similar to Spanglish between Nahuatl and Spanish, that is, a hybrid language that borrows from both, yet has its own distinct characteristics? I've heard some people refer to it as *Nahuañol*.

JS: I'm not familiar with studies on how Indigenous languages have influenced the development of regional varieties of Mexican Spanish. But yes, there is a lot of mixing of Nahuatl and Spanish in middle-aged speakers and the younger generations, although I don't know if it could be considered stable enough to be called a hybrid language.

IS: When did the first attempt take place to make a dictionary of Nahuatl? Who was behind it?

JS: The first attempt to create a Nahuatl dictionary was probably the *Vocabulario trilingüe*, which, as its name suggests, is actually a Nahuatl-Spanish-Latin vocabulary, based on Antonio de Nebrija's Castilian-Latin dictionary, and prepared by an unknown author or authors sometime between 1540 and 1570.[2] The manuscript is catalogued as MS 1478 in the Ayer Collection at the Newberry Library in Chicago. All of the many Nahuatl grammars and scarcer Nahuatl vocabularies and dictionaries produced during the colonial period were sanctioned and written within the institution of the Catholic

---

[2] *Vocabulario trilingüe*, ca. 1540–1570, MS 1478 in the Ayer Collection, Newberry Library, Chicago; Elio Antonio de Nebrija, *Vocabulario latino-español* (Salamanca, 1492); *Vocabulario español-latino* (Salamanca, 1495?).

IS: Church in order to facilitate the work of the priests who were Christianizing Nahuas, that is, ministering to the newly Christianized populations.

IS: Were there multiple editions of the *Vocabulario trilingüe*? And the Nahual vocabularies you refer to, how many were published? Were any of them done by Indigenous lexicographers? Was their readership different than that of the *Vocabulario trilingüe*? Is it possible to reflect on the impact they had on Nahuatl speakers?

JS: While the *Vocabulario trilingüe* is mentioned by two writers during the colonial period, very little is known about its circulation or the number of copies that were made. The Nahuatl dictionaries and vocabularies produced at this time were designed for the consumption of priests, although Pedro de Arenas' *Vocabulario manual de las lenguas castellana y mexicana* (1611) went through eleven editions, so one could assume that it might have also been used by non-Indigenous people who needed to learn Nahuatl for personal or commercial reasons.[3] Except for Faustino Chimalpopocatl Galicia, who published his *Silabario de idioma mexicano* in 1849, Nahuatl dictionaries published by Indigenous authors are a very recent phenomenon: they don't appear until well into the second half of the twentieth century.[4] Reflecting on the impact that Nahuatl dictionaries have had on speakers of Nahuatl for the past five centuries is a very short exercise. What possible benefit could a dictionary or a vocabulary, whose only Nahuatl content is its headwords, offer a speaker of Nahuatl?

IS: What happened with dictionaries of Nahuatl during the so-called period of independence in Mexico, in the nineteenth century?

JS: There were three Nahuatl dictionaries published in the nineteenth century: Bernardino Biondelli's *Glossarium Azteco-Latinum et Latino-Aztecum* (1869), Rémi Siméon's *Dictionnaire de la langue nahuatl* (1885), and Cecilio A. Robelo's *Vocabulario comparativo castellano y náhuatl* (1888).[5] Faustino Chimalpopocatl Galicia published the *Silabario de idioma mexicano* in 1849, but it was a pedagogical work, combining a pronunciation guide, a Nahuatl-Spanish glossary, and readings.

IS: Talk to me about each of them. Who was behind it? How rigorous were they? In what way did their agenda – linguistic, ideological – differ from the lexicons produced during the colonial period? In other words, were they tools of a new kind of nationalism connected with independent Mexico?

JS: Rémi Siméon (1822–90) was a French ethnographer, linguist, and philologist. His Nahuatl-French dictionary was based mostly on Alonso de Molina's Nahuatl-Spanish dictionary,[6] with some additions from the colonial grammars

---

[3] Pedro de Arenas, *Vocabulario manual de las lenguas castellana y mexicana* (Mexico: Henrico Martínez, 1611).

[4] Faustino Chimalpopocatl Galicia, *Silabario de idioma mexicano* (Mexico: Imprenta de las Escalerías, 1849), www.cervantesvirtual.com/obra/silabario-de-idioma-mexicano/.

[5] Bernardino Biondelli, *Glossarium Azteco-Latinem et Latin-Aztecum* (Milan: Valentier et Mues, 1869), https://archive.org/details/glossariumazteco00blon/mode/2up; Rémi Siméon, *Dictionnaire de la langue nahuatl ou mexicaine* (Paris: Imprimérie Nationale, 1885); Cecilio A. Robelo, *Vocabulario comparativo castellano y náhuatl* (Cuernavaca: Luis G. Miranda, 1888).

[6] Alonso de Molina, *Vocabulario en lengua castellana y mexicana y mexicana y castellana* (1555–1571), Colección "Biblioteca Porrúa" 44 (Mexico: Porrúa, 1977).

of Horacio Carochi, Andrés de Olmos, and Francisco Xavier Clavijero.[7] He classifies headwords using the basic lexical categories of Western European languages, such as noun, verb, pronoun, adjective, adverb, verbal adjective, deverbal noun, participle, etc. He uses Molina's system of inflectional prefixes to specify the transitivity of verbs and whether they can take human and/or nonhuman subjects, as well as citing the preterite form to show verb class. And whereas Molina includes phrases as separate headwords, Siméon includes them under a single entry, the stem of their nominal or verbal component. He also identifies the components of compounds.

As for Bernardino Biondelli (1804–86), he was an Italian academic whose research focused on dialectology, Indo-European studies, and both the archeology and languages of pre-Columbian civilizations. His Nahuatl-Latin dictionary has basically the same lexicographical characteristics as Siméon's. These two works are in line with the European trend of the time to study language as a lay, scientific endeavor, departing from the previous model in which American languages were documented to aid in the preparation of Catholic missionaries.

Then there is Cecilio A. Robelo (1839–1916), a Mexican magistrate, politician, historian, archeologist, and philologist, who studied Nahuatl language and culture. He is also the author of the influential *Diccionario de aztequismos* (1904).[8] Robelo wrote his dictionary in order to answer a "philological questionnaire formulated by the General Office of Statistics of the Mexican Republic." It consists of 255 numbered Spanish headwords, not in alphabetical order, suggesting that the list was supplied by the Office of Statistics. The entries begin with one or more Nahuatl equivalents of the Spanish headword, followed by a narrated explanation of the word's composition, inflectional prefix usage, meaning nuances, pertinent grammatical notes, and cross references to other headwords. In this sense, Robelo's work resembles an encyclopedia more than a dictionary and represents a departure from the religious oriented texts of the colonial period, completely in line with the European scientific focus of Siméon and Biondelli.

There is also Faustino Chimalpopocatl Galicia (died 1877), a native speaker of Nahuatl who worked as a lawyer, translator, and administrator. The glossary of his *Silabario* was divided into sections that grouped words according to their number of syllables, and each headword was divided into syllables with dashes. The work was written as an aid for non-native speakers who wished to learn to speak Nahuatl.

---

[7] Horacio Carochi, S. J. *Grammar of the Mexican Language with an Explanation of Its Adverbs* (1645), trans. and ed. with commentary by James Lockhart, UCLA Latin American Studies Volume 89 (Stanford, CA: Stanford University Press, 2001); Andrés de Olmos, *Arte de la lengua mexicana* (1547), ed. Heréndira Téllez Nieto (Madrid: Iberoamericana, 2022); Francisco Xavier Clavijero, *Reglas de la lengua mexicana con un vocabulario* (ca. 1770–87), introduction and notes by Arthur J. O. Anderson, Instituto de Investigaciones Históricas (Mexico: Universidad Nacional Autónoma de México, 1974).

[8] Cecilio Agustín Robelo, *Diccionario de aztequismos o sea catálogo de las palabras del idioma nahuatl, azteca o mexicano introducidas al idioma castellano bajo diversas formas* (Cuernavaca: Printed by the author, 1904).

As a pedagogical tool that did not include the lexicographical innovations found in the works of Siméon, Biondelli, and Robelo, the *Silabario* is best classified within the colonial model of the sixteenth through eighteenth centuries, especially since Chimalpopocatl resisted the liberal project for the removal of religious instruction from the educational system. The *Silabario* cannot, therefore, be considered a tool of the national project of independent Mexico, which by the way, did not contemplate Indigenous languages or peoples as part of the new nation.

Chimalpopocatl, as a lawyer, defended Indigenous people and communities who were impacted by the Ley Lerdo, an 1856 law designed to transfer eclesiastical and Indigenous corporately owned property into private hands, and he favored the incorporation of Indigenous languages in the school curriculum, albeit for religious instruction. Ignacio Manuel Altamirano was the only other Mexican intellectual of the nineteenth century who actively campaigned for the use of Indigenous languages in the educational system and for the inclusion of Indigenous people in the national project.

Finally, colonial and nineteenth-century lexicography share a fundamental characteristic: dictionaries were bilingual; in other words, they were not designed for the consumption of Indigenous people.

IS: What about modern Nahuatl dictionaries? Specifically, I'm thinking of the twentieth century. In what way have they been shaped by recent theoretical and technological advances in the field of lexicography?

JS: The production of Nahuatl dictionaries and vocabularies, as well as glossaries contained in descriptive and pedagogical grammars, has increased tremendously since the twentieth century.

The majority have not kept pace with advancements in our understanding of Nahuatl grammar. It is common to see headwords: (1) that include inflectional affixes; and (2) that are either not labeled regarding their lexical category or employ Western European categories (adjective, adverb, preposition, conjunction, pronoun, etc.) that do not apply to Nahuatl. There has never been a standard Nahuatl orthography; in fact, writing systems have proliferated. Most of them are haphazardly applied to texts, so it is not uncommon to see a word spelled in multiple ways in a single work.

The most complete and rigorous dictionary published in the twentieth century is Frances Karttunen's *An Analytical Dictionary of Nahuatl* ([1983] 1992).[9] There is a very heartening trend consisting of local Indigenous academics who document their variants of Nahuatl in the form of published vocabularies, although their circulation is limited. All are bilingual; hopefully these works will begin to be produced monolingually. The most important innovation of this period is the online, searchable database.

When I began teaching Nahuatl in Mexico in the 1990s, my students and I would use hard copies of Molina's and Karttunen's dictionaries, and this went on for many years; but, as we know, books are now falling out of use. Today, with very few exceptions, my students use one of two online databases to look

---

[9] Frances Karttunen, *An Analytical Dictionary of Nahuatl* (Norman: University of Oklahoma Press, [1983] 1992).

up words in Nahuatl: the *Online Nahuatl Dictionary*, created by Stephanie Wood at the University of Oregon, and the *Gran Diccionario Nahuatl*, produced by academics at the Universidad Nacional Autónoma de México.[10]

When one looks up a word in these online databases, one is provided with definitions, and in the case of the Oregon dictionary, grammatical information and contextualized citations from multiple sources, each with its associated metadata. The *Compendio Encíclopédico Náhuatl (CEN)* contains a text editor, a morpheme analyzer, and a collection of pictographic dictionaries, as well as access to the *Gran Diccionario Nahuatl*.[11] It is also available in an app from the Apple Store and Google Play.

The efficiency of their interfaces, which hopefully will be available in Nahuatl at some point, the breadth of their sources, and the power of their analytic and synthetic capabilities should only increase with time. These are not dictionaries: they are valuable repositories of information for the teaching and study of Nahuatl. With the exception of *Tlahtolxitlauhcayotl*, today's native speakers still lack an authority, in print or digital form, that they can consult in their own language, when they have doubts regarding the spelling, lexical category, inflectional prefixes (subject, possessor, object, tenses, plural form), derived forms, definitions, contextual use, and morphological analysis of a word.[12]

There is no reason why an app cannot combine the quick reference function of a dictionary with access to broader information provided by the three online databases mentioned above. This would be the dictionary of the future.

IS: Like other Indigenous languages in Latin America, Nahuatl has been looked down on by modernity. What is behind its survival?

JS: Nahuatl was not looked down on by the Spanish Empire. Its pre-Hispanic role as a lingua franca was strengthened after the conquest when it was used both orally and in its newly alphabetized form by the Catholic Church as a general tool of Christianization and by the viceregal apparatus, which included local, traditional Indigenous governments, to record city council minutes, land sales and disputes, criminal proceedings, and petitions.

As the Indigenous population slowly became more Hispanicized, spheres for the public use of Nahuatl began to shrink. Its use today is largely confined to the family and certain traditional aspects of community life. The single most important factor in the decline of Nahuatl language and culture is the creation of the modern Mexican state after the Mexican Revolution and its policy of ethnocide implemented by public education, literature, and the media. Nahuatl has survived only in geographically isolated regions. As roads, schools, and cellphone towers are built, the shift to Spanish accelerates.

IS: What is in your view the most important dictionary of Nahuatl?

---

[10] Stephanie Wood, ed., *Online Nahuatl Dictionary* (Wired Humanities Projects, College of Education, University of Oregon, 2000), https://nahuatl.wired-humanities.org; *Gran Diccionario Náhuatl* (online), Universidad Nacional Autónoma de México (Ciudad Universitaria, México D.F.), www.gdn.unam.mx.

[11] CEN, Compendio Enciclopédico Náhuatl, https://cen.sup-infor.com/.

[12] Sullivan et al., *Tlahtolxitlauhcayotl: Chicontepec, Veracruz*, Totlahtol Series (Warsaw: IDIEZ/ University of Warsaw, 2016).

JS: Molina's *Vocabulario en la lengua castellana y mexicana* and *Vocabulario en la lengua mexicana y castellana* (1555–71). Alonso de Molina was an infant when he arrived in Mexico in 1522 with his parents from Spain. He grew up playing with Indigenous children and became fluent in Nahuatl. After becoming a Franciscan, he prepared a grammar and doctrinal materials in Nahuatl, but his most important contribution was two versions of a Spanish-Nahuatl dictionary (1555, 1571), and a Nahuatl-Spanish dictionary (1571), which continue to be useful to scholars of older and modern variants of Nahuatl today. He set the standard for defining Nahuatl dictionary entries by stripping nominal, verbal, and relation words to their stems. He created a system using inflectional prefixes to indicate human subjects, possession, and transitivity; and he used the preterite to indicate verb classes. There are two more major works of Nahuatl lexicography: Fran Karttunen's *An Analytical Dictionary of Nahuatl* and Joe Campbell's lexical database, including all words in Molina's dictionaries and Sahagún's *Florentine Codex*.[13]

IS: I'm interested in Karttunen's analytical dictionary. I believe she taught at Texas and the dictionary was published by the University of Oklahoma Press.

JS: Fran published *An Analytical Dictionary of Nahuatl* in 1983 through the University of Texas Press, and it was subsequently published in 1992 by the University of Oklahoma Press. After Molina's work, this is the most important dictionary of Nahuatl ever written, and along with Molina, it is a valuable tool, even today, for scholars of modern variants of Nahuatl.

Each entry begins with a bold, capitalized headword, in which vowel length is marked with a macron, and glottal stops or aspirations are represented with the letter "H." Absolutive suffixes are separated from noun stems with a dash, and if a stem-initial or final vowel is lost in combining or possessed forms, it is enclosed in parentheses. Verb classes are inferred by enclosing a final vowel in parentheses (class 2) and by specifying the preterite form in capital letters (class 4). Capital letters are also used to specify all irregular forms and stem-altered forms, as well as the constituents of compounds and the origin of derived forms, both of which can be found in the form of their own entry, elsewhere in the dictionary.

Definitions are in English and Spanish, with labels for those corresponding to transitive and/or reflexive forms, and a definition's source is identified with a code. There is abundant commentary, including where sources provide

---

[13] R. Joe. Campbell, *A Comprehensive Dictionary of Classical Nahuatl: Combining original and standardized spellings along with morphological analyses for all lexical items from Molina's three dictionaries and from Sahagun's Florentine Codex* (in preparation); Bernardino de Sahagún, Antonio Valeriano, Alonso Vegerano, Martín Jacobita, Pedro de San Buenaventura, Diego de Grado, Bonifacio Maximiliano, Mateo Severino, et al., *Historia general de las cosas de Nueva España* (Florentine Codex), Ms. Mediceo Palatino 218–20, Biblioteca Medicea Laurenziana, Florence, MiBACT, 1577; Charles E. Dibble and Arthur J. O. Anderson, eds., *The Florentine Codex: General History of the Things of New Spain, In Thirteen Parts* (Santa Fe: School of American Research and the University of Utah, 1950–69); Digital Florentine Codex/Códice Florentino Digital, edited by Kim N. Richter, Alicia Maria Houtrouw, Kevin Terraciano, Jeanette Favrot Peterson, Diana Magaloni, and Lisa Sousa (Los Angeles: Getty Research Institute, 2023), https://florentinecodex.getty.edu.

contradictory information. The Nahuatl orthography used in the dictionary is a modified version of the traditional, semi-standardized spelling system found in Carochi's seventeenth-century grammar.

I like to call it the ACK orthography, because it was developed simultaneously by Richard Andrews, R. Joe Campbell, and Frances Karttunen. Alphabetization groups headwords together that begin with the Nahuatl digraphs ch-, cu-, hu-, tl-, and tz-. Finally, it is important to mention that of the dictionary's ten sources, three are from modern variants of Nahuatl. On the one hand, this was necessary to complement the scarce information on vowel length and the glottal stop or aspiration, contained in older sources; on the other hand, Frances Karttunen is making an important statement with regard to Nahuatl studies.

IS: How about Campbell's lexical database: What sort of impact has it had?

JS: Joe Campbell's database has not yet been made available to the public, and for this reason its impact has been minimal. I have two extracts, one in the form of a 4,350 page-long pdf, with Nahuatl headwords and definitions in English and Spanish, which is my go-to "dictionary" when working with classical Nahuatl manuscripts and published works, as well as a list of the approximately 1,500 morphemes that form the building blocks of the language.

Fifty years ago, Joe began digitalizing the three Molina dictionaries and the entire Florentine Codex, *on punch-cards*. He added standardized spelling – the ACK system I mentioned before – and supplied notation for vowel length and the glottal stop or aspiration that was missing from the original sources. He proceeded to parse *every single word* in the corpus into its constituent morphemes, using codes that he created for this purpose. He has also identified and corrected Molina's and Sahagún's mistakes! He continues to process the corpus today, identifying and correcting errors in his own analysis, and working on what he calls "hard things," morphological problems in the data that he has not yet been able to resolve. He uses SPITBOL, an evolution of SNOBOL, a programming language created at Bell Laboratories in the 1960s.

When the database is made available to the public, researchers will be able to make queries for words and strings of words, in isolation or in context, as well as morphemes and strings of morphemes, in progressive or regressive order. And I'm sure that some enterprising scholar, either human or artificial, will be happy to mark the corpus for syntax. With this database, we may be able to answer some very interesting questions.

Do each of Nahuatl's multiple verbalizing suffixes have preferences for certain kinds of stems? Is there an unmarked sentence order for verb, subject, and object? We know that *cihuatl* means "woman." But what will we learn about its full semantic field when we can consider all its attestations in a large corpus, including its adjectival function as a compound, its adverbial use as an incorporated noun, and its derived forms? And, with a little tweaking, just as with the online databases I've talked about previously, it can become a very useful digital Nahuatl dictionary, perhaps the most important dictionary and research tool for the study of Nahuatl ever created.

IS: The dictionary you co-edited, *Tlahtolxitlauhcayotl*, published by the Instituto de Docencia e Investigación Etnológica de Zacatecas and Warsaw University, is monolingual. What is the history that led to it?

JS: I began to work as a professor at the Universidad Autónoma de Zacatecas in 1993, and toward the end of the decade, I became aware that there were native speakers of Nahuatl from the Huasteca studying there as undergraduates. So, I used my stipend from the Mexican National System of Researchers (Sistema Nacional de Investigadores, SNI) to pay some of them to teach me modern conversational Nahuatl. I had heard that what was left of modern Nahuatl variants was a diminished form of the rich and complex language encountered by the Spaniards in the sixteenth century.

Soon it became apparent that this was a lie or, at best, a statement born out of ignorance. I had already done some introductory work in learning how to read older Nahuatl manuscripts with James Lockhart, and I immediately recognized, (1) that these young people, all children of subsistence farmers from isolated towns and villages in the Huasteca, whose primary and secondary education had been only in Spanish, were capable of carrying out high-level thinking and eloquently expressing themselves in Nahuatl, and (2) the Nahuatl that they spoke was as lexically rich and grammatically complex as anything I had been reading with Lockhart.

While I was taking lessons with them, I would work with them in Spanish on some of these older manuscripts, but as I became more fluent it hit me that every minute I spent working with them in Spanish was a minute that I was engaging in ethnocide. At that moment, our work became exclusively monolingual, and I realized that if we were going to conduct high-level academic work in Nahuatl we would need to generate monolingual reference materials: a dictionary, a grammar, and an encyclopedia, for starters. And so, we began to work collectively on the dictionary and continued to do so until it was published sixteen years later.[14]

You refer to us as coeditors of the dictionary, but that's not quite right. Dictionaries in Western languages are basically compilations, some would say "thefts," of material created by others in the past. In our case, there were no other monolingual dictionaries of Nahuatl to extract material or formatting from. Each one of the 12,000 or so entries, including headwords, grammatical categories, definitions, example sentences, derived forms, and morphological analyses were generated and written by the nine coauthors who participated in the project.

IS: What entities are in charge of sponsoring Nahuatl dictionaries? Are they serving the proper role?

JS: Dictionaries and vocabularies of different modern variants of Nahuatl are routinely published by the Mexican National Institute of Indigenous Languages, Mexican universities, state and local cultural institutions, as well as foreign universities and funding agencies. Few undergo a serious process of editorial revision, but this is because scholars who could carry out this work are scarce.

And if their role is to document Nahuatl lexicon for non-Indigenous consumers and institutions, then they are definitely fulfilling it. I should also mention that the Summer Institute of Linguistics, an international, evangelical Christian organization, produces an enormous amount of quality language documentation, including dictionaries and grammars, as well as bible translations in a number of modern variants of Nahuatl.

---

[14] Sullivan et al., *Tlahtolxitlauhcayotl*.

IS: You talk about non-Indigenous consumers. It strikes me, then, that Nahuatl dictionaries have a "tourist" approach to the culture, by which I mean their target audience is outsiders. To myself, I imagine a dystopian landscape in which English-language dictionaries were produced only for foreigners.

JS: This is exactly what I ask my students. Imagine that the only dictionary available to you as a native speaker is one whose instructions, grammatical information and definitions are all in another language. What would this teach you about the value of your language, about its capacity for use in critical and creative thinking? And then I pose another issue to them.

What if a think tank received a very large amount of money to work on a major problem: war, hunger, gun violence, sexism, racism, etc.? Would that think tank hire 100 clones of the same brain (people who speak the same language and are from the same culture, people who have studied at the same prestigious schools, people of the same gender, etc.) to work on solutions to that problem? Or would they endeavor to hire the most diverse group of people possible, in order to attack the problem from a multiplicity of perspectives?

A language provides its speakers with a unique set of tools for critical and creative thinking that can be used to solve the problems that affect us all. Stifling the academic development of minority languages just doesn't make sense. Monolingual reference materials are an investment in the future of humanity.

The academy is complicit in this problem in two ways. First, linguistics encourages academics to work for a short period of time on multiple languages, in order to gain insight into language in general. And after all, no one who works long enough on a single language to become fluent and integrate themself into the community is going to get tenure. Second, how many universities in the United States and Mexico hire speakers of Indigenous languages to carry out monolingual teaching and research activities? That's a rhetorical question. So yes, dystopia and tourists.

IS: What is the role of bilingual Nahuatl dictionaries?

JS: Bilingual Nahuatl dictionaries and vocabularies do document Nahuatl lexicon, but this is not their most important function. Western culture is founded on the idea that European languages are the only valid vehicle for conducting educational activities and research endeavors; in other words, for generating, recording, and transmitting knowledge.

It is no accident that in the last 500 years, only two monolingual dictionaries of Indigenous languages, including ours, have been produced anywhere in the Americas. A bilingual dictionary teaches a native speaker of an Indigenous language that meaning only exists outside of their language. And it teaches speakers of European languages that all languages and cultures of the world and the knowledge that they contain, are reducible to and accessible through European languages. In this situation, everyone loses.

Suggested Readings

Arenas, Pedro de. *Vocabulario manual de las lenguas castellana y mexicana*. Mexico City: Universidad Nacional Autónoma de México, [1611] 1982.

Biondelli, Bernardino. *Glossarium Azteco-Latinem et Latin-Aztecum*. Milan: Valentier et Mues, 1869. https://archive.org/details/glossariumazteco00blon/mode/2up

Brewer, Forest, and Jean G. Brewer. *Vocabulario mexicano de Tetelcingo, Morelos*. Mexico City: Summer Institute of Linguistics, 1971.

Campbell, R. Joe. *A Morphological Dictionary of Classical Nahuatl: A Morpheme Index to the Vocabulario en lengua mexicana y castellana of Fray Alonso de Molina*. Madison, WI: Hispanic Seminary of Medieval Studies, 1985.

Carochi, S. J. Horacio. *Grammar of the Mexican Language with an Explanation of Its Adverbs* (1645). Translated and edited with commentary by James Lockhart. UCLA Latin American Studies Volume 89. Stanford, CA: Stanford University Press, 2001.

Compendio Enciclopédico Náhuatl (CEN). SUP-INFOR. Ediciones sur supports informatiques. https://cen.sup-infor.com

Chimalpopocatl Galicia, Faustino. *Silabario de idioma mexicano*. Mexico City: Imprenta de las Escalerías, 1849. www.cervantesvirtual.com/obra/silabario-de-idioma-mexicano/

Clavijero, Francisco Xavier. *Reglas de la lengua mexicana con un vocabulario*. Introduction and notes by Arthur J. O. Anderson. Instituto de Investigaciones Históricas. Mexico City: Universidad Nacional Autónoma de México [(ca. 1770–87)] 1974.

Frawley, William, Kenneth C. Hill and Pamela Munro, eds. *Making Dictionaries: Preserving Indigenous Languages of the Americas*. Berkeley: University of California Press, 2002.

Gran Diccionario Náhuatl. Mexico City: Universidad Nacional Autónoma de México, 2012. http://www.gdn.unam.mx.

Hernández Beatriz, Marcelino. *Vocabulario náhuatl-español de la huasteca hidalguense*. Cruzhica: Edición Xochipouali, 2001

Karttunen, Frances. *An Analytical Dictionary of Nahuatl*. Norman: University of Oklahoma Press, [1983] 1992.

Key, Harold, and Mary Ritchie de Key. *Vocabulario de la Sierra de Zacapoaxtla*. Mexico City: Summer Institute of Linguistics, 1953.

Matías Alonso, Marcos y Constantino Medina Lima. *Vocabulario náhuatl-español de Acatlán, Guerrero*. 2nd ed. Mexico City: Centro de Estudios Superiores en Antropología Social/Plaza y Valdés, 1996.

Molina, Alonso de. *Vocabulario en lengua castellana y mexicana y mexicana y castellana*. Colección "Biblioteca Porrúa" 44. Mexico: Porrúa, [(1555–71)] 1977.

Olmos, Andrés de. *Arte de la lengua mexicana*. Edited by Heréndira Téllez Nieto. Madrid: Iberoamericana, [(1547)] 2022.

Ramírez, Cleofas de Alejandro, and Karen Dakin. *Vocabulario náhuatl de Xalitla, Guerrero*. Cuadernos de la Casa Chata 25. Mexico City: Centro de Investigaciones Superiores del Instituto Nacional de Antropología e Historia, 1979.

Robelo, Cecilio A. *Vocabulario comparativo castellano y náhuatl*. Cuernavaca: Luis G. Miranda, impresor, 1888.

Siméon, Rémi. *Diccionario de la lengua náhuatl o mexicana* (1885). Mexico City: Siglo XXI, 1993.

Sullivan, John, Eduardo de la Cruz Cruz, Abelardo de la Cruz de la Cruz, Delfina de la Cruz de la Cruz, Victoriano de la Cruz Cruz, Sabina Cruz de la Cruz, Ofelia Cruz Morales, Catalina Cruz de la Cruz and Manuel de la Cruz Cruz. *Tlahtolxitlauhcayotl: Chicontepec, Veracruz*. Totlahtol Series. Warsaw: IDIEZ/University of Warsaw, 2016.

Vocabulario trilingüe. MS 1478 in the Ayer Collection, Newberry Library, Chicago, ca. 1540–70.

Wolgemuth Walters, Joseph Carl, Marilyn Minter de Wolgemuth, Plácido Hernández Pérez, Esteban Pérez Ramírez, Christopher Hurst Upton. *Diccionario náhuatl de los municipios de Mecayapan y Tatahuicapan de Juárez, Veracruz*, 2nd ed., digital. Mexico City: Instituto Lingüístico de Verano, 2002. https://www.sil.org/system/files/reapdata/85/18/08/8518081951523477324992367140025803 6256/nhx_diccionario_ed2.pdf

Wood, Stephanie, ed. *Online Nahuatl Dictionary*. Wired Humanities Projects, College of Education, University of Oregon, 2000. https://nahuatl.wired-humanities.org

15 Yiddish

Gitl Schaechter-Viswanath

In the constellation of Jewish languages (from Judeo-Spanish, aka Ladino, and Judeo-Portuguese to Hybriya, aka Judeo-Arabic, and Judeo-Persian, and not counting biblical and Modern Hebrew), Yiddish, or Judeo-German, is unquestionably the most popular. Its development over a millenium is attested, among other things, by the variety of dictionaries it has produced, the earliest one dating back to the end of the sixteenth century. For centuries, Yiddish flourished in the Pale of Settlement, the region in Central and Eastern Europe where the Russian Czar allowed Jewish settlements, until the Holocaust, when 6 million Jews were murdered by the Nazis, many of them Yiddish speakers. Decades before, Yiddish followed the route of immigration to Israel, the United States, Argentina, Australia, Canada, South Africa, Mexico, and elsewhere, where modern dictionaries continued to appear before and after World War II. Factoring that Yiddish is considered an "endangered" language, the conversation concentrates on the most recent lexicon, *Comprehensive English-Yiddish Dictionary*.[1]

***

ILAN STAVANS: As far as I know, the oldest Yiddish dictionary was a multilingual endeavor: Yiddish, Hebrew, German, and Latin. It was compiled in 1592, that is, about fifty years before Glückel of Hameln – meaning Hamburg, Germany – was born. We no longer produce lexicons of such ambition. The first Yiddish-English dictionary was made in 1891 by Alexander Harkavy,[2] who also translated *Don Quixote* into Yiddish. He eventually produced a Yiddish-English-Hebrew lexicon.[3] Harkavy's endeavor was a companion to the Yiddish-speaking

---

[1] Gitl Schaechter-Viswanath with Paul Glasser, eds., *Comprehensive English-Yiddish Dictionary* (Bloomington: Indiana University Press, 2016; revised 2nd ed., 2021).

[2] Alexander Harkavy, ed., *Complete English-Jewish Dictionary* (New York: Hebrew Publishing Company, 1891).

[3] Alexander Harkavy, ed., *Yidish-English-Hebreisher Verterbukh* (New York: Hebrew Publishing Company, 1928).

immigrants from the Pale into America. I'm interested in your view as a Yiddish lexicographer. How does a dictionary come to be?

GITL SCHAECHTER-VISWANATH: Every lexicographer could probably give you a different story of how his/her dictionary came to be. But the bottom line – *di untershte shure* – is that a dictionary comes into being because someone sees a need for a different kind of lexicon. Perhaps a paucity of content in existing dictionaries. Previous dictionaries may include outdated words or expressions, either linguistically, culturally, or sociologically. Or new words have come into the language – either through necessary neologisms that address new concepts, or borrowings from surrounding languages. Or a language has been mostly an oral language (e.g. oral Indigenous tongues which are in danger of vanishing), and the dictionary is intended to preserve the language in writing for future generations.

As you mentioned, the first Yiddish multilingual lexicon was published more than 400 years ago. But the first English-Yiddish dictionary, by Alexander Harkavy, wasn't published until 1891, after the historic waves of Jewish immigration had begun from Europe to America in the later nineteenth century. Prior to those mass migrations, there really was no need for an English-Yiddish lexicon, as there was no significant community or society in which such a dictionary would play a needed role. By 1924, however, approximately 2.5 million (mostly Yiddish-speaking) Jews had entered the United States. In order to acculturate them to the new English-speaking world – where they would need to find a home, a job, perhaps learn a different trade from the one they practiced back in the "old country," and become a productive member of society – the Harkavy dictionary was reprinted a number of times, and republished in several editions, the last one in 1928. Forty years (and a Holocaust) were to pass before a new English-Yiddish dictionary was published: Uriel Weinreich's *Modern English-Yiddish Yiddish-English Dictionary* (1968).[4] And nearly fifty years before the next one was published. In the case of the *Comprehensive English-Yiddish Dictionary* (*CEYD*), it was a decades-long and intergenerational effort. But we can discuss that a bit later.

Incidentally, the Yiddish language is unusual in that it is not a state language, although in 1999 it was declared an official "national minority language" in Sweden. Still, it is spoken all over the world, in many countries, and in different dialects. Standardizing the language within the context of a dictionary, yet making it accessible to all Yiddish speakers, is no simple task. Lexicographical history has recorded the difficulties that Harkavy experienced with standardizing the gender of various nouns – which may have different genders depending on which dialect one is speaking. By the time he got to the second letter, *beyz*, he had dispensed with indicating gender altogether and just indicated the part of speech (e.g. "*n.*").

---

[4] Uriel Weinreich, *Modern English-Yiddish Yiddish-English Dictionary* (New York: YIVO Institute for Jewish Research/McGraw Hill, 1968).

IS: Tell me more about that first multilingual dictionary: Yiddish, Hebrew, German, and Latin. What needs did its creation respond to? Who was behind it and who were its users? For instance, it predates the *Haskalah*, the Jewish Enlightenment. Dictionaries that aren't regularly updated die a slow death. Were there attempts to prolong the life of this one?

GSV: I probably don't know much more than you do on this one. *Shemot Devarim* (Yiddish: *Shemos Devorim*, meaning "Names of Things," 1542), by Elia Levita, is a thirty-two-page compendium of professional words, including names of diseases, pharmaceuticals, and technical words relating to other professions.[5]

The work is alphabetical according to the Yiddish *alef-beys* and translated in parallel columns into the three other languages – Hebrew, German, and Latin. Levita, a lexicographer and writer (much better known for his authorship of the hugely popular *Bove-Bukh*, the first Yiddish novel)[6] published the lexicon in Isny, a small town in southeastern Germany, near modern-day Liechtenstein, where permission had been granted for Hebrew works to be printed through the press opened by Paul Fagius – a Renaissance scholar of Biblical Hebrew and, interestingly, a protestant reformer – with whom Levita worked closely in the printing press.

Who used it? Doctors, nurses, pharmacists (or the medieval equivalents of these modern titles), and other artisans or craftsmen. Perhaps it provided a window (or opened a door) into non-Yiddish-speaking circles for Jewish practitioners to wield their craft outside their own communities.

IS: The YIVO Institute for Jewish Research in New York (originally, Yidisher Visnshaftlekher Institut) has a collection of over 100 dictionaries. The vast majority were published in the twentieth century. Exceptions include Y. Lifshits' *Rusish-Yudisher Verterbukh* (1880), published in Kiev, and I. Dreyzin's *Russish-Yudishes Verter Bukh* (1886), released in Warsaw.[7] What happened between 1592 and the end of the nineteenth century?

GSV: Well, there was the *Haskalah* (Jewish Enlightenment), and, with it, the related rise in literacy over time that came with its impact on traditional Jewish society. People were able to read and wanted to read books.

From a purely economic point of view, the nineteenth century saw the development of more efficient printing methods and the sourcing of paper from wood pulp (where printers up until this time had used various materials, e.g. cotton rags and hemp). Paper became much cheaper, with a resulting decline in book prices, which made literature much more available and accessible to the masses. And of course, reading literature – especially for immigrants learning a new language – necessitated the creation of new, particularly bilingual, dictionaries.

IS: Alexander Harkavy (1863–1939) is an engaging figure. Born in what is today Belarus, he lived an itinerant life in Paris, New York, Montreal, and Baltimore, among other places. He wrote the first history of the Jews in Canada and rendered portions of the Masoretic versions of the Torah into English, including *Genesis*

---

[5] Elia Levita, ed., *Shemos Devorim* (Isny: Paul Fagius, 1542).
[6] Elia Levita, *Bovo-Bukh* (Isny: Paul Fagius, 1541).
[7] Y. Lifshits, ed., *Rusish-Yudisher Verterbukh* (Kiev: 1880); I. Dreyzin, ed., *Russish-Yudishes Verter Bukh* (Warsaw: 1886).

and *Psalms*. He also translated parts of *Don Quixote* into English, not from Spanish but, like Chaim Nakhman Bialik, from German. But he is best known for his bilingual Yiddish-English dictionary.

GSV: A multifaceted individual. As a child in Navaredok, he received a traditional education and studied several languages; later in Vilna he worked as an accountant in the Romm publishing house and took up writing poetry and essays in Russian, Hebrew, and Yiddish. He joined a youth group, Am-Oylem, which was planning on organizing Jewish agricultural colonies in America. After arriving in America in 1882, Harkavy worked at a number of odd jobs not usually associated with Yiddish lexicographers. He was – according to his obituary in the *New York Times* – a "jack-of-all-trades," who worked for two years in New York as a longshoreman, factory worker, dishwasher, and assistant in a matzo bakery.[8] He also apparently spent time on a farm in upstate New York, milking cows. All during this time, he continued studying languages and became fluent in English. He moved to Montreal, where he taught Hebrew and published the first Yiddish newspaper in Canada (*Di Tsayt* [The time]). Only one single issue of this paper was published; later he founded another Yiddish newspaper, in Baltimore, called *Der Yidisher Progres*, which had a slightly longer life (nine issues). Harkavy published both bilingual (English-Yiddish and Yiddish-English) dictionaries, as well as a trilingual one (Yiddish-English-Hebrew), which were hugely popular among the immigrants from Eastern Europe.[9]

IS: These are all either bilingual or multilingual dictionaries. What about the tradition in Yiddish of monolingual lexicons? Did it get its wings clipped?

GSV: The *Groyser Verterbukh fun der Yidisher Shprakh* is arguably the most famous Yiddish monolingual lexicon.[10] There were several attempts in the early twentieth century to create a comprehensive monolingual lexicon for Yiddish. They failed for a variety of reasons (not the least of which were Stalin and Hitler). Harkavy, in addition to his bilingual dictionaries, also compiled a 50,000-word monolingual (Yiddish-Yiddish) dictionary, tentatively titled "Yidisher folks-verterbukh," but it remained unfinished and unpublished by the time he died in 1939. In the 1950s, the well-known Yiddish linguist Yudel Mark was commissioned by YIVO to begin work on a new comprehensive Yiddish dictionary.

After four hefty volumes of words beginning with the letter *alef* (a huge proportion of Yiddish words happen to start with *alef*), the project stalled and ended with that first letter of the *alef-beyz* and never saw another volume past the first letter. Those four volumes, published between 1961 and 1980, contain an absolute treasure of words (as does Nahum Stutchkoff's *Der Oytser fun der Yidisher Shprakh*, the definitive Yiddish thesaurus),[11] but the *Groyser*

---

[8] "Alex. Harkavy, 76, author, is dead," *New York Times*, Nov. 28, 1939.
[9] Alexander Harkavy, ed., *Complete English-Jewish Dictionary* (New York: Hebrew Publishing Company, 1891); Alexander Harkavy, *Yiddish-English Verterbukh: A Dictionary of the Yiddish Language* (New York: Hebrew Publishing Company, 1898 [later printing, c. 1925]); Harkavy, *Yidish-English-Hebreisher Verterbukh*.
[10] Judah A. Joffe, with Yudel Mark, eds., *Groyser Verterbukh fun der Yidisher Shprakh*, 4 vols. (New York: Komitet farn Groysn verterbukh fun der yidisher shprakh, 1961–80).
[11] Nahum Stuchkoff, *Der Oytser fun der Yidisher Shprakh* [The thesaurus of the Yiddish language] (New York: YIVO, 1950).

Verterbukh ceased production partly due to lack of funds and available manpower.

There was a subsequent collaborative effort on the part of both Columbia University and Hebrew University to produce a fifth and sixth volume – which reportedly would have included English and Hebrew glosses as well, and Latin-letter transcriptions of every Yiddish entry word – but no new volumes were subsequently published. During those years, however, a devoted team of lexicographers and linguists from these two universities spent innumerable hours editing, and supplementing, the original manuscripts. This resulted in the astounding (one could even say miraculous) news this past year that the scans of the nearly complete typewritten manuscripts for volumes five (letters *beyz* and *giml*) and six (*daled* and *hey*) are now publicly available online, allowing open access to this latest treasure of the Yiddish language.[12] (There's also a new chamber opera based on the history and travails of Yudel Mark and the *Groyser Verterbukh*, but that's a story for another day.)[13]

Regarding bilingual vs. monolingual dictionaries: I would also mention that as an itinerant wandering people, Jews were so often finding themselves in new locales, having to learn new languages. And that reality likely played a role in the publication of a much greater proportion of bilingual, rather than monolingual, dictionaries – supporting the need to learn new languages, as well as the assimilation into new cultures and societies.

IS: The *Modern English-Yiddish Yiddish-English Dictionary* by Uriel Weinreich (1926–67) is, in my mind, a university endeavor, since Weinreich taught at Columbia, where he developed his concept of "interlanguage" and his studies of Yiddish. What does it mean for a dictionary to emerge from an academic context?

GSV: For one thing, it reflects the reality that Ashkenazi Jews (other than the various Hasidic communities who continue to use Yiddish as a daily language) don't live in a Yiddish-speaking geographical area, or in an area where Yiddish is the first language. Non-Hasidic people speaking Yiddish today are likely second-, third-, or fourth-generation learners of the language. Since we don't have an official Yiddish-speaking environment to call our own and have to continually create such spaces, the newly taught Yiddish speakers by necessity come mostly out of the academic setting.

Incidentally, one of the fundamental principles of the *CEYD* is that Yiddish users of the dictionary should have access to language used in all aspects of life, not just the limited fund of words utilized in the narrow academic setting. Students of Yiddish can't really become fluent in all areas of the language when the context is purely an academic one. Weinreich seemingly attempted to address some of those issues by including, for example, a number of expressions to counter the natural tendency of language learners to use calques from their primary language. In addition, he included accent marks to indicate the appropriate stress, which is especially helpful in words such as, for

---

[12] https://yiddish5-6.com/
[13] "The Great Dictionary of the Yiddish Language" (composer: Alex Weiser; librettist: Ben Kaplan).

example, סאַלאַט [SALÁT], the Yiddish word for "salad," which is accented differently in the two respective languages.

An important note (with thanks to Alec Leyzer Burko): although Uriel Weinreich wasn't appointed professor of Yiddish language, literature, and culture at Columbia University until 1959, he had already completed a basic draft of his dictionary as early as 1949; it still needed to be edited and, of course, there were funding issues, which were eventually resolved, finally allowing for its publication in 1968.

IS: Let's move to your *Comprehensive English-Yiddish Dictionary*. You come from a distinguished family of Yiddishists: your father was Romanian-born linguist Mordkhe Schaechter, who taught Yiddish at Columbia, Yeshiva University, and the Jewish Theological Seminary, was the third editor of the Yiddish magazine *Afn Shvel* (1957–2004) and associate editor of *The Great Dictionary of the Yiddish Language*, and your son, Arun Schaechter Viswanath, translated *Harry Potter and the Philosopher's Stone* (2020) into Yiddish.[14] I'm just referring to two relatives in a galaxy of luminaries. You said dictionaries come about when someone sees a need for a different kind of lexicon.

GSV: My father lived and breathed Yiddish every moment of his life. An arrival in New York in 1951 as a survivor and newly minted PhD in Linguistics (University of Vienna), he immersed himself in research, writing, and teaching, with the ever-optimistic approach that Yiddish would continue to live and prosper – in the US and elsewhere – if we only will it to be so. Of course, in order to ensure this, we needed textbooks, terminologies, and dictionaries to support these efforts. The publication in 1968 of Weinreich's *Modern English-Yiddish Yiddish-English Dictionary* was a monumental achievement, a high-quality contemporary dictionary consisting of 20,000 entries.

A little-known fact for those who are familiar with Weinreich's dictionary is that it was intended as an initial attempt, the first edition, which would be followed by improved and expanded editions. Weinreich unfortunately died in 1967, at the young age of forty, and didn't even live to see the publication of his oeuvre. From that point onward, no one undertook to revise or expand the corpus of the dictionary, although subsequent printings continued for decades, to this very day. This was the dictionary used in most university-level Yiddish classes. At 20,000 entries (which seemed like a lot at the time), this pioneering work became increasingly more limited as time went on, yet many existing words/expressions in Yiddish just didn't appear there. Just a few examples:

flea market (דער פֿלייִמאַרק/וואַנצנמאַרק) [DER FLÉYMARK/VÁNTSNMARK]
flip a coin (וואַרפֿן גורל) [VARFN GOYRL]
shake sb. down (אויספּרעסן) [ÓYSPRESN]
hit pay dirt (געפֿינען גאָלד; אַרײַנפֿאַלן אין אַ שמאַלצגרוב) [GEFÍNEN GOLD; ARÁYNFALN IN A ShMÁLTSGRUB]

---

[14] Yudel Mark and Judah A. Joffe, eds., *The Great Dictionary of the Yiddish Language*, 4 vols. (New York: Yiddish Dictionary Committee, 1961–80); J. K. Rowling, *Harry Potter and the Philosopher's Stone*, (Yiddish) trans. Arun Schaechter Viswanath (Lund: Olniansky Text, 2020).

Thousands of other words were missing – for example, terms of anatomy and physiology, sex and intimacy, chemistry, art, music, sports, cuisine, medicine – many thousands of verbs and nouns and adjectives and adverbs that had long existed (you think they didn't do these things, or speak of these things, in Eastern Europe?), but a dictionary of 20,000 simply couldn't include them all.

Dr. Schaechter, a philologist with an interest in compiling specific terminologies, gradually became more and more intent on the need to create a new dictionary. As a field researcher for YIVO's Language and Culture Atlas of Ashkenazic Jewry, he travelled to all five boroughs of New York City on the subway, shlepping a humongous tape recorder, his *magnetofon*, to interview hundreds of Jews who had lived in Eastern Europe and were now transplanted to a different country. He would interview them about their trade or profession, and record their Yiddish dialects, including the subtle differences within even one spoken dialect.

He interviewed tailors, shoemakers, farmers, teachers, professional athletes, scientists, cooks/*balebustes*, former soldiers in the Russian army, and many more specialists, all of whom used Yiddish in their daily work. Aside from that, he read every manner of Yiddish newspaper and magazine being published in the world – you can't even imagine what my childhood dining-room table looked like. He voraciously read literature, memoirs, prose, poetry, essays – and that's how he collected all those words – one by one, by transcribing them onto 3″ x 5″ index cards. He estimated that over the years he had amassed around a million words.

Based on this accumulated treasure, he was able to publish several terminological dictionaries, among them: *English-Yiddish Dictionary of Academic Terminology* (1988); *Pregnancy, Childbirth and Early Childhood: An English-Yiddish Dictionary* (1991); and *Plant Names in Yiddish* (2005).[15] He also compiled unpublished terminologies e.g. the sports terminology, compiled for use at the weeklong Yiddish immersion retreat (*Yidish-vokh*), organized by Yugntruf Youth for Yiddish.

Finally, at the beginning of the new millennium, he began to devote much of his time, together with several of his colleagues, to compiling all those words in a manageable format. I was tasked with and involved in data-entering the words on those index cards onto a computer, after which it took nearly two years for him to compile a first draft of the letter "A." He then became ill, was unable to continue, and the work ground to a halt. (In the Yiddish lexicographical world it seems we have a history of not getting beyond the letter *alef* or "A.")

With enthusiasm, tempered with a considerable amount of doubt (yet without truly understanding how raw the material still was and what the scope of this effort would be), we decided to carry on with the project. The undertaking was expanded to include many more additional entries that were missing from

---

[15] Mordkhe Schaechter, *English-Yiddish Dictionary of Academic Terminology* [English-Yidish Verterbikhl fun Akademisher Terminologye] (New York: Yiddish Language Resource Center/League for Yiddish, 1988); *Pregnancy, Childbirth and Early Childhood: An English-Yiddish Dictionary* [Trogn, Hobn un Friike Kinder-Yorn: An English-Yidish Verterbikhl] (New York: Yiddish Language Resource Center/League for Yiddish, 1991); *Plant Names in Yiddish* [Di Geviksn-Velt in Yidish] (New York: YIVO Institute for Jewish Research, 2005).

Schaechter's corpus that should be a necessary part of any bilingual dictionary. It took sixteen years, but the 83,000-plus-word *CEYD* was finally published by Indiana University Press in 2016, and republished in 2021 in a second revised edition with approximately 1,000 additional words, some of them in active use in contemporary Hasidic Yiddish.

IS: What about the criteria of word selection as well as the protocols in shaping each definition?

GSV: The word selection came directly from the collections of Mordkhe Schaechter. Although thousands of additional words not found on those index cards were added during the process of expanding and editing the *CEYD*, the glosses were generally drawn from other existing dictionaries – either Yiddish-only (e.g. Stutchkoff *Oytser*, Mark's *Groyser Verterbukh*) or English-Yiddish (e.g. Weinreich) or Russian-Yiddish (e.g. Shapiro and Spivak, 1984).[16] Neologisms were, for obvious reasons, handled separately and were selected based on consultations with other Yiddish language experts – as well as (Yiddish-speaking) professionals in a variety of fields, usually the sciences or technology, or even a field as timeless as music, because the editors of this dictionary have their own limited vocabularies when it comes to specialized fields.

IS: What do you make of Uriel's father Max Weinreich's dictum: "A language is a dialect with an army and a navy." Yiddish has never had either of them. It has also not had a territory, unless we count the infamous episode of Birobidzhan, the administrative locus of Jewish life created by Josef Stalin on the Trans-Siberian Railway, near the China–Russia border. Does having no homeland force a language to have a different relationship to dictionaries than their peers with an address and everything that comes with it?

GSV: That saying is attributed to Max Weinreich who, in any case, was the one who popularized it. He was being facetious, as he believed with his entire being that Yiddish was a language that stood on its own. The border between a language and a dialect – at what point a dialect is recognized as a language – is difficult to pinpoint, although that determination becomes much more concrete, so much easier to ascertain, when you attach an entire military – an inherent and necessary corpus of a political system – to the language. Weinreich's dictum reflected the historical social and political position of Yiddish and the resulting manner in how it is viewed by other communities.

IS: Does Yiddish therefore have a different relationship to dictionaries?

GSV: No doubt. A Yiddish dictionary for the Yiddish student and even the advanced Yiddish speaker/professor/linguist is an absolute must if they are to navigate literature (in the passive use of the language) or day-to-day life (e.g. when trying to raise young children with Yiddish). In the case of an official language of a country, the residents/citizens/tourists in that country constantly absorb words spoken, heard, and written all around them, displayed on signs and billboards: old words used in new contexts, new words reflecting novel ideas and products, catchy expressions, words that have been vetted by the country's official

---

[16] M. Shapiro, with E. Spivak and M. Shulman, eds., *Rusish-Yidisher Verterbukh* (Moscow: Russkiy Yazik, 1984).

"language panel" – all of which easily and naturally become part of the local language.

Without a homeland, the Yiddish speaker – unless they are lucky enough to live in a Yiddish-speaking environment where everyone speaks the language fluently and grammatically correctly, without creating calques or loan translations from the surrounding environment (in itself a heavy lift) – is by default reliant on the written compilation, the "bible" of words that is the dictionary.

IS: Are you the first woman ever to publish a Yiddish dictionary?

GSV: Definitely not. First of all, I should mention here that without my coeditor-in-chief, Paul (Hershl) Glasser, the *CEYD* would not have crossed the finish line. The same should be said as well for our associate editor, Chava Lapin. The *CEYD* may be the most extensive dictionary ever edited by a woman, but I know of several, including the tiny English-Yiddish Lilliput dictionaries edited or compiled by Dr. Zina (Paula) Horowitz, and published in Leipzig.[17] The first edition was published around 1920 and republished a number of times through the 1950s, I believe. I have a copy of this 621-page, 12,000-word palm dictionary, and it's a bit difficult – even with my reading glasses – to read the words clearly, but it's definitely the most portable dictionary.

IS: Yet the shaping of dictionaries, or at least the leadership behind such endeavors, remains a male endeavor. Am I wrong? Of course, the irony in the case of Yiddish cannot be ignored. It started as a language of women, children, and the average folk.

GSV: You're right that the history of the making of Yiddish dictionaries (you could possibly even say the same about dictionaries in other languages) was almost exclusively male-only. But again, most of those Yiddish dictionaries were produced in the late nineteenth through the second half of the twentieth century. Certainly, there were exceptions, but women were generally not out there breaking down the walls of Yiddish academia or linguistics to find a place for themselves. The sociological reasons for this don't need much explanation.

I read a great line in an article by the contemporary female lexicographer Kory Stamper, who said "Lexicography moves so slowly that scientists classify it as a solid."[18] Dictionary-making is incredibly time-consuming and may not lend itself to a decision to devote years of one's life for a person who may have other clocks and responsibilities in mind. And is it possible that the occasional highly qualified woman was politely excluded from lexicographic circles? Not sure, but it may be something to think about...

IS: The updated edition of *CEYD* is laudable. But as you know, dictionaries in the twenty-first century thrive – let me be humble here: survive – online.

GSV: You are absolutely correct. And as a matter of fact, you'll be thrilled to know that the *CEYD* has had an online presence since September 2021, accessible at englishyiddishdictionary.com. The online version is updated regularly, with new entries, subentries, synonyms, and expressions, and is the most current version of any English-Yiddish dictionary extant in the world today. It's also

---

[17] Zina Horowitz, ed., *Liliput Dictionary: English-Yiddish* (Leipzig, ca. 1920).
[18] Kory Stamper, "Falling in Love with Words: The Secret Life of a Lexicographer," Longreads.com, March 14, 2017.

interactive, in the sense that it allows subscribers to write us with comments regarding words or expressions that may be missing, or with other questions or remarks.

IS: As you look back at the development of Yiddish as a language, might it be said that dictionaries propelled it to achieve its own maturity?

GSV: Yes, I believe so. The more people became literate and wanted access to reading material, the more they needed dictionaries to explain many of those words. And with the publication in time of additional dictionaries (some of them specialized, others more generalized), the more varied and multidimensional became the sources available to teachers and students of Yiddish, in the further learning and development of Yiddish. Dictionaries also play a certain role in standardizing the written language, which contributes partly to the maturity of a language.

IS: By the way, Gitl, do you have a sense of how many Yiddish speakers there are worldwide today? The statistics I see range widely, from 200,000 to a million. I ask not only out of curiosity but because, obviously, lexicography and demographics go hand in hand. The more users a language has, the vaster the need for dictionaries. Do you think otherwise?

GSV: I agree, of course, that the need for dictionaries grows with the number of users of a given language. Two hundred thousand seems a bit low, though, given the prevalence of Yiddish as a daily language among many Haredim and Hasidim (usually generically referred to as "ultra-Orthodox"), together with their high birth rate (one study showed the birthrate among Haredi Jews in Israel to be seven children compared with three among non-Haredi and/or secular Jews). The numbers that I'm familiar with – 500,000 to a million – place most of those speakers in the Haredi communities.

IS: What, in your view, is the future of Yiddish lexicography?

GSV: I'm sure you recall Isaac Bashevis Singer's famously immortal words in his Nobel acceptance speech: "There are some who call Yiddish a dead language, but so was Hebrew called for 2,000 years. ... Yiddish has not yet said its last word."[19] The same could be said about Yiddish lexicography, and all the more so. Yiddish dictionaries of various kinds continue to be published in the twenty-first century: Yiddish bilingual dictionaries in various languages (French, English, Russian, Dutch, Hebrew, amongst others), a cultural dictionary, a dictionary of place names, dictionaries of Jewish given names and surnames, and other specialized dictionaries. Some of these dictionaries can be found online and can, therefore, be easily edited and updated "in real time," so to speak, which renders the art of Yiddish dictionary-making significantly more manageable. No question that Yiddish lexicography will be around for quite some time.

IS: Are there any attempts, in your knowledge, within the Haredi community, to engage in dictionary-making?

GSV: Of course! I have a copy of a 6,000-word Yiddish-Yiddish thesaurus targeted to the *haymish* (read "ultra-Orthodox") community. The book was published back in 2009, expanded and republished in 2011, with subsequent editions as recently

---

[19] Isaac Bashevis Singer, Nobel lecture, December 8, 1978, www.nobelprize.org/prizes/literature/1978/singer/lecture/.

as 2019 that I know of.[20] There's at least one other plan that I'm aware of to produce a dictionary for the Haredi community, but I don't believe that project has made much headway. Oh, and by the way, the above-mentioned dictionary was written by a woman called "A. Roth."

Suggested Readings

Dreyzin, I., ed. *Russish-Yudishes Verter Bukh*. Warsaw, 1886.
Harkavy, Alexander, ed. *Complete English-Jewish Dictionary*. New York: Hebrew Publishing Company, 1891.
   Yidish-English-Hebreisher Verterbukh. New York: Hebrew Publishing Company, 1928.
Horowitz, Zina, ed. *Liliput Dictionary: English-Yiddish*. Leipzig, ca. 1920.
Joffe, Judah Achilles, with Yudel Mark, eds. *Groyser Verterbukh fun der Yidisher Shprakh*. 4 vols. New York: Komitet farn Groysn verterbukh fun der yidisher shprakh, 1961–80.
Levita, Elia. *Bovo-Bukh*. Isny: Paul Fagius, 1541.
   ed. *Shemos Devorim*. Isny: Paul Fagius, 1542.
Lifshits, Y., ed. *Rusish-Yudisher Verterbukh*. Kiev: 1880.
Roth, A., ed. *Idish Verter-Oytser*. Monsey, NY: Eastern Book Press, 2009.
Schaechter, Mordkhe. *English-Yiddish Dictionary of Academic Terminology* [English-Yidish Verterbikhl fun Akademisher Terminologye]. New York: Yiddish Language Resource Center/League for Yiddish, 1988.
   Pregnancy, Childbirth and Early Childhood: An English-Yiddish Dictionary [Trogn, Hobn un Friike Kinder-Yorn: An English-Yidish Verterbikhl]. New York: Yiddish Language Resource Center/League for Yiddish, 1991.
   Plant Names in Yiddish [Di Geviksn-Velt in Yidish]. New York: YIVO Institute for Jewish Research, 2005.
Schaechter-Viswanath, Gitl. *Plutsemdiker Regn/Sudden Rain*. Introduction by Sheva Zucker. Tel Aviv: Israel Book, 2003.
Schaechter-Viswanath, Gitl, with Paul Glasser, eds. *Comprehensive English-Yiddish Dictionary*. Bloomington: Indiana University Press, 2016; revised 2nd ed., 2021.
Shapiro, M., with E. Spivak and M. Shulman, eds. *Rusish-Yidisher Verterbukh*. Moscow: Russkiy Yazik, 1984.
Stamper, Kory. "Falling in Love with Words: The Secret Life of a Lexicographer," Longreads.com, March 14, 2017.
Stutchkoff, Nahum. *Der Oytser fun der Yidisher Shprakh* [The thesaurus of the Yiddish language]. New York: YIVO, 1950.
Weinreich, Uriel. *Modern English-Yiddish Yiddish-English Dictionary*. New York: YIVO Institute for Jewish Research/McGraw Hill, 1968.

---

[20] A. Roth, ed., *Idish Verter-Oytser* [Yiddish Thesaurus] (Monsey, NY: Eastern Book Press, 2009); A. Roth, ed., *Yiddish Verter Oytser* (Roth Publishers, 2019).

16   Portuguese

Rute Costa and Ana Salgado

One of the most influential languages, Portuguese is spoken by over 250 million individuals worldwide. The tension at its core emerges from standardization and the influence of one variant over others. Yet the Portuguese people, from Portugal to Brazil to Africa and elsewhere, share deep cultural and historical bonds. The linguistic variations, therefore, are the result of vast richness and diversity inherent to the broader Portuguese-speaking world. This conversation delves into the making of dictionaries, first in Portugal, then – although insufficiently – in Brazil. A large portion is about Aurélio Buarque de Holanda Ferreira's *Novo dicionário da língua portuguesa*, popularly known as the *Dicionário Aurélio*, as well as Antônio Houaiss's *Dicionário Houaiss da língua portuguesa*.[1] This conversation is supported by (1) the MORDigital – Digitalização do Diccionario da Lingua Portugueza de António de Morais Silva project financed by the Portuguese National Funding through the Fundação para a Ciência e Tecnologia; and (2) Portuguese National Funding through the Fundação para a Ciência e Tecnologia as part of the project Centro de Linguística da Universidade NOVA de Lisboa.

***

ILAN STAVANS: Let me start with a personal question. How did the two of you become interested in the life of words?
RUTE COSTA: I was raised in a rich, multilingual environment that left a lasting impact on my personality and worldview. Regularly engaging with multiple languages was a shared experience among those who grew up with me. As I progressed through university, my interest in languages in contact, minority languages, and the meticulous documentation of lexical units and their variations deepened. My academic pursuits led me to delve into scientific disciplines such as lexicology, lexicography, and terminology.

---

[1] Aurélio Buarque de Holanda Ferreira, *Novo dicionário da língua portuguesa* (Rio de Janeiro: Editora Nova Fronteira, 1975); Antônio Houaiss, *Dicionário Houaiss da língua portuguesa* [CD-ROM] (Rio de Janeiro: Editora Objetiva, 2001).

                    Within this academic setting, I developed methodological approaches rooted in theoretical reflections, consistently underscoring the inherent value of words. My focus revolved around issues related to meaning and definitions, fostering a lasting connection with the organization of knowledge. The creation of new words, including their denotations and connotations, became a central area of fascination for me, and there's no turning back from this passionate exploration.

ANA SALGADO: From a young age, my interest in words felt almost innate. It was a natural inclination, a genuine passion for language that seemed to be part of who I am. As I grew, this fascination only intensified, and words became my companions on a journey of exploration. I was an avid reader, and through books, I discovered the enchanting world of language. It was this early immersion in literature that fueled my enthusiasm for words. Eventually, I decided to delve deeper into the intricacies of language by studying Portuguese. The sound and meaning of words, their nuances, and the stories they tell have always held a profound fascination for me. Those moments of uncovering a new word, feeling its weight and rhythm, and understanding the power it held were like small revelations. Each word became a piece of a puzzle, contributing to the beauty of language. I vividly remember a moment during my studies when the sound of a particular word struck me. My passion for words guided my educational path and continues to shape my career. I found myself naturally drawn to fields where language is not just a tool but a canvas for expression. It has influenced the way I communicate, write, and connect with others. The intricate dance between sound and meaning became the focus of my academic journey. This passion has translated into a career where I explore the richness of language and contribute (I hope) to its understanding and appreciation. My favorite book is always a good dictionary. Even today, I am enchanted, especially with old editions.

IS: Switching to the historical realm, my understanding is that the first dictionary in the Portuguese language was a Latin-Old Portuguese glossary of 2,930 verbs of the fourteenth century.

AS: Portuguese lexicography, like other European languages, originated from bilingual dictionaries encompassing Latin and the vernacular languages. One of the most notable contributions to early Portuguese lexicography was rendered by Jerónimo Cardoso (c. 1508–1569), a distinguished Portuguese humanist scholar and missionary renowned for his compilation of the *Dictionarium ex Lusitanico in Latinum Sermonem* (1562),[2] regarded as a dictionary that represents a significant milestone in the art and craft of dictionary-making in Portugal.

---

[2] J. Cardoso, *Hieronymi Cardosi Lamacensis Dictionarium ex Lusitanico in Latinum Sermonem* (Lisbon: Joannis Alvari, 1562).

Portuguese 197

This dictionary registers approximately 12,000 entries, providing equivalents and explanations of Latin words in Portuguese. The work you mention is a verb glossary containing roughly 2,930 medieval Latin verbs and corresponding Old Portuguese glosses. It corresponds to a manuscript from the Alcobaça collection published by Henry Hare Carter (1905–2001) in 1953, which is in the National Library of Lisbon.

IS: What were some of the historical forces that played a significant role in shaping the development of early lexicography?

RC: We can identify various historical factors that influenced the development of early lexicography. These factors include linguistic evolution, cultural exchange, and standardization efforts. During the Middle Ages, the Latin language, referred to as Vulgar Latin, had already undergone significant changes compared to classical Latin, used in universities, liturgy, and law. Consequently, the practice of glossing texts emerged where difficult words were explained through notes.

These glosses were inserted between the lines or in the margins of the texts, introducing the term "interlinear gloss" (written between the lines) and later evolving into "marginal gloss" (written in the margins). Medieval bilingual glossary listings, primarily Latin-Vernacular, were published to assist in learning Latin during that period. In terms of cultural exchange, Portugal, as a prominent nation, needed to understand and communicate with individuals who spoke Latin and other languages. The compilation of dictionaries facilitates the teaching and learning of emerging vernacular languages. Lastly, these early lexicographic works played a critical role in establishing standards for vocabulary, spelling, and grammar.

IS: The age of colonization in Portugal opened up new territories in various parts of the world. Portuguese was exported to them. How did dictionaries in the early days of colonization account for the linguistic variety in the colonies?

RC: During the period of colonization, as Portuguese territories expanded across diverse regions worldwide, the multifaceted linguistic landscape and interactions with local languages presented challenges to lexicographers and dictionary-makers. In the colonial context, early dictionaries undertook the intricate effort of embracing this vast linguistic diversity, integrating the lexicon, and embracing the unique linguistic characteristics of the local tongues. Missionaries played a crucial role in lexicography during this period. They actively engaged with local communities, studying and documenting their languages.

They created dictionaries and grammars to facilitate translation, language learning, and the spread of Christianity. Bilingual dictionaries assumed importance in facilitating effective communication and comprehension between Portuguese-speaking communities and Indigenous populations. These lexicographic works often included articles (entries) related to local customs, flora, fauna, and specific cultural allusions, thus providing invaluable insights into the Indigenous cultures and fostering a deeper understanding.

IS: I'm particularly interested in the tension between Portuguese in Portugal and Portuguese in Brazil. Is this tension similar to the one between the Spanish of Spain and the Spanish of Latin America?

AS: There are no justifiable reasons for the existence of such tensions. The diverse varieties of the Portuguese language, including Brazilian, African, and Asian variants, contribute to the enrichment of the Portuguese language and can harmoniously coexist. Linguistic diversity plays a vital role in Portuguese as a global language, with distinct pronunciation patterns, grammatical differences, and a wide range of vocabulary.

IS: Yet as in the case of the Real Academia Española in Madrid and Spanish speakers throughout Hispanic America, a feeling of colonialism prevails. Until rather recently, intellectuals of all persuasions complain that Iberian lexicography is rigid, not allowing for the plurality of voices from the former colonies. How is it in the Portuguese-speaking world?

RC: The issue of colonialism and linguistic representation in the Portuguese-speaking world, particularly in the context of lexicography, has some similarities to the concerns expressed in the Spanish-speaking world. Probably the dynamics are different, but there has been an ongoing debate about how well the linguistic diversity of the Portuguese-speaking world is represented and whether there is a sense of colonialism in the standardization and regulation of the language.

In recent years, there has been a growing recognition of the need to promote the linguistic and cultural diversity within the Portuguese-speaking world. Efforts have been made to incorporate words and expressions from different Portuguese-speaking regions, including former colonies, into lexicographic resources. Additionally, there has been a push to recognize the various dialects and creole languages spoken in former Portuguese colonies.

IS: Are the same dictionaries popular in Portugal today the ones people favor in Brazil?

AS: In general, there are some common Portuguese dictionaries that are recognized and used in both Portugal and Brazil. However, there are also differences in preferences due to linguistic variations and the accessibility of the dictionaries themselves. The choice of a dictionary can be influenced by factors such as the target audience, the intended use of the dictionary, and individual preferences. Here are some dictionaries that are commonly used in both countries:

Dicionário Priberam da língua portuguesa (https://dicionario.priberam.org/): This is a contemporary Portuguese dictionary that is widely used in both Portugal and Brazil, produced by Priberam, a Portuguese company. Currently, it comprises around 165,000 lexicographic entries, including expressions and phraseologies. Its nomenclature encompasses general vocabulary and the most common terms from the primary scientific and technical fields.

Infopédia. Dicionários Porto Editora (https://www.infopedia.pt/dicionarios): Porto Editora is a well-known Portuguese publishing house that primarily produces dictionaries for the Portuguese market. The Porto Editora dictionaries are commonly used in Portugal. This website contains dictionaries in Portuguese, Portuguese Sign Language, English, Spanish, French, German, Italian, Dutch, Chinese, Tetum, Greek, and Swedish.

Dicionário Houaiss da língua portuguesa: Houaiss is another respected dictionary used in both Brazil and Portugal. This Portuguese language dictionary, of Brazilian origin, was elaborated by the Brazilian lexicographer Antônio Houaiss (1915–99). The first edition was launched in 2001 in Rio de Janeiro by the Instituto Antônio Houaiss. It is known for its extensive coverage and linguistic accuracy. The continuity of the work was ensured by the Antonio Houaiss Institute of Lexicography and Portuguese Language Database, an institute founded in 1997 in Rio de Janeiro by Antônio Houaiss, Francisco Manoel de Mello Franco, and Mauro de Salles Villar. While it originated in Brazil, this dictionary is also appreciated by Portuguese speakers, having two adapted versions in Portugal – the first in 2002 and the second in 2005, both published by Círculo de Leitores.

Dicionário Aurélio da língua portuguesa: Aurélio is a widely recognized and respected dictionary in Brazil. This dictionary was originally launched in late 1975. The original version resulted from the work of lexicographer Aurélio Buarque de Holanda Ferreira (1910–89), spanning more than three decades. It's known for its comprehensive coverage of Portuguese vocabulary and is often used by students, writers, and the general public.

Users in each country may have preferences for dictionaries that are more tailored to their specific linguistic needs. It's not uncommon for people to use a combination of dictionaries, including those designed for their region and more comprehensive options, to address both regional and international language nuances. Of course, I also want to reference two digital dictionaries, published by two academies: the one from the Academia Brasileira de Letras (Brazilian Academy of Letters) and the one from the Academia das Ciências de Lisboa (Academy of Sciences of Lisbon).[3]

IS: How do words from the former colonies get incorporated into Portuguese dictionaries published in Lisbon?

RC: In recent years, there has been a growing awareness and commitment to including words from former colonies in Portuguese dictionaries published in Lisbon. The incorporation of words and expressions from these colonies reflects the evolving nature of language and the recognition of linguistic diversity. This process typically involves several steps: researching to document the words and expressions used in the former colonies, such as collecting texts, and collaborating with local language experts to understand the linguistic nuances of these regions.

Additionally, it includes evaluating the relevance and frequency of these units in everyday language. Sometimes, these units need to be standardized to fit the rules and conventions of standard Portuguese. Another important aspect is the labeling of these units in dictionaries. They are typically marked to indicate their regional origin. Lastly, language is dynamic, and new words and expressions continue to emerge.

Therefore, dictionaries must be updated regularly to reflect changes in the language and to include new terms from former colonies. It's essential to note that this process is part of a broader effort to recognize and celebrate the linguistic diversity within the Portuguese-speaking world.

IS: The Academia das Ciências de Lisboa was created in 1789. Was it in order for the Portuguese to have an academy similar to the French, Italian, and Spanish?

---

[3] www.academia.org.br/; www.acad-ciencias.pt/

AS: The creation of the Academia das Ciências de Lisboa (ACL) in 1789 was driven by the desire to establish a prestigious scientific institution in Portugal, similar to the academies in France, Italy, and Spain. It aimed to promote scientific research, intellectual exchange, and cultural development in line with the European intellectual climate of the time.

The ACL, originally Academia Real das Sciencias de Lisboa due to its royal protection, was founded in 1779, during the reign of Dona Maria I. The leading proponents of this academic project, D. João Carlos de Bragança e Ligne de Sousa Tavares Mascarenhas da Silva (1719–1806), second Duke of Lafões, and José Francisco Correia da Serra (1750–1823), better known as Abade Correia da Serra, were influenced by Enlightenment trends and institutions that were already emerging across Europe. Since its foundation, the ACL has established that among its *"utilissimos intentos, que a composição de hum Diccionario da mesma lingoa fizesse parte dos seus primeiros trabalhos"* (useful intentions, that the composition of a dictionary of that language was part of its first works).[4]

The ACL plays a crucial role in promoting and disseminating scientific knowledge in Portugal. It supported research and publication and organized scientific meetings and lectures. The academy's members contributed to various fields of knowledge. Currently, among its missions, the ACL is responsible for encouraging scientific research, stimulating the study of the Portuguese language and literature, and promoting the study of Portuguese history and its relations with other countries.

Pursuant to its current charter, the ACL remains an *"órgão consultivo do Governo português em matéria linguística"* (advisory body to the Portuguese Government on linguistic matters).[5] The lexicographic activities of the ACL are part of the responsibilities of the Instituto de Lexicologia e Lexicografia da Língua Portuguesa (ILLLP).

IS: And what about the *Vocabulário ortográfico da língua portuguesa* published in 1940 by the ACL?[6]

RC: The *Vocabulário ortográfico da língua portuguesa* of 1940 was a significant orthographic dictionary that aimed to establish a standard for the spelling of the Portuguese language. It was published by the ACL and was an authoritative reference for spelling norms in Portugal. Besides being the first in a series of subsequent vocabularies, this lexicographic work has great historical and linguistic value.

The twentieth century was productive in the field of Portuguese lexicography, with the publication of several orthographic vocabularies, not only by institutions like the ACL or the Academia Brasileira de Letras (ABL), but also private editions authored by various philologists and linguists, both Portuguese and Brazilian, as well as abridged versions.

---

[4] Academia das Ciências de Lisboa, "Planta para se formar o Diccionario da lingoa portugueza," in *Diccionario da lingoa portugueza*, t. 1, A, i–xx (Lisbon: Academia Real das Ciências de Lisboa, 1793), s.p.

[5] Decreto-Lei n. 157/2015, art. 5.

[6] Academia das Ciências de Lisboa, *Vocabulário ortográfico da língua portuguesa* (VOLP-1940) (Lisbon: Imprensa Nacional, 1940).

We have an ongoing project on the Linguistics Research Centre of NOVA University Lisbon (NOVA CLUNL), *Digital Edition of the Vocabularies of the Academy of Sciences* project, which aims to digitize the spelling vocabularies of the ACL in order to create a digital lexicographic corpus bringing together the printed versions of all these lexicographical reference works – the 1940, 1947, 1970, and finally the 2012 editions.[7]

AS: It is also important to mention that in 1966 the *Vocabulário da língua portuguesa* by Rebelo Gonçalves was published.[8] This work continues to be a reference work for many language professionals, even with the application of new spelling rules. In the twenty-first century, as a matter of fact in 2010, the Instituto de Linguística Teórica e Computacional (Institute of Theoretical and Computational Linguistics [ILTEC]) published the *Vocabulário ortográfico do português*.[9]

This same vocabulary served as the working basis for the *Vocabulário ortográfico comum da língua portuguesa*, an instrument for language policy constructed by countries with Portuguese as an official language.[10] Meanwhile, since 2018, the ACL has also made available a digital vocabulary.[11] The first digital version contains over 215,000 entries with their respective grammatical classification and other helpful information. This vocabulary follows the officially established spelling system – the Acordo Ortográfico da Língua Portuguesa (Orthographic Agreement of the Portuguese Language [1990]). It covers Modern Portuguese, the linguistic period that extends from the sixteenth century to the present.

IS: Let's talk about António de Morais Silva and his *Diccionario da lingua portugueza*, first published in 1789.[12]

RC: The Morais dictionary represents a great legacy since it marks the beginning of Portuguese dictionaries, having served as a model for all subsequent lexicographic production throughout the nineteenth and twentieth centuries. The first edition of the known Morais dictionary is entitled in its main edition (1789) *Diccionario da lingua portugueza, composto pelo Padre D. Rafael Bluteau, reformado, e accrescentado por Antonio de Moraes Silva, natural do Rio de Janeiro* (*Diccionario da Lingua Portugueza* composed by Father D. Rafael Bluteau, retired, and accredited by Antonio de Morais Silva, born in Rio de Janeiro).

The information that immediately stands out concerns the authorship attribution since Morais does not claim to be the author, assigning this condition to

---

[7] Academia das Ciências de Lisboa, *Vocabulário ortográfico da língua portuguesa* (VOLP-1940) (Lisbon: Imprensa Nacional, 1940); Academia das Ciências de Lisboa, *Vocabulário ortográfico resumido da língua portuguesa* (VOLP-1947) (Lisbon: Imprensa Nacional, 1947); Academia das Ciências de Lisboa, *Vocabulário ortográfico resumido da língua portuguesa* (VOLP-1970) (Lisbon: Imprensa Nacional, 1970); Academia de Ciências de Lisboa, *Vocabulário ortográfico atualizado da língua portuguesa* (VOALP) (Lisbon: Imprensa Nacional – Casa da Moeda, 2012).
[8] F. Rebelo Gonçalves, *Vocabulário da língua portuguesa* (Coimbra, 1966).
[9] www.portaldalinguaportuguesa.org/vop.html   [10] https://voc.cplp.org/
[11] www.acad-ciencias.pt/vocabulario/
[12] A. de Morais Silva, *Diccionario da lingua portugueza, composto pelo padre D. Rafael Bluteau, reformado, e accrescentado por Antonio de Moraes Silva, natural do Rio de Janeiro*, 2 vols (Lisbon: Simão Thaddeo Ferreira, 1789).

Rafael Bluteau (1638–1734), author of the *Vocabulario portuguez e latino*. However, Morais recognizes in the "Prólogo ao Leitor" (Prologue to the reader) that his additions to the dictionary are pretty relevant. Morais further developed Bluteau's work and systematically considered most entries and definitions.

In NOVA CLUNL, we are now working on the first three editions of the Morais dictionary. We decided to create a project a few years ago: MORDigital. The main goal is to encode the selected editions. The project has the support of Portuguese national funding through FCT (Fundação para a Ciência e Tecnologia) as a project submitted to the IC&DT Project Competition in all scientific domains. MORDigital follows a new paradigm in lexicography, which results from the convergence between lexicography, terminology, computational linguistics, and ontologies. The MORDigital project addresses a significant gap in Portuguese-speaking countries, where there is a lack of searchable online retro-digitized dictionaries that adhere to current data-sharing standards.

Moreover, MORDigital operates in an era marked by the emergence of mass digitization projects, revolutionizing the field of lexicography. These initiatives aim to preserve heritage materials and simplify access to historical documents, emphasizing the importance of best practices in ensuring data quality and integrity. Technological progress has taken us beyond mere scanned texts. Our ultimate goal is to transform printed dictionaries into computational, readily exploitable lexical resources, enhancing searchability.

IS: Could you provide additional information regarding the Morais editions?

AS: The first edition of Morais' dictionary (1789) is titled *Diccionario da lingua portugueza composto pelo Padre D. Rafael Bluteau, reformado, e accrescentado por Antonio de Moraes Silva, natural do Rio de Janeiro* [Dictionary of the Portuguese language composed by Father D. Rafael Bluteau, revised, and augmented by Antonio de Moraes Silva, born in Rio de Janeiro]. This edition was published in two volumes: the first covering the letters A to K, totaling 752 pages, and the second covering the letters L to Z, with 541 pages. The printing of the work was carried out by the publisher Simão Thaddeo Ferreira in Lisbon.

It is worth noting that Morais does not claim authorship of the work, attributing it to Bluteau as Rute said before. Nevertheless, in the "Prólogo ao Leitor," Morais acknowledges the importance of the additions he made to the dictionary. The second edition (1813) of the dictionary, corrected and expanded, is considered a substantial overhaul, due to both its increased content and updates.[13] This new edition, published in two volumes (A–E; F–Z), also originated in Lisbon, at Typographia Lacerdina.

On this occasion, Antonio de Morais Silva explicitly claimed authorship of the dictionary on the title page, describing the work as *Diccionario da lingua portugueza, recopilado dos vocabularios impressos ate agora, e nesta segunda edição novamente emendado, e muito accrescentado, por Antonio de Moraes Silva natural do Rio de Janeiro* (Dictionary of the Portuguese language, compiled

---

[13] A. de Morais Silva, *Diccionario da lingua portuguesa, recopilado dos vocabulários impressos até agora, e nesta segunda edição novamente emendado, e muito accrescentado*, 2 vols. (Lisbon: Typographia Lacerdina, 1813).

from printed vocabularies until now, and in this second edition, again corrected and greatly augmented by Antonio de Morais Silva born in Rio de Janeiro).

Finally, the third edition was published ten years later, in 1823, under the title *Diccionario da lingua portugueza, recopilado de todos os impressos até o presente, por Antonio de Moraes Silva, natural do Rio de Janeiro* (Dictionary of the Portuguese language compiled from all prints until the present, by Antonio de Morais Silva, native of Rio de Janeiro).[14]

IS: I'm interested in the transition between printed dictionaries of Portuguese and online dictionaries. As in the rest of the world, I assume the latter are winning without much competition.

RC: The move from printed dictionaries to online versions is a global phenomenon, and it's reshaping how we engage with language, not just in Portuguese but worldwide. It's been a game-changer. Online dictionaries are now easily accessible to anyone with an internet connection. This inclusivity is particularly crucial for Portuguese speakers in various regions, including those with limited access to printed resources. The digital shift has democratized access to language tools.

IS: What about staying current with language changes?

AS: That's another significant advantage. Online dictionaries can be updated more frequently, ensuring they provide the most current information on language usage and evolving vocabulary. It's about staying in tune with the dynamic nature of language.

IS: Are there features that enhance the user experience? How about multimedia elements?

RC: Absolutely. Online dictionaries come with powerful search features, making them incredibly user-friendly. Users can find specific words or information swiftly, streamlining the learning process. Online dictionaries can incorporate audio pronunciations, example sentences, and even video content. These features not only enhance the learning experience but also cater to different learning styles. Users can often customize online dictionaries to their preferences, saving favorite words or utilizing language translation features. It adds a personal touch to the learning journey.

AS: While online dictionaries have become the primary choice for many, printed dictionaries have not disappeared entirely. They continue to be valuable references for some, particularly in academic and library settings. Some people may also prefer the tactile experience of using a printed dictionary. In the Portuguese-speaking world, both printed and online dictionaries coexist, but the trend is undoubtedly toward the increasing use of online resources due to their accessibility and convenience.

IS: How have people's habits in their use of dictionaries changed as a result of online versions?

RC: Now, with online dictionaries, a world of language resources is at our fingertips. Users can instantly access word meanings, translations, and more by simply typing a word into a search bar.

---

[14] A. de Morais Silva, *Diccionario da lingua portuguesa, recopilado de todos os impressos até o presente, por Antonio de Moraes Silva, natural do Rio de Janeiro* (Tip. M. P. de Lacerda, 1823).

IS: That's a significant convenience. How has this ease of access affected how people use dictionaries?
RC: The impact is profound. The ease of access has led to a surge in dictionary use. People are more inclined to look up words or phrases they encounter in their daily activities – whether reading, writing, or engaging in conversations.
IS: And it's not just about definitions, is it?
AS: Exactly. Online dictionaries often go beyond traditional definitions. They incorporate multimedia elements like audio pronunciations, images, and videos, enhancing understanding and making language learning more engaging.
IS: Are there specific tools that cater to their needs?
RC: Absolutely. Online dictionaries serve as invaluable tools for language learners and teachers alike. They provide not only word meanings but also language examples, idiomatic expressions, and grammar information.
IS: What about bridging language gaps?
RC: Online dictionaries often include translation features, making it easier for users to navigate foreign languages and broaden their linguistic horizons.
IS: And staying current with language changes?
RC: Precisely. Online dictionaries can be updated in real time, ensuring users have access to the latest language developments, new words, and evolving meanings.
IS: What about advanced search features?
AS: Online dictionaries offer advanced search features such as autocomplete, suggest corrections, and related words. These features empower users to find the information they need quickly and efficiently.
IS: It sounds like a comprehensive transformation. Does this shift foster a sense of community among users?
AS: Indeed, some online dictionaries allow users to contribute by suggesting new words, reporting errors, and sharing language insights. This is the case at ILLLP, where we receive a significant number of contributions from our users daily. It fosters a collaborative environment, creating a sense of community among language enthusiasts.
IS: I would like you to reflect on the role of the vernacular, or the plural vernaculars, in Portuguese today, and their relationship to dictionaries. How long does it take for a vernacular word to be accepted?
RC: The acceptance of vernacular words into dictionaries is a dynamic process influenced by linguistic, cultural, and social factors. The role of dictionaries is to reflect the evolving nature of language and to celebrate the diverse voices and identities within the Portuguese-speaking world. As the language continues to evolve, dictionaries will adapt to accommodate new words and expressions. The acceptance of vernacular words can be a complex and evolving process. The time it takes for a vernacular word to be accepted into dictionaries can vary widely. Some units may be recognized relatively quickly if they gain prominence, while others may take years or even decades to be formally acknowledged.

This is also influenced by cultural and social factors. Terms related to cultural practices, traditions, or social movements may be more readily accepted due to their significance. As communities interact and language changes, new words emerge, and existing words may take on new meanings or usage. Dictionaries need to keep pace with these shifts. The media, including television, the internet, and social media, can accelerate the recognition and spread of vernacular words. Words that gain popularity through these channels may find their way into dictionaries more quickly.

Suggested Readings

Academia das Ciências de Lisboa. *Catalogo dos livros, que se hão de ler para a continuação do diccionario da lingua portugueza: Mandado publicar pela Academia Real das Sciencias de Lisboa.* Lisbon: Academia das Ciências de Lisboa, 1799. https://bibdig.biblioteca.unesp.br/handle/10/28356

Dicionário da língua portuguesa. Coord. A. Salgado. Lisbon: Academia das Ciências de Lisboa, 2024. https://dicionario.acad-ciencias.pt/

Academia das Ciências de Lisboa. *Dicionário da língua portuguesa contemporânea.* 2 vols. Coord. J. M. Casteleiro. Lisbon: Academia das Ciências de Lisboa and Editorial Verbo, 2001.

Instituto de lexicologia e lexicografia da língua portuguesa. Lisbon: Academia das Ciências de Lisboa, 1987.

Plano de estatutos, em que convierão os primeiros socios da Academia das Sciencias de Lisboa, com beneplacito de sua Magestade. Lisbon: Regia Officina Typografica, 1780.

"Planta para se formar o Diccionario da lingoa portugueza." In *Diccionario da lingoa portugueza*, t. 1, A, i–xx. Lisbon: Academia Real das Ciências de Lisboa, 1793.

Relatório da Comissão encarregada de propor à Academia Real das Sciencias de Lisboa o modo de levar a efeito a publicação do Diccionario da lingua portugueza. Lisbon: Academia das Ciências de Lisboa, 1870.

Vocabulário ortográfico da língua portuguesa. Coord. A. Salgado. Lisbon: Academia das Ciências de Lisboa, 2024. https://volp-acl.pt/

Bluteau, R. *Vocabulario portuguez e latino, áulico, anatómico, arquitectónico, bélico, botânico, brasílico, cómico, crítico, químico, dogmático, dialéctico, dendrológico, eclesiástico, etimológico, económico, florífero, forense, fructífero ... autorizado com exemplos dos melhores escritores portugueses, e latinos...*, Vols. 1 and 2: Coimbra: Collegio das Artes da Companhia de Jesu, 1712; Vols. 3 and 4: Coimbra: Collegio das Artes da Companhia de Jesu, 1713; Vol. 5: Lisbon: Officina de Pascoal da Sylva, 1716; Vols. 6 and 7: Lisbon: Officina de Pascoal da Sylva, 1720; Vol. 8: Lisbon: Officina de Pascoal da Sylva, 1721; Suplemento I: Lisbon: Officina de Joseph Antonio da Sylva, 1727; Suplemento II: Lisbon: Patriarcal Officina da Musica, 1712–28.

Cardoso, J. *Hieronymi Cardosi Lamacensis Dictionarium ex Lusitanico in Latinum Sermonem.* Lisbon: Joannis Alvari, 1562.

Costa, R., and A. Salgado. "Le projet lexicographique MORDigital: Une nouvelle approche au service des dictionnaires numériques." *Ela. Études de linguistique appliquée* 3, no. 211 (2024): 315–84. Paris: Klincksieck Editions.

Costa, R., A. Salgado, F. Khan, A. Carvalho, L. Romary, B. Almeida, M. Khemakhem, M. Ramos, R. Silva, and T. Tasovac. "MORDigital: The Advent of a New Lexicographical Portuguese Project." *Proceedings of the eLex 2021 Conference*, Brno, 321–24, 2021.

Houaiss, Antônio. *Dicionário Houaiss da língua portuguesa* [CD-ROM]. Rio de Janeiro: Editora Objetiva, 2001.

Grande dicionário Houaiss da língua portuguesa. Instituto Antônio Houaiss and Bloco Gráfico, Lda. Lisbon: Círculo de Leitores, 2015.

Morais Silva, A. de. *Diccionario da lingua portugueza, composto pelo padre D. Rafael Bluteau, reformado, e accrescentado por Antonio de Moraes Silva, natural do Rio de Janeiro*. 2 vols. Lisbon: Simão Thaddeo Ferreira, 1789.

Diccionario da lingua portuguesa, recopilado dos vocabulários impressos até agora, e nesta segunda edição novamente emendado, e muito accrescentado. 2 vols. Lisbon: Typographia Lacerdina, 1813.

Diccionario da lingua portuguesa, recopilado de todos os impressos até o presente, por Antonio de Moraes Silva, natural do Rio de Janeiro. Lisbon: Tip. M. P. de Lacerda, 1823.

Porto Editora. *Dicionário Infopédia da língua portuguesa*. Porto: Porto Editora, 2024. www.infopedia.pt/

Priberam. *Dicionário Priberam da língua portuguesa*, 2024. https://dicionario.priberam.org/

Salgado, A., and R. Costa. "O projeto Edição Digital dos Vocabulários da Academia das Ciências: o VOLP-1940." *Revista da Associação Portuguesa de Linguística* 7 (2020): 275–94.

Salgado, A., A. Simões, A. Iriarte, R. Vieira, M. Ferreira, R. Carmo, and C. Pinheiro. "Dicionário da língua portuguesa: A New Lexicographic Resource of Academia das Ciências de Lisboa." In *Electronic Lexicography in the 21st Century (eLex 2023): Invisible Lexicography*, ed. M. Medveď, M. Měchura, C. Tiberius, I. Kosem, J. Kallas, M. Jakubíček, and S. Krek, Book of Abstracts, 72–75. Brno: Lexical Computing, June 27–29, 2023.

Verdelho, T. "O dicionário de Morais Silva e o início da lexicografia moderna." In *História da língua e história da gramática: Actas do encontro*, 473–90. Braga: ILCH, Universidade do Minho, 2003.

Verdelho, T., and J. P. Silvestre, orgs. *Dicionarística portuguesa, inventariação e estudo do património lexicográfico*. Aveiro: Universidade de Aveiro, 2007.

17 Japanese

Yukio Tono

Japanese, a language spoken by some 130 million people, comes from Old Japanese (these words are called *yamato kotoba*), words that come from Chinese (*kango*), and hybrid words that come from European languages, especially English (*gairaigo*). This last variety is called *wasei-eigo*, that is, "made-in-Japan English." All this is to say that Japanese is a hodgepodge tongue, one whose prehistory is little known. The language seems to have produced more dictionaries compared to other standardized linguistic habitats. This is one of the topics of the following conversation, which also inevitably delves into the formation of Japanese as a language. It also contemplates the impact that other languages have had on Japanese lexicography – for instance, the desire to have a lexicon similar to the *Oxford English Dictionary* (*OED*) – and explores bilingual dictionaries as well as electronic resources.

***

ILAN STAVANS: Japan has an extraordinary abundance of dictionaries...

YUKIO TONO: The Japanese language has a complex writing system comprising kanji, hiragana, and katakana, each with its own uses and historical origins. This intricacy necessitates a range of dictionaries to address the various aspects of reading, writing, and understanding the language. Secondly, Japan has a long history of lexicography dating back to the Heian period (794–1185). Over time, this has led to a rich tradition of dictionary compilation and the development of a collective skill set in the field, resulting in a substantial number of high-quality dictionaries.

Another contributing factor is Japan's high valuation of education and literacy. This cultural emphasis creates a demand for a wide array of dictionaries to support educational needs at all levels, from elementary schools to universities and beyond. Additionally, Japan boasts a robust tradition of scholarship in literature and linguistics, with scholars frequently producing specialized dictionaries to support the study and teaching of Japanese as well as the study of classical and regional texts.

More recently, Japan's recovery from the war and subsequent economic success have enabled the Japanese market to demonstrate a willingness to invest in education, which, in turn, has spurred the publishing business, including dictionary production. We take pride in the fact that Japan is among the few countries where books in every discipline from around the world can be made available in our own language.

IS: Could you elaborate on the evolution of Japanese dictionaries in the post-World War II era?

YT: In the latter half of the twentieth century, while a plethora of dictionaries hit the shelves in Japan, two notable trends emerged. Firstly, general-purpose, single-volume desk dictionaries gained immense popularity, with the *Kōjien* 広辞苑 becoming a bestseller.[1] Another significant stride was the compilation of a comprehensive, unabridged dictionary of the Japanese language, grounded in historical principles, known as the *Nihon Kokugo Daijiten* 日本国語大辞典.[2]

IS: And what constitutes a bestseller in the dictionary market?

YT: For the *Kōjien*, the metrics are quite impressive. According to Iwanami Shoten 岩波書店, the first edition sold over a million copies. By the year 2000, the fifth edition had pushed cumulative sales past 11 million. Given that this edition included 230,000 headwords across 2,996 pages, totaling approximately 14 million characters, it is remarkable that it became an essential household reference, demonstrating the value placed on language and knowledge in Japanese society.

The *Kōjien* is a renowned medium-sized Japanese-language dictionary published by Iwanami Shoten and edited by Shinmura Izuru 新村出. It is based on the earlier *Jien* 辞苑, which Shinmura compiled and Hakubunkan 博文館 published in 1935.[3] After Hakubunkan declined to continue publication due to wartime damages, Iwanami Shoten acquired it and renamed it *Kōjien*. Subsequent rights disputes over the original content between Iwanami Shoten and Hakubunkan led to a lawsuit. Postwar editing was arduous due to reforms in the Japanese language, such as changes to kana usage and kanji shapes, and the introduction of new words. Nevertheless, the diligent efforts of Shinmura Izuru and his team culminated in the first edition's release in 1955.

A distinctive feature of the *Kōjien* is the addition of 10,000 to 20,000 new words with each revision, typically every decade. Its hybrid nature as a comprehensive Japanese dictionary and an encyclopedia has been widely embraced. The digitization of the *Kōjien* began early on; by 1987, a CD-ROM version was available, later integrated into Casio and other electronic dictionaries for modest royalties, sparking a surge in electronic dictionaries featuring the *Kōjien* content. The latest, seventh edition, published in 2018, contains approximately 250,000 words.

Following the *Kōjien*, several other desk dictionaries emerged, such as the *Daijirin* 大辞林 (1988), *Nihongo Daijiten* 日本語大辞典 (1989), and *Shūeisha*

---

[1] *Kōjien* 広辞苑, ed. Shinmura Izuru 新村出 (Iwanami-shoten, 1955 [1st ed.] – 2018 [7th ed.]).
[2] *Nihon Kokugo Daijiten* 日本国語大辞典, ed. Nihon Daijiten Kankokai 日本大辞典刊行会 (Shogakukan, 1972–76 [1st ed.]; 2000–2002 [2nd ed.]).
[3] *Jien* 辞苑, ed. Shinmura Izuru 新村出 (Hakubunkan, 1935).

Kokugo Jiten 集英社国語辞典 (1993).[4] Yet, none have matched the *Kōjien*'s popularity. Its entries are frequently cited and debated by intellectuals, reflecting on the appropriateness of inclusions in what is considered a reference for the populace. The discourse surrounding new entries often spills over into reviews and critical columns, underlining *Kōjien*'s unique status as a touchstone in Japanese lexicography, whether viewed favorably or contentiously.

IS: Great. Let's move to the production of an unabridged dictionary on historical principles.

YT: For Japanese lexicographers, it has long been an ambition to compile a dictionary akin to the *OED*, grounded in historical principles. The Japanese language boasts a history nearly as rich as English, yet the origins of the Japanese language family remain elusive. This endeavor is a spiritual successor to the *Dainihon Kokugo Jiten* 大日本國語辭典 (1915–1919) edited by Ueda Kazutoshi 上田万年 and Matsui Kanji 松井簡治.[5] In 1964, Shōgakukan 小学館, a Japanese general publisher, which also produced the famous anime series *Pokemon*, intrigued by the citation slips collected by Matsui Kanji's son Matsui Tadashi 松井驥 and grandson Matsui Eiichi 松井栄一, initiated the publication of the *Nihon Kokugo Daijiten*, enlisting leading linguists such as Kindaichi Kyōsuke 金田一京助, Shinmura Izuru (compiler of the *Kōjien*), and Morohashi Tetsuji 諸橋轍次, noted for his extensive Kanji-Japanese dictionary, as editorial advisors.

Over 200 authors contributed to the work, the *Nihon Kokugo Daijiten* was published across five years from 1972 to 1976, culminating in a comprehensive twenty-volume series with 450,000 entries and 750,000 examples. The supplementary volume included a list of major citation sources, dialect data, and additional information. Upon completion in 1976, the dictionary received a special prize at the 30th Mainichi Publication Culture Awards.

The first edition features 450,000 entries spanning common Japanese words, dialects, foreign words, Buddhist terms, historical concepts, and specialized fields such as flora and fauna, alongside 50,000 names of people, places, and other proper nouns. The entries are historically structured, detailing changes in meanings, and the 750,000 citations are drawn from a wide array of sources, including classical and contemporary literature, records, ancient documents, and Buddhist scriptures. The dictionary stands out for its linguistic depth, offering insights into ancient etymological theories, excerpts from historical dictionaries, and the evolution of word pronunciations and accents.

Twenty-four years after the original, the second edition was published from 2000 to 2002 in thirteen volumes, boasting 500,000 entries and 1,000,000 examples, plus an Indexes volume, which addressed previous criticisms by dating all citations. This edition expanded dialect coverage, referencing the *Nihon*

---

[4] *Daijirin* 大辞林, ed. Matsumura Akira (Sanseido, 1988 [1st ed.]; 2006 [3rd ed.]); *Nihongo Daijiten*日本語大辞典 (Kodansha, 1989); *Shūeisha Kokugo Jiten* 集英社国語辞典, ed. Morioka Kenji, Tokugawa Soken, Kawabata Yoshiaki, Nakamura Akira, and Hoshino Koichi (Shūeisha, 1993).

[5] *Dainihon Kokugo Jiten* 大日本國語辭典, ed. Ueda Kazutoshi 上田万年 and Matsui Kanji 松井簡治 (Fuzambo, 1915–19).

Hogen Daijiten 日本方言大辞典 (1989).⁶ In 2005, the essential edition of the dictionary (日本国語大辞典精選版) was released, containing 300,000 entries with an equal number of examples. This edition is set to be featured in Casio and Seiko's portable electronic dictionaries. Today, the *Nihon Kokugo Daijiten* is recognized as the most comprehensive and high-quality Japanese language dictionary in Japan.

IS: Let's move to Japanese-English or English-Japanese dictionaries.

YT: Japan also has contributed to the development of bilingual lexicography, especially in the area of English learners' dictionaries. Here, I don't have time to elaborate on the history of English bilingual lexicography in Japan in greater detail, so I will just summarize the major developments. If you are interested, you should read Isamu Hayakawa's seminal work on English-Japanese lexicography (2016).⁷ After the Meiji period (1868–1912), English became a primary source of information from the West, and the need for the production of good English-Japanese dictionaries was pressing. Most English-Japanese dictionaries in the Meiji era were based on four dictionaries: Peter Austin Nuttall's *Routledge's Diamond Dictionary of the English Language* (1861), Noah Webster's *An American Dictionary of the English Language* (1864), and John Ogilvie's *Imperial Dictionary* (1850) and *Student's English Dictionary* (1866).⁸

Apparently, there was no influence of Samuel Johnson's dictionary on English bilingual lexicography in Japan, which was rather surprising, but it showed that Japanese users of English bilingual dictionaries at that time needed the information about current English words and usages and might not find such academic works as Johnson's dictionary informative.

IS: Tell me how those British and American dictionaries influenced English-Japanese dictionaries.

YT: The first several years of the Meiji era saw a series of English glossaries, but it wasn't until 1873 that the first substantial work of English-Japanese dictionaries was published. It was entitled the *Fuon Sōzu Eiwa Jii* 附音挿図英和字彙 (1873), compiled by Shibata Masayoshi 柴田昌吉 and Koyasu Takashi 子安峻. It had 55,000 entries and 500 pictorial illustrations and was influenced by both British and American dictionaries such as those by Ogilvie and Webster.

Prior to that, James Curtis Hepburn, an American missionary and doctor, had published a Japanese-English dictionary called the *Waei Gorin Shūsei* 和英語林集成 (1867), which contained 20,772 Japanese-English entries and 10,030 English-Japanese entries. Hepburn's dictionary also focused on the language spoken by ordinary Japanese citizens at that time and its editorial policy and

---

⁶ *Nihon Hogen Daijiten* 日本方言大辞典, ed. sup. Tokugawa Sōken 徳川宗賢, 3 vols (Shogakukan, 1989).

⁷ Hayakawa Isamu, *A Critical History of English-Japanese Lexicography* (Kindle Books, 2016, ASIN: B01LXK2NO8).

⁸ *Routledge's Diamond Dictionary of the English Language* ed. P. Austin Nuttall (London: Routledge, 1861); *An American Dictionary of the English Language*, comp. Noah Webster, Chauncy Goodrich, Noah Porter, and James Hadley (Springfield: G. & C. Merriam, 1864); *The Imperial Dictionary of the English Language*, ed. John Ogilvie (London: Blackie & Son, 1850); *The Student's English Dictionary*, ed. John Ogilvie (London: Blackie & Son, 1866).

format became an excellent model for subsequent bilingual dictionary making in Japan.

During the 1880s, many English-Japanese dictionaries were compiled. The *Meiji Eiwa-Jiten* 明治英和字典 (1884–89) compiled by Seki Shinpachi 尺振八 showed a very strong influence from Webster's dictionary. They began to include more entries using Webster's unabridged dictionary. Additionally, diacritics used in Webster's spelling book, a popular school speller at the time, were also adopted in these dictionaries. This period marked the beginning of English-Japanese dictionaries including detailed subject or technical field labels for meanings.

In the Taishō period (1912–26), two figures stood out in English lexicography in Japan: Saitō Hidesaburō 斎藤秀三郎 and Inouye Jūkichi 井上十吉. Inouye Jūkichi and Saitō Hidesaburō each led the way in English dictionaries during the Taishō period, but their backgrounds were quite different. Inouye had long experience of using English in his work, having studied in England for a long period and then serving as a second secretary stationed overseas, whereas Saitō had acquired an astonishingly high level of English almost entirely in Japan, and made a name for himself as an English scholar.

Saitō was a linguistic innovator in the field of English grammar and developed his own theory of "idiomology," which bears a resemblance to what is now known as "phraseology." However, Saitō's theory was deeply rooted in a cross-linguistic comparison between Japanese and English. He compiled two notable bilingual dictionaries: *Saito's Idiomological English-Japanese Dictionary* (熟語本位英和中辞典, 1915) and *Saito's Japanese-English Dictionary* (斎藤和英大辞典, 1928).[9] Around this time, the first edition of the *Concise Oxford Dictionary of Current English* (*COD*) was published. This marked a shift in lexicographical practice, with most lexicographers beginning to follow the *COD* rather than Webster's dictionaries as a model for compiling bilingual dictionaries with a focus on lexical and usage information. Inouye Jūkichi translated the *COD* and compiled *Inouye's English-Japanese Dictionary* (1915), followed by Inouye's Japanese-English Dictionary (井上和英大辞典, 1922).[10]

During the Taishō period (1911–24) and the prewar Shōwa period (1925–45), a significant event that influenced bilingual lexicography in Japan was the appointment of Harold E. Palmer as the "linguistic advisor" for the Ministry of Education and the subsequent founding of the Institute for Research in English Teaching (IRET). Palmer made many contributions, including the publication of the *Interim Report on Vocabulary Selection* (1930) and the *Second Interim Report on English Collocations* (1933).[11] He also planned a monolingual learner's dictionary and recruited A. S. Hornby to assist in Japan. In 1936,

---

[9] *Saito's Idiomological English-Japanese Dictionary* (熟語本位英和中辞典), comp. Saito Hidesaburo 斎藤秀三郎 (Nichieisha, 1915); *Saito's Japanese-English Dictionary* (斎藤和英大辞典), comp. Saito Hidesaburo 斎藤秀三郎 (Nichieisha, 1928).

[10] *Inouye's English-Japanese Dictionary* 井上英和大辞典, comp. Inouye Jūkichi 井上十吉 (Shiseido, 1915); *Inouye's Comprehensive Japanese-English Dictionary* 井上和英大辞典, comp. Inouye Jūkichi 井上十吉 (Shiseido, 1922).

[11] *Interim Report on Vocabulary Selection* (Gogaku Kyoiku Kenkyujo, 1930); H. E. Palmer, *Second Interim Report on English Collocations* (Kaitakusha, 1933).

Palmer returned to the UK, and Hornby assumed responsibility, compiling the *Idiomatic and Syntactic English Dictionary* (ISED) in 1940.[12] This dictionary was later published by Oxford University Press as *A Learner's Dictionary of Current English* (1948), which eventually evolved into the renowned *Oxford Advanced Learner's Dictionary of Current English* (OALD).[13]

The OALD set a precedent as the first monolingual learner's dictionary and inspired other British publishers to produce similar works, including the *Longman Dictionary of Contemporary English* (LDOCE, 1978) and the *Cambridge International Dictionary of English* (CIDE, 1995).[14] Furthermore, the competition among learner's dictionaries led to the publication of the first corpus-based monolingual learner's dictionary, the *Collins COBUILD English Dictionary* (1987), which catalyzed a shift toward corpus-based approaches in major monolingual learner's dictionaries.[15]

This transition also affected the development of English-Japanese dictionaries. In the postwar Shōwa period (1945–89), various bilingual learner's dictionaries were released, drawing inspiration from the ISED or the OALD. Among these were the *New CROWN English-Japanese Dictionary* (ニュークラウン英和辞典) (1954), *Kenkyusha's New Collegiate English-Japanese Dictionary* (研究社英和中辞典) (1966), and the *Anchor English-Japanese Dictionary* (アンカー英和辞典) (1972) for senior high school students.[16] Additionally, Obunsha's *Comprehensive English-Japanese Dictionary* (旺文社英和中辞典) (1975) and the *Progressive English-Japanese Dictionary* (プログレッシブ英和中辞典) (1980) catered to college students and the general readership.[17] All these dictionaries have been revised or renamed several times and are still on the market today.

---

[12] *Idiomatic and Syntactic English Dictionary*, comp. A. S. Hornby, E. V. Gatenby, and A. H. Wakefield (Kaitakusha, 1942).

[13] *A Learner's Dictionary of Current English*, comp. A. S. Hornby, E. V. Gatenby, and A. H. Wakefield (Oxford: Oxford University Press, 1948); *Oxford Advanced Learner's Dictionary of Current English*, comp. A. S. Hornby, E. V. Gatenby, and A. H. Wakefield (Oxford: Oxford University Press, 1948 [1st ed.] – 2020 [10th ed.]).

[14] *Longman Dictionary of Contemporary English* (Harlow: Longman, 1978 [1st ed.] – 2014 [6th ed.]).
Cambridge International Dictionary of English, ed. Paul Procter (later, *Cambridge Advanced Learner's Dictionary*) (Cambridge: Cambridge University Press, 1995).

[15] *Collins COBUILD English Dictionary* (later, *Collins COBUILD Advanced Learner's Dictionary*), ed. John Sinclair (Glasgow: Harper Collins, 1987 [1st ed.] – 2018 [9th ed.]).

[16] *New CROWN English-Japanese Dictionary* 新クラウン英和辞典, ed. Kawamura Jūjirō 河村重治郎 (Sanseidō, 1939 [1st ed.] – 1995 [5th ed. by Tajima Shingo 田島伸悟]); *Kenkyusha's New Collegiate English-Japanese Dictionary* (新英和中辞典), ed. Iwasaki Tamihei 岩崎民平 (Kenkyūsha, 1966 [1st ed.] – 2003 [7th ed. by Takebayashi Shigeru, et al. 竹林滋 他]); *Anchor English-Japanese Dictionary* (アンカー英和辞典), ed. Shibata Tetsushi 柴田徹士 (Gakushū Kenkyūsha, 1972).

[17] *Obunsha's Comprehensive English-Japanese Dictionary* (旺文社英和中辞典), ed. Takahashi Genji 高橋源次 (Ōbunsha, 1975); *Progressive English-Japanese Dictionary* (プログレッシブ英和中辞典), ed. Konishi Tomoshichi 小西友七, Yasui Minoru 安井稔, Kunihiro Tetsuya 国広哲弥 (Shōgakukan, 1980 [1st ed.] – 2012 [5th ed.]).

From the 1990s to the 2000s, the *GENIUS English-Japanese Dictionary* (ジーニアス英和辞典) (1987) gained significant popularity.[18] This surge was partly due to the harsh – often unjustified – criticism leveled at Kenkyūsha's dictionaries that a cram school English teacher, Soejima, made in his controversial book, which scrutinized the quality and accuracy of Kenkyūsha's illustrative examples and usage descriptions.[19] The controversy led to a court case, which Soejima lost. Nevertheless, the case cast a negative light on Kenkyūsha's works, adversely affecting their sales. It was regrettable that such unfounded criticism tarnished the reputation of Kenkyūsha's well-regarded dictionaries.

Concurrently, the market for pocket electronic dictionaries was expanding, with brands like Casio, Seiko Instruments, Sharp, and Sony incorporating full-content dictionaries into their compact devices. This trend coincided with the decision by most manufacturers to opt for the *GENIUS English-Japanese Dictionary* for their devices, contributing to its market success. Indeed, *GENIUS* was recognized for its meticulous grammar and usage notes, underpinned by a comprehensive review of preceding dictionaries from within and outside Japan. Ironically, it was a nonacademic event that inflicted lasting damage on Kenkyūsha's standing in the dictionary market – a situation from which the publisher struggled to recover for an extended period.

IS: How about unabridged English-Japanese dictionaries?

YT: Among unabridged English-Japanese dictionaries, *Kenkyusha's New English-Japanese Dictionary* (研究社新英和大辞典) stands out as one of the most authoritative.[20] Despite the criticisms aimed at Kenkyūsha's dictionaries mentioned above, the unabridged dictionary has maintained its status due to its extensive coverage and precision. Since its first publication in 1927, it has distinguished itself from earlier dictionaries by including a wealth of synonyms, word origins, idioms, and proverbs. Its comprehensive scope and accuracy have established it as the most scholarly unabridged English-Japanese dictionary available.

In the preface of the sixth edition, editor-in-chief Shigeru Takebayashi 竹林滋 highlighted the comprehensive update of the dictionary's content. Emphasizing its encyclopedic nature, the new edition boasted a significant addition of terms across diverse fields such as IT, society, politics, economics, science, medicine, and more. Reflecting English's status as a global lingua franca, it included varied vocabulary from English-speaking regions beyond the UK and the US, as well as notable non-English proper names. Traditional literature such as the King James Bible and Shakespeare's works had also been preserved and expanded upon. Moreover, the dictionary had undergone meticulous refinement in word meanings, usage examples, idioms, and pronunciation, among other aspects, to ensure

---

[18] *GENIUS English-Japanese Dictionary* (ジーニアス英和辞典), ed. Konishi Tomoshichi 小西友七 (Taishūkan, 1987 [1st ed.] – 2022 [6th ed.]).

[19] Soejima Takahiko, *Kekkan Eiwa-Jiten no Kenkyū* (欠陥英和辞典の研究, Research on Defective English-Japanese Dictionaries) (JICC Press, 1989).

[20] *Kenkyusha's New English-Japanese Dictionary* 研究社新英和大辞典,ed. Takebayashi Shigeru 竹林滋 (Kenkyūsha, 1927 [1st ed.] – 2002 [6th ed.]).

rigor and relevance to contemporary social conditions, updating any previously unsuitable descriptions.

Another notable achievement was the *Shogakukan Random House English-Japanese Dictionary* (小学館ランダムハウス英和大辞典), the bilingual edition of the *Random House Dictionary of the English Language*.[21] The second edition featured 345,000 entries, surpassing *Kenkyusha's New English-Japanese Dictionary*, which contained 260,000 entries in its sixth edition. This edition not only added 30,000 headwords and 50,000 definitions absent from the US second edition but also augmented it with 110,000 example sentences, increasing the total from the US edition's 65,000 to an impressive 175,000. However, the original *Random House Dictionary* project eventually ceased, overtaken by the rising influence of free online dictionaries globally, which also led to the discontinuation of its bilingual version.

IS: In most ecosystems of standardized languages, online dictionaries today are the most frequently used. I assume that is also the case in Japan.

YT: Japan has one of the most distinctive developments in electronic and online dictionaries in the world, largely due to its rapid economic growth in the 1960s and its subsequent dominance in the global precision instruments market, including electronic calculators, cameras, Walkman, and video game devices, among others.

The earliest electronic "word list" was the *Pocket Denyakuki* ポケット電訳機 (IQ-3000) released by Sharp in 1979, which contained a bilingual word list of approximately 2,800 English-Japanese and 5,000 Japanese-English words. Throughout the 1980s, companies such as Canon, Casio Computer, Sanyo Electric, and Seiko Instruments entered the electronic dictionary market. January 1992 saw the launch of the TR-700 by Kenkyūsha and Seiko Instruments, the first full-fledged integrated circuit (IC) electronic dictionary in Japan. Known as a full-content dictionary, it included all text from two volumes of *Kenkyusha's New English-Japanese* and *New Japanese-English Dictionaries*. This release marked a shift in the market to IC electronic dictionaries, which then split into two categories: comprehensive full-content versions and the more affordable "standard" dictionaries. From 1996 to 1999, Japan's IC electronic dictionary market expanded significantly as costs for IC memory and liquid crystal displays (LCD) decreased, leading to the advent of full-content electronic dictionaries with large LCD screens and multiple dictionaries.

By 2000, the variety of dictionaries and product options had broadened. Falling semiconductor prices and access to digitized dictionary data allowed devices to host numerous dictionaries, spurring the release of multidictionary products. Competition intensified as companies vied to increase the number of dictionaries included in their products and to cater to a diverse user base that ranged from high school students to the elderly and women, each with specific needs. This variety led to a surge in full-content electronic dictionary options and continued market

---

[21] *Shogakukan Random House English-Japanese Dictionary* 小学館ランダムハウス英和大辞典. ed. Konishi Tomoshichi, Yasui Minoru, Kunihiro Tetsuya, and Horiuchi Katsuaki (Shogakukan, 1973 [1st ed.] – 1993 [2nd ed.]); *Random House Dictionary of the English Language*, ed. Jess Stein (New York: Random House, 1966; 1987 [2nd ed.]).

growth. The market reached 2 million units in 2000 and maintained sales over 2 million units annually for the following decade.

Companies sought to distinguish their products by adding unique features, including voice pronunciation, expandable memory cards, color LCD screens, and handwriting input systems. The content expanded beyond traditional dictionaries and encyclopedias to include specialized, large, and national language dictionaries, as well as a vast array of educational materials, hobby guides, and practical handbooks. However, with the advent of smartphones, the proliferation of dictionary apps, and the rise of free dictionary sites on the internet, sales volumes declined steadily from 2008 onward. Despite these difficulties, however, demand for electronic dictionaries for high school and university students remains strong.

IS: How have online dictionaries evolved while pocket electronic dictionaries were so popular in Japanese?

YT: With the advent of internet technology, online dictionaries also developed rapidly. It was back in 1999 when internet protocol (IP) connections on mobile phones were made possible that a subscription-based mobile dictionary service began, first with Sanseido offering three resources, including the Kokugo dictionary *Daijirin*, for a monthly fee of fifty yen, creating a new market for membership-based mobile dictionary sites. In 2001, the World Wide Web saw the launch of several dictionary services: Sanseidō's *Web Dictionary* (a subscription service), Shōgakukan Group's (Net Advance) *Japan Knowledge* in April, and the user-contributed free encyclopedia *Wikipedia* Japanese edition in May.[22]

Pioneers of free dictionary search sites operated by portal sites included *goo Dictionary* (launched in August 1999) and *Yahoo! Dictionary* (launched in July 2000, then merged with *Kotobank* in 2013), with many Japanese portal sites following their lead.[23] While many online paid dictionary services have struggled due to the rise of free online dictionaries and encyclopedias, Japan Knowledge has successfully carved out a stable operation by tapping into the B2B market. *Kotobank*, established by the Asahi Shimbun Company and several publishers, has implemented a revenue model based on search-linked advertising (keyword advertising), providing free dictionary services to consumers. These sites have been alive and accepted by users with different reference needs.

IS: How has online lexicography changed the making and usage of dictionaries in Japanese?

YT: There are notable developments in this area. The *Weblio* stands out as a portal site offering access to a wide array of dictionaries serving both general and specialized needs.[24] Significantly, the *Weblio* does not compile dictionaries; it provides a platform for accessing dictionary content. They have agreements with content providers who supply data from dictionaries tailored to specific fields. By 2019, the *Weblio* hosted over 563 different sets of terminological dictionaries, all appropriately credited to their respective contributors. As of November 2018, the platform boasted approximately 10 million entries and garnered over 300 million page views per month.

---

[22] https://japanknowledge.com/; https://ja.wikipedia.org/wiki/
[23] https://dictionary.goo.ne.jp/; https://kotobank.jp/   [24] https://www.weblio.jp/

Another highly successful commercial venture is the *Eijirō* 英辞郎 (ALC Press), born from a bilingual phrase database initially contributed by a community of translators.[25] Users can look up words or phrases in English or Japanese, and the *Eijirō* presents the results in a parallel text format. This layout is particularly useful for translating challenging phrases, including complex colloquialisms and contemporary jargon. Researchers and translators frequently turn to the *Eijirō* when dealing with neologisms and nuanced language.

IS: Do you find any issues or problems related to the current lexicographical practice or user behavior?

YT: For a while, the abundance of dictionaries in a single device led many users to search within pocket electronic dictionaries without being familiar with the distinct titles and characteristics of each dictionary. This resulted in an increased number of searches conducted without a full understanding of the individual dictionary features. However, with the entrenchment of the internet and the rise in popularity of smartphones in the 2010s, the availability of free online dictionaries soared. As the display resolutions of smartphones and tablets improved, an increasing number of dictionaries became accessible via apps. This shift to digital platforms, compared to previous behaviors, was beneficial in that it allowed users to interact with individual dictionaries, thereby enhancing their understanding of each one's unique characteristics, much like the interaction with physical dictionaries.

Conversely, there are significant global trends: the number of users bypassing traditional dictionary consultation in favor of translation software such as Google Translate or DeepL is surging. Instead of navigating to a dictionary website, users simply input a word into a search bar and immediately receive definitions. As these integrated dictionary functions become more user-centric, the visibility and recognition of the dictionaries themselves diminish. Moreover, the cognitive processes traditionally associated with dictionary use, such as comparing multiple meanings under the entry, discerning senses from examples, and understanding grammatical context, are becoming less prevalent, a phenomenon I refer to as the "degeneration of dictionary search skills." I am concerned that this trend could be detrimental, particularly for those in the initial stages of learning a foreign language, as it bypasses critical thinking and deep understanding of how words are used in context.

IS: Let's go back to the beginning of the history of Japanese lexicography. In the fourth century CE, the Chinese writing system was imported to Japan. I understand that Japanese history books, such as *Kojiki* 古事記, showed up in the eighth century. When did the first attempt at cataloging words – that is, the forerunner of our present conception of dictionaries – emerge?

YT: *Kojiki* is a book of Japanese history, containing historical facts as well as mythology about the origin of the country and the imperial family. It is the oldest existing document in Japan. In the book, there was a description of importing Buddhist texts (*butten* 仏典) and Chinese classics (*kanseki* 漢籍) from China. The Japanese Buddhist monks had to learn how to read and write Chinese, so they probably consulted imported Chinese monolingual dictionaries, such as the

---

[25] https://eow.alc.co.jp/

Erya 爾雅 (c. 3rd century BCE), the *Shuowen jiezi* 説文解字 (100 CE), and the *Yupian* 玉篇 (543 CE).[26] The first Kanji dictionary compiled in Japan was called the *Niina* 新字 (682 CE).[27] *Nihon Shoki* 日本書紀 (the oldest chronicles of Japan, 720 CE) described that Emperor Tenmu 天武天皇 ordered Sakaibe no Iwatsumi 坂合部磐積 to compile the forty-four volumes of the *Niina* in 682 CE.[28]

IS: Could you tell me more about what the *Niina* is like?

YT: Unfortunately, the *Niina* is a lost literary work, and no surviving copies are known to exist. We can only speculate about the reasons for its compilation. There are several theories regarding the nature of the *Niina*. One theory suggests that it stipulated Japanese pronunciations for Chinese characters. Another posits that it compiled a list of Japan-made Chinese characters authorized by the imperial family. A third theory argues that it was established to aid in compiling Japanese history books during the Emperor Tenmu period, specifically for the accurate notation of archaic words.

IS: How did Japanese lexicography develop in the Heian period, between the years 794 and 1185, a period that also saw the rise of Buddhism in Japan?

YT: The oldest existing dictionary in Japan is the *Tenrei Banshō Meigi* 篆隷万象名義 (830–835 CE) compiled by the prominent Heian period monk and scholar Kūkai 空海. This was based on the Chinese *Yupian* dictionary. Since the *Yupian* dictionary was also a lost literary work, the researchers in China tend to consider this *Tenrei Banshō Meigi* as an important record to provide some evidence about the organization of the original *Yupian* dictionary. From Japanese lexicographical viewpoints, however, this dictionary was still a copy of the Chinese dictionary, showing a list of 16,000 characters with the Chinese character in ancient seal script, Chinese pronunciation in *fanqie* (a method of indicating the pronunciation of a character by using two other characters, each giving part of the pronunciation), and definition, all copied from the *Yupian*.

Here, I want to make a distinction of two types of readings, *on-yomi* 音読み and *kun-yomi* 訓読み. The former is the Japanese approximation of the base Chinese pronunciation of the character at the time it was introduced, so basically it is the same as Chinese. In English, we translate *on-yomi* to "Sino-Japanese readings." For the Chinese character 波, which means "wave," the pronunciation is ha in *on-yomi* and nami in *kun-yomi*. *Kun-yomi* (Japanese readings) is a reading based on the pronunciation of a native Japanese word, or *yamato kotoba* 大和言葉, which closely approximated the meaning of the Chinese character when it was introduced. As Chinese characters became more and more established in Japan, we modified them into *manyō-gana* 万葉仮名 to denote sounds, so the character 波 started to denote the sound [ha] in the Japanese sound system, which later developed into its cursive style called hiragana (は) and, its simplified form, katakana (ハ). Also, we invented our own "Chinese" characters, called

---

[26] *Erya* 爾雅, author unknown (c. 3rd century BCE); *Shuowen jiezi* 説文解字, comp. Xu Shen 許慎 (25–206 CE); *Yupian* 玉篇, comp. Gu Yewang 顧野王 (543 CE).
[27] *Niina* 新字, comp. Sakaibe no Iwatsumi 坂合部磐積 (682 CE).
[28] T. Okimori, "Jodai no jisho: Niina ha jitsuzai shitaka" (上代の辞書：『新字』は実在したか), *Yukyu* 悠久 139 (2015): 27–41.

kokuji 国字 (national characters); for example, 峠, which means "mountain pass," is a character unique to Japanese and does not have an original Chinese reading (*on-yomi*). Knowing these character differences is essential in understanding types of Japanese dictionaries and their historical development.

A later Heian dictionary, the *Shinsen Jikyō* 新選字鏡 (898–901 CE) was the first to include Japanese readings for Chinese characters. It was compiled by the Buddhist monk Shōjū (昌住). This dictionary was unique in several points. The first innovation was its original semantic organization. Instead of following the Chinese dictionaries, Shōjū introduced a novel Japanese system of 160 radicals (*bu* 部) that exhibit semantic organization.

For example, the first seven are heaven (天), sun (日), moon (月), meat (肉), rain (雨), air (气), and wind (風). The *Shinsen Jikyō* not only reduced the number of radical headings but also logically arranged them by meaning. It also for the first time provided Japanese equivalents (*wakun* 和訓), which means each Chinese character had a *kun-yomi* originated from a Japanese reading, which was more familiar to the Japanese users. Whilst the *Tenrei Banshō Meigi* was compiled for Japanese monks and scholars for the purpose of understanding Chinese texts, the *Shinsen Jikyō* provided information for Chinese characters used in Japanese. It noted over 3,700 Japanese pronunciations and cited early texts, for instance, the *Nihon Ryōiki* 日本霊異記 (*Accounts of Miracles in Japan*, c. 822 CE).[29] The *Shinsen Jikyō* is also the first Japanese dictionary to include *kokuji* invented in Japan.

IS: Please establish the difference between the graphically organized dictionaries, the semantically organized dictionaries, and the phonetically organized dictionaries.

YT: Absolutely. The Japanese language has three distinct character sets: kanji (Chinese characters), hiragana, and katakana. For instance, the word *jiten* (dictionary) can be written using kanji (辞典) or in hiragana (じてん). If one wants to know the meaning of a kanji, they can consult a graphically organized dictionary known as a *kan-wa jiten* 漢和辞典 (kanji-Japanese dictionary). In this case, you would look up the character 辞 under the radical 舌 to find its meaning. Hopefully, you can also find the most typical example like 辞典 under that entry in a *kan-wa jiten*. The earliest dictionaries, such as the *Niina* or the *Tenrei Banshō Meigi*, belong to this group of graphically organized dictionaries, with each Chinese character entry classified by radicals. The *Shinsen Jikyō* added Japanese readings but still followed the macro-structure of this Chinese character dictionary format.

For factual or encyclopedic information, semantically organized dictionaries like a thesaurus or an onomasiological dictionary are useful. In the Heian period, the *Wamyō Ruijushō* 和名類聚抄 (934 CE) was the first semantically organized dictionary. It was compiled by Minamoto no Shitagō 源順 (911–83 CE), who categorized Chinese characters into twenty-four subject headings such as "universe," "humans," "body," "sickness," "arts," etc. It was considered an antecedent of Japanese encyclopedias. More recently, these types of encyclopedic dictionaries are also called *jiten*; but they often use different characters, such as *jiten* 事典 (sometimes referred to as *koto-ten*), or *hyakka-jiten* 百科事典,

[29] *Nihon Ryoiki* (日本国現報善悪霊異記), comp. Keikai 景戒 (Kyoto, c. 822 CE).

indicating that they are dictionaries of "general knowledge and things." In recent times, many encyclopedic dictionaries adopt phonetically organized indexes. The strictly semantically organized dictionaries are called thesaurus (シソーラス), following the Western tradition.

Finally, if one wanted to know the meaning of a given Japanese word like *jiten*, they could refer to phonetically organized dictionaries and search for the word *jiten* (じてん) directly in the entries. This type of dictionary mainly focuses on language or the linguistic information of a word, thus they are called *jiten/kotoba-ten* 辞典 and distinguished from *jiten* 字典, meaning *kan-wa jiten*.

The first phonetically organized dictionary was the *Iroha Jiruishō* 色葉字類抄 (1144–65). *Iroha-jun* いろは順 is a method of arranging kana characters in Japanese, which was once very popular as the arrangement of the Japanese kana system but has now been overtaken by the *gojūon jun* 五十音順 (a-i-u-e-o) system. The *Iroha Jiruishō* was the first Heian period dictionary to collate characters by pronunciation rather than by logographic radical (like *Tenrei Banshō Meigi*) or word meaning (like *Wamyō Ruijushō*). The *Iroha Jiruishō* actually has a complex history. The original two-fascicle edition was compiled by an unknown editor in the late Heian period (c. 1144–65). This was followed by a three-fascicle edition by Tachibana Tadakane 橘忠兼 (c. 1177–88). Finally, another anonymous editor compiled the expanded ten-fascicle edition, entitled 伊呂波字類抄 (with *iroha* written 伊呂波 instead of 色葉) in the beginning of the Kamakura period (1185–1333).

After the Edo period (1603–1867), ordinary citizens started to consult dictionaries, and most of them preferred to use phonetically organized dictionaries. So, most dictionaries compiled after the Edo period for general users used dictionaries ordered phonetically by *iroha-jun* until the Meiji period (1868–1912). Besides the *Iroha Jiruishō*, *Setsuyōshū* 節用集 and *Onkochishinsho* 温故知新書 (1484) are worth mentioning as phonetically organized dictionaries. *Setsuyōshū* is a Japanese dictionary organized by a Japanese *iroha* syllabary, which was produced in the mid Muromachi period (1469–87). It was almost the first dictionary of this style and nature, and it was welcomed by the general public as a practical book for its simplicity at the time. It was revised and edited in various ways until the early Meiji period. Because of its long life, *Setsuyōshū* occupies an extremely important position in the history of Japanese dictionaries. Among the general public in the Edo period, the term *Setsuyōshū* was even a synonym for a dictionary with *iroha* indexes. The everyday vocabulary of the time was arranged in *iroha* order according to the first syllable and then classified into about twelve categories ranging from heaven and earth to language, with some appendices. Each word was written in Chinese characters and kana (mostly katakana), and sometimes the meaning and etymology were provided. It is a practical dictionary for looking up the kanji notation of a word from its *iroha*-reading. *Onkochishinsho* was published in 1484 during the Muromachi period (1336–1573), edited by Ōtomo Hirokimi 大伴広公. This was the oldest Japanese dictionary to collate words in the now standard *gojūon* order (a-i-u-e-o) instead of the *iroha* order (i-ro-ha-ni-ho). The dictionary contains 13,000 words, collated by *gojūon*, then by twelve subject classifications. The contents were quite similar to *Setsuyōshū*, but the *gojūon* system was not as popular as the *iroha* system back then, and *Setsuyōshū* became more accepted by the users.

IS: I'm interested in the impact of the Jesuit Mission Press in the development of dictionaries in Modern Japanese.

YT: In the sixteenth century, as part of their mission, Jesuits compiled and published what are known as *Kirishitan-ban* キリシタン版 (Christian editions), which were instrumental in evangelization efforts. These editions included a variety of works, from literature to language dictionaries, and even moral and doctrinal texts. A standout among these is the *Nippo Jisho* 日葡辞書, also known in Modern Portuguese as *Vocabulário da língua do Japão*. This Japanese-Portuguese dictionary from 1603 catalogued over 32,000 Japanese words with their Portuguese definitions, marking the first time Japanese was systematically documented for a European language. Notably, it captured the spoken language and colloquial expressions prevalent at that time, which is quite rare for dictionaries of that era.

The *Nippo Jisho* had a special purpose for Jesuits. It was crafted to aid missionaries in learning spoken Japanese, with careful attention to regional dialects, written and spoken forms, and even distinctions in language used by different social groups, such as women and children, or in terms of elegance or vulgarity.

Many words recorded in the *Nippo Jisho* had never been seen in written form before, and its romanization reflects the phonetics of the sixteenth-century Japanese language, offering invaluable insights to modern linguists about the language during the Sengoku period (1467–1603) and its evolution. The dictionary also provides details on aspects like rhyming words, pronunciation, meanings, usage, and even cultural elements such as names of flora and fauna, popular phrases, and customary practices of that time.

IS: Tell me about the subsequent development of monolingual dictionaries in Japan.

YT: I already mentioned *Setsuyōshū* of the fifteenth century, often referred to as a *jibiki* 字引 (character dictionary); however, it was not a kanji dictionary but an essential reference for daily life, listing words by their *iroha* pronunciation. Although it only provided many kanji idioms with their kana readings, without any word meanings, it was deemed sufficient for everyday writing. Numerous editions of *Setsuyōshū* are recorded. During the Edo period, *Setsuyōshū* had become a household name, a term synonymous with dictionaries themselves.

The narrative continues into the early modern period with Kaibara Yoshifuru's 貝原好古 1688 publication of the *Wa-ji-ga* 和爾雅, taking inspiration from the Chinese *Ji-ga* 爾雅. This is a kanji dictionary similar to the *Shinsen Jikyō*. The nineteenth century saw innovative works like Ishikawa Masamochi's 石川雅望 *Gagen Shūran* 雅言集覧 (1826, 1849). The dictionary contains examples of ancient words mainly from kana literature books of the Heian period, as well as from *Konjaku Monogatari Shū* 今昔物語集, *Monzen* 文選, and other Chinese classics, arranged in order of their usage and sometimes with brief explanations.[30]

---

[30] *Konjyaku Monogatari Shū* (今昔物語集), author unknown, 31 vols., c. 1120; *Monzen* 文選, *Wen Xuan* (Selections of Refined Literature), comp. Xiao Tong. c. 520s.

The examples are arranged in order of *iroha* and are sometimes accompanied by brief explanatory notes. The compilation was intended to serve as a standard for creating pseudoclassical texts at the time. Ōta Zensai 太田全斎 compiled the *Rigen Shūran* 俚言集覧 (1797–1829), which catalogued the slang of the era and is akin to Modern Japanese language dictionaries in the sense that the entries were ordered in *a-ka-sa-ta-na* style, using the *gojūon* style horizontally.

Another important work in the Edo period is *Wakun no Shiori* (和訓栞) by Tanigawa Kotosuga 谷川士清. It contains Parts 1–3 in ninety-three volumes, which were published between 1777 and 1877. The first two parts contain a collection of ancient words (*kogo* 古語 or *jōdai-go* 上代語) and courtesy words (*ga-go* 雅語, or *chūko-go* 中古語 words in the Heian period). Part 3 mainly contains slang words, colloquialisms, and dialects (*zoku-go* 俗語), arranged in Japanese syllabary order up to the second syllable, with sources, explanatory notes, and illustrative examples. It is notable as the first Modern Japanese language dictionary in Japan and has had a significant influence on dictionaries in the following eras. The current version, the *Zouho Gorin Wakun no Shiori* 増補語林和訓栞, enlarged and reorganized by Inoue Yorikuni 井上頼圀 and Kosugi Sugimura 小杉榲邨 in 1898, does not include the second part of the dictionary.

IS: Let's talk about Ōtsuki Fumihiko 大槻文彦.

YT: Certainly. Ōtsuki Fumihiko, a colossus in the field, is celebrated for his seminal work, the *Genkai* 言海 (*The Sea of Words*), a cornerstone in the realm of Japanese dictionaries in the Meiji period. His diverse educational background at Kaiseijo 開成所, a forerunner to the University of Tokyo and Tokyo University of Foreign Studies, where he immersed himself in Western studies, English, and mathematics, equipped him for this monumental task. In 1872, his career path led him to the Ministry of Education, where he embarked on a mission to compile a comprehensive Japanese dictionary – a project that spanned over a decade, from 1875 to 1886. Ōtsuki first thought he could produce a Japanese dictionary by translating English dictionaries into Japanese. He actually attempted to translate *Webster's Royal Octavo Dictionary* (1871) and the manuscripts of this bilingual dictionary still remains at the Waseda University library.[31] However, he gave up the idea due to the fundamental differences between the two languages. Borrowing the dictionary format from English dictionaries, he studied the Japanese language carefully and came up with a new grammatical description for the Japanese, which was fully described in the *Gohō Shinan* 語法指南 (Usage instructions) in the *Genkai*.

Despite completing the manuscript, the ministry could not publish it due to the lack of budget. It was not until 1889 that he was requested by the ministry to publish it at his own expense. The *Genkai* contains 39,103 entries ordered in the *gojūon* system in 1,000 pages. It was soon republished and expanded in commercial editions that went through over a thousand printings by the middle of the twentieth century. Ōtsuki's *Genkai* not only set a benchmark for subsequent

---

[31] *An American Dictionary of the English Dictionary: Webster's Royal Octavo Dictionary with 10,000 New Words*, ed. Noah Webster, rev. Chauncey A. Goodrich (Philadelphia: Lippincott, 1871).

Japanese dictionaries but also reflected a global movement toward the standardization of national languages and the consolidation of lexicographical knowledge. His insistence on including pronunciation, parts of speech, etymology, definitions, and citation sources laid the groundwork for the structure of Modern Japanese lexicography.

Ōtsuki's innovative approach mirrored the lexicographical advancements of his contemporaries in the West. Notable parallels include the *Webster's American Dictionary of the English Language* in the US and the *OED* in the UK, both emblematic of their respective linguistic heritages. Similarly, Émile Littré's work in France and the Brothers Grimm's dictionary in Germany were indicative of this world-historical trend toward crafting comprehensive national lexicons.[32] Moreover, during the period of compilation of the *Genkai*, English bilingual dictionaries such as Hepburn's *Waei Gorin Shūsei* or the *Fuon Sōzu Eiwa Jii* by Shibata Masayoshi and Koyasu Takashi were published, which inspired Ōtsuki to produce a relatively concise dictionary of the Japanese language for general users. In that sense, Ōtsuki's *Genkai* is also a testament to Japan's participation in this lexicon-building epoch.

IS: After the *Genkai*, more comprehensive, unabridged dictionaries of the Japanese language were compiled, such as the *Dainihon Kokugo Jiten*.

YT: Yes, everyone was impressed by Ōtsuki's *Genkai*, but at the same time they realized that lexicography in the West saw a remarkable progress in the description of the language families and the roots of the language, which inspired lexicographers to compile dictionaries on historical principles such as the *OED*. The *Dainihon Kokugo Jiten* was edited by Ueda Kazutoshi and Matsui Kanji.

Ueda Kazutoshi established the foundation of Modern Japanese linguistics. After graduating from the Department of Japanese Literature at the Imperial University, he went to Germany and France to study linguistics. After returning to Japan, he introduced Western European methods of language study to the research conducted by Japanese language scholars up to that time. He reexamined conventional research and pioneered new research on the history of Japanese linguistics, Japanese phonology, Japanese language history, and linguistic typologies, etc. He was also involved in national language policy and research by helping to establish the National Language Research Committee (1900; reorganized as the National Language Council in 1949) and worked to foster many outstanding young scholars.

This dictionary with Matsui Kanji was one of his monumental works. More than 200,000 Japanese, Chinese, and foreign words from the Nara period (710–84) to the Taishō period (1912–26) are arranged in Japanese syllabary order using the historical kana syllabary system, with pronunciations indicated by furigana, and abundant examples of usage given, especially for words from the early, middle, and modern periods.

Although the glossary is simple, with few etymological theories, and the medieval words are relatively brief, this is an unprecedentedly excellent dictionary of the Japanese language, and together with the *Daigenkai* 大言海, edited by

---

[32] *Dictionnaire de la langue française*, ed. Émile Littré (Paris: Hachette, 1873); *Deutsches Wörterbuch*, ed. Brothers Grimm (Leipzig: Weidmann's, 1854).

Ōtsuki Fumihiko,[33] it has enduring value. Many scholars consider that this dictionary was the mother of the twenty-volume *Nihon Kokugo Daijiten*.

Following the release of the *Dainihon Kokugo Jiten*, Ōtsuki embarked on the ambitious project of compiling the *Daigenkai*, a comprehensive and enlarged edition of the *Genkai*. Despite dedicating sixteen years to this endeavor, Ōtsuki passed away after completing about one-third of the work. It was Ōkubo Hatsuo 大久保初男 who stepped in to finish the dictionary in 1935, which ultimately contained 98,000 entries spanning Old, Middle, and Modern Japanese.

The *Daigenkai*, alongside the *Dainihon Kokugo Jiten*, stands as one of the two most influential modern-style dictionaries in the Japanese language, significantly shaping subsequent lexicography. Ōtsuki's distinctive approach to defining words, particularly his focus on etymology, is a hallmark of this work. It is evident that the methodology of the *OED* and other historically grounded dictionaries played a role in influencing Ōtsuki's methods of word definition and explanation.

Suggested Readings

Hayakawa, Isamu. *A Critical History of English-Japanese Lexicography*. Kindle Books, 2016. ASIN: B01LXK2NO8.

Tono, Yukio. "The Lexicography of Japanese." In *International Handbook of Modern Lexis and Lexicography*, ed. Patrick Hanks and Gilles-Maurice de Schryver. Berlin: Springer, 2022. https://doi.org/10.1007/978-3-642-45369-4_86-1

Tono, Yukio. "Lexicography across Languages." In *The Encyclopedia of Applied Linguistics*, ed. Carol A. Chapelle. Oxford: Blackwell, 2013. http://doi.org/10.1002/9781405198431.wbeal0700

Tono, Yukio. "Japanese lexicography." Edited by Keith Brown. *Encyclopedia of Language and Linguistics* 14, no. 6 (2005): 105–9.

Dictionaries

Dictionaries (Chinese)

Erya 爾雅. Author unknown, c. 3rd century BCE.
Shuowen jiezi 説文解字. Compiled by Xu Shen 許慎, 25–206 CE.
Yupian 玉篇. Compiled by Gu Yewang 顧野王, 543 CE.

Dictionaries (Japanese)

Niina 新字. Compiled by Sakaibe no Iwatsumi 坂合部磐積, 682 CE.
Tenrei Banshō Meigi 篆隷万象名義. Compiled by Kūkai 空海, 830–835 CE. Kyoto.
Shinsen Jikyō 新選字鏡. Compiled by Shōjū 昌住, 898–901 CE. Kyoto.
Wamyō Ruijushō 和名類聚抄. Compiled by Minamoto no Shitagō 源順, 934 CE. Kyoto.

---

[33] *Daigenkai* 大言海, ed. Ōtsuki Fumihiko 大槻文彦 (Fuzambo, 1932–37).

Iroha Jiruishō 色葉字類抄/伊呂波字類抄. Compiled by Tachibana Tadakane 橘忠兼 and anonymous editors. Around the late 12th century. Kyoto.

Ruiju Myōgishō 類聚名義抄. Author unknown. 11th–12th century.

Kagakushū 下学集. Compiled by Tōroku Hanō 東麓破衲. 1444. Kyoto.

Onkochishinsho 温故知新書. Compiled by Otomo Yasuhiro 大伴泰広. 1484. Kyoto.

Setsuyōshū 節用集. Author unknown. Various editions from the mid 15th to 18th centuries.

Rakuyōshū 落葉集. Compiled by Japan Jesuit Mission. 1598.

Nippo Jisho 日葡辞書 (or Vocabulário da Língua do Japão), 1603.

Wa-ji-ga 和爾雅. Compiled by Kaibara Yoshifuru 貝原好古. 1688.

Wakun no Shiori 和訓栞. Compiled by Tanigawa Kotosuga 谷川士清. 93 vols. 1777–1877.

Gagen Shūran 雅言集覧. Compiled by Ishikawa Masamochi 石川雅. 1826–49.

Rigen Shūran 俚言集覧. Compiled by Ōta Zensai 太田全斎. Early 19th century.

Genkai 言海. Compiled by Ōtsuki Fumihiko 大槻文彦. 1889–91.

Zōho Gorin Wakun no Shiori 増補語林和訓栞. 3 vols. Compiled by Inoue Yorikuni 井上頼圀 and Kosugi Sugimura 小杉榲邨. 1898.

Dainihon Kokugo Jiten 大日本國語辞典. Edited by Ueda Kazutoshi 上田万年 and Matsui Kanji 松井簡治. Fuzambo, 1915–19.

Daigenkai 大言海. Edited by Ōtsuki Fumihiko 大槻文彦. Fuzambo, 1932–37.

Jien 辞苑. Edited by Shinmura Izuru 新村出. Hakubunkan, 1935.

Kōjien 広辞苑. Edited by Shinmura Izuru 新村出. Iwanami-shoten, 1955 (1st ed.) – 2018 (7th ed.).

Nihon Kokugo Daijiten 日本国語大辞典. Edited by Nihon Daijiten Kankokai 日本大辞典刊行会. Shōgakukan, 1972–76 (1st ed.); 2000–2002 (2nd ed.).

Daijirin 大辞林. Edited by Matsumura Akira 松村明. Sanseidō, 1988 (1st ed.) – 2006 (3rd ed.).

Nihon Hogen Daijiten 日本方言大辞典. Editorial supervisor Tokugawa Sōken 徳川宗賢. 3 vols. Shōgakukan, 1989.

Nihongo Daijiten 日本語大辞典. Kodansha, 1989.

Shūeisha Kokugo Jiten 集英社国語辞典. Edited by Morioka Kenji 森岡健二, Tokugawa Sōken 徳川宗賢, Kawabata Yoshiaki 川端善明, Nakamura Akira 中村明, and Hoshino Kōichi 星野晃一. Shūeisha, 1993.

Nihon Kokugo Daijiten Seisenban 日本国語大辞典精選版. Edited by Nihon Kokugo Daijiten Editorial Office. Shogakukan, 2006.

Dictionaries (English bilingual)

Waei Gorin Shūsei 和英語林集成. Compiled by James Curtis Hepburn. 1867.

Fuon Sōzu Eiwa Jii 附音挿図英和字彙. Compiled by Shibata Masayoshi 柴田昌吉 and Koyasu Takashi 子安峻. 1873.

Meiji Eiwa-Jiten 明治英和字典. Compiled by Seki Shinpachi 尺振八. 1884–89.

Saito's Idiomological English-Japanese Dictionary 熟語本位英和中辞典. Compiled by Saitō Hidesaburō 斎藤秀三郎. Nichieisha, 1915.

Kenkyusha's New English-Japanese Dictionary 研究社新英和大辞典. Edited by Okakura Yoshisaburō 岡倉由三郎. Kenkyūsha, 1927 (1st ed.) – 2002 (6th ed, chief editor: Takebayashi Shigeru 竹林滋).

Saito's Japanese-English Dictionary 斎藤和英大辞典. Compiled by Saitō Hidesaburō 斎藤秀三郎. Nichieisha, 1928.

New CROWN English-Japanese Dictionary 新クラウン英和辞典. Edited by Kawamura Jūjirō 河村重治郎. Sanseidō, 1939 (1st ed.) – 1995 (5th ed. by Tajima Shingo 田島伸悟).

Kenkyusha's New Collegiate English-Japanese Dictionary (新英和中辞典). Edited by Iwasaki Tamihei 岩崎民平. Kenkyūsha, 1966 (1st ed.) – 2003 (7th ed. by Takebayashi Shigeru, et al. 竹林滋 他).

Anchor English-Japanese Dictionary (アンカー英和辞典). Edited by Shibata Tetsushi 柴田徹士. Gakushū Kenkyūsha, 1972.

Shogakukan Random House English-Japanese Dictionary (ランダムハウス英和大辞典). Edited by Kunihiro Tetsuya 国広哲弥 and Konishi Tomoshichi 小西友七. Shōgakukan, 1973 (1st ed.); 1993 (2nd ed.).

Obunsha's Comprehensive English-Japanese Dictionary (旺文社英和中典). Edited by Takahashi Genji 高橋源次. Ōbunsha, 1975.

Progressive English-Japanese Dictionary (プログレッシブ英和中辞典). Edited by Konishi Tomoshichi 小西友七, Yasui Minoru 安井稔, Kunihiro Tetsuya 国広哲弥. Shōgakukan, 1980 (1st ed.) – 2012 (5th ed.).

GENIUS English-Japanese Dictionary (ジーニアス英和辞典). Edited by Konishi Tomoshichi 小西友七. Taishūkan, 1987 (1st ed.) – 2022 (6th ed.).

Dictionaries (English monolingual)

Routledge's Diamond Dictionary of the English Language. Edited by P. Austin Nuttall. London: Routledge, 1861.

An American Dictionary of the English Language. Compiled by Noah Webster, Chauncy Goodrich, Noah Porter, and James Hadley. Springfield: G. & C. Merriam, 1864.

The Comprehensive English Dictionary, Explanatory, Pronouncing, and Etymological. Compiled by John Ogilvie. London: Blackie & Son, 1864.

An American Dictionary of the English Dictionary: Webster's Royal Octavo Dictionary with 10,000 New Words. Edited by Noah Webster, rev. by Chauncey A. Goodrich. Philadelphia: Lippincott, 1871.

A New English Dictionary on Historical Principles. (Later, the *Oxford English Dictionary.*) Edited by James A. H. Murray. Oxford: Oxford University Press, 1884–1928.

The Concise Oxford English Dictionary. Compiled by H. W. Fowler and F. G. Fowler. Oxford: Oxford University Press, 1911.

Idiomatic and Syntactic English Dictionary. Compiled by A. S. Hornby, E. V. Gatenby, and A. H. Wakefield. Tokyo: Kaitakusha, 1942.

A Learner's Dictionary of Current English. Compiled by A. S. Hornby, E. V. Gatenby, and A. H. Wakefield. Oxford: Oxford University Press, 1948.

Oxford Advanced Learner's Dictionary of Current English. Compiled by A. S. Hornby, E. V. Gatenby, and A. H. Wakefield. Oxford: Oxford University Press, 1948 (1st ed.) – 2020 (10th ed.).

Random House Dictionary of the English Language. Edited by Jess Stein. New York: Random House, 1966; 1987 (2nd ed.).

Longman Dictionary of Contemporary English. 1978 (1st ed.) – 2014 (6th ed.). Harlow: Longman.

Collins COBUILD English Dictionary. (Later, *Collins COBUILD Advanced Learner's Dictionary*.) Edited by John Sinclair. Glasgow: Harper Collins, 1987 (1st ed.) – 2018 (9th ed.).

Dictionaries (online portal sites)

goo Dictionary URL: https://dictionary.goo.ne.jp/
Kotobank URL: https://kotobank.jp/
Japan Knowledge URL: https://japanknowledge.com/
Weblio URL: https://www.weblio.jp/
Eijiro on the Web URL: https://eow.alc.co.jp/

18 Russian

Mikhail Kopotev

Alexander Pushkin, the father of modern Russian literature, used an original, nuanced language. He dramatically expanded the Russian lexicon by borrowing from other languages. Much variety springs from his innovative approach. No wonder Pushkin, a lover of dictionaries, is such a canonical figure in a language spoken by close to 260 million people. This conversation explores the tradition of Russian dictionaries, concentrating on Jacob Grot's *Dictionary of the Russian Language*, Dmitry Ushakov's *Explanatory Dictionary of the Russian Language*, Sergey Ozhegov's *Dictionary of the Russian Language*, and *The Great Academic Dictionary of the Russian Language*.[1] It also contemplates regional varieties and Russian as an international language, as well as bilingual dictionaries. And it reflects on Pushkin's standing in the language.

***

ILAN STAVANS: Russians are avid dictionary-makers. How do you explain this passion?

MIHAIL KOPOTEV: While it is true, as you say, that Russians have been avid dictionary-makers, this engagement has a relatively short history. Unlike Western Europe, the Old Rus, a common ancestor of Belarusian, Russian, and Ukrainian cultures, did not reveal an advanced lexicographic practice. We know only limited and mainly non-original and non-systematic word lists (*slovniki*) and onomasticons (*imenniki*), which were in use in translation or exegesis of ecclesiastical texts; for example, "The speech of

---

[1] Yakov Grot, Словарь русского языка [Dictionary of the Russian language] (Санкт-Петербург, Типография Императорской Академии наук, 1891–1995); Dmitry Ushakov, *Толковый словарь русского языка* [Explanatory dictionary of the Russian language] (Moscow: State Publishing House of Foreign and National Dictionaries, 1935–1940); Sergey Ozhegov, Словарь русского языка [Dictionary of the Russian language] (Moscow: State Publishing House of Foreign and National Dictionaries, 1949); Большой академический словарь русского языка [The great academic dictionary of the Russian language], Vols. 1–27 (St. Petersburg: Russian Academy of Sciences, 2004–).

	the Jewish language as translated into (Old) Russian" (Рѣчь Жидовьскаго іазыка преложена на Роускоую), or "The interpretation of not-convenient [words] for understanding in written speech" (Толкование неудобь познаваемымъ в писанiихъ речемъ).
IS:	In spite of this short history, to me it seems as if Russians have produced what seems like an endless number of dictionaries, whether lexicographical or technical, historical, literary, and so on.
MK:	The genesis of East Slavic lexicography is tightly connected to modernity. Starting from the sixteenth century and gradually increasing during the seventeenth, Western European culture interfered, mainly through Ukrainian and Belarusian influencers, in the turbulent East Slavic cultures. The most prominent linguistic shift during that period was the embrace of new cogitation patterns: while in Old Rus, written texts were typically memorized and reproduced, the advent of linguistic analysis in Eastern Europe during the modern era led to a more analytical approach toward texts.
	The key innovative publications that reflected that change were rhetorical and grammatical treatises, as well as dictionaries – both translated and original. The latter, initially presented in the form of alphabetically organized lists (*azbukovniki*), quickly became the mainstream of early modern linguistic research of East Slavic scholars. The first dictionary, Lexis (Лєксис сирѣчъ реченїа, въкратъцѣ събранны) by Ukrainian scholar Lavrentij Zyzanij, was published in 1596.[2] During the seventeenth century, at least fifteen dictionaries and dozens of phrase-books (*razgovorniki*) were published. One reason why the lexicographic tradition in East Slavic countries was bolstered during that period is simple: dictionaries served as repositories of knowledge and cultural history, enabling the East Slavic people to conceptualize and represent a changing world. A new world requires new words.
IS:	New words are needed to catch up with scientific, technological, and other advances. But neologisms also come from imperial quests, tourism, immigration, and the sheer movements of modernity.
MK:	Memoirs from the Petrine time (beginning of the seventeenth century) reveal that Muscovites and inhabitants of the newly elevated Saint Petersburg literally did not understand each other due to the large number of foreigners flocking to the new capital. New words always indicate changes in society. By examining neologisms that entered the Russian language during a specific period, we can discern both the direction of influence and the areas where the old language lacked certain concepts.
	For example, in the seventeenth and eighteenth centuries, Germanic and Romance civilizations were considered the main sources of both word-borrowing and technological progress. Many of these loanwords continue to exist in the modern language, such as *admiral*, *storm*, and *flagman* (from Dutch), *flag*, *graf*, and *gas* (German); *aria* and *solo* (Italian); *ball*, *band*, and *balkon* (French). Less known, but also significant, were the influences from Slavic languages: *borscht* and *Cossack* (Ukrainian); *akademia*, *monopolia*, and the most curious one, *vodka* (Polish).

---

[2] Lavrentii Zyzanii, Лексис [Lexis] (Vilnius, 1596).

IS: Tell me about the *Leksikon vokabulam novym po alfavitu* (Лексикон вокабулам новым по алфавиту), a Russian dictionary of foreign words written, though not published, during the reign of Peter the Great. It is attributed to Fedor Polikarpov-Orlov and possible date of publication, according to some scholars, is 1715.

MK: The reforms conducted by Peter the Great can be seen as the culmination of long-lasting changes that were evident in various aspects, reflected in lexicons and dictionaries. These linguistic resources served the purpose of either preserving the "proper old treasure" or legitimizing new words and concepts. One intellectual who addressed both of these needs was Fedor Polikarpov-Orlov (c. 1670–1731), a man of education – and Muscovite.

A prominent representative of the Enlightenment, Polikarpov-Orlov was one of the most influential scholars and officials in Peter's court of his time. He was born in Moscow and received a classical Westernized education at the Slavic-Greek-Latin Academy there. He served in the Moscow Print Yard and later became a director of this publishing house. During his life, he engaged in translation work, delivered lectures, and wrote books. His main works include *Abecedarium* (Алфавитарь рекше букварь, 1701) and the *Trilingual Lexicon* (Лексиконъ треязычный, сирѣчь реченій славенскихъ, єллино-греческихъ и латінскихъ сокровище, 1704), both of which were used in education for decades, as well as an unpublished "Lexicon of New Words" (Лексиконъ вокабуламъ новымъ по алфавиту).[3]

The "Lexicon of New Words" is a collection of foreign lexemes that was not published at the time and is likely attributed to Polikarpov-Orlov. This dictionary exemplifies the lexicographic trend mentioned earlier, which signifies yet another Western influence on Russian civilization. The dictionary follows an alphabetical organization, with each entry presenting the foreign word, its Russian equivalent, and a concise definition. The entries encompass various subjects such as science, technology, religion, and culture. The dictionary is particularly notable for its inclusion of many technical and scientific terms that were new to the Russian language at the time (e.g. *arest, komedia, kompas*, etc.). It also reflects Peter the Great's interest in modernizing Russia and bringing it into closer contact with Western Europe. Despite its historical significance, the "Lexicon" was not published until much later. Scholars believe that it was completed in 1715, but the manuscript was not discovered until the nineteenth century and was fully transcribed and published in the twentieth century.[4]

---

[3] Fedor Polikarpov-Orlov, *Алфавитарь рекше букварь* [Alphabet book, also called a primer] (Moscow: Moscow Print Yard, 1701); Fedor Polikarpov-Orlov, *Лексикон треязычный сирѣчь реченій славенскихъ, эллино-греческихъ и латинскихъ сокровище* [Trilingual lexicon, or treasury of Slavonic, Hellenic-Greek, and Latin sayings] (Moscow: Moscow Print Yard, 1704).

[4] N. A. Smirnov, *Словарь иностранных слов, вошедших в русский язык в эпоху Петра Великого* [Dictionary of foreign words that entered the Russian language in the era of Peter the Great], *Proceedings of the Department of Russian Language and Literature* 88, no. 4(2) (St. Petersburg: Russian Academy of Science, 1910), 363–82.

Polikarpov-Orlov's main lexicographic opus, the *Trilingual Lexicon*, includes 17,328 entries, organized alphabetically, and provides definitions of words in three "languages": Slavic (here Russian and Church Slavonic), Greek, and Latin. The entries also include information on the origins of the words and their usage in various contexts. One of the main purposes of the *Trilingual Lexicon* was to aid in the translation of religious texts. It was also intended to help Russian scholars and intellectuals better understand and communicate with their Western European counterparts. The *Trilingual Lexicon*, considered a significant contribution to the history of Russian lexicography, reflects the growing interest in preserving national heritage and the importance of cross-cultural communication in eighteenth-century Russia. Along with other dictionaries published at that time, it also demonstrates the role of dictionaries as tools for language learning, translation, and cultural exchange.

IS: What needs in Russian culture was Polikarpov-Orlov's endeavor responding to?

MK: As Russia sought to modernize and establish closer ties with Western Europe under the reign of Peter the Great, there was a need to expand the Russian language to encompass new concepts and ideas from various fields. Polikarpov-Orlov's dictionaries aimed to bridge the gap between the Russian language and the influx of foreign intellectual traditions. The *Trilingual Lexicon* specifically addressed the need for interpreting religious terminology, while also incorporating a broader cultural perspective, such as ancient Greek. The *Lexicon* facilitated the process of integration by providing translations and explanations, enabling Russian intellectuals to comprehend other traditions in their native language. Moreover, the *Lexicon* aimed to showcase the closer relations between Eastern and Western cultures by emphasizing the fact that the same concepts could be expressed equally in all three "languages."

IS: I want to move to Russian Romanticism, particularly the Archaists and Karamzinists. Pushkin was a product of these trends. I'm interested in its connection to dictionaries.

MK: The early nineteenth century in Russia saw the emergence of two fundamentally opposite groups of thinkers, known at that time as *Shishkovists* and *Karamzinists*, who questioned the prevailing Rationalist ideology. The Archaists, led by Alexander Shishkov, sought to revive the language and literature of ancient Rus, believing that the Russian language had become corrupted by foreign influences. They aimed to purify the language by returning to the old Slavonic written tradition and create a national literature that reflected Russian heritage.

Their work often included archaic words and forms that were not commonly used in contemporary discourse, not to mention that some were of Church Slavonic origin, not East Slavic. Their lexicographic efforts resulted in the first dictionary of the Russian Academy of Science, a six-volume compendium of almost 50,000 words attributed as *slavenorossijskije,* (lit. Slavonic-Russian, meaning "Church Slavonic") and published in 1794, which aimed to standardize the Russian language by providing clear definitions and usage examples.

In contrast, the Karamzinist movement, named after Nikolai Karamzin, aimed to construct a new language suited for the aesthetic needs of secular educated readers, including women. Karamzin – a *Russian Sterne*, as he was called – played an important role in the development of the Russian language toward innovation. As part of this effort, he compiled a *History of the Russian State*, a fundamental twelve-volume compilation that included thought-provoking facts and romantic hyperboles about the Russian past.[5] As a writer, he created sentimental stories written in a modernized, "French" style.

Overall, the Shishkovists and Karamzinists were important contributors to the development of the Russian language and its vocabulary, although, in terms of lexicographic practice, only the Archaists have created a fundamental dictionary.[6]

Alexander Pushkin (1799–1837), often glorified – ideologically, in part – as the father of Modern Russian language and literature, was a product of both trends, influenced and criticized by both the Archaists and Karamzinists. His poetry and prose drew on archaic and classical forms and vocabulary. An example of his ambiguous position can be found in *Eugene Onegin* (1833), where Pushkin's ironic comments are directed against both modern borrowings and the archaic Academic dictionary.[7] This translation is by James E. Falen. All italics are in the original:

> Your interest piqued and doubtless growing
> In current fashions of *toilette*,
> I might describe in terms more knowing
> His clothing for the learned set.
> This might well seem an indiscretion,
> Description, though, is my profession;
> But *pantaloons, gilet,* and *frock* –
> These words are hardly Russian stock;
> And I confess (in public sorrow)
> That as it is my diction groans
> With far too many foreign loans;
> But if indeed I overborrow,
> I have of old relied upon
> Our *Academic Lexicon.*[8]

Pushkin's contributions to Russian language and literature were widely recognized already at his time; he was among the first to be promoted as a member of the Russian Academy of Science, although he did not make significant contributions to lexicography or any other linguistic studies. Instead, Pushkin's works provided a blueprint for shaping the "Russian literary

---

[5] Nikolai Karamzin, История государства Российского [History of the Russian state] (St. Petersburg: Gretsch Publishing House, 1816–18).
[6] Словарь Академии Российской [Dictionary of the Russian Academy], Vols. 1–6 (St. Petersburg, 1806–22).
[7] Alexander Pushkin, Евгений Онегин [Eugene Onegin] (St. Petersburg: Alexander Smirdin Printing House, 1833).
[8] Alexander Pushkin, *Eugene Onegin: A Novel in Verse*, trans. James E. Falen (Oxford: Oxford University Press, 1995), 16.

language," a concept that was fundamentally developed by Soviet scholars and attributed to Pushkin as the main (and sometimes the only) legitimate source of the standard language. His legacy continues to influence language policy today, with Pushkin and "his" language being a battlefield.

IS: Let's talk about what is perhaps the most famous Russian dictionary ever assembled – the *Explanatory Dictionary of the Living Great Russian Language (Tolkovyj slovar' zhivogo velikorusskogo yazyka)*. This massive project was begun in 1918 by Vladimir Dal'. It was published in four volumes from 1863 to 1866.

MK: I will start with a fun fact: the real "living Russian language" is censored twice in the *Dictionary*. Initially, Vladimir Dal' intentionally did not include obscene words in the dictionary. Later, a Polish-Russian linguist, Jan Baudouin de Courtenay, enriched the vocabulary with many words, including the crispest ones, but Soviet lexicographers blacked them out again.[9]

Despite this fact, it is perhaps the most famous Russian dictionary ever assembled. The project was initiated by Dal', who – another trivia – in the capacity of a professional doctor attested Pushkin's death in 1837. By that day, Dal' had been compiling the *Dictionary* for almost twenty years, and it would be almost thirty-five more years until it was sent to print in 1863.

The dictionary was based on the extensive fieldwork conducted by Dr. Dal', who practiced throughout Russia, while also collecting examples of the language. He was particularly interested in preserving the language of the common people and their folklore. In this sense, the dictionary was in opposition to the lexicographic practice of the Russian Academy. Dal's dictionary aimed to provide a comprehensive explanation of the meanings of potentially all Russian words, to capture the rich diversity of Russian dialects. The dictionary included over 200,000 entries, with detailed definitions, usage examples, and etymological information.

In addition to its linguistic and lexicographic importance, the *Explanatory Dictionary of the Living Great Russian Language* has also played an important role in preserving Russian culture and identity: it helped to establish a common ground before and after the Revolution. With all considerations in mind, this dictionary was, by all odds, distorted at a minimum by the Soviet censorship, remaining the only publicly available pre-Revolutionary lexicographic source for several generations. No wonder that Aleksandr Solzhenitsyn leaned largely on that of Dal' in creating his *Russian Dictionary of Language Expansion* (Русский словарь языкового расширения).[10]

IS: The Soviet Orthography Reform of 1917 was pursued by Alexander Shakhmatov shortly after the Revolution. It is probably the single most significant change to Russian orthography that endures to this day.

---

[9] Vladimir Dal', *Толковый словарь живого великорусского языка* [Explanatory dictionary of the living great Russian language], 3rd ed., ed. Jan Baudouin de Courtenay, Vols. 1–4 (St. Petersburg: Academy of Sciences, 1903–9).

[10] Alexandr Solzhenitsyn, *Русский словарь языкового расширения* [Russian dictionary of language expansion] (Moscow: Nauka, 1990).

It removed a few mostly undistinguished old Cyrillic characters. But notably, Russian emigres did not adopt these changes immediately.

MK: A common assumption suggests that the reform was initiated and conducted by Bolsheviks. In fact, Alexander Shakhmatov, an academician of the Imperial Academy of Science, first reported on that matter in 1904, shortly after the orthographic committee had been established under the auspices of Grand Duke Konstantin Konstantinovich of Russia. The reform was supported by many scholars and teachers and was officially declared by the provisional government in May 1917. When the Bolsheviks came to power, they reapproved the reform in December 1917.

You are absolutely right that the reform was a significant change to the Russian orthography. It aimed to simplify the Russian writing system and bring it more in line with the spoken language. One of the key changes introduced by the reform was the removal of several old Cyrillic characters that were considered archaic and unnecessary; these included the letters ѣ (*yat*), Ѳ (*fita*), and others; some morphological forms were also unified. These changes were intended to make the Russian writing system more accessible to the general population and to reduce illiteracy rates.

Despite the fact that the reform was initially supported by conservative forces, including the royal family, it was not, as you mentioned, immediately adopted by Russian emigres, who continued to use the pre-reform orthography in their writing. This was partly due to momentum, as no new textbooks or dictionaries were available, but the main reason was indisputably political, as many Russian emigres were opposed to the Soviet government and its policies, while not fully aware of the historical background of the reform.

It was not until the 1940s, when the Soviet Union began to exert greater influence on the international Russian-speaking community that the new orthography began to be more widely adopted outside of the Soviet Union. Today, the orthography reform of 1917 is still in use in Russia and other countries that use the Russian language, and it is considered an important milestone in the development of the Modern Russian writing system.

IS: How about *Ushakov's Dictionary*, whose full name is *Explanatory Dictionary of the Russian Language,* published in 1935–40.

MK: The *Explanatory Dictionary of the Russian Language* (Большой толковый словарь русского языка), one of the most comprehensive dictionaries of the Russian language, was created during the Soviet era. At the same time, it reflects and is influenced by Soviet lexicographic practice.

It was edited by Dmitry Ushakov (1873–1942), a prominent Soviet linguist and lexicographer, and was published in four volumes between 1935 and 1940. On the one hand, the dictionary includes over 200,000 entries, with detailed definitions, information on the pronunciation and inflection of words, and usage examples. It is noteworthy for its comprehensive coverage of the vocabulary of the Russian language, including many archaic and dialectal words. On the other hand, despite its many strengths, the dictionary has been criticized for its emphasis on literary rather than spoken language. It is focused on the norms of the Soviet literary language and does not adequately reflect the diversity of Russian, as can be seen in the entry explaining the meaning of символизм (symbolism): "... 2. A movement in the art of the late nineteenth and early twentieth centuries that expressed the decadent reactionary moods of the bourgeoisie, creating symbols of mystical experiences and representations in artistic images" (my translation).

IS: In major lexicographic traditions, the twentieth century has seen a bonanza of dictionaries. This is the result of advanced technology, including the wide accessibility of online resources.

MK: The same happened in Russia, resulting in the countless dictionaries that can be found on library bookshelves today. There is a common perception for the Soviet fascination with dictionaries: the complexity and richness of the Russian language itself, as well as its wide spread across the globe. Russian is a highly inflected language with a rich and diverse vocabulary, and its grammar is notoriously difficult for both native and non-native speakers to master. As such, the production of dictionaries has been essential for preserving and advancing the language and associated culture.

However, there was a deeper reason for the boom in Soviet lexicography, which was politically driven and connected with what today would be called a need to colonize other nations, where dictionaries became a tool for ideological expansion. In the early Soviet period, many dictionaries for numerous languages were created that reflected a uniformed view of the world. For many languages spoken in the USSR, thousands of words were introduced in dictionaries with a "proper" interpretation. The socioeconomic background for new dictionaries to appear was massive internal migration, urbanization, and technological progress. These factors brought into view people who did not have a good command of Russian or did not possess specific terminology – the problems that could be addressed with dictionaries and unified education available to a wider audience.

Yet, Soviet lexicographic practice was grounded on the theory of the "literary language" (литературный язык), which was understood as "the superior form of the language existence" (my translation of the definition of литературный язык from *Linguistic Encyclopedic Dictionary*, published in the final year of the USSR's existence in Moscow).[11] This ideological construct presupposed creating dictionaries that were prescriptive yet addressed different social groups, from schoolchildren to foreign speakers.

To sum up, the Russian passion for dictionary-making is rooted in a tradition of Westernized intellectualism and the pursuit of knowledge that started in the late sixteenth century. During the era of Enlightenment and beyond, dictionaries evolved into a reflection of their times, either preserving old traditions or adopting a more modern and relaxed approach to word usage. In the twentieth century, the need to serve Communist ideology and support the industrial revolution with many people being relocated to cities resulted in a wealth of lexicographical, technical, historical, and literary dictionaries that played a vital role in preserving and advancing the Russian language within Soviet culture.

---

[11] Victoria Yartseva, ed., *Лингвистический энциклопедический словарь* [Linguistic encyclopedic dictionary] (Moscow: Soviet Encyclopedia, 1990).

IS: In other words, Russians, like other cultures, embraced dictionaries because France, Italy, England, and others already had them.

MK: Indeed, lexicography in Russia has been influenced by various traditions since its inception. Medieval word lists were often bilingual or multilingual, reflecting a leaning toward either Western or, in many cases, Byzantine intellectual tradition. In modernity, many lexicographers across Europe pursued similar goals, driven by the Enlightenment. Over time, however, lexicography in Russia evolved into a distinct discipline, and later, especially during the Soviet era, several unique lexicographic programs were established. One of the most well-known is the Meaning-Text theory, developed by Igor Mel'čuk and his colleagues. From a lexicographic perspective, the theory highlights the significance of capturing and representing the underlying semantic and syntactic structures and their holistic representation in dictionaries.

IS: Does this mean that during the Soviet period, dictionaries functioned not only as self-preservation tools?

MK: The vast majority of Soviet lexicographic production mainly served self-preservation aims, somewhat reminiscent of Jorge Luis Borges' *The Library of Babel*, which also aimed to preserve every possible ordering of information.[12] Some of them were purely descriptive, such as the dictionary of Pushkin's language (Словарь языка А. С. Пушкина) or the *Dictionary of the Names of Freshwater Fishes of the USSR* (Словарь названий пресноводных рыб СССР).[13] Others were, directly or indirectly, ideologically loaded, like Ushakov's dictionary of the Russian language or the *Dictionary of Word-Stress for Radio and Television Announcers* (Словарь ударений для работников радио и телевидения).[14] The latter, supposedly intended for a technical purpose, provides a notable example of how Soviet power sought to monopolize language. First, it assumed that there was only one normative variant of each word, and second, it presumed that linguists from Moscow knew it better. Specifically, many long-standing place names, which had been used by local residents for centuries, were appropriated and "normalized" in the dictionary.

Despite that, Soviet linguists developed dictionaries based on strong theoretical foundations. Until now, these resources represent the highest achievements in lexicography. One of the most famous ones is the *Grammatical Dictionary* (Грамматический словарь) compiled by Andrey Zaliznyak in 1977.[15] The dictionary may appear a bit cryptic (see Figure 18.1 to view three

---

[12] Jorge Luis Borges, *La biblioteca de Babel* [The library of Babel], *El jardín de senderos que se bifurcan* (Buenos Aires: Sur, 1941).

[13] Viktor Vinogradov, ed., *Словарь языка А. С. Пушкина* [Dictionary of A. S. Pushkin's language] (Moscow: Academy of Sciences, 1956); Georgy Lindberg and Aleksandr Gerd, *Словарь названий пресноводных рыб СССР на языках народов СССР и европейских стран* [Dictionary of names of freshwater fish of the USSR in the languages of the peoples of the USSR and European countries] (Leningrad: Nauka, 1972).

[14] Florentsia Ageenko and Maya Zarva, *Словарь ударений для работников радио и телевидения* [Dictionary of word-stress for radio and television announcers] (Moscow: Sovetskaya entsiklopediya, 1960).

[15] Andrey Zaliznyak, *Грамматический словарь русского языка* [Grammatical dictionary of the Russian language] (Moscow: Russian Language, 1977).

печь	ж	8e, П₂
печь	нсв	8b/b (-к-), ё
запе́чь	св	8b/b (-к-), ё ◐II

Figure 18.1 A fragment from the *Grammatical Dictionary*

complete dictionary entries), but it contains all Russian words with clear indices of their declensions and stress patterns. It enables the automatic generation of all word forms, which was quite an impressive feat considering the complexity of Russian morphology and lack of computers at that time.

Another extraordinary example is the *Explanatory Combinatorial Dictionary of Modern Russian* (Толково-комбинаторный словарь русского языка), edited by Igor Mel'čuk and Alexander Zholkovsky.[16] Due to political sanctions against the editors, its publication was significantly delayed, eventually seeing release in Vienna in 1984. Despite its modest size of only 282 entries, the dictionary's importance far exceeds its volume.

First, it is based on a rigorous theoretical approach that encompasses a holistic description of words, including morphological, semantic, stylistic, and idiomatic information, as well as government patterns, and encyclopedic information necessary for the correct usage of each headword. Second, it introduces the concept of *lexical functions*, which enable the representation of deep semantic relations between lexemes. For instance, the lexical function MAGN "to a very high degree" is manifested by different adjectives when used with different nouns:

- MAGN(illness) = severe
- MAGN(applause) = thunderous
- MAGN(joy) = great

IS: Today multilingual dictionaries – that is, a lexicon in three or more languages – are almost exclusively the domain of academic research. Is it the case in Russia as well? Of course, I'm excluding bilingual dictionaries, say Russian-English, Russian-French, Russian-Italian, which are favorites among a broad range of users.

MK: Yes and no. On the one hand, we have witnessed a decline in the use of traditional paper dictionaries, including multilingual ones, in recent decades. They are less practical for looking up words and are cumbersome to carry. On the other hand, electronic dictionaries have thrived. Various IT and EdTech companies have developed online dictionaries that offer quick and combined searches, easily accessible on devices that can fit in your pocket. The concept of simultaneously searching multiple multilingual paper sources was once unimaginable, but now one can combine as many sources as one

---

[16] Igor Mel'čuk and Alexander Zholkovsky, eds., *Толково-комбинаторный словарь русского языка* [Explanatory combinatorial dictionary of the Russian language] (Vienna: Wiener Slawistischer Almanach, 1984).

IS: needs in as many languages as one comprehends, filter results based on topics, genres, or specific keywords – and *voilà*.

IS: *Voilà*, indeed. How has Russian lexicography absorbed foreign traditions?

MK: Today, Russian lexicography is a rich and vibrant practice. It has absorbed venerable foreign traditions while also developing its own distinct profile. This profile encompasses two fundamental and non-mutually exclusive trends: prescriptive and descriptive.

The first trend is evident in the strong interest of those in power in controlling the language, which they perceive as a tool for manipulation. This interest extends to dictionaries as well. The most recent example of their activity is the State Language Act, passed in 2005 (and updated in 2024), which established that language norms are recorded, among other sources, in normative dictionaries. The list of these dictionaries is determined by the government of the Russian Federation.

The second trend is a flourishing academic lexicographic practice, which combines fundamental achievements from the Soviet era with cutting-edge computational approaches based on large collections of real language data. A brilliant example of this trend is the dictionaries prepared or edited by Juri Apresjan. Among them, the most ambitious one is the Russian "Active Dictionary" (Активный словарь русского языка),[17] which aims to provide a holistic description of living language phenomena based on real data. The ultimate outcome of which trend will prevail remains to be observed.

IS: In a number of linguistic habitats worldwide, governments, which play a role in safekeeping the language and are even the fiscal sponsors of dictionaries (think of the *Diccionario de la lengua española* in Madrid),[18] engage in a dialectical relationship with commercial enterprises whose business is to sell lexicons (*Merriam-Webster* in English, for example). What is the relationship between government-sponsored and business-oriented dictionaries in Russia today?

MK: In Russia, major lexicographic projects usually receive support through government grants or dedicated funding. This makes sense when you consider that these projects may span decades and require significant investments. For instance, the *Dictionary of the Old East Slavic Language* (Словарь русского языка XI–XVII веков) was initially thought up in 1925, saw its first issue published in 1975, and the most recent one in 2019 – and it's still ongoing.[19] Looking at it from this angle, these fundamental projects do not exactly scream commercial success. On the bright side, many of them are freely available online. However, smaller dictionaries, tailored to specific audiences, can turn a decent profit. This is particularly true for school or learner's dictionaries, whose demand is directly tied to the curriculum.

---

[17] Juri Apresjan, "Active Dictionary." In *Encyclopedia of Slavic Languages and Linguistics Online*, ed. Marc L. Greenberg (Leiden: Brill, 2020), https://doi.org/10.1163/2589-6229_ESLO_COM_032490.

[18] Real Academia Española-Asociación de Academias de La Lengua Española, *Diccionario de la lengua española*, tricentenial edition, 23rd printing (Madrid: Real Academia Española, 2014).

[19] *Словарь русского языка XI–XVII веков* [Dictionary of the Old East Slavic language] (Moscow: Nauka, 1975–).

A commonly seen practice, not just in Russia but also in other countries, is for new lexicographic projects to be funded by research foundations, governmental or private, with the distribution managed by publishing houses. Projects where the creation of a dictionary from scratch, without grant support, has been profitable are few and far between. This state of affairs has its advantages and drawbacks. On the one hand, fundamental lexicographic projects are mostly secured for years (if not centuries) until completion; on the other, the authorities might use this setup to enforce prescriptive norms by endorsing projects that align with their interests.

IS: How do you see Russian lexicography in the future?

MK: It's tough to predict what lies ahead, especially in the midst of such uncertainty. Setting aside potential economic and political fallout that could stem from the Russian invasion in Ukraine, I would like to shift attention to the linguistic implications. The rich lexicographic tradition, which I described above, will survive, as it has done many times before. However, one notable change is that the concept of Russianness is no longer monopolized by Russia. As we are observing right at the moment, numerous individuals are being displaced from Ukraine and Russia, and many Russian-speaking communities are distancing themselves from the Kremlin, whose ownership of the language has expired. This is leading to the emergence of a multicentered, globally distributed Russian-speaking populace, which has no single center of power.

This situation somewhat mirrors the aftermath of the Bolsheviks' rise to power, a time when many emigrants integrated into their host cultures. However, there is a key difference: in many countries like Kazakhstan, Belarus, or Latvia, the Russian language serves as a lingua franca – to say the very least. Before the full-scale invasion, Russian diaspora communities often adopted an opportunistic stance toward the "motherland," aligning with its linguistic norms. Today, the landscape is evolving and becoming more fragmented: from now on, dictionaries printed in Russia may no longer be considered the gold standard for "proper" language use – a situation that is already evident with fiction and textbooks published in Russia. These circumstances bear some resemblance to global English and its regional varieties, although significantly more work still needs to be done to decolonize the Russian language.

I anticipate that we will see initiatives popping up that aim to record local language usage, including regional vocabularies. It is tough to predict whether these endeavors will resonate with local communities, which may be at risk of the full assimilation into the broader linguistic environment. However, if a community is sufficiently large and tight-knit, it might be more inclined to shift away from the norms dictated by Moscow. From a lexicographic standpoint, I expect the development of dictionaries that capture and preserve local varieties of the language.

Regarding lexicographic practice in Russia, I believe that in the long run it will weather even the darkest storms. However, scholars currently stand at a crossroads: they can either choose (wholeheartedly or reluctantly) to adhere to conservative, prescriptive norms and politically driven dictionary use, or they could strive to reassess their practices and foster greater language diversity.

	The latter would entail embracing more flexible regional norms, compiling non-Russian-centric dictionaries for the languages spoken in Russia, and, perhaps, even reevaluating the titles of dictionaries. To begin with, this should be applied to historical dictionaries like that of the Old Russian Language 11th–14th centuries (Словарь древнерусского языка (XI–XIVвеков) (emphasis added), which cover a period when three East Slavic languages – Belarusian, Russian, and Ukrainian – had not yet even diverged.[20]
IS:	What about the tension between online and print in dictionaries? Is the latter becoming absolute in Russian? How are online Russian dictionaries reinventing their lifelong mission?
MK:	The benefits offered by electronic dictionaries will likely position them as primary lexicographic resources in the future. Moreover, their further transformation is already underway. For instance, the lexicographic platform Gramota.ru is expanding beyond providing electronic versions of existing dictionaries. It now offers a meta-dictionary, which amalgamates various lexicographic resources into a single, user-friendly, and interactively linked system. Looking ahead, I envision future dictionaries as comprehensive and multidimensional databases, empowered by AI. These would not only offer full semantic descriptions of each word but also include information on constructional and idiomatic usage, semantic embedding, and real-time usage statistics. Essentially, this future system will evolve beyond mere word definitions to become an interactive information hub, a format that fundamentally differs from traditional paper representations. Would it still be called a dictionary?

Suggested Readings

Apresjan, Juri. "Active Dictionary." In *Encyclopedia of Slavic Languages and Linguistics Online*, edited by Marc L. Greenberg. Brill, 2020. https://doi.org/10.1163/2589-6229_ESLO_COM_032490

Apresjan, Juri. *Systematic Lexicography.* Oxford: Oxford University Press, 2000.

Benson, Morton. "A Step Forward in Russian Lexicography." *Slavic and East European Journal* 39 no. 3 (1995): 429–35.

Bobunova, M. A. *Russkaja leksikografija XXI veka* [Russian lexicography of the twenty-first century]. Moscow: Flinta, 2013.

Bogatova, Galina, ed. *Отечественные лексикографы XVIII—XX века* [National lexicographers of the eighteenth to twentieth centuries] Moscow: Nauka, 2020.

Comrie, Bernard S., Gerald Stone, and Maria Polinsky. *The Russian Language in the Twentieth Century.* Oxford: Oxford University Press, 1996.

Dubichinsky, Volodimir. *Українська лексикографія: історія, сучасність та комп'ютерні технології* [Ukrainian lexicography: History, modernity, and computer technologies]. Kharkiv: National Technical University, 2004.

---

[20] *Словарь древнерусского языка (XI–XIV веков)* [Dictionary of the Old Russian language, 11th–14th centuries] (Moscow: Russian Language, 1988–).

Eberhard, D. M., G. F. Simons, and Ch. D. Fennig, eds. "Russian." In *Ethnologue: Languages of the World*. 27th ed. Dallas: SIL International, 2024. Online version: www.ethnologue.com/language/rus.

Jachnow, Helmut. "Russische Lexikographie." In *Wörterbücher, Dictionaries, Dictionnaires: Ein internationales Handbuch zur Lexikographie*, ed. F. J. Hausmann, O. Reichmann, H. E. Wiegand, and L. Zgusta. Pt. 2, 2309–29. Berlin: De Gruyter, 1990.

Karpova, Olga. "Russian Lexicography." In *Oxford Encyclopedia of Language and Linguistics*, Vol. 10, edited by K. Brown, 704–15. Oxford: Elsevier, 2005.

Kiselev Yuri, Andrew Krizhanovsky, Pavel Braslavski, Ilya Menshikov, Mikhail Mukhin, and Nataly Krizhanovskaya. "Russian Lexicographic Landscape: A Tale of 12 Dictionaries." In *Dialogue*, edited by V. Selegey, Vol. 1(1), 254–71. Moscow: Russian State University for the Humanities (RSUH), 2015.

Kozyrev, Vladimir, and Valentina Chernyak. *Вселенная в алфавитном порядке: Очерки о словарях русского языка* [The universe in alphabetical order: Essays on the dictionaries of the Russian language]. St. Petersburg: Herzen State Pedagogical University, 2000.

Mel'čuk, Igor, and Tilmann Reuther. "Explanatory Combinatorial Dictionary." In *Encyclopedia of Slavic Languages and Linguistics Online*, edited by M. L. Greenberg. Brill, 2020. https://doi.org/10.1163/2589-6229_ESLO_COM_032020

Mel'čuk, Igor, André Clas, and Alain Polguère. *Introduction à la lexicologie explicative et combinatoire*. Brussels: Duculot, 1995.

Miznikov, Sergey, and Olga Krylova, eds. *Sovremennaya russkaja leksikografija* [Modern Russian lexicography]. St. Petersburg: Nauka, 2010.

Müller, O. "Lexikographie." In *Handbuch der sprachwissenschaftlichen Russistik und ihrer Grenzdisziplinen*, edited by H. Jachnow, 290–320. Wiesbaden: Harrassowitz, 1999.

Ryazanova-Clarke, Larissa, and Terence Wade. *The Russian Language Today*. London: Routledge, 2002.

Shestakova, Larisa. *Russkaya avtorsakaya leksikografiya: Teoriya, istoriya, sovremennost'* [Russian authorial lexicography: Theory, past, present]. Moscow: Yazyki slavyanskikh kultur, 2011.

Sorokoletov, Fyodor, ed. *История русской лексикографии* [History of Russian lexicography]. St. Petersburg: Nauka, 2001.

Vinogradov, Viktor. *История слов* [A history of words]. Moscow: Az, 1999.

Zhivov, Viktor. *Language and Culture in Eighteenth Century Russia*. Boston: Academic Studies Press, 2009.

19   Quechua

Odi Gonzales

There is a Quechuan version of Miguel de Cervantes' *Don Quixote of la Mancha*. It was done by Demetrio Túpac Yupanqui, and it is called *Yachay sapa wiraqucha dun Qvixote Manchamantan* (2005).[1] The principal language of the Inca Empire, Quechua, among the most widely known pre-Hispanic languages, is the most popular Indigenous language of the Andes region in South America, was the tongue of the Inca Empire, and is spoken today by between 7 and 12 million people. Alongside Spanish, Quechua is an official language in Bolivia, Ecuador, and Peru, where it is spoken by almost 15 percent of the population. In his conversation, translated from Spanish by Gabriel Mandereau, Odi Gonzales reflects on the tradition of Quechua dictionaries and places in context his own *Quechua-Spanish-English-Dictionary: A Hippocrene Trilingual Reference* (2018), which he edited with Christine Mladic Janney, and Emily Fjaellen Thompson.[2]

***

ILAN STAVANS: How did the *Quechua-Spanish-English Dictionary* come to be? It's a trilingual dictionary. Today very few dictionaries have more than two languages.

ODI GONZALES: About nine years ago, two of my graduate students (now anthropologists) and I began to concretize the idea of a trilingual dictionary; there was very little material of this kind, and what little there was did not fit the needs of students in the United States and Latin America, so we set out to fill that void using a vast glossary from my courses on Quechua language and culture at New York University.

---

[1] Demetrio Túpac Yupanqui, *Yachay sapa wiraqucha dun Qvixote Manchamantan* (Lima: Ediciones El Comercio, 2005).
[2] Odi Gonzales, Christine Mladic, Emily F. Thompson, *Quechua-Spanish-English Dictionary* (New York: Hippocrene Books, 2018).

IS: How were decisions made as to which words to include? I suppose the answer has to do with the target audience of the dictionary.

OG: We tried to select the most relevant verbs and include, whenever possible, conjugated constructions or terms linked to the arduous suffixes that act as kind of "dirigibles" that transmute each Quechua word into a precise, meticulous, and specific word.

IS: Let's talk about the history of Quechua lexicography. What are the origins of Quechua?

OG: Although it can be written with the Spanish alphabet, Quechua remains an oral language, and that is what differentiates it most from Spanish, English, and other "written" languages. There is no single Quechua; Quechua is a mishmash of mutually intelligible variants, despite their peculiarities. Quechua derives from ancestral Andean languages (proto-Quechua); its vocabulary is shaped by terms originating from the Aymara, Puquina, Qulli, Chinchaysuyu, and the ensemble of Amazonian languages. The name Quechua is inexact; it is the result of a historical error. What we know as Quechua, the Quechua language, native speakers call *Runasimi*, which translates to "language of the people." The term *Quechua* refers to a geographical space; it is equivalent to "temperate valley."

IS: And how did Runasimi become Quechua?

OG: In the sixteenth century, the first Quechua-Spanish dictionary, written by the learned Hispanic priest Domingo de Santo Tomás, was called *Diccionario quechua*; however, its author wasn't referring to the name of the language but to the place where he had compiled the material, in the central and southern valley of Peru.[3] Since then, the predominance of writing over orality determined and legitimized that improper name, among others.

IS: At its pre-Hispanic apogee, how many people spoke Quechua?

OG: I couldn't say exactly; the global figures, while larger and more abstract and rhetorical, do not reconcile with Andean language or culture; what is essential are manageable quantities; for example, a population of 100 people that form part of a million. Perhaps there were 8 million speakers, or 10. The thing is that in those times, one had to speak *la lengua del inka* (the language of the Inca), or what the Spaniards would later call *lengua general* (general language), a kind of lingua franca, but that didn't keep individuals from communicating with their people in the variant of their community.

IS: Was Spanish repression in any way a stimulus for Quechua? Today, we think of it as a driving force of resistance, but it is a modern concept.

OG: Spanish and Quechua are particularly dissimilar and irreconcilable languages, and I don't believe it was a stimulus for Quechua except to the extent of being a dominant language that diminishes the vocabulary of the dominated language and urges it to subsist with neologisms and linguistic borrowings. During these almost six centuries of coexistence, a mutual and binding influence has undoubtedly been generated. For example, there are Quechua terms that flow into Latin American Spanish: *pampa, kancha, carpa, puma, papa, mate, shakira*, and "Quechuized" terms of Castilian origin: *sintikuy* (to resent); *turiyay* (to bother;

---

[3] Domingo de Santo Tomás, *Lexicón o vocabulario de la lengua general de los indios del Perú, llamada Quichua* (Valladolid, 1560).

to tease), *susigo* (calm, slow: *sosiego* "tranquility/ quiet/ peace"); *wapu* (daring; handsome); *kasukuy* (to obey; to heed).

IS: At what point did Quechua transition from an oral to a written language?

OG: Quechua has not lost its oral character, even when it is written with the Spanish alphabet. The first texts of evangelization (*Doctrina Christiana*, 1584), dictionaries, and treatises on Quechua grammar, established in writing the dynamic oral nature of the Quechua language.[4] Since then, there has been an ongoing and irreconcilable struggle between orality and writing that underlies the diction of every bilingual mestizo. Andean chroniclers (Guamán Poma, Inka Garcilaso, Santa Cruz Pachakuti) experienced it and tried to reconcile it; in the twentieth century, the writer and poet José María Arguedas mentioned the "hellish struggle with language."[5]

IS: Arguedas' image of the "hellish struggle with language" is, I would say, characteristic of any language. Even in Spanish, one of the imperial languages, there is still a tension between spoken and written forms when listening to street slang, the speech of immigrants, or the language in certain fields like sports or commerce. But in Indigenous languages, hell takes on a special significance. What images of hell exist in Quechua?

OG: The hellish struggle referenced by Arguedas speaks to the conflict between orality and writing, to the duel between a language inclined toward concrete actions and performative verbs that configure precise, concise, and specific terms; and the other language that abounds in concepts, rhetorical expressions, pure abstractions, and set phrases. This struggle is not universal; it concerns, in this case, only bilinguals and mestizos, genuinely oral Andean individuals who take on writing. This was the struggle of the Andean chronicler Guaman Poma, who had to use drawings to configure his intricately scrambled speech because written language was insufficient. For example, the Quechua lexicon omits the verb *gustar* (to like) because it does not entail any action, it does not even express a desire; it is considered empty rhetoric. Moreover, academic language is the opposite of oral languages: it is composed of concepts, abstractions, rhetorical jargon, and metalanguage (artificial language) understood only by themselves.

IS: In the early years of the twenty-first century, I translated *Don Quixote of La Mancha* into Spanglish,[6] in part to push for the consolidation of this hybrid tongue spoken by millions of people in the United States. I also did a Spanglish dictionary.[7] I am thrilled to be in the company of Demetrio Túpac Yupanqui's *Yachay sapa wiraqucha dun Qvixote Manchamantan*. When did the first Quechua dictionary appear? Who was in charge of the project, and what audience did they have in mind?

---

[4] *Doctrina christiana y catecismo para instrucción de los indios* (Lima: Editorial de Antonio Ricardo, 1584).
[5] José María Arguedas, "La novela y el problema de la expresión literaria en el Perú" (Lima, 1950).
[6] Miguel de Cervantes, *Don Quixote of La Mancha*, English and Spanglish editions, adapted by Ilan Stavans, illustrated by Roberto Weil (Philadelphia: University of Pennsylvania Press, 2018).
[7] Ilan Stavans, *Spanglish: A Dictionary* (New York: Perseus Books, 2001).

OG: The first Quechua-Spanish dictionary appeared in Valladolid, Spain, in 1560.[8] Its author, the Spanish Dominican Domingo de Santo Tomás, worked on it for a decade in Peru. Notwithstanding its significant contribution, Santo Tomás' dictionary is also a document in which the first resemantizations, manipulations, and alterations occurred at a formal and content level.

IS: What are you referring to specifically?

OG: Before the arrival of Europeans, the Quechua lexicon lacked terms with Christian connotations such as *sin, hell, heaven, God*, etc. A society that didn't use money wouldn't have verbs like *buying* and *selling*, and the notion of wealth in the Andes was incompatible with that in Europe. That is where the first interventions occurred: based on Quechua terms, neologisms were re-elaborated, distorting the semantic essence of Quechua cultural categories. *Hucha* is *pecado* (sin) in dictionaries, but oral tradition preserved its original essence: *hucha* refers to the condition of being at fault for not being reciprocal.

IS: All dictionaries exercise a kind of tyranny.

OG: But there are options. Taking these documents as bearers of absolute truth is a vulgar surrender. There are countless Quechua terms that have survived with two meanings, sometimes opposites: one that appears in the dictionaries of the sixteenth and seventeenth centuries, and one that the community of speakers has preserved until today. Domingo de Santo Tomás' dictionary was aimed at the Hispanic public and the first mestizos.

IS: And afterwards, what have been the important Quechua dictionaries?

OG: The dictionary titled *Arte y vocabulario en la lengua general del Perú* (Art and vocabulary in the general language of Peru) was authored by an anonymous writer and published in Peru in 1586.[9] The Jesuit Diego González Holguín published another valuable dictionary and grammar treatise in 1608.[10] And many more followed from there. In my opinion, the most valuable and inescapable contribution to the Quechua language is still the vast, living, dynamic, and irreducible dictionary of the community of speakers, of oral memory. Very few scholars turn to it; they rely solely on the sixteenth-century dictionaries; they ignore the rest, and most likely their work is destined to fail.

IS: Orality doesn't catalog, doesn't systematize. How do speakers establish a common agreement regarding definitions, spelling, semantics, and so on?

OG: What you say is correct. However, that perspective isn't Andean but Western. Why should a non-Western culture be analyzed with Western cultural categories? Cataloging, systematizing, defining, orthography and semantics are rhetorical concepts that do not converge in an oral language; Quechua is action, not abstraction.

IS: So far, the Quechua dictionaries you've referred to are efforts by the Spanish. Could you speak of a moment when Indigenous people assumed the production, that is, the control, of their own dictionaries?

---

[8] Domingo Santo Tomás, *Lexicón o vocabulario de la lengua general de los indios del Perú, llamada quichua* (Valladolid, 1560).

[9] Anonymous, *Arte y vocabulario en la lengua general del Peru, llamada quichua, y en la lengua española: El mas copioso y elegante que hasta agora se ha impreso* (Lima: Imprenta de Antonio Ricardo, 1586).

[10] Diego Gonzalez Holguín, *Vocabulario de la lengua de todo el Perú, llamada lengua qqichua o del inca* (Lima: Editorial de la Universidad Nacional Mayor de San Marcos, [1608] 1989).

OG: The creators of the language are the speakers, not the compilers. The chronicles of Guamán Poma, Inka Garcilaso, and Santa Cruz Pachakuti are documents that encompass more than a dictionary.[11] In the Cusco variant and in the twentieth century, there were rigorous dictionaries like those of the Cusco priest Jorge Lira, the grammarian Antonio Cusihuaman, César Guardia Mayorga, and, with its excesses and shortcomings, that of the Academia Mayor de la Lengua Quechua de Cusco (High Academy of the Quechua Language of Cusco).[12]

IS: In the history of Spanish, the formation of the Real Academia Española, in the eighteenth century, inaugurated the conviction that dictionaries should be a tool for linguistic centralization. And then came the wars of independence in Latin America, which began in the early nineteenth century. What happened to Quechua in those centuries?

OG: There was a consolidation and predominance of the dominant language over the native Andean languages. The book – the written word – prevails over orality; writing is an instrument of power, of prestige; a recourse that legitimizes. During that time, no Quechua dictionaries or grammar treatises were published; a type of Andean theater emerged that, while written in Spanish, included Quechua terms, themes, and characters based on real events that occurred in Inca history.

IS: And in the twentieth century, supposedly when Latin America modernized, did Quechua also enter a period of modernization?

OG: That's right. Arguedas' volume of Quechua poetry, *Katatay* (1972), is an example of this new vigor.[13] The compelling poetry of Andrés Alencastre, who wrote under the Quechua pseudonym Kilku Warak'a, combines European techniques with Andean sentiment. These were followed by an upsurge of oral testimonies collected in Quechua and published in bilingual editions.

IS: How does Quechua compare with other Indigenous languages in Latin America in terms of its dictionaries?

OG: Bolivia publishes many Quechua dictionaries, but abundance doesn't necessarily imply thoroughness. In Peru, regional dictionaries are published that capture the lexicon and vocabulary of a particular variant.

IS: On a personal level, I have an enduring interest in hybrid languages in contact: Spanglish, Franglais, Hibríya, and the like. You recently reflected on orality. Tell me about the marriage, or the divorce, of Quechua with Spanish. What kind of relationship do they maintain with each other? Do they overlap? Do they respect each other?

---

[11] Felipe Guamán Poma de Ayala, *Nueva crónica y buen gobierno* [1615], www.herbogeminis.com/IMG/pdf/El_sitio_de_Guaman_Poma.pdf; Inca Garcilaso de la Vega, *Comentarios reales de los Incas*, Vol. 1, ed. Carlos Araníbar (Lima: Fondo de Cultura Económica, 1991); Santa Cruz Pachakuti, *Relacion de antigüedades deste reino del Piru* (Lima: Instituto Frances de Estudios Andinos, 2014).

[12] Jorge Lira, with Mario Mejía Huaman, *Diccionario Quechua-Castellano* (Lima: Editorial Universitaria, Universidad Ricardo Palma, 2008); Antonio Cusihuaman, *Gramática quechua Cuzco-Collao* (Lima: Ministerio de Educación, Instituto de Estudios Peruanos (IEP), 1976); César Guardia Mayorga, *Gramatica Kechwa* (Lima: Ediciones los Andes, 1973); Academia Mayor de la Lengua Quechua; *Diccionario quechua-español-quechua* (Cusco: Ediciones de la Municipalidad, 1995).

[13] José María Arguedas, *Katatay* (Lima: Editorial Instituto Nacional de Cultura, 1972).

OG: Between Spanish and Quechua, there is a coexistence with clashes and quarrels, yet it is a coexistence nonetheless. During these almost six centuries, the two languages have assimilated influences and borrowings that flow into the daily speech of Spanish and Quechua speakers. Quechua does not accommodate terms related to the operation of machines and audiovisual devices, and in such cases, it adopts terms from Spanish or English to configure its grammatical constructions. This always implies gains and losses.

IS: Are different variants of Quechua spoken in Bolivia, Ecuador, and Peru? Or in specific geographical regions within these countries? For example, are there differences in vocabulary? Dialects?

OG: Quechua is a marvel of variants and subvariants, and that diversity is its vitality and strength; unifying or reducing it, as populist governments want, would lead to its extinction. They aren't completely different; there are always links, ties, and structures that allow a Kichwa from Otavalo in Ecuador to communicate with a Quechua speaker from Cochabamba, Bolivia or a Chanka from Apurimac or Ayacucho, Peru.

IS: How do the language policies of Bolivia, Ecuador, and Peru regarding Quechua differ?

OG: It seems to me that in Bolivia and Ecuador, there is a tendency toward the unification of the variants, or the imposition of one variant over the others, promoted by government bureaucracies. In Peru, the latter also occurs; Quechua newscasts on national radio and television are broadcast exclusively in one variant without a rotation that could show the other variants. On the other hand, there's a long-standing disagreement about Quechua writing: whether it should be with three or five vowels. In this debate are the academics and the bureaucrats: both ignore the community of speakers.

IS: Your dictionary was made in New York. To what extent is the geographical distance from Quechua in Peru an advantage and a disadvantage?

OG: I can assure you that my Quechua improved in New York. In Peru, I speak it, but in New York, I teach and analyze it; that imposes a rigor, a commitment akin to a mission. My courses are trilingual (Quechua, Spanish, English), and in recent years, I have been expanding toward Andean studies and Andean linguistic anthropology, translation of sixteenth- to twenty-first-century documents, among others.

IS: You are a poet. In what way does your artistic work inform your linguistic work, and vice versa?

OG: My poetry feeds on my research; I have always worked on poetry books connected to the Andean world. I have a couple of books in Quechua, and the rest in Spanish but with Quechua interpolations. I'm a poet who writes like an oral narrator.

Suggested Readings

Academia Mayor de la Lengua Quechua. *Diccionario quechua-español-quechua.*
    Cusco: Ediciones de la Municipalidad, 1995.
Anonymous. *Arte y vocabulario en la lengua general del Peru, llamada quichua, y en la lengua española: El mas copioso y elegante que hasta agora se ha impreso.*
    Lima: Imprenta de Antonio Ricardo, 1586.

Calderon Quillatupa, Francisco. *Diccionario ideológico runasimi*. Huancayo: Gráfica E. Calderón, 2009.

Cerron Palomino, Rodolfo. *Quechua sureño: Diccionario unificado*. Lima: Biblioteca Nacional del Perú, 1994.

Condori, Gregorio, Carmen Escalante, Asunta Quispe, and Ricardo Valderrama. *Autobiografía de Gregorio Condori Mamani*. Cusco: Centro de Estudios Rurales Andinos Bartolomé de las Casas, 1977–82.

Cusihuaman, Antonio. *Gramática quechua Cuzco-Collao*. Lima: Ministerio de Educación, Instituto de Estudios Peruanos (IEP), 1976.

Chipana Curo, Lorenzo. *Rimayqelqa: Diccionario bilingüe*. Arequipa: Ediciones Unas, 2012.

Direccion Provincial de Educacion Intercultural Bilingue de Napo D. Kichwa shimita yachasunchik. Ecuador: Tuna/Napo, 2011.

Figueroa, Zenón, and Daniel Tunque. *Quechua: Academia Mayor de la Lengua Quechua: Manual para el aprendizaje del idioma*. Cusco: Editorial Graficolor, 2007.

Garcilaso de la Vega, Inca. *Comentarios reales de los Incas*. Vol. 1. Edited by Carlos Araníbar. Lima: Fondo de Cultura Económica, 1991.

Gonzales, Odi. *Runasimi: Lengua y cultura quechua I, II, III, IV*. New York: Center for Latin American and Caribbean Studies CLACS-NYU, 2016.

Gonzales, Odi; Molina Almanza, and Mario Molina. *Walaycho Qorilazo: Memoria oral quechua en los Andes*. Lima: Pakarina Ediciones, 2017.

Gonzales, Odi, Christine Mladic, and Emily F. Thompson. *Quechua-Spanish-English Dictionary*. New York: Hippocrene Books, 2018.

Gonzalez Holguín, Diego. *Gramática y arte nueva de la lengua general de todo el Peru llamada lengua qquichua o lengua del Inca*. Lima, [1607] 1842.

Vocabulario de la lengua de todo el Perú, llamada lengua qqichua o del inca. Lima: Editorial de la Universidad Nacional Mayor de San Marcos, [1608] 1989.

Guamán Poma de Ayala, Felipe. *Nueva crónica y buen gobierno* [1615]. www.herbogeminis.com/IMG/pdf/El_sitio_de_Guaman_Poma.pdf

Lira, Jorge, with Mario Mejía Huaman. *Diccionario quechua-castellano*. Lima: Editorial Universitaria, Universidad Ricardo Palma, 2008.

Santo Tomás, Domingo. *Lexicón o vocabulario de la lengua general de los indios del Peru, llamada quichua*. Valladolid, 1560.

20 Scandinavian

Lars Trap-Jensen

No such thing as "Scandinavian" exists. In general, the term refers to the cultural region of Denmark, Norway, and Sweden, whereas geographically, the Scandinavian Peninsula comprises Norway, Sweden, and parts of Finland. If one wants to include Finland, the Faroe Islands, Iceland, and sometimes even Greenland, it is common to speak about the Nordic countries. Thus, the term "Scandinavian" refers to a family of languages of North Germanic origin dating back to the Viking Age (c. 750–1050), when the expansion of Nordic peoples resulted in a Scandinavian speech – at times called "Danish" – brought along by dialectal differences, which were consolidated as languages thanks to the arrival of the Roman Catholic church. This conversation explores how each cultural region developed its own dictionaries, such as Nynorsk and Bokmål's *Norwegian Dictionary* (1930–), the *Swedish Academy Glossary* (1898–), the *Swedish Etymological Dictionary* (1922–), and the *Den Danske Ordbog* (1955–).[1]

***

ILAN STAVANS: I want to know your story. How did you become interested in words?

LARS TRAP-JENSEN: I think the fascination with words has always been there. I could read and write before I started school, learning from my elder sister. According to our family chronicle, I would be waiting impatiently for her to return from school: "What kind of homework do we have today?" I remember a similar fascination when I first started learning a foreign language: it opened a window into a new world.

---

[1] *Bokmålsordboka og Nynorskordboka*, https://ordbokene.no; https://svenska.se, dictionary portal with access to *Svenska Akademiens ordbok* (*SAOB*), *Svensk ordbok utgiven av Svenska Akademien* (*SO*) and *Svenska Akademiens ordlista* (*SAOL*); *Den Danske Ordbog*, https://ordnet.dk/ddo.

IS: How many languages do you speak?

LTJ: As you know, language mastery varies in degrees; it is not a question of either-or, and it needs constant maintenance. I speak Danish, English, and German without problems, and of course easily understand Swedish and Norwegian. I have also studied Greenlandic, Russian, Latin, ancient Greek, and to a lesser degree Icelandic, French, and Spanish, but I cannot claim that I speak these languages at a conversational level today.

IS: When talking about dictionaries, the moniker "Scandinavian languages" is in itself a challenge. These are the North Germanic languages that are Danish, Swedish, Norwegian, Icelandic, and Faroese. But not Finnish, which is a Uralic language of the Finnic branch. The Scandinavian languages are divided into East (Danish and Swedish) and West Scandinavian (Norwegian, Icelandic, and Faroese) groups. Do they have similar histories when it comes to the making of dictionaries?

LTJ: Linguistically, Scandinavian is often used synonymously with the North Germanic languages Danish, Swedish, Norwegian, Faroese, and Icelandic, also known as the Nordic languages. Although there are similarities in the lexicographic traditions, history, politics, and culture play a significant role in shaping them, as much as linguistic affinity. Many languages are spoken in the Nordic countries today, but only eight are recognized as official languages. In addition to the five North Germanic languages there are another three, all non-Indo-European languages: Finnish, Sami (a group of Uralic languages spoken in northern Finland, Sweden, and Norway), and Greenlandic (the Inuit language spoken in Greenland).

IS: Let's approach the various lexicographical traditions in their own terms, starting with your own Danish. It wasn't until the sixteenth century when, under the Protestant Reformation, a number of dialects coalesced into a national language – derived from Old Norse – around the dialect of Copenhagen and Malmö. This time marks the beginning of Early Modern Danish, whereas Danish split from Swedish during the medieval period, Old Danish being set to 1100–1500. When does the first dictionary of Danish come about, and what are the forces behind its appearance?

LTJ: As was common in the Renaissance, the first dictionaries that emerged were bilingual Latin-Danish glossaries, primarily used in grammar schools. During this period, education and scholarly pursuits were primarily controlled by the clergy, with Latin serving as the language of learning. During the Renaissance era, a notable collection of Latin-Danish glossaries surfaced, although a few glossaries also existed in the opposite direction due to Latin's active role in scholarship.

One noteworthy example is Christiern Pedersen's *Vocabularium ad usum Dacorum*, which can rightfully claim the title of the first Danish dictionary.[2] Pedersen, a canon from Lund Cathedral and a trusted aide to King Christian

---

[2] Christiern Pedersen, *Vocabularium ad usum dacorum* (Paris, 1510) (available as: Christiern Pedersen, *Vocabularium ad usum dacorum*, published by Inger Bom and Niels Haastrup. Det 16. århundredes danske vokabularier 1. Copenhagen: Universitets-Jubilæets danske Samfund, 1973).

II, not only authored this dictionary but also significantly influenced the standardization of the Danish language (responsible, among other things, for the first translation of the New Testament).

Published in 1510 in Paris, his dictionary contained approximately 13,000 Latin headwords with their corresponding Danish translations, arranged alphabetically and encompassing all parts of speech. Besides word equivalents, Pedersen's work provided grammar and morphology information for the Latin terms.

Intriguingly, the third edition of Pedersen's dictionary, printed in Leipzig in 1518, featured appendices contributed by Henrik Smith, another canon, which covered subjects such as plants, minerals, food and drink, and kinship terms. These appendices, compiled independently from Pedersen's list, represent the first thematically ordered lexicographical work known in Danish and were likely inspired by similar works popular in European lexicography at the time.

IS: Did this effort immediately result in a full-fledged Danish dictionary?

LTJ: No, it was not until around 1700 that the first major Danish dictionary appeared, crafted by Matthias Moth. Moth, a remarkable figure who served as a senior official to King Christian V, held several pivotal positions in the government. Apart from his governmental responsibilities, Moth distinguished himself as an industrious polyhistor, actively engaged in translation and lexicography.

Drawing inspiration from the dictionary of the Académie française and various German dictionaries of the period,[3] Moth embarked upon an ambitious plan to create a comprehensive dictionary that would reflect the cultural significance of Denmark under his absolute monarch, King Christian V. Moth's dictionary also deviated from established norms in several ways. Notably, his approach encompassed a broad view of language.

In 1697, while holding the position of titular privy councillor and head of the chancellery, Moth issued instructions to all Danish bishops, including those in Norway, urging them to gather lexical material for his dictionary. He specifically sought words that were regionally specific or used by peasants in their daily lives. Moth's inclusive approach ensured that no word, regardless of rarity or coarseness, was excluded. Consequently, the dictionary offers valuable insights into the language of common people during that era.

Fortunately for us and the dictionary, Moth faced dismissal and subsequent decline when King Christian V passed away in 1699, granting him ample time to devote himself fully to the monumental task of creating the dictionary. Over the course of his lifetime, Moth diligently worked on the dictionary, resulting in the production of approximately 9,000 handwritten pages. While the lemma list and source language were Danish, Moth used Latin as the metalanguage. Ultimately, he divided the material into a verbal dictionary and an encyclopedia in the final edition.

IS: What was the reaction to Moth? I'm interested in user's responses. Did the Danish feel proud?

---

[3] *Dictionnaire de l'Académie française* (Paris, 1694).

LTJ: Regrettably, Moth's dictionary did not receive the recognition it truly deserved when compared to, for example, Samuel Johnson's dictionary in England later in the same century.[4] This lack of recognition is primarily due to the fact that Moth's dictionary remained unpublished and only survived within the confines of a storeroom at the Royal Library.

A portion of the work, containing the letters P and R, as well as parts of the letter O, were lost during the English bombardment of Copenhagen in 1807. It was not until 2015 that Moth's dictionary was finally published, marking a significant milestone and serving as a testament to the richness of Danish lexicography. However, Moth's work, despite being unpublished for centuries, continued to be a highly influential resource, even if its reputation remained limited to a select group of experts.

IS: What other dictionaries followed?

LTJ: Throughout the eighteenth century, the Royal Danish Academy of Sciences and Letters prepared an ambitious dictionary project inspired by the legacy of Moth. The work drew inspiration from the Académie française and Samuel Johnson's dictionary and also incorporated the contents of Moth's dictionary manuscript, handed to the king by Moth's heirs in 1753. After several revisions of the dictionary plan, the first volume was published in 1793, while the eighth and final volume did not appear until 1905.[5]

The editorial process was marked by multiple changes regarding both editors and editorial principles. The resulting work showed a noticeable inconsistency, even when we consider the inevitable transformation of its subject matter during the 112 years of preparation.

IS: In most European linguist tradition, the nineteenth century represented significant breakthroughs in lexicography.

LTJ: In the nineteenth century, the two-volume *Dansk Ordbog* (Danish dictionary) by Christian Molbech gained considerable, popular success.[6] Molbech, a librarian, philologist and historian, also worked as an editor for the Royal Danish Academy of Sciences and Letters' dictionary. His work was also rooted in the tradition of the Académie française, only allowing words into the dictionary that were found to be of lasting value and usable in higher style. The role of the dictionary was aimed – to quote from Molbech's preface – "to function as a guide for the correct and refined utilization of written language in contemporary society."

---

[4] Samuel Johnson, *A Dictionary of the English Language* (London: printed by W. Strahan for J. and P. Knapton et al., 1755).

[5] *Dansk Ordbog udgiven under Videnskabernes Selskabs Bestyrelse*, 8 vols. (Copenhagen: N. Møller & Søn, 1793–1905).

[6] Christian Molbech, *Dansk Ordbog indeholdende det danske Sprogs Stammeord: tilligemed afledede og sammensatte Ord, efter den nuværende Sprogbrug forklarede i deres forskiellige Betydninger, og ved Talemaader og Exempler oplyste* (Copenhagen: Gyldendal, 1833); 2nd ed.: *Dansk Ordbog: Indeholdende det danske Sprogs Stammeord tilligemed afledede og sammenfattede Ord, efter den nuværende Sprogbrug forklarede i deres forskiellige Betydninger, og ved talemaader og Exempler oplyste. Anden forøgede og forbedrede Udgave* (Copenhagen: Gyldendal, 1859).

The prescriptive paradigm came to an end with the publication of *Ordbog over det danske Sprog* (*ODS*, Dictionary of the Danish language), a dictionary compiled in the descriptive tradition of the comprehensive dictionaries of the Germanic languages that were initiated in the nineteenth century.[7] Somewhat smaller in scale than its counterparts the *Oxford English Dictionary* (*OED*), Grimm, and the Dutch and Swedish projects,[8] *ODS* was completed expeditiously in twenty-eight volumes from 1918 to 1956. With five subsequent supplementary volumes it constitutes a high point in Danish lexicography, covering the period from around 1700 to 1950. Post-1950 modern language is covered by *Den Danske Ordbog* (The Danish dictionary), the first corpus-based Danish dictionary, initially published in six volumes (2003–2005) and then converted into an online dictionary, available free of charge alongside a digitized version of *ODS*.[9]

IS: Talk to me, Lars, about the first official Danish spelling dictionary: Svend Grundtvig's *Dansk Haandordbog*, published in 1872.[10]

LTJ: Well, a development toward orthographic consistency gained significant momentum during the nineteenth century in response to a growing demand. Among the interested parties were the educational institutions that recognized an apparent need for a standardized spelling. However, despite their obvious and fair request, they struggled to gain the attention of the education authorities, who dismissed their concerns and instead pointed to the practices of prominent authors of that era. These authors often deviated from the orthographic guidelines set forth by pioneers such as Rasmus Rask and N. M. Petersen earlier in the century.

Meanwhile, a more fruitful endeavor emerged through efforts to coordinate and bring the Scandinavian languages closer together. This movement aligned with the broader Romantic Scandinavian movement that had gained momentum in the preceding decades. A series of meetings took place during the 1860s, culminating in a pivotal orthography meeting held in Stockholm in July 1869. During this gathering, a range of decisions were reached to address and solve spelling concerns.

Svend Grundtvig played a central role in implementing these decisions. First, he put the result into practice in his *Dansk Retskrivningsordbog* (Danish spelling dictionary), a rather strict and uncompromising work.[11]

---

[7] *Ordbog over det danske Sprog*, 28 vols., Det Danske Sprog- og Litteraturselskab (Copenhagen: Gyldendal, 1918–56).

[8] *Deutsches Wörterbuch von Jacob Grimm und Wilhelm Grimm*, 16 vols. [1–32] (Leipzig: Hirzel, 1854–1971), www.woerterbuchnetz.de/DWB1; M. de Vries and L.A. te Winkel, *Woordenboek der Nederlandsche taal*, 43 vols. (The Hague: Nijhoff, 1864–2001); *Ordbok över svenska språket, utgiven av Svenska Akademien*, Vols. 1–39 (Lund, 1893–2023).

[9] K. Kristensen and E. Hjorth, *Den Danske Ordbog*, 6 vols., Det Danske Sprog- og Litteraturselskab, (Copenhagen: Gyldendal, 2003–5).

[10] S. Grundtvig, *Dansk Haandordbog: Med den af Kultusministeriet anbefalede Retskrivning* (Copenhagen, C.A. Reitzels Publishers, 1872).

[11] S. Grundtvig, *Dansk Retskrivnings-Ordbog* (Copenhagen: C.A. Reitzel, 1870).

After extensive revisions, however, a more balanced version, the *Dansk Haandordbog* (Danish concise dictionary), was published.[12]

So, the journey toward standardized spelling and the creation of authoritative dictionaries unfolded in response to various factors. While the school system's plea for consistency faced challenges, the efforts to harmonize the Scandinavian languages proved more fruitful. The culmination of these initiatives, marked by the publication of the *Danish Concise Dictionary*, was ultimately recognized and sanctioned by the Ministry of Church and Education in 1872.

IS: When was the Danish Language Council formed?

LTJ: The Danish Language Council was formed in 1955 following a significant spelling reform that took place in 1948. Among its first tasks was the creation of an official spelling dictionary to encapsulate the effects of the reform. The result was the first edition of *Retskrivningsordbogen* (The spelling dictionary) in 1955.[13]

Since then, one of the Council's primary responsibilities has been to observe the evolution of the Danish language, establish standardized Danish orthography, and document their decisions in the official spelling dictionary. Subsequent editions of *Retskrivningsordbogen* were published in 1986, 1996, 2001 and 2012, and the latest edition in 2024.[14]

IS: How does the council operate?

LTJ: It operates as a governmental body under the Ministry of Culture, with its responsibilities regulated by law under the Orthography Act of 1997. In their standardization practice, the Language Council adheres to two basic principles: the principle of tradition and the principle of language use. The former principle preserves the spelling of the existing vocabulary, even in the face of evolving pronunciations, while the latter allows for adjustments in spelling based on the written language practices of "good and confident language users."

IS: Let's move to the other Scandinavian languages. How does the development of Danish dictionaries compare to those in Norwegian and Swedish?

LTJ: In Sweden, the foundation of the Swedish Academy by King Gustav III in 1786 marks a new era in Swedish lexicography. The academy – today probably best known for awarding the Nobel prizes – was formed with the Académie française as a model to promote the country's language and literature and work for the "purity, vigour and majesty" of the language.

The ambition was right from the start to publish a normative dictionary that would lead to the further development and refinement of the Swedish language. But although work began shortly after, the preparatory phase dragged on, and it was not until 1883 that a plan had been prepared and

---

[12] Grundtvig, *Dansk Haandordbog*.
[13] *Retskrivningsordbog*, published by Dansk Sprognævn (Copenhagen: Dansk Sprognævn, Gyldendal, 1955).
[14] *Retskrivningsordbogen* (Copenhagen: Aschehoug, 1986); *Retskrivningsordbogen*, 2nd ed. (Copenhagen: Aschehoug, 1996); *Retskrivningsordbogen*, 3rd ed. (Copenhagen: Aschehoug, 2001); *Retskrivningsordbogen*, 4th ed. (Copenhagen: Alinea, 2012); *Retskrivningsordbogen*, 5th ed. (Copenhagen: Alinea, 2024); all published by Dansk Sprognævn.

editorial work began, with the first volume being published in 1898. After 140 years of work, the thirty-ninth and final volume came out in 2023, making the *Swedish Academy Glossary* (*SAOB*) the largest reference work ever published in the Scandinavian area, comprising 33,111 pages and about 500,000 entries. It covers the Swedish language from 1521 (roughly marking the starting point of Modern Swedish) to the present.

Even if the creation period was long, SAOB was among the pioneers when it comes to digitization. As early as 1983, work began with converting the text to the digital format, and the dictionary has been available online since 1997, since 2011 in a new, improved digital format. The academy is also responsible for two other dictionaries: the so-called Academy word list (*SAOL*), a spelling dictionary that is widely used in the educational system as a de facto norm for the correct spelling and inflection of some 125,000 words, and a medium-size monolingual dictionary of contemporary Swedish, *Svensk ordbok* (*SO*, Swedish dictionary), both available online in free versions.[15]

You may already have noticed parallel developments in the Danish and Swedish traditions. This can be taken even further if we look at older works. Where Molbech's two-volume dictionary was popular in Denmark in the nineteenth century, Sweden had A. F. Dalin's *Ordbok öfver svenska språket* (Dictionary of the Swedish language), also in two volumes.[16] And just as Molbech was involved in the editing of the Danish Academy's dictionary, so Dalin participated in the Swedish Academy's preparatory dictionary work. For the description of the early language period, Sweden has K. F. Söderwall's *Ordbok öfver svenska medeltidsspråket* (Dictionary of medieval Swedish), where Danish has O. Kalkar's *Ordbog over det ældre danske Sprog* (1300–1700) (Dictionary of the older Danish language, 1300–1700), in addition to the still unfinished *Gammeldansk Ordbog* (Old Danish dictionary), initiated in the 1950s.[17]

By contrast, the Norwegian tradition starts later. After its independence from Denmark in 1814, Norway had to accept a personal union with Sweden but in practice only the Crown and foreign policy were common to the two countries, and Sweden accepted the newly prepared Norwegian constitution. As a result, Norway had full internal self-government and the necessary institutions needed for nation-building and the creation of the associated cultural resources. It is against this background that one must see the distinctive Norwegian development with two standard languages.

The century-long Danish presence in the Norwegian capital had led to the Norwegian written language being replaced by Danish and a general convergence toward Danish, especially in educated speech. Following the newly gained political status, the nineteenth century saw an effort to restore the

---

[15] https://svenska.se
[16] A. F. Dalin, *Ordbok öfver svenska språket*, 2 vols. (Stockholm: J. Beckman, 1850–53).
[17] K. F. Söderwall, *Ordbok öfver svenska medeltids-språket*, 2 vols. (Stockholm: Svenska fornskriftsällskapet, 1884–1918); O. Kalkar, *Ordbog til det ældre danske Sprog (1300–1700)*, 5 vols. (Copenhagen: Thieles Bogtrykkeri, 1881–1918).

original language and unify the Norwegian dialects in a new common language. The name associated with this effort is Ivar Aasen, who untiringly traveled the country to gather linguistic material and study the country's dialects.

In 1848, he published *Det norske Folkesprogs Grammatik* (Grammar of the Norwegian vernacular), and in 1850 *Ordbog over det norske Folkesprog* (Dictionary of the Norwegian vernacular) came out.[18] At the same time, another effort to standardize the dominating Danish-Norwegian language of the educated classes emerged. It was connected to influential writers like Bjørnstjerne Bjørnson and Henrik Ibsen and especially to Knud Knudsen, a Norwegian school teacher and linguist. His aim was to create a distinct Norwegian standard based on regular phonetic principles, and he was a central figure in the above-mentioned orthography meeting in Stockholm in 1869. Eventually, many of Knudsen's proposals were adopted, and he is generally known as the father of Bokmål, as this standard is called today.

Aasen's work resulted in what is now known as Nynorsk. Corresponding to the two standards, there are two major monolingual dictionaries, *Norsk Ordbok* (Norwegian dictionary) for Nynorsk and *Det Norske Akademis Ordbog* (*NAOB*, Norwegian Academy dictionary) for Bokmål.[19] Both projects were initiated in the 1930s and were published at a somewhat uneven pace, for different reasons.

Norsk Ordbok covers the Norwegian dialects as well as the written standard Nynorsk and aims ambitiously at an exhaustive description. Work progressed rather slowly, and before the turn of the millennium only three volumes and about a quarter of the work had been completed. *NAOB* was originally compiled in four volumes between 1937 and 1957, to which were added two supplementary volumes in the 1990s. Since the supplementary volumes were half the size of the original work, there was soon a demand for a new edition that would merge the six volumes into a single alphabetical list and update the lexicographic content.

In this situation, both projects developed ambitious plans for future work. For *Norsk Ordbok* it involved a speedy completion of the remaining nine volumes, and for *NAOB* a digitized, updated, and integrated edition. Both projects managed to get substantially increased funding from the Ministry of Culture, which wanted to see the dictionary works completed in time for the celebration of the 200th anniversary of the constitution in 2014.

Even though they didn't quite make it to the anniversary, it happened a few years later, and it means that today we have two comprehensive dictionary descriptions of the two official standard language variants. The twelve volumes of *Norsk Ordbok* comprise almost 10,000 pages and describe more than 330,000 entries. A full digital version is currently under way. The *NAOB* is already available in an online version, giving access to 225,000

---

[18] I. Aasen, *Det norske Folkesprogs Grammatik* (Kristiania: C. C. Werner & Co., 1848); I. Aasen, *Ordbog over det norske Folkesprog* (Kristiania: C. C. Werner & Co., 1850).
[19] *Norsk Ordbok I–XII: Ordbok over det norske folkemålet og det nynorske skriftmålet* (Oslo: Samlaget, 1966–2016); *Det Norske Akademis Ordbok* (*NAOB*), https://naob.no.

IS: entries, freely available and continuously updated.[20] In addition to these, a concise dictionary that gives simultaneous access to both language variants also exists. It was initiated in the 1980s and has undergone several revisions.[21] It is now available online, hosted by the University of Bergen.[22]

IS: Let's talk about Finnish, Faroese, and Icelandic dictionaries. Did they appear in the middle of the nineteenth century?

LTJ: Finland, Iceland, and the Faroe Islands went through a development that is comparable to that of Norway. As in the case of Norway, these areas were all under foreign administration for a long period. Finland was under Swedish administration until 1809, then under Russian administration from 1809 to its independence in 1917, whereas Iceland and the Faroe Islands were under Danish administration. As a consequence of the political situation, the language of administration and education was traditionally that of the dominating country. But with the rise of Romanticism, national consciousness grew, and language played an important role in the development.

After the Finnish War of 1808–9, Finland was allotted to the Russian Empire but enjoyed a considerable degree of autonomy as a Grand Duchy. This meant that, even if Swedish continued to be the language of administration, Finnish could develop as a literary language during the nineteenth century. A written standard was created in the latter half of the century, and in 1902 Finnish was recognized as an official language. The first monolingual Finnish dictionary, *Nytt Finskt Lexicon* (New Finnish lexicon), had been compiled as early as 1787 by the curate Christfrid Gananders, but this was not published until much later (in facsimile 1937–1940, as print edition 1997).[23]

It served as the main source for Kustaa Renvall's dictionary *Suomalainen Sana-Kirja: Lexicon linguae Finnicae, cum interpretatione duplici, copiosiore Latina, breviore Germanica* (Finnish dictionary: Lexicon of the Finnish language, with a double interpretation, more extensive in Latin, briefer in German) that appeared in 1823–26.[24] However, the most influential dictionary of the nineteenth century was Elias Lönnrot's *Suomalais-Ruotsalainen Sanakirja/Finskt-Svenskt Lexikon* (Finnish-Swedish dictionary) which was published in instalments 1866–80.[25]

Like its predecessors, this is a bilingual dictionary on the face of it, but its primary goal was to elevate the Finnish vocabulary. The Swedish words are not so much equivalents in a bilingual dictionary as they are used as a

---

[20] *Det Norske Akademis Ordbok* (*NAOB*), https://naob.no.
[21] M. I. Landrø and B. Wangensteen, *Bokmålsordboka: Definisjons- og rettskrivningsordbok* (Oslo: Universitetsforlaget/Kunnskapsforlaget, 1986); M. Hovdenak, L. Killing-Bergtrø, A. Lauvhell, S. Nordlie, M. Rommetveit, and D. Worren, *Nynorskordboka: Definisjons- og rettskrivingsordbok* (Oslo: Det Norske Samlaget, 1986).
[22] *Bokmålsordboka og Nynorskordboka*, https://ordbokene.no.
[23] C. Ganander, *Nytt Finskt lexicon* (Porvoo: Werner Söderström Osakeyhtiö, 1786–87).
[24] G. Renvall, *Suomalainen Sana-kirja: Lexicon linguæ finnicæ, cum interpretatione duplici copiosiore latina, breviore germanica*, 2 vols. (Turku: Typis Frenckellianis, 1826).
[25] E. Lönnrot, *Suomalais-Ruotsalainen Sanakirja/Finskt-svenskt lexikon*, 2 vols. (Porvoo: Werner Söderström Osakeyhtiö, 1874–80).

	metalanguage to describe and explain the semantic field of the Finnish words. With an estimated 240,000 entries, Lönnrot's dictionary was for a long period the largest dictionary compiled in the Nordic area.
IS:	When was the first monolingual Finnish dictionary published?
LTJ:	The first purely monolingual Finnish dictionary was *Nykysuomen sanakirja* (Dictionary of Modern Finnish), which contains over 200,000 entries and was published in six volumes from 1951 to 1961, after about thirty years of work.[26] The entry list reflects the changes in society, language, and lexicography, and differs considerably from Lönnrot's. The dictionary has a clear academic orientation, but it was widely acclaimed and had a huge impact on the standardization of the Finnish vocabulary.
	It also had a good sales record for many years. However, it was never updated and the present-day user will find many lexical gaps. Therefore, a new dictionary was created in the 1990s, in three volumes and about half the size of *Nykysuomen sanakirja*.[27] This dictionary was later published as a CD-ROM (1997) and then as an online dictionary (2004).[28] The current online version, *Kielitoimiston verkkosanakirja* (Online dictionary of the language institute), has over 100,000 entries and is regularly updated.[29]
IS:	How about Iceland and the Faroe Islands?
LTJ:	They didn't have monolingual dictionaries for their languages until the twentieth century. Ever since the Middle Ages, these communities have linguistically found themselves in comparable situations characterized by diglossia, with Danish as the language of administration, and Icelandic and Faroese as the language of day-to-day life, although not in the classic sense and not quite in the same way. Icelandic in particular was well-established as a written language, not least as a literary language, and with a full translation of the Bible in 1584, Icelandic also served as the church language as well as the language of instruction in schools.
	By contrast, the Faroe Islands did not receive a complete Bible translation until 1949. Both languages were still strongly influenced by Danish, sometimes so much that there was concern for their survival: in 1813, the Danish linguist Rasmus Rask predicted that Icelandic would become extinct if nothing was done to prevent it.
	Toward the end of the eighteenth century, the first Faroese dictionary was compiled by Jens Chr. Svabo, comprising a list of Faroese words with Danish and Latin translations.[30] His work was primarily motivated by the idea that

---

[26] *Nykyssuomen sanakirja* [Modern Finnish dictionary], 6 vols. (Porvoo: Suomalaisen Kirjallisuuden Seura, 1951–61).

[27] *Suomen kielen persussanakirja* [Basic dictionary of the Finnish language], 3 vols. (Helsinki: Valtion painatuskeskus and Kotimaisten kielten painatuskeskus, 1990–94).

[28] *CD-Perussanakirja* (Helsinki: Kotimaisten kielten tutkimuskeskus, Lingsoft Oy, Kustantaja, 1997); *Kielitoimiston sanakirja* (Helsinki: Kotimaisten kielten tutkimuskeskus, Kielikone OY, 2004 [digital], 2006 [print]).

[29] *Kielitoimiston verkkosanakirja* [Online dictionary of the Language Council], www.kielitoimistonsanakirja.fi/#/

[30] The work was not published in Svabo's time and only existed as a manuscript. It was later published as: J. C. Svabo, *Dictionarium Faeroense, Faersk-dansk-latinsk Ordbog*, published

otherwise it would be too late and the language cease to exist. Fortunately, this did not happen, and during the nineteenth century nationalism grew there as elsewhere leading to a consolidation of both languages. In their struggle to elevate the local languages to full-fledged national languages, efforts to keep the dominant language from influencing them were significant, for understandable reasons.

In the nineteenth century, bilingual dictionaries between each of the two languages and Danish were dominant but, as in the case of Finland, the entry lists also served as a way of canonizing the vocabularies. In the Faroe Islands, Jakob Jakobsen's Faroese-Danish dictionary from 1891 was very much focused on the puristic effort to suppress the Danish-influenced words and reinstate the original or "genuine" Faroese vocabulary.[31] One way of doing this was by using cross-references: the more widespread Danish-influenced words were not omitted from the lemma list, but rather than having translations they functioned as mere references to the "good" or "correct" Faroese words. This tradition continued throughout most of the twentieth century.

A similar situation is seen in Iceland. By no means the first of its kind (Icelandic dictionaries exist from as early as the seventeenth century for Latin and bilingual dictionaries between Icelandic and Latin, Danish or English were published in the eighteenth and nineteenth century), Sígfus Blöndal's *Icelandic-Danish Dictionary* (1920–24) is considered one of the most influential for Icelandic lexicography, whether monolingual or bilingual.[32]

Blöndal also addresses the correctness issue, by adding question marks to lemmas of dubious (i.e. Danish or other foreign) origin. This tradition is also found in the first monolingual dictionary of Icelandic, Árni Böðvarsson's *Íslensk orðabók handa skólum og almenningi* (Icelandic dictionary for school and the general public) (1963), but no longer in the modern dictionaries, such as *Íslex* and *Íslensk nútímamálsorðabók* (Icelandic contemporary dictionary).[33]

In Modern Faroese dictionaries, on the other hand, the element of pedagogical, or puristic, guidance is still noticeable, for instance in J. H. W. Poulsen et al., *Føroysk orðabók* (Faroese dictionary, 1998), and Z. S. Hansen and H. Joensen's *Føroysk-donsk orðabók* (Faroese-Danish dictionary, 2010).[34]

---

from the manuscripts by Chr. Matras (Munksgaard: Selskabet til Udgivelse af Færøske Kildeskrifter og Studier, 1966).

[31] J. Jacobsen, *Ordsamling og Register*, Vol. 2 of V. U. Hammershaimb, *Færøsk Anthologi* I–II (Copenhagen: Møller & Thomsen, 1891).

[32] S. Blöndal, *Íslensk-dönsk ordabók* (Þ. B. Þorlákssonar, Reykjavík, 1920–24); see also, e.g. G. Andrésson, *Lexicon Islandicum* (Reykjavík: Orðabók Háskólans, 1683; 2nd ed., 1999); J. Árnason, *Nucleus Latinitatis* (Reykjavík: Orðabók Háskólans, 1738; 2nd ed., 1994); *Vocabula Gallica* (copy from the 18th century) and *Vocabula Biscaica*, two manuscripts with Basque-Icelandic glossaries from the 17th century (accessed from: https://arnastofnun.is/is/basknesk-islensk-ordasofn).

[33] https://islex.arnastofnun.is/is; https://blondal.arnastofnun.is; A. Böðvarsson, *Íslensk orðabók handa skólum og almenningi* (Reykjavík: Menningarsjóðs, 1985).

[34] J. H. W. Poulsen, et al., *Føroysk orðabók* (Tórshavn: Føroya Fróðskaparfelag, 1998); Z. S. Hansen, and H. Joensen, *Føroysk-donsk orðabók* (Tórshavn: Føroya Fróðskaparfelag, 2010).

IS: In what way does the advance of lexicography, say in Denmark, affect the field in Norway and Sweden, or vice versa?

LTJ: Mutual influence is primarily a matter of networking and human interaction. The Nordic lexicographers have a long history of close cooperation and use various channels to collaborate. The most important channel nowadays is undoubtedly the Nordic Association of Lexicography, which has organized biennial conferences and annual symposiums since the early 1990s. The association publishes two journal series, *LexicoNordica* and *Nordic Studies in Lexicography*, and has also worked to develop the technical language of the Scandinavian languages by coordinating decisions on lexicographical terminology. This happened with the publication of the common *Nordisk Leksikografisk Ordbog* (Nordic lexicographical dictionary).[35]

IS: Are there women in the field of dictionary-making? We have been talking exclusively about men.

LTJ: That is a good observation, and true, too. Today, there are probably as many women as men engaged in the field, but historically the situation was different. I will give you two notable exceptions. In Denmark, the person in charge of the monumental twenty-eight-volume *Ordbog over det danske Sprog* (*ODS*) was Lis Jacobsen (1882–1961), a language historian and runologist. She earned her doctorate in 1910 and just five years later she was entrusted with the compilation of the great dictionary project. Contributing modestly to the editing of entries herself, she was responsible for all financial and administrative matters as well as the organization of the work.

The other example is the Icelandic Björg Carítas Þorláksson (1874–1934), the first Icelandic woman to earn a doctorate. She was the wife of Sígfus Blöndal and sacrificed her personal academic ambitions to assist him with his Icelandic-Danish dictionary over a twenty-year period. Although her contribution to the dictionary was substantial, she did not receive proper recognition, and the couple divorced after its completion.

IS: I'm interested in the vernacular in Scandinavian languages. As you know, it is often left out of official dictionaries.

LTJ: There are many fine examples of dialect lexicography in the Scandinavian area. We do not have time to cover them all, but let me mention a few. First of all, the special situation of Norway must be kept in mind. Norway has a richness of dialectal variation, arguably the richest of all the countries, and dialects enjoy more prestige in Norway than, for example, Denmark, where dialects are disappearing as a result of increasing mobility and the lack of prestige. As mentioned earlier, one of the two official written forms of the Norwegian language, Nynorsk, was based on vernacular forms, and for this reason many of these items are treated in *Norsk Ordbok* rather than in separate dialect dictionaries.

---

[35] H. Bergenholtz, I. Cantell, R. V. Fjeld, D. Gundersen, J. H. Jonsson, B. Svensén, *Nordisk leksikografisk ordbok* (Nordisk forening for leksikografi: Universitetsforlaget A/S, 1997).

In Denmark, the dialects can be divided into three main groups, each having their own dictionary: *Jysk Ordbog* (Jutlandic dictionary) for the western dialects of mainland Jutland, *Ømålsordbogen* for the insular dialects, and *Bornholmsk Ordbog* for the easternmost dialect.[36] The first two of these are ambitious long-term academic projects, dating back to the first third of the twentieth century and still active today; the latter were initiated around the same time but remained dormant for a long time until it was brought to life recently. The object of description is primarily the language of the traditional farming community around the year 1900.

Equally ambitious are the two main dialect dictionaries in Finland. With a similar focus on the period around 1900, they are both long-term academic projects, initiated around the same time as their Danish counterparts and still works in progress. *Ordbok över Finlands svenska folkmål* (Dictionary of Finland's Swedish vernaculars) covers the Swedish dialects in the coastal regions of Finland, whereas *Suomen murteiden sanakirja* (Dictionary of Finnish dialects) describes the Finnish vernaculars.[37] Both dictionaries began to appear as printed volumes in the 1980s but are now also available online on the same website alongside a separate dictionary for Karelian dialects.[38]

The dialectal diversity of Sweden was documented lexicographically in 1862–67 when *Svenskt dialektlexikon* (Swedish dialect lexicon) was published.[39] There are no current projects comparable to those in Denmark and Finland, but a rich archive of collected material exists, and a dictionary of selected dialect words is planned to be published in the near future.

I hope you have gained an appreciation for the richness of lexicographic practice in the Scandinavian region, encompassing both historical traditions and the diversity in the coverage of the languages. I have aimed to convey the commonalities that emerge from the linguistic similarities between them, as well as the differences that arise from the unique political and cultural developments of each country.

---

[36] *Jysk Ordbog*, Vol. 1, tome 1-4 (Århus: Institut for Jysk Sprog og Kulturforskning (ed.), Universitetsforlaget, 1970–79); O. Rasmussen, V. Sørensen, T. Arboe, I. Schoonderbeek Hansen, and N. Grøftehauge, eds., *Jysk Ordbog* (Århus: Peter Skautrup Centret, Institut for Kommunikation og Kultur, Aarhus Universitet, 2000–), www.jyskordbog.dk/jyskordbog/ordbog.html; *Ømålsordbogen: En sproglig-saglig ordbog over dialekterne på Sjælland, Lolland-Falster, Fyn og omliggende øer* (Copenhagen: Center for Dialektforskning, Københavns Universitet and Universitets-Jubilæets danske Samfund, 1992–); *Bornholmsk Ordbog* (Copenhagen: Institut for Nordiske Studier og Sprogvidenskab, 2018–), https://bornholmskordbog.ku.dk.

[37] *Ordbok over Finlands svenska folkmål* (Helsinki: Forskningscentralen for de inhemska språken, Skrifter utgivna av Forskningscentralen for de inhemska språken, 1982–).

[38] www.kotus.fi/en/dictionaries

[39] J. E. Rietz, *Svenskt dialektlexikon: ordbok öfver svenska allmogespråket* (Lund: C. W. K. Gleerups Förlag, 1862–67).

Suggested Readings

Bokmålsordboka og Nynorskordboka. https://ordbokene.no
Den Danske ordbog. https://ordnet.dk/ddo
Det Norske Akademis ordbok (NAOB). https://naob.no
Hauksdóttir, Auður. "The Role of the Danish Language in Iceland." *Linguistik Online* 79, no. 5 (2016): 77–91.
Íslensk-dönsk orðabók eftir Sigfús Blöndal. https://blondal.arnastofnun.is
Íslensk nútímamálsorðabók. https://islenskordabok.arnastofnun.is
Íslex, multilingual dictionary with Icelandic as source language. https://islex.arnastofnun.is/is
Jacobsen, Jógvan í Lon, and Zakaris Svabo Hansen. "The Lexicography of Faroese." In *International Handbook of Modern Lexis and Lexicography*, edited by Patrick Hanks and Gilles-Maurice de Schryver, 1–7. Berlin: Springer, 2022.
www.kotus.fi/en/dictionaries, website with access to Finnish and Swedish monolingual, bilingual, and dialectal dictionaries.
Lorentzen, Henrik. "The Danish Dictionary at Large: Presentation, Problems and Perspectives." In *Proceedings of the Eleventh EURALEX International Congress*, edited by Geoffrey Williams and Sandra Vessier, 285–94. Lorient, 2004.
Malmgren, Sven-Göran, and Emma Sköldberg. "The Lexicography of Swedish and Other Scandinavian Languages." *International Journal of Lexicography* 26, no. 2 (2013): 117–34.
Moths Ordbog. https://mothsordbog.dk
Nilstun, Carina. "Den digitale ordbokens innvirkning på den praktiske leksikografien." In *Nordiska studier i lexikografi*, Vol. 15, edited by Caroline Sandström, Ulla-Maija Forsberg, Charlotta af Hällström-Reijonen, Maria Lehtonen, and Klaas Ruppel, 245–52. Helsinki, 2020.
Norsk Ordbok I–XII: Ordbok over det norske folkemålet og det nynorske skriftmålet. Oslo: Samlaget, 1966–2016.
Ordbog over det danske Sprog (ODS). https://ordnet.dk/ods
Sandström, Caroline. "Perspektiv på svensk lexikografi i Finland med Ordbok över Finlands svenska folkmål och Finlandssvensk ordbok som eksempel." In *Framtidens lexikografi: Rapport från ett symposium i Göteborg 5 oktober 2012* (Meijerbergs institut för svensk ordforskning 42), 75–110. Gothenburg, 2016.
Sigurðardóttir, Aldis, Anna Hannesdóttir, Håkan Jansson, Halldóra Jónsdóttir, Lars Trap-Jensen, and Þórdís Úlfarsdóttir. "ISLEX: An Icelandic-Scandinavian Multilingual Online Dictionary." In *Proceedings of the 13th EURALEX International Congress*, edited by Elisenda Bernal and Janet DeCesaris, 779–89. 2016.
Sköldberg, Emma, Louise Holmer, Elena Volodina, and Ildikó Pilán. "State-of-the-Art on Monolingual Lexicography for Sweden." *Slovenščina 2.0* 7, no. 1 (2019): 13–24.
Sprotin. https://sprotin.fo, dictionary portal with access to over twenty monolingual and bilingual Faroese dictionaries.
https://svenska.se, dictionary portal with access to *Svenska Akademiens ordbok (SAOB), Svensk ordbok utgiven av Svenska Akademien (SO)* and *Svenska Akademiens ordlista (SAOL).*

Trap-Jensen, Lars. "State-of-the-Art on Monolingual Lexicography for Denmark (Danish)." *Slovenščina 2.0* 7, no. 1 (2019): 1–12.

Troelsgård, Thomas, and Marita Akhøj Nielsen. "Moth's Danish Dictionary: Publishing a Dictionary with a 300-year Delay." In *Proceedings of the 17th EURALEX International Congress*, edited by Tinatin Margalitadze and George Meladze, 622–34. 2016.

Úlfarsdóttir, Thórdís, and Kristín Bjarnadóttir. "The Lexicography of Icelandic." In *International Handbook of Modern Lexis and Lexicography*, edited by Patrick Hanks and Gilles-Maurice de Schryver, 1–12. Berlin: Springer, 2017.

Vikør, Lars S. "Norsk Ordbok: The Crown of Nynorsk Lexicography?" In *Proceedings of the 7th EURALEX International Congress*, edited by Martin Gellerstam, Jerker Järborg, Sven-Göran Malmgren, Kerstin Norén, Lena Rogström, and Catalina Röjder Papmehl, 705–13, 1996.

21   Spanish

Francisco Javier Pérez

Spanish is spoken by roughly 475 million people globally. This conversation, translated from Spanish by Hipólito Slomianski, starts with Antonio de Nebrija's bilingual Latin-Spanish dictionary, published in the *annus mirabilis* 1492, then switches to the role Andrés Bello, the most influential South American philologist of the age of independence and author of *Gramática de la lengua castellana, destinada al uso de los americanos*, approached not only the Spanish language but the Indigenous tongues as well.[1] It discusses Sebastián de Covarrubia's *Tesoro de la lengua castellana o española* and the canonical *Diccionario de autoridades*, which served as the foundation of the *Diccionario de la lengua española*, produced by the Real Academia Española (Royal Academy of the Spanish Language).[2] It also contemplates the role played by the groundbreaking female lexicographer María Moliner, and it reflects on the tension between particular forms of Spanish (Argentinisms, Colombianisms, Cubanisms, Ecuatorianisms, Venezuelanisms, etc.) and a global Spanish used in the media and for international pedagogical purposes.

***

ILAN STAVANS: Antonio de Nebrija, who descended from converts, had the sharp idea of publishing his *Grammar* almost when Christopher Columbus undertook his journey across the Atlantic Ocean, the Reconquista in Spain finally consolidated, and the Jews were expelled. It is not unfair, therefore, to refer to 1492 as the miraculous year. In his prologue to *Gramática de la lengua castellana* (1492),

---

[1] Antonio de Nebrija, *Gramática de la lengua castellana* [1492], ed. Antonio Quilis (Madrid: Editora Nacional, 1980); Andrés Bello, *Gramática de la lengua castellana, destinada al uso de los americanos* [1847], in *Obras completas*, Vol. 4 (Caracas: Ministerio de Educación, 1951).
[2] Sebastián de Covarrubias, *Tesoro de la lengua castellana o española* [1611], edited by Martín de Riquer (Barcelona: Alta Fulla, 1987); Real Academia Española, *Diccionario de autoridades* [1726–39], 6 vols, 3rd centennial ed. (Madrid: Real Academia Española, 2013); Real Academia Española-Asociación de Academias de La Lengua Española, *Diccionario de la lengua española*, tricentenial ed., 23rd printing (Madrid: Real Academia Española, 2014).

	Nebrija told Queen Isabel La Católica that Spanish was "the companion of empire." He remains a controversial figure, doesn't he?
FRANCISCO JAVIER PÉREZ:	The controversies surrounding Nebrija have long passed. His figure has been established as the founder of the grammar and lexicography of the Castilian romance. This does not prevent recognition that Alonso de Palencia, with his *Vocabulario universal en latin y en romance* from 1490, also made a significant contribution.[3] Nebrija's study program was more ambitious and better accomplished than Palencia's, and as a result, his influence was very decisive and enduring. The history of the early descriptions of the language is organized around his work, distinguishing him from other authors of his time.
IS:	The *Tesoro de la lengua castellana o española* by Sebastián de Covarrubias was published in 1611, almost exactly between the first part of *Don Quixote of La Mancha* and the second. It is an astonishing book in many ways.
FJP:	With Covarrubias, another moment in Spanish lexicography begins: that of monolingual dictionaries, of which he is considered the undisputed father. Never before had Spanish vocabulary been explained using the language itself, detached from Latin and rather understood as a language with sufficient metalinguistic independence to explain itself. Although it may not seem so today, this was a giant leap in the modernization of language study. The precious relationship you suggest between Covarrubias and Cervantes only enhances the figure of the lexicographer, to the point of establishing a parallel between the father of modern novels and the father of modern lexicography.
IS:	Besides, Covarrubias, as a Spanish lexicographer, propels the study of this language beyond many other European languages, such as French, Italian, and German.
FJP:	Exactly – therein lies its modernity, as its creative influence spreads to other European lexicographic traditions, which begin to become as modern as that of Spanish. With Covarrubias, bilingual lexicography comes to an end as a means of providing the vocabulary of modern languages, as these compilations are based on Latin, conditioning the description and establishing linguistic material in the realm of classicist dependence.
IS:	Although I wish I could stay longer with Covarrubias, I am moving to the next major lexicographic revolution in the Spanish language, the *Diccionario de autoridades*, which depends on Covarrubias, in a benchmark in the history of Hispanic civilization.
FJP:	The first dictionary of the Real Academia Española (RAE), known as the "dictionary of authorities" due to the testimonial reinforcement that each entry receives from literary texts by renowned authors, has been considered the most perfect of lexicographical works dedicated to Spanish. This is true in many respects, given the vigor with which it undertakes the study of vocabulary and the mastery of explanations, many of which remain relevant to this day. The collective effort in

---

[3] Alonso de Palencia, *Vocabulario universal en latín y en romance* [1490], 2 vols (Madrid: Comisión Permanente de la Asociación de Academias de la Lengua Española, 1967).

creating this work has shaped the destiny of the RAE to the present day, which still employs a unique method of compilation.

This method involves making the language dictionary a polyphonic work, where academicians from the twenty-three academies and diverse multinational lexicographer teams contribute. A plural and pan-Hispanic language requires an equally plural and pan-Hispanic methodology. Having said that, it must be concluded that the *Diccionario de autoridades*, with which academic lexicography was born as a specific field of linguistic work on Spanish, inherited all previous descriptive experiences, with Covarrubias at the forefront.

IS: How did lexicographers harvest the entries contained in *Autoridades*? What did they leave out? I'm not sure the word "lexicographer" is correct in this case. They were dictionary-makers before there was a discipline called lexicography.

FJP: The verb "harvest" aptly describes what this dictionary aimed to achieve, as it sought to offer explained and documented lists of words that, when arranged alphabetically, would become the largest and best collections of words ever undertaken for the Spanish language. And, indeed, as a collection, much was accomplished and much was left out; such is the fate of a collector. In any case, it provides a comprehensive account of the state of knowledge of the Spanish vocabulary in the eighteenth century.

IS: Let's talk about Andrés Bello, the cornerstone in Hispanic American lexicography. To what extent was Bello interested in Indigenous languages?

FJP: Bello's project involved the study of the Spanish language in general and the American language in particular. He aimed to distance himself from principles that, in his time, still adhered to Latin grammar, which were more general. Bello focused solely on the postulates specific to a particular description of grammar. For Bello, each language had its grammar, and therefore, he only believed in the specific grammar, contradicting what Noam Chomsky would later call "Cartesian linguistics," almost exclusively referring to the Port-Royal school.

In this context, it might seem curious that Bello was interested in Indigenous languages. However, considering that this is a subject pending in-depth study, it can be said that there is an indigenist aspect to Bello. We find it in his historical works, in the fragments of Alexander von Humboldt's work that he translates and edits in the magazines he publishes in London (whose titles would be the *Biblioteca americana* (1823) and the *Repertorio americano* (1826–27). In his famous silvas ("Alocución a la poesía" and "La agricultura de la Zona Tórrida"), we can trace indigenist traces embedded in the lexicon regarding the continent's flora, as well as in place names.

IS: Why not then take an interest in the particular grammar of one or more Indigenous languages? I think, for example, of Sor Juana Inés de la Cruz, who died less than 100 years before Bello was born. Sor Juana wrote a handful of verses, rhymes in Nahuatl, partially or entirely. Although she makes mistakes in grammar and commits spelling errors, these exercises at least help us think about her relationship with the Indigenous languages that surrounded her. I also think of the text "Para que los indios aprendan el castellano" (1769) by Archbishop Antonio de Lorenzana y Buitrón, which serves to understand the ecclesiastical regulations aimed at the Hispanicization of the Indigenous people of New Spain.

FJP: In the history of American linguistics, Bello's time is distinct. Bello's interests, in particular grammar, were focused on breaking away from describing Spanish according to the parameters of Latin grammar. His interest in Indigenous languages appears to be more of a cultural topic than linguistics, which, on the other hand, also addresses a peculiarity of modern linguistics. At this juncture, Bello ceases to look to the past to observe a future he would not witness, but one that all nineteenth-century linguistics seems to anticipate: cultural linguistics.

IS: Bello is famous for his *Gramática de la lengua castellana destinada al uso de los americanos* (1847). And, in particular, for his interest in spelling. Did he ever consider the creation of a dictionary?

FJP: In my book *Estudios sobre nuevos temas de lingüística bellista* (2016), I devoted a lengthy study to the significance that dictionaries had in shaping the intellectual and scientific personality of Bello.[4] It was confirmed that dictionaries as a genre of linguistic description and dictionaries as aids to research were of paramount importance to this scholar, even though he had not compiled any dictionaries himself. Lexicographical examples would be found in the "Glosario al Cantar de Mio Cid" and the vocabulary of some of his literary works.[5]

IS: Once again, is it curious that, despite his astonishing and diverse productivity, he never directed his attention to a dictionary before?

FJP: Bello undertook such demanding tasks that I don't believe he would have had time for another one, such as creating a dictionary of Spanish. His idea of building the Nation (American, Venezuelan, or Chilean) led him to unfold a polymathic task never before attempted in America and rarely afterwards. That's why we see in the entirety of his works occupations as diverse as language, literature, philosophy, law, history, science, journalism, etc. Furthermore, if he had been able to compile a dictionary of Spanish, he would have single-handedly closed the perfect circle of linguistic research: grammar, vocabulary, spelling, and pronunciation.

IS: Let's focus on the idea of creating *Diccionario hispano-americano* (1866), by Ramón Sotomayor Valdés, a Chilean immersed in the conservative politics of his country. His goal is to preserve the linguistic identity of the continent.

FJP: Authors who defended the Spanish language in the nineteenth century as if it were an immovable heritage were numerous. They sought to exert cultural power through language, where anything other than purity was repudiated as ignoble forms of speech and, consequently, as ways of expressing a cultural poverty believed to be caused by diversity. Sotomayor Valdés is one among hundreds of language scholars who preferred to deny the particularities of American Spanish in favor of a general language that existed only as a tool for understanding and work.

Recognizing that the greatness of Spanish came from the variety of its developments did not fit into the thinking of these nineteenth-century enthusiasts. His dictionary, however, paved the way for unity as a form and process to make American Spanish a standard language. Lexicography and dialectology in the late nineteenth century soon would discard these ideas and instead embrace the principle that we are a great and powerful language by accepting that diversity

---

[4] Francisco Javier Pérez, *Estudios sobre nuevos temas de lingüística bellista* (Valencia: Aduana Vieja, 2016).

[5] Andrés Bello, "Glosario," *Poema del Cid* [1862], in *Obras completas*, Vol. 7 (Caracas: La Casa de Bello, 1986).

strengthens unity, by reaffirming it in the face of a common realm of phenomena, and not the other way around.

IS: Let's talk about the maxim: la diversidad fortalece la unidad (diversity strengthens unity). I'm interested in the role that academies play in the health of contemporary Spanish. In your opinion, have we moved beyond Iberocentrism? Is it possible?

FJP: We have made significant progress in the struggle against linguistic hegemonies. The American academies of the nineteenth century were established as corresponding institutions to the RAE. Today, while still acknowledging that connection, none of the academies would subscribe to subordinate adherence to the RAE. On the contrary, since the creation of the Association of Spanish Language Academies (ASALE) in 1951 in Mexico, the Spanish language academies have been consolidating a pan-Hispanic language policy that anchors its principles and actions in a polycentric theory that dismantles traditional linguistic power centers, conceiving an image of the language that derives its identity from a plurality of prestigious modalities, explaining the essence of a unitary language characterized by its rich dialectal variety.

This paradox makes sense in the practice of a language where we can communicate with very few hurdles from the Rio Grande to Patagonia and from Equatorial Guinea to the Philippines. However, this does not exempt us from lowering our guard regarding linguistic power instances that constantly strive to return to outdated frameworks. The cohesion and fraternity achieved by the twenty-three language academies are confirmation of the outlined achievements. Vigilance over such a vast language remains a crucial issue of the present time.

IS: The *Diccionario de la lengua española* (*DLE*), just as the Academia behind it, takes a prescriptive approach to language. This has led to numerous criticisms. Don't you think it is time to opt for description rather than prescription? People might take both institutions more seriously.

FJP: Traditionally, grammatical academic works had to be prescriptive, guided by a norm that facilitated many speakers in handling the language appropriately. For a long time, the dictionary was also influenced by this imprint. However, increasingly, the language dictionary, while understanding the crucial importance of its creed for the majority of speakers, is transforming into a dictionary that attempts to describe the lexicon of Spanish objectively and in accordance with the polycentric codes dictated by pan-Hispanic policies. I agree with you that the dictionary should be the most descriptive (= scientific) genre that exists, although it must also be said that it is not always easy to sustain explanations that simply explain and do not seek to impose conditioned ways of evaluating the idea of the language.

IS: I've always found it curious that English – unlike Spanish, French, Italian, and many other languages – does not have an academy to standardize, fix, and give splendor to it. This doesn't mean that there haven't been attempts to organize such an entity. Intellectuals and politicians like Daniel Defoe and John Adams, among others, have advocated for it. But for one reason or another, there has never been a Royal Academy of the English Language. What explanation do you give?

FJP: This question is very pertinent as it points to the heart of the essentiality of language academies on both sides of the Atlantic. These academies understood that unity represented a maximum value of the language and set out to try to preserve it by creating institutions that guided speakers toward the best uses. In many cases, specifically in the nineteenth century, this guidance gave rise to the aberrant species of "linguistic purism," causing many academies and their members to play sanctioning roles regarding what were then considered poor forms of speech.

As linguists and language scientists entered the language academies, purism diminished, and by the twentieth century, the situation changed completely. However, residues of purism still exist as recessive forces and occasionally resurface. Regarding English, it was a language planted in the United States, a modern country where democracy took root strongly and where there was never a monarchy. The situation in the rest of the languages you mentioned grew in monarchical countries where democracy faced many setbacks until well into the twentieth century. Just as we continue to work for the "democracy of language," we must also understand that there was a "dictatorship of language," exercised from power as in many other social and cultural matters. For that reason, I have titled my most recent book *Por una democracia de la lengua: Escritores, filólogos y academias frente al panhispanismo lingüístico* (2023).

IS: One of the most remarkable examples in Hispanic lexicography is María Moliner (1900–81), whom I deeply admire. As far as I know, she is the only woman who has single-handedly created a dictionary, in the manner of Samuel Johnson, in the Spanish language. Do you know if this exclusivity is also at a global level? Either way, I'm interested in your opinion on Moliner, whom Gabriel García Márquez considered one of the titans of our civilization.

FJP: Like you, I also wholeheartedly admire María Moliner. I believe there hasn't been any other author who, on her own, has undertaken the immense task of compiling a dictionary of her language. Her work is considered exemplary in terms of the work method, the management of the revision of the academic dictionary, and the richness of the forms she noted to understand the value that usage holds when conceiving a dictionary for a specific era. María Moliner embraces and values lexicographic tradition, infusing it with an energy that seemed to have been lost. In another sense, she embodies the "internal exile" demanded by lexicographic work, as explained very well in the biography that Inmaculada de la Fuente wrote in 2011 about this philologist.[6]

IS: How have things changed? Or is the preparation of dictionaries still primarily a matter of men in the Hispanic world?

FJP: On the contrary, nowadays there are more women working in lexicography than men. This is not because institutions have done something to reverse the masculinity of the discipline, but because the task has been approached with more dedication by lexicographers, perhaps following the virtuous example of Moliner. In any case, I believe that each era generates its own forces, and they do not depend on whether men or women carry out the task.

As curious as it may sound, I believe more in astrological aspects than in the gender of lexicographers. Let me explain. The perseverance and dedication,

---

[6] Inmaculada de la Fuente, *El exilio interior: La vida de María Moliner* (Madrid: Editorial Turner, 2011).

patience and discipline required for compiling a dictionary can only be initiated by someone, whether male or female, born under the sign of Capricorn. This sign has virtues such as systematic and long-term work, knowing that by laying just one brick each day, the building will be completed thoroughly.

IS: Similarly, I am interested in knowing if there is diversity in the preparation of the *DLE* in its various forms: age, origin, class, linguistic variant, etc. Or is it still mainly a group of Spaniards determining how we should use our language?

FJP: I must say that is no longer the case. The *DLE* is a dictionary compiled by a group of academics and specialists with diverse characteristics in terms of age, place of birth, social stratum, and dialectal competence. Pan-Hispanic linguistic policy has reversed the situations of uniformity in dictionary compilation, and today it is established that the twenty-three academies are the authors of the work.

This enriches the dictionary with the natural diversity of nationalities, ages, origins, and sociocultural conditions of the teams that compile the work in each academy and across all of them. The *DLE* has ceased to be a dictionary made by Spaniards to become one that represents the entire Spanish language in its simultaneous unity and diversity. Today, the language academies are pan-Hispanic corporations and institutions advocating for linguistic polycentrism.

IS: Is this polycentrism also evident in the academies? For example, to what extent does the collection of linguistic material in a country like Colombia not limit itself to major cities like Bogotá, Cali, Medellín, etc., but rather includes voices from all corners of the national landscape? I am interested in the dialectic between city and province, young and old, women and LGBTQ+, Indigenous groups, and other minorities.

FJP: Polycentrism is a principle that conditions everything we do to study, describe, and disseminate the nature of the Spanish language today. This understanding of linguistic tasks has been a proposal from the academies and ASALE to the point that we have not wavered for an instant in fulfilling it. We implement it as a sign of equality and democracy of language, leaving aside any form of linguistic nationalism and, especially, social exclusions of any kind.

For Colombia and any other Spanish-speaking country, we are interested in what is spoken in the capitals as well as in rural areas, what individuals of any social, economic, and cultural stratum say, women and men, people from any minority group or those who might be excluded due to their sexual or affective preference, race, skin color, or any human condition. We are interested in how people speak, and therefore, we must be respectful to all of them.

IS: In many parts of the world, online dictionaries are now the most commonly used. In the English-speaking world, the number of users of *Merriam-Webster* and the *Oxford English Dictionary* is enormous. The online page of the *DLE* is comparatively much less sophisticated than that of these dictionaries. How has the internet changed lexicography in the Spanish-speaking world?

FJP: The current monthly query figures for the *DLE* on the internet amount to around 100,000 searches. This has fundamentally changed the relationship between speakers and the dictionary, as it has become a constant, massive, and widespread instrument for understanding the language. On the other hand, this figure requires the RAE and ASALE website to keep pace with these achievements for the Spanish-speaking world. Perhaps this is the most urgent task that our institutions must undertake, as some of them are still not equipped with these tools.

IS: In the English-speaking world, dictionaries have stopped focusing solely on written words for many years. Since 1963, the ecosystem includes popular culture: TV, radio, cinema, the internet, and more. *Merriam-Webster*, in its historical zeal, provides specific citations from movies or TV programs where a neologism first appeared. This approach is opposite to that of Samuel Johnson, or the *OED* until the mid 1980s. Has the same happened in the Spanish-speaking world?

FJP: Of course, the same has happened for Spanish. Today's linguists are more interested in the living language, the language of the street, the language of the media. This does not imply a rejection of cultured speech, which clearly also belongs to the state of the language at a specific moment of analysis.

IS: What is the relationship between the *DLE*, a government enterprise, and commercial dictionaries? My question relates to capitalism. Do you think the competition between these two ways of preparing and selling lexicographic artifacts improves the final product?

FJP: Although I understand that dictionaries end up being commercialized, I prefer to understand that there are good and bad dictionaries. They can be created from both institutional and commercial sectors. However, I do believe that competition leads to an improvement in the quality of lexicographic products. The increase in the number of copies sold can provide some clues about the acceptance of a dictionary and its achievement as a representation of a society, community, or human group. What we should demand from a dictionary is that it offers our best cultural image in the selection and description of the lexicon it gathers. To achieve this, it no longer matters whether the goal is commercial or not, but whether it aims to be the lexical mirror of a specific time and context.

IS: In the English-speaking world, academic institutions (universities, graduate programs, etc.) are crucial for the analysis of linguistic transformations. In fact, it could be said that without these institutions, whether commercial or nonprofit, dictionaries would visibly suffer. How do you assess the contribution to verbal studies from that academic sphere in the Spanish-speaking world?

FJP: Well, I believe that no one would doubt in the Spanish-speaking world about the influence that academies have had on the development of language studies. Sometimes due to excessive interference and paternalism, but always with a benevolent intention toward preserving the best practices, academies have made more than significant contributions. Fortunately, these have been accompanied by scientific advancements produced in universities and specialized linguistic centers.

There have been moments in the past where the disconnect between these two realms has resulted in a significant decline in the quality of contributions (I refer to the mismatch between the traditionalism of academies and the scientific forge of universities in the birth of linguistic modernity during the early decades of the twentieth century). The current state of this situation has been resolved since academies have drawn from and continue to draw from university professionals, researchers, and technicians, either as academics or collaborators.

IS: I want to return to the topic of indigenism. Does the RAE understand well the role played by these languages in the Spanish-speaking world?

FJP: Indigenism is a pending matter, not only for the RAE but for all of us who study Spanish. Regarding the presence of the Indigenous element in American Spanish, work has been done since the nineteenth century. Just to mention two masters,

Rodolfo Lenz (*Diccionario etimológico de las voces chilenas derivadas de lenguas indígenas americanas,* 1905–10) and Lisandro Alvarado (*Glosario de voces indígenas de Venezuela,* 1921), the former from Chile and the latter from Venezuela, laid very solid foundations for determining words of varied Indigenous origins spoken in some areas of the continent.[7]

Their studies document the impact that the major families of Indigenous languages had on the shaping of American Spanish. One of my teachers, the Capuchin missionary Fray Cesáreo de Armellada, delivered a valuable inaugural speech at the Academia Venezolana de la Lengua, "Las lenguas indígenas venezolanas y el castellano (sus relaciones y mutuo enriquecimiento durante 500 años)" (1978),[8] where he studied the relationships between Castilian and Indigenous languages. In a way, this text should be considered one of the scientific manifestos of contemporary American linguistics. Returning to your question, the RAE has not been and cannot be a reference for indigenist research, as this subject falls outside its scientific competencies.

IS: As for normativity, do you think the *DLE* reflects the subtle changes in gender, race, and class taking place in today's society?

FJP: I must say that the *DLE* makes efforts to record the mentioned changes. However, they are not sufficient, as sometimes the speed at which neologisms that reflect these social realities are generated challenges the pace of dictionary development. Concrete examples of what I mean can be seen in the review that was done a few years ago with all activities and professions defined in the masculine, even though they are currently performed by both men and women.

The entire dictionary was reviewed, and "person" was substituted where appropriate. Another case, this time related to human groups treated disrespectfully in the definitions, proposed more respectful terms. This was the case in entries related to American Indigenous groups, where the use of the term *indio* was improper and changed to the more neutral and anthropologically appropriate term, *indígena*.

IS: Let's talk about the future of Spanish dictionaries. How do you see it?

FJP: Although apocalyptic views about the death of dictionaries are tempting, there is no such death. The solidity of this genre of works and the robustness of lexicographic discipline are the best confirmation of the vitality of these types of works. What has changed is the incorporation of the digital medium, presentation formats, and search mechanisms.

I don't think anyone today questions the delights of computer resources in dictionary development and the information storage capacity it provides for lexicographic research. These are the aspects we should focus on when announcing the death of paper dictionaries, which, due to their different nature, made some of these operations more challenging. Dictionaries have a great future

---

[7] Rodolfo Lenz, *Diccionario etimológico de las voces chilenas derivadas de lenguas indígenas americanas* [1905–10], ed. Mario Ferreccio Podestá (Santiago: Universidad de Chile, 1979); Lisandro Alvarado, *Glosario de voces indígenas de Venezuela* [1921], prologue by Francisco Javier Pérez (Caracas: Monte Ávila Editores, 2008).

[8] Cesáreo de Armellada, *Las lenguas indígenas venezolanas y el castellano* (Caracas: Academia Venezolana de la Lengua, 1978).

because they contain such crucial matters as the semantic management of language and, along with it, the cultural consideration of dictionaries.

I assign great value to the latter because nothing reflects our moods, sensibilities, affections, ways of thinking, and views of the world more than the ways dictionaries describe the words of a language. Hence, lexicographic work is not only linguistic but accompanied by a hermeneutics that reveals the reading dictionaries make of life. For this reason, the lexicographer, in addition to linguistics, engages in anthropology, ethnography, historiography, sociology, and philosophy of societies. Dictionaries are nothing more than the virtuous result of these dedications.

IS: I'm interested in talking about the encounter between literary language and popular language and its scientific fertility for Spanish. You have referred to this intersection as "los diccionarios infusos, encubiertos o escondidos" (infused, covert, or hidden dictionaries).

FJP: The study of what is left unnoticed in lexicography caught my attention from my early days as a researcher. I understood it as part of a larger area of knowledge that I titled "pequeños dominios lexicográficos" (small lexicographic domains), contrasting with the large domains that dictionaries in uppercase letters constituted. It was about tracing in lexicographic traditions the presence of vocabularies, glossaries, repertoires, or word lists annexed to non-lexicographic writings: novels, stories, poems, histories, scientific treatises, etc., which functioned as lexicographic supplements to these works and whose seemingly minor importance was not minor at all. On the contrary, these pieces constituted a lexicographic genre until now unnoticed, where popular and literary lexicons established a very fertile dialogue. I then set out to collect those related to Venezuelan literature, and so far I have isolated more than 100 texts from the nineteenth to the twenty-first century.

The cumulative lexical knowledge they contain is so significant that they constitute the most authentic and expressive dictionary of Venezuelan Spanish, largely not covered in general dictionaries of Venezuelan terms. Lexicographic research into these small domains has led me to organize a theoretical book on this subject and to provide references based on Hispanic-American and Venezuelan samples in particular. The relationship of literature and lexicography is meant to bring us surprises.

Suggested Readings

Alvar Ezquerra, Manuel. *De antiguos y nuevos diccionarios del español*. Madrid: Arco/Libros, 2002.

Alvarado, Lisandro. *Glosario de voces indígenas de Venezuela* [1921]. Prologue by Francisco Javier Pérez. Caracas: Monte Ávila Editores, 2008.

Álvarez de Miranda, Pedro. *Los diccionarios del español moderno*. Gijón: Ediciones Trea, 2011.

Armellada, Cesáreo de. *Las lenguas indígenas venezolanas y el castellano*. Caracas: Academia Venezolana de la Lengua, 1978.

Azorín Fernández, Dolores. *Los diccionarios del español en su perspectiva histórica*. Alicante: Universidad de Alicante, 2004.

Bello, Andrés. "Glosario," *Poema del Cid* [1862], in *Obras completas*, Vol. 7. Caracas: La Casa de Bello, 1986.

Bello, Andrés. *Gramática de la lengua castellana, destinada al uso de los americanos* [1847], in *Obras completas*, Vol. 4. Caracas: Ministerio de Educación, 1951.

Coseriu, Eugenio. *Tradición y novedad en la ciencia del lenguaje: Estudios de historia de la lingüística*. Madrid: Editorial Gredos, 1977.

Covarrubias, Sebastián de. *Tesoro de la lengua castellana o española* [1611], edited by Martín de Riquer. Barcelona: Alta Fulla, 1987.

Haensch, Günther. *Los diccionarios del español en el umbral del siglo XXI*. 2nd ed., augumented by Carlos Omeñaca. Salamanca: Ediciones Universidad de Salamanca, 2004.

Lenz, Rodolfo. *Diccionario etimológico de las voces chilenas derivadas de lenguas indígenas americanas* [1905–10], edited by Mario Ferreccio Podestá. Santiago: Universidad de Chile, 1979.

López Morales, Humberto. "Diccionarios generales de americanismos" [2001], in *Obra selecta*, edited and with a prologue by Francisco Javier Pérez, 161–87. Valencia: Aduana Vieja, 2022.

Moliner, María. *Diccionario de uso del español*. 2 vols. Madrid: Editorial Gredos, 1966–67.

Nebrija, Antonio de. *Gramática de la lengua castellana* [1492], edited by Antonio Quilis. Madrid: Editora Nacional, 1980.

Palencia, Alonso de. *Vocabulario universal en latín y en romance* [1490]. 2 vols. Madrid: Comisión Permanente de la Asociación de Academias de la Lengua Española, 1967.

Pérez, Francisco Javier. *Diccionarios, discursos etnográficos, universos léxicos: Propuestas teóricas para la comprensión cultural de los diccionarios*. Caracas: Universidad Católica Andrés Bello/ Fundación Centro de Estudios Latinoamericanos Rómulo Gallegos, 2000.

Por una democracia de la lengua: Escritores, filólogos y academias frente al panhispanismo lingüístico. Prologue by José Manuel Blecua. San Millán: Fundación San Millán de la Cogolla, 2023.

Real Academia Española. *Diccionario de autoridades* [1726–39]. 6 vols. 3rd centennial ed. Madrid: Real Academia Española, 2013.

Real Academia Española-Asociación de Academias de La Lengua Española. *Diccionario de la lengua española*. Tricentenial ed., 23rd printing. Madrid: Real Academia Española, 2014

Seco, Manuel. *Estudios de lexicografía española*. Madrid: Paraninfo, 1987. 2nd ed.: Madrid: Editorial Gredos, 2003.

Torner, Sergi, Paz Battaner, and Irene Renaud. *Lexicografía hispánica/The Routledge Handbook of Spanish Lexicography*. London: Routledge, 2023.

Epilogue
The Total Dictionary

The entrance was unassuming, a building in midtown with no memorable characteristics. A man behind a desk was distracted with his iPhone. I told him I wanted to purchase a ticket. He asked for my name. After I gave it to him, he said the curators had told him I would be coming. "Still, the exhibit at the Grolier Room is free," he added.

He pointed me to a door, which led to an ample oblong gallery that was exquisitely built with mahogany. The walls were made of large case windows that displayed artifacts of various sizes, mostly books but also daguerreotypes and photos, dactylography machines, cassettes and CD-ROMs, and plain old fashion letters.

A month or so earlier, I had received an invitation by mail. The exhibit was called "Hardly Harmless Drudgery," a reference to Samuel Johnson's definition of *lexicographer* as "a harmless drudge that busies himself in tracing the original, and detailing the signification of words." It was made to coincide with the release of a 500-year pictorial anthology of "the geniuses, sciolists, plagiarists, and obsessives" who defined the English language. I knew well the exhibit curators and anthology editors: Bryan A. Garner and Jack Lynch. I had sent a congratulating email to them, saying I would visit on a particular day.

Neither of them wrote back.

I was thrilled to see first and facsimile editions of books I had only read about, such as Robert Cawdrey's *A Table Alphabeticall, conteyning and teaching the true writing, and understanding of hard usuall English wordes* (1604), published in London while Shakespeare was at the height of his playwrighting career and before the King James Bible was completed. It defined about 2,500 "hard usuall English wordes," mostly learned imports from Latin and Greek. The sole copy of the first edition of Cawdrey's book is in the Bodleian. Apparently, the Bodleian refused to lend that book to the Grolier Club because Grolier would display it in an exhibit hall where food and drinks were to be served. Consequently, what I had before my eyes was a duplicate. (Facsimile versions are available even through Amazon.)

Nearby was John Minsheu's *The Guide into the Tongues* (1625), the first multilingual dictionary with English headwords, surveying eleven languages.

Perhaps the most exciting item was Samuel Johnson's *Plan of a Dictionary of the English Language; Addressed to the Right Honourable Philip Dormer, Earl of Chesterfield* (1747), which is the first systematic statement of lexicographic principles in English. Johnson had received a publisher's advance of £1,575 to do his dictionary, but the sum wasn't enough. The plan was a strategy to raise money, which explains the Earl of Chesterfield as the addressee.

Johnson's dictionary was itself in the exhibit. If I'm right, it was open to the letter "j," displaying his fanciful definition of *Jobbernowl*, "Loggerhead; blockhead." I saw a semblance of James A. H. Murray, the titanic lexicographer credited for bringing to life the early volumes of the *Oxford English Dictionary*. Noah Webster's face was also behind the case windows, as was that of J. R. R. Tolkien, whose love for *Beowulf* (he translated it) led him to create Middle Earth so that he could devise an array of concocted languages.

My list might suggest, mistakenly, a heavy-handed exhibit. There was Hester Lynch Piozzi's *British Synonymy; or, An Attempt at Regulating the Choice of Words in Familiar Conversation* (1794), undeniable proof that thesauruses sometimes intrude on each other. I stayed for a while with Philip B. Gove's *Webster's Third New International Dictionary* (1961), which ignited a storm that is still with us. Humorously, there was a response by E. B. White to Oliver Jensen (1970), one of the editors of *American Heritage Dictionary*, declining an invitation to write an endorsement to his lexicon. It ended with a delightful "I must return to the kitchen now and continue with my preparation of vichyssoise."

For the hour or so I wandered around, there was never anyone else in the gallery. I told myself it was exactly the way such an exhibit should be appreciated: alone and in silence. Then, as I prepared to leave, a gentle woman with a hat and a colorful flower dress entered the room and immediately looked at me.

At first, I felt uncomfortable but then ignored her presence. A few minutes later, she was standing next to me.

"Are you enjoying it?"

I smiled. "Very much."

"It is remarkable how much might be cramped into eight display windows."

"Yes."

There was a silence.

"Are you Professor Stavans?"

I was surprised. "I am, madame. How did you know?"

"Mr. Garner and Mr. Lynch let us know we should expect you today."

"Mmmm. I communicated with them but didn't get a response."

"Well, they surely anticipated your arrival. Neither of them is here. But Mr. Pappernick would be most honored if you agreed to see him."

I had never heard of Mr. Pappernick, so I asked her.

"He knows you well, having followed your work for years. In fact, he has a large collection of your books in his personal library, which is rather large. He knows you also collect dictionaries."

"I do, indeed."

"What kinds of dictionaries, Professor?"

"All kinds. Quite a few in Spanish, starting with a folio edition of Antonio de Nebrija's *Vocabulario español-latino*, Sebastián de Covarrubias' *Tesoro de la lengua castellana o española*, and María Moliner's *Diccionario de uso del español*. I have dictionaries in Esperanto, Yiddish, Chinese, German, Hebrew, Nahuatl, Quechua, French..."

"Mr. Elias Pappernick's office is a few blocks away, on Madison Avenue."

"I'm sorry, but I have a busy day," I responded.

"I know you do, and Mr. Pappernick does too."

"Why would he want to see me?"

"Mr. Pappernick will explain in detail. He funded this exhibit. He also underwrote a number of your projects. He is interested in talking to you about an idea. Would you be available at 3pm today? Or else, tomorrow for breakfast? Mr. Pappernick knows you come to New York City briefly, for two to three days, and are likely to leave soon. He doesn't want to miss the opportunity."

"What precisely does he want to discuss with me?"

"I would be remiss to answer your question, yet I assure you the topic is of your interest."

"Might you be more specific?"

"If you are ready to spare an hour, Mr. Pappernick will explain the details of a plan."

"A plan? Like Johnson's *Plan of a Dictionary of the English Language*?"

"Maybe. Although it might be better called a proposal. Anyway, I shouldn't speak. It's between Mr. Pappernick and you, or at least I hope so. Can I have a taxi pick you up?"

I was suspicious. "Maybe. I would need to arrange my schedule." I paused. "Do you have a copy? I'm eager to see it."

"Of what?"

"The plan."

"Oh, no, I don't. Please ask Mr. Pappernick."

At my place an hour later, I got an email to meet Mr. Pappernick for breakfast. I moved around my schedule. Next morning, a limo picked me up early and drove me to a luxurious building. The guard at the lobby knew who I was. He asked me to take the elevator to the last floor.

The door opened into a luxurious office with views on the back to the entire city. A secretary welcomed me, then walked me to a conference room with an

Epilogue 277

ovoid table in the middle, leather chairs, a shelf of antiquarian books on one side, and a large TV screen on another side. She asked me to wait. "Mr. Pappernick will be with you shortly."

A few minutes later, a waiter brought a fruit bowl, yogurt, scrambled eggs, a loaf of bread, marmalade, coffee, milk, and other accoutrements. He placed them gently on the table. As soon as he left, he was followed by a businessman dressed elegantly with suit and tie, cleanly shaved and with salt-and-pepper hair, and, most visibly, a liberal smile. I estimated his age to be in the mid eighties.

"Professor Stavans, I'm humbled by your visit."

"Gracias, Mr. Pappernick, although I'm not sure I understand the reason."

"Not to worry," he answered. "First and foremost, I wanted to meet you. I have followed you for years. I have dreamt of possible conversations you and I have had. Please, eat your breakfast. In particular, try the marmalades. I know you have a sweet tooth."

"My reputation precedes me."

After preparing our dishes, each of us made our way to our respective place on the conference table.

"How long are you in the city? For a couple of days, I guess. You probably have to resume classes. Your students must be very bright."

"That's right."

His knowledge of me made me somewhat uneasy.

For a while we talked about a variety of light subjects until Mr. Pappernick finally made his way to his main theme. "I don't mean to intrude in your schedule, Professor. I want to talk about an idea I have. Let me reiterate: it is just an idea, which might lead to a plan. I should say that I'm a practical person. By this I mean that time is precious, yours and mine; I don't intend to waste either of them. Fortunately, you are known for making things happen."

He paused. "I understand you visited the exhibit at the Grolier Room yesterday. I hope you enjoyed it. It took a few years to materialize and I was happy to help with the logistics. You also have a collection of dictionaries, so your personal library must feel like a museum, although perhaps not to you. I know of your uncommon interest in various dictionary traditions. It is uncommon because most people, when they see a dictionary, they think it just appeared out of the blue. But none of them did. There is a complex history behind them... To be more precise, I have been made aware of the conversations you've been having with lexicographers all over the world – in Lebanon, in Tel Aviv, in Tokyo, in Lima, in Warsaw, and in other places – about their respective national quests for the perfect lexicon."

"Yes, Mr. Pappernick. It has been enormously rewarding." I sighed. "The perfect lexicon is a Platonic archetype: an unattainable yet worthwhile dream."

"You are imperfect beings." He looked at the city outside the windows. "How does the *OED* define *perfection*? Free from defect, flawlessness, faultlessness, purity. Rather cumbersome, don't you think? You are a consultant to the *OED*, so you know the tricks of the trade. And you've edited your own dictionary of Spanglish. A language I confess to be somewhat frightened about."

"Don't be frightened, Mr. Pappernick. Languages aren't subversive; people are."

"Anyway, I would like you to consider a project: creating an *absolute* dictionary."

"Absolute?"

"Well, the right word is *total*, Professor Stavans. How about making a dictionary that would comprise everything? I would provide you with the funds you need for it to become a reality. I know this proposal is absurd. In fact, I have read what you said once: there is no such thing as an unabridged dictionary. It is sheer hubris. All dictionaries are abridged."

"I didn't say it, Mr. Pappernick. Jack Lynch, one of the curators of the exhibit 'Hardly Harmless Drudgery' did."

"Ah, but in my mind, you said it. At any rate, you have put your eyes on countless dictionaries: in Bengali, in Esperanto, in Norwegian, in Portuguese. Why not create a dictionary that would contain all others? Please don't underestimate its potential. Who uses dictionaries today? Young people might think they are unnecessary; at least those who don't grow up with dictionaries at their side. It doesn't matter because sooner or later they become users. Professor Stavans, you have written extensively about the word *Quixotic*, meaning "impractical." This idea might appear impractical at first sight. Yet we need impractical ideas, now more than ever. An impractical idea is rash, extravagant, and romantic, but it might be the foundation of a new way of looking at things. The first dictionary, regardless of the language it showed up in – was it Greek? or Arabic? – must have been regarded as an absurd artifact. To corral, in between covers, all the words in one language? Foolish. Today we cannot live without dictionaries. For it is through dictionaries that we catalog the world around us. You're interested in the concept of *lexilalia*, right?"

"Yes, I am."

"Lexilalia is the need to copy other people's words. And copy the copy. *Merriam-Webster* defines it as "the frequent pathological repetition of words as an attempt to capture their fleeting meaning. Like Melville's Bartleby the Scrivener and Flaubert's Bouvard et Pecuchet."

"People might copy other people's words. But only the original copyists leave a legacy."

"Mallarmé believed that '*tout, au monde, existe pour aboutir à un livre.*'"

"Exactly. Something similar might be said of dictionaries: all dictionaries are snapshots of the time and place in which they came to be. Together, they make a Platonic vessel, a dictionary of dictionaries – total, unabridged. God, who created language in order to make the world, is the Great Lexicographer, witnessing how the universe changes by means of the feeble repetition of words, which are fragile and ephemeral, and how words splinter into new words, fresh and full of life. It is through dictionaries that we humans exercise our will to live and stamp our personality on things, defying as emphatically as possible the inevitability of death. Why then not make a dictionary that encompasses all dictionaries? It is actually rather simple: the total dictionary would coalesce, in a single point, all the words every created, past, present, and future. It is the quest of humankind to bring in totality to our knowledge. It would be a response to the myth of the Tower of Babel, in Genesis 11:1–9. There are similar Sumerian and Mesopotamian versions. We went up the ziggurat with one universal language and came down with a thousand. Returning to the pristine stage of a universal language is impossible. The Esperantists know that firsthand. No, *The Total Dictionary* isn't that foolish. It would be a centripetal force, an Aleph – I'm talking about a writer you love, Professor – were "the milk of paradise" would be drank whole."

"That's not Borges but Samuel Taylor Coleridge."

"It doesn't matter."

"What are you proposing?"

"I will be concrete. I don't propose that you quit your job. Do as much as I like. But sign a contract with me whereby you receive a handsome yearly salary, three times as large as your current one, whereby you commit to produce, in a span of no more than five years, a dictionary that contains all other dictionaries ever produced."

"Five years?"

"Five years. Aside from the aforementioned salary..."

"Is it a bribe or a salary?"

"It is both. All salaries are bribes. Aside from the bribe, you will have an office in this magisterial city where everything converges, and a staff of as many as two dozen people supporting the endeavor."

"Are you imagining *The Total Dictionary* as a digital technology?"

"Of course, unless you, Professor Stavans, are able to also produce a physical artifact. That, in my view, is impossible. But I might be wrong."

"All the languages in the world..."

"Every single one. How many are there? I read that currently there are around 7,000 and that cumulatively there have been around 31,000."

"Are you aware of the limits of the project your proposing? 31,000 languages cataloged in a single dictionary in five years?"

"Yes."

"Is it a joke?"

"I would never be irreverent to you. I'm perfectly conscious of the immensity of my invitation. In those five years, you would have little time to focus on other matters. Knowing you, though, I'm sure you would succeed in doing other activities. I'm happy with that as long as our contractual parameters are respected."

I sighed. "The breakfast is delicious, Mr. Pappernick."

"Have as much as you please."

I waited a few minutes before I asked: "What is there for you?"

He responded without delay. "Nothing. The glory would be yours alone, Professor Stavans. My name wouldn't appear anywhere, not even in the acknowledgments. In the past, I have donated funds to various ambitious projects. I always make sure to do so anonymously. In fact, the contract would include that provision: I don't what anyone to know I'm behind it, not now and not ever. I find pleasure in the sole existence of these artifacts. Nothing else is at stake."

"Mr. Pappernick, how did you make your fortune?"

"The answer is trivial: in hedge funds. Nothing interesting... But that is why I find traction in ideas like this. Making money isn't the point. Honestly, it is a rather mechanical effort. What matters is what one does with one's capital, be it money, intellectual, or emotions."

"Sorry but I have yet another question, one no doubt indiscreet."

"Sure."

"You're an old man, Mr. Pappernick. What if you die before I complete the so-called *The Total Dictionary*?"

"First of all, don't 'so-call' it. It is an idea that will grow on you, I assure you. Second, you too aren't young. There are two decades in between us. I'm 83 years old. At the moment, I am healthy, but health – this isn't news to you – is a lottery. The contract would provide an escort account that continues to pay for the project irregardless."

"*Irregardless* – perhaps my answer is in that word. What to do with words that aren't correct, so to speak?"

He laughed. "I threw in the word to see how engaged you are with my proposal. Happily, you seem fully engaged. Of course, it would be up to you to decide what goes in and what is left out. Isn't that what dictionary-makers do, no matter the language? Isn't that what the controversy between prescription and description is about?"

"Yes," I responded. "But if I leave out *irregardless*, if I leave out slang, if I leave out slurs, if I leave out youthful creations such as *frenemy*, am I really editing *The Total Dictionary*?"

"Isn't that what the *OED* does? Is it truly the *Oxford Dictionary of the English Language* or is it the *Oxford Dictionary of Whatever the Oxford Dons*

Deem Appropriate for inclusion? Still, they call it the *OED* and not the *OAOED*, the *Oxford Almost-All-of-English Dictionary*."

I laughed.

"Do you know about *Hyper-Webster*? It's an infinite dictionary with all the words, existent and nonexistent, in the English language. That doesn't interest me, as it is only a game to explore the contours of Georg Cantor's set theory. I'm talking about a living dictionary that will feature pictorial, word, and other languages. Only a few might be organized alphabetically, as you know from your explorations on Japanese, Chinese, and other languages. It would focus not on oral but exclusively on written forms of communication. Hittite from Anatolia, Phoenician, Sogdian, Eblaite, Ge'ez, Old Turkic, Mycenaean Greek – all would be included. Why don't you think about it, Professor? Take a week or two, maybe a month. Any organizing principles should be sorted out through rational principles. Your life would be infinitely richer for having tried and so would those of the potential users if the effort indeed came to be."

"And what if it doesn't? What if in the process I find that, as I suspect, the idea is ridiculous?"

"You don't need time to come to that conclusion: it *is* ridiculous, which makes it all the more important. I know you to be a serious scholar. In any case, if you're ready to entertain the prospect, I will take the risk."

Suddenly, it felt to me as if I was not in a skyscraper in New York City but in a dream, starting with my arrival to the Grolier Room. There was something illogical in the experience. Was Mr. Pappernick considering that once *The Total Dictionary* was up and running, it would require daily actualization? In spite of his insistence it wasn't a vanity project, it felt like one. Who would use such a lexicon? People only go to their "local" dictionary, the one pertaining to their own language, or at most they use a bilingual one. But one with all the languages in the universe? Not even a handful of scholars would find value in it.

I thought of the last three lines of Coleridge's "Kubla Khan; Or, a Vision in a Dream":

> And close your eyes with holy dread
> For he on honey-dew hath fed,
> And drunk the milk of Paradise.

The woman in the flowery dress I had seen the day before reappeared. It was clear her presence was announcing the end of my encounter with Mr. Pappernick. After thanking me profusely for coming, she said he was due for a morning nap. He said goodbye with his handsome smile. She walked me to the elevator and said goodbye, but not before stating that, should I say yes, the contract would be prepared in a manner of days.

Still, the idea was acquiring shape in my mind. The fact that it was described as Quixotic made it all the more alluring. Did he want me to prepare a plan, like Samuel Johnson had made for the Earl of Chesterfield? I recalled that Johnson had promised his publisher he could do *A Dictionary of the English Language* in three years, but it took many more.

I asked the woman if I could write a thank-you note to Mr. Pappernick. She replied, "Only if you do it in multiple languages."

Index

Aasen, Ivar, 254
   Det norske Folkesprogs Grammatik
      (Grammar of the Norwegian vernacular),
      255
   Nynorsk and, 255
   Ordbog over det norske Folkesprog
      (Dictionary of the Norwegian vernacular),
      255
Abade Correia da Serra, 200
Abān b. Rabāḥ, 111
Abdel-Nour, J., 116
Abecedarium (Алфавитарь рекше букварь),
   229
Aboriginal peoples, 133
Abrogans, 28, 30
Abū ʿUbayd al-Qāsim b. Sallām, 112
Abū Ḥanīfa ad-Dīnawarī, 112
Abū Hayra al-Aʿrābī
   Kitāb al-Ḥašarāt, 111
   Kitāb aṣ-ṣifāt, 112
Abū Mālik ʿAmr b. Kirkira
   Kitāb al-hayl, 112
Academia Brasileira de Letras (ABL), 200
Academia das Ciências de Lisboa (Lisbon
   Academy of Sciences) (ACL), 199–201,
   206
   *Vocabulário ortográfico da língua
      portuguesa*, 200
Academia Mayor de la Lengua Quechua de
   Cusco (High Academy of the Quechua
   Language of Cusco), 245
Academia Real das Sciencias de Lisboa, 200,
   see also Academia das Ciências de Lisboa
   (Lisbon Academy of Sciences) (ACL)
Academia Venezolana de la Lengua, 271
academic institutions, influence of, 270
academic language, 243
Académie française, 60, 83, 86–88, 101, 102,
   164, 250, 251, 253
Academy of Esperanto, 16, 26
Academy of Sciences of Lisbon, 199
Academy of the Hebrew Language, 127–28

Accademia della Crusca, 86, 94, 101–3
   INCIPIT Group and, 102
   online site of, 102, 105
Accademia d'Italia, 101
ACK orthography, 179
Adams, John, 267
Adelung, Johann Christoph, 29, 30, 31, 32
   Grammatisch-kritisches Wörterbuch, 32, 33
Afn Shvel, 189
Africa
   Arabo-Islamic invasion of, 157
   dictionary culture in, 169–70
   European colonization of, 157
African American vernacular English, 58, 65
African language dictionaries
   availability of, 161
   online, 162
   oral, 160–61
African languages, 156–70
   Arabic languages and, 157
   converting oral forms into literary forms,
      159–60
   European languages and, 157, 168
   European orthography and, 159–60
   illiteracy and, 160
   tension between oral and written spheres,
      160–61
African Languages Lexical (ALLEX) Project,
   164, 166
African Languages Research Institute, 163,
   164, 166
African lexicography, 156–70
   future of, 170
   impact of technology on, 166
   role of academic institutions in, 162–63
   undermined by limited commercial viability,
      162
Afrikaans, 163
Afro-Asiatic languages, 166–67
Akan, 168
Akiva, Rabbi, 120
Alberti, Leon Battista, 84

283

Alcalá, Pedro de, *Vocabulista aravigo en letro castellana*, 108
ALECSO Arabization Coordination Bureau, 116
al-Muʿjam al-ʿarabī al-'asāsī, 109
Alencastre, Andrés (Kilku Warak'a), 245
Algonquian languages, 135
Alkalay, Reuven, 125
alphabetic languages, 43
Altuigurisches Wörterbuch, 39
Alvarado, Francisco de, *Vocabulario en lengua misteca*, 135
Alvarado, Lisandro, *Glosario de voces indígenas de Venezuela*, 271
Amazonian languages, 242
American English, 60, 81
  British English and, 82
  development of, 60
  dictionaries of, 60–61
American Heritage Dictionary, 60, 275
American linguistics, 265, 271
American Spanish, 66, 266–67, 271
Americanisms, 81
Amharic, 156
Amherst College, 3
Anchor English-Japanese Dictionary, 212
Andalusia, 107
Andean languages, 242, 245
Andersen, Hans Christian, 21
Anderson, Patricia, *Revitalization Lexicography: The Making of the New Tunica Dictionary*, 135
Andrews, Richard, 179
anglicisms, 65, 88, 89
Antonini, Annibale, *Dictionnaire italien latin et françois*, 100
Antonio Houaiss Institute of Lexicography, 199
Apresjan, Juri, Russian Active Dictionary (Активный словарь русского языка), 237
Arabic, 60, 107–17, 121, 157, 166
  Andalusian dialects of, 107, 108
  dialects spoken in Africa, 157
  as dominant language in African countries, 157
  Modern Standardized Arabic (MSA), 116–17
  morphology based on internal inflection, 110
Arabic Academy of Cairo, 110, 116–17
Arabic dictionaries
  classification by roots in, 109, 110
  classification by words in, 110–11
  Modern Standardized Arabic (MSA) and, 116–17
  rotating around families of words, 109–10

Arabic Hebrew, 128
Arabic lexicography, 107–17
  genesis of, 111–12
  reach of, 117
Arabic-French dictionaries, 109
Arabic-Hebrew dictionaries, 127
Arabic-Latin dictionaries, 108
Arabic-Persian dictionaries, 115
Arabs, 129
Archaists, 230, 231
Arenas, Pedro de, *Vocabulario manual de las lenguas castellana y mexicana*, 174
Arguedas, José María, 243
  Katatay, 245
Aristotle, 7
Armellada, Cesáreo de, 271
Arte y vocabulario en la lengua general del Perú, 244
Asahi Shimbun Company, 215
Ashkenazi Jews, 61, 129, 188
Association for African Lexicography (AFRILEX), 164
Association of Spanish Language Academies (ASALE), 267, 269
Augst, Gerhard, *Wortfamilienwörterbuch*, 35
Auitanian, 134
Auld, William, 22
Austen, Jane, 21
authority, dictionaries and, 26, 61
Avneon, Eitan, 125
Ayalon, David, 127
Aymara, 242
al-Azharī, *Tahdīb al-luġa*, 114
Aznavour, Charles, 67
Aztec Empire, 172, 173

Baalbaki, Mounir, 116
BABADADA, kreol morisien - Australian English, diksioner viziel - visual dictionary: Mauritian Creole - Australian English, visual dictionary, 169
Baciroa, 134
Bahasa Indonesia, 26
Bahat, Shoshana, 126
Bajadir, Bir, *Nepali-Thami-English Dictionary*, 139
Balaibalan, 16
Bantu languages, 157, 158
Baretti, Giuseppe, *A Dictionary of the English and Italian Languages*, 100
Barton, Helen, 3
Basalenque, Diego, *Arte de la lengua tarasca*, 135
Bastiano de' Rossi, *Vocabolario degli Accademici della Crusca*, 99

Battaglia, Salvatore, 100
Baumgartner, Walter, 123
Bayt al-Ḥikma, 115
Baza Radikaro Oficiala, 16
Bedouins, 111
Bein, Kazimierz, 16
Belarusian, 239
Bello, Andrés, 265, 266
  Gramática de la lengua castellana, destinada al uso de los americanos, 263, 266
Ben Amotz, Dan, 127
Ben Mrad, Ibrahim, 117
Ben Yehuda, Eliezer, 124–25, 126, 127
  Hamilon Ha-Gadol (The big dictionary), 124
Ben Yehuda, Netiva, 127
Ben Zeev, Yehuda Leib, *Otsar Ha-Shorashim* (Roots' treasure), 123
Berber, 167
Berber dialects, 157
Bhreathnach, Póilín, 153
Bialik, Chaim Nakhman, 187
the Bible, 7, 21
  editions of, 6
  as engine of development of lexicography, 86
  translations of, 6, 85–86, 158, 159
bible software, 11–12
biblical lexicography, 122, 123
biblical philology, history of, 14
biblical studies, 85
Bierce, Ambrose, *The Devil's Dictionary*, 1, 2, 76
bilingual dictionaries. *See also under specific languages and language combinations*, 83, 95, 100, 107, 108–9, 145, 210–14, 244, 258
  in African languages, 163
  of African languages, 159
  in Arabic tradition, 115–16
  in Gabon, 165
  globalization and, 115–16
  Hebrew, 126–27
  Irish and, 147, 148–49
  Japanese, 222
  Nahuatl and, 175–76, 181
  in Portuguese, 197
  seen as colonial tools, 161
  in South Africa, 164
  Yiddish and, 187, 188, 193
bilingual dictionaries. *See also under specific languages*
  for African languages, 161, 165
  of African languages, 159

in African languages, 163
in Arabic tradition, 115–16
in Gabon, 165
globalization and, 115–16
Hebrew, 126–27
Irish and, 147, 148–49
Japanese, 222
Nahuatl and, 175–76, 181
in Portuguese, 197
seen as colonial tools, 161
in South Africa, 164
Yiddish and, 187, 188, 193
bilingual glossaries. *See also under specific language combinations*, 249
bilingual lexicography, 210–14
bilingualism
  in Canada, 133
  hybrid languages and, 67
  Yiddish speakers and, 62
Biondelli, Bernardino,
  Glossarium Azteco-Latinum et Latino-Aztecum, 174, 175, 176
Björg Carítas Þorláksson, 259
Bjørnson, Bjørnstjerne, 255
Blair, Eric, 25
Blöndal, Sígfus, *Icelandic-Danish Dictionary*, 258
Bluteau, Rafael
  Diccionario da Lingua Portugueza composto pelo Padre D. Rafael Bluteau reformado, e accrescentado por Antonio de Moraes Silva, natural do Rio de Janeiro, 201, 202
  Vocabulario Portuguez e Latino, 201
Boccaccio, Giovanni, 84, 101, 102
Bochtor, Ellious, 108
Böðvarsson, Árni, *Íslensk orðabók handa skólum og almenningi* (Icelandic dictionary for school and the general public), 258
Bokmål, 248, 255
Bolivia, language policies of, 246
Bolsheviks, 233, 238
Bolze (French and Swiss German), 61
The Book of Ancient Texts, 45
The Book of Changes, 45
The Book of Rites, 45
The Book of Songs, 45
bopomofo phonetic notations, 48
border zones, 58, 67
Borges, Jorge Luis, 25, 56, 73, 235, 279
Bornholmsk Ordbog, 260
Boyle, Margaret, 58
Boym, Michał, 55
Brazilian Academy of Letters, 199

Brazilian Portuguese, 198–99
Breton, 26
Brian Boru, 146
Brill Dictionary of Ancient Greek, 12
British English, American English and, 82
Buddhism, 54–55
Bureau of die Woordeboek van die Afrikaanse Taal, 165
Burko, Alec Leyzer, 188–89
Bustānī, Buṭrus al-, *Muḥīṭ al-muḥīṭ*, 116, 117
Byzantine Empire, 7
Byzantine intellectual tradition, 235

Cai Yuanpei 蔡元培, 53
calepin, 84
Calepino, Ambrogio, *Dictionarium Latinum*, 6, 84–85, 86, 88, 96
Call My Bluff, 73
calligraphic standardization, 42
Calvin, John, 86
Cambridge Greek Lexicon, 10, 12
Cambridge Handbook of the Dictionary, 14
Cambridge International Dictionary of English (CIDE), 212
Cambridge University Press, 166
Cameron, James, 67
Campbell, R. Joe, 178, 179
  lexical database by, 179
Canada
  Aboriginal peoples in, 133
  multilingualism in, 133
Canadian Constitution, 133
Cangjie 仓颉, 47
Canon, 214
Canones Lexicographici, 81
Cantor, Georg, 281
Caomhánach, Muiris (Kruger), 150
Cape Verdean Creole or Kriolu (Crioulo Caboverdiano), 168
Cape Verdean Dictionary, 168
Cardoso, Jerónimo, *Dictionarium ex Lusitanico in Latinum Sermonem*, 196–97
Carochi, Horacio, 174, 179
Carolina Algonquian, 135
Carroll, Lewis, 21
Carter, Henry Hare, 197
Cartesian linguistics, 265
Cartier, Jacques, 135
Casio, 210, 213, 214
Castilian, 108, *see also* Spanish
Castilian-Latin dictionaries, 173
Catalan, 26
Catholic Church, 86, 173, 177, 248
Catholicism, 86
Caussin de Perceval, A., 109

Cawdrey, Robert, *A Table Alphabeticall, conteyning and teaching the true writing, and understanding of hard usuall English wordes*, 274
Celts, 145–54
Centre for Kiswahili Lexicography and Grammar, 162
Centro de Linguística da Universidade NOVA de Lisboa project, 195
Cervantes, Miguel de
  Covarrubas and, 264
  Don Quixote, 21, 63–65, 241, 243, 264
Chadic, 167
Chadic langauges, 157
Chadwick, John, 9, 10
Chanka, 246
character writing, 45
Chen Tingjing 陈廷敬, 52
China
  class reconciliation through language and culture, 51–52
  dictionaries as a central vehicle of campaign against illiteracy in, 53
  Esperanto in, 23
  Han dynasty, 43, 46, 50
  Ming dynasty, 51, 55
  publishing in modern, 53
  Qin dynasty, 42, 43, 45, 51
  Qing dynasty, 52, 55
  Shang dynasty, 43
  Song dynasty, 48, 55
  Sui dynasty, 48
  Tang dynasty, 44, 48, 49, 54, 55
  Warring States period, 45
  Western Han dynasty, 43, 51
  Zhou dynasty, 43, 45
China Illustrata, 55
Chinchaysuyu, 242
Chinese Academy of Social Sciences, 54
Chinese characters
  character dictionaries, 52
  character-making, 42, 47
  evolution of, 43–44, 46–48
  explanation and interpretation of, 45, 55
  historiography of, 47
  resilience of, 52
  Six Categories (*liu shu* 六书) of making, 47
  Xu Shen's model of arranging, 46–48
Chinese dictionaries, 42–56, 217, 220
  character dictionaries, 52
  contemporary dictionary-making, 52–54
  cultural legitimacy and, 51
  exegesis of classics and, 45
  first, 45–46
  future of, 56

Index

monolingual, 216–17
prototypes of, 42–45
role of state agencies in creating, 50–52
word dictionaries, 52
Chinese Romanization system, 55, 56, *see also* Chinese, Latinization and
Chinese writing system, 216, *see also* Chinese characters
Chinese, Latinization and, 42, 53, 60, 207
Chinese-English dictionaries, 55–56
Chinese-French dictionaries, 55
Chinese-Latin dictionaries, 55
Chinglish (Chinese and English), 61
Chomsky, Noam, 265
Christian II, King, 249
Christian V, King, 250
Christianity, 197, 244
Church Slavonic, 230
Cicero, 6
Círculo de Leitores, 199
Classical antiquity, 5
Classical Latin, 197
Clavijero, Francisco Xavier, 174
Close, Rev. Maxwell, 151
codebreaking, 10
code-switching, 58, 62
Coleridge, Herbert, 8
Coleridge, Samuel Taylor, 279, 281
collaboration, 132
Collins, 56
Collins COBUILD English Dictionary (COBUILD), 212
Collins, Isabel, 3
colonialism, 63, 81, 107–9, 135
  in Africa, 157, 158, 159
  African lexicography and, 159, 163
  bilingual dictionaries and, 161
  English lexicography and, 80–82
  hybrid languages and, 61
  Indigeneity and, 133, 134
  Nahuatl lexicography and, 173
  Portuguese and, 197–98
Colotlan, 134
Columbia University, 188, 189
Columbus, Christopher, 132, 263
Commercial Press (Shangwu yinshu guan 商务印书馆), 53
Commission on the Unification of Pronunciation (China), 53
Communist ideology, 234
comparative lexicography, Latin-German, 31
Compendio Enciclopédico Náhuatl (CEN), 177
Complete Dictionary of Esperanto (known as PV), 24, 25

Complete Illustrated Dictionary of Esperanto (known as PIV), 24, 26
Comprehensive English-Yiddish Dictionary (CEYD), 184, 185
Concise Oxford Dictionary, 79
Concise Oxford Dictionary of Current English (COD), 211
Confucian scholars, 46, 47, 50
Confucianism, 50, 52, 53, 55
Confucius, 46, 50
  Erya 尔雅, 45–46
Conicari, 134
Consejo Superior de Investigaciones Científicas, 10
Consiglio Nazionale delle Ricerche (CNR), 101
Considine, John, 8
Constantinople, fall of, 7
Conversos, 63, 65
Corca Dhuibhne (West Kerry) Iri, 150
Cormac mac Cuileanáin, 146, 148
Corpus na Gaeilge, 152, 153
Corriente, Federico, 108
Cortese, Giuseppina, 94
Cortez, Hernan, 172
Costa, Rute, 195–205
Cottez, Herni, 89
Courtenay, Jan Baudoin, 232
Covarrubias, Sebastián de
  as father of Spanish lexicography, 264, 265
  Tesoro de la lengua castellana o española, 96, 99, 263, 264, 276
Cree dictionaries, 136
creole dictionaries, 83
creole languages, 58, 168–69, 198
Croidhe Cainnte Chiarraighe, 149–50
Crystal, David, 72
Cubonics, 65, 66
cultural exchange, 197
cultural linguistics, 266
Cushitic, 166
Cusihuaman, Antonio, 245
Cyrillic, 232, 233
da Silva, D. João Carlos de Bragança e Ligne de Sousa Tavares Mascarenhas, 200

Daijirin 大辞林, 208, 215
Dainihon Kokugo Jiten 大日本國語辭典, 209, 222–23
Dal', Vladimir, 232
Dalin, A. F., 254
Danish, 248, 249, 254, 257, 258
  Faroese and, 258
  spelling standardization and, 252, 253
Danish Academy, 254
Danish Concise Dictionary, 253

288 Index

Danish Language Council, 253
Danish lexicography, 249–53, 259
Danish orthography, standardized, 253
Dante Alighieri, 2, 21, 84, 94, 96, 102
　Commedia, 97, 98
　Convivio, 98
　De vulgari eloquentia, 96–98
　Vita nova, 98
Dao (Chinese and Tibetan), 61
Dasypodius, Petrus, 31
David ben Abraham al-Fasi, Kitāb Jāmiʿ al-Alfāz, 122
David Qimhi (Radaq), Rabbi, Sefer Ha-Shorashim (The book of roots), 122
dazhuan 大篆 (large seal script), 45
de Bhaldraithe, Tomás, 150, 152–53
de Serra, José Francisco Correia, 200
De vulgari eloquentia, 94
dead languages, 4–5
Debove, Josette, 89
DeepL, 216
Defoe, Daniel, 22, 267
Del Bailo, Francesco, Fabrica del mondo, 94
Delauney, Père, 136
Den Danske Ordbog (The Danish dictionary), 248, 252
Denmark, 248
Det Norske Akademis Ordbog (Norwegian Academy dictionary or NAOB for short), 255–56
Deutsches Fremdwörterbuch, 37
Deutsches Wörterbuch (Grimm), 28, 29, 30–31, 33–34, 37, 39, 74
dialectology, 266
dialects. See also under specific languages
　African languages and, 156
　definition of, 156
　dialect surveys, 49
　dictionaries collecting, 49
　distinguishing from languages, 134
　Scandinavian, 259–60
dialetti, 98–99
Diccionario Clave, 65
Diccionario de autoridades, 263, 264–65
Diccionario de la lengua española (DLE), 237, 263, 267, 269, 270, 271
　online, 269
　Spanglish and, 65
Diccionario de uso del español, 276
Diccionario della lengua castellana, 32
Diccionario español-árabe, 108
Diccionario griego-español (DGE), 10–11, 13
Diccionario y gramática chibcha, 135
Dicionário Aurélio da língua portuguesa, 199
Dicionário lexical santome–português, 169

Dicionário livre santome/português—Livlunglandji santome/putugêji, 169
Dicionário Priberam da língua portuguesa, 198
Dickens, Charles, 22
dictionaries
　authoritative, 253
　bilingual, 35–36, 54–56, 108–9
　capitalism and, 270
　development from one-person to team efforts, 75–76
　digitized, 151
　etymological, 38
　experience of creating, 129
　grassroots, 21
　historical, 38, 104, 239
　historiography of language and, 42
　history of, 34
　by Indigenous people, 244–45
　literacy and, 53
　monolingual, 35, 44, 87
　multilingual, 165
　national, 38
　nationalism and, 163–64
　online, 26, 79, 105, 129, 137
　oral, 160–61
　orientalist, 107–9
　portable electronic, 210, 213
　prescriptive vs. descriptive, 126
　preservation of languages and, 62
　in print, 79
　regional, 38
　as respositories of knowledge and cultural history, 228
　as response to need for regulation/standardization, 74
　specialized, 166
　translation and, 54, 62
　tyranny exercised by, 244
Dictionaries (journal), 58
Dictionaries Knowledgebase, 137
Dictionarium Latino-Anglo-Hibernicum, 148
Dictionarium Latinogermanicum, 31
dictionary culture, 169–70
dictionary entries
　components of, 77
　length of, 76–78
Dictionary of American English, 78
Dictionary of A. S. Pushkin's Language (Словарь языка А. С. Пушкина), 235
Dictionary of Esperanto, 58
Dictionary of Irish Biography, 152
Dictionary of Medieval Latin from Celtic Sources, 152
A Dictionary of Modern Written Arabic, 115

Index 289

Dictionary of Old English, 78
Dictionary of the Irish Language: Based Mainly on Old and Middle Irish Materials (DIL), 151–52
Dictionary of the Names of Freshwater Fishes of the USSR (Словарь названий пресноводных рыб СССР), 235
Dictionary of the Old East Slavic Language (Словарь русского языка XI–XVII веков), 237
dictionary-making, translation and, 44
Dictionnaire alphabétique et analogique de la langue française, 89, *see also* Grand Robert
Dictionnaire de l'Académie française, 32
Dictionnaire de la langue nahuatl, 174
Dictionnaire des dictionnaires de médecine français et étrangers, ou traité complet de médecine et de chirurgie pratiques, 115
Dictionnaire des termes anciens et modernes des sciences médicales, naturelles et vétérinaires, 116
Dictionnaire étymologique des créoles portugais d'Afrique, 169
Dictionnaire français-créole mauricien, 169
Dictionnaire italien latin et françois, 100
Dictionnaires Le Robert, 83, 88–90, 91
differentia specifica, 32
Diggle, James, 10
Digital Himalaya Project, 132
Digitales Wörterbuch der deutschen Sprache (*DWDS*), 35
diglossia, 59, 61, 257
Dinka, 167
Dinneen, Fr. Patrick S., 149, 153
Diogenes, 4
diplomatic and translation institutions, 55
Discorides, *De materia medica*, 115
Dizionario francese-italiano, 100
Doke, Clement, *English-Zulu Dictionary*, 158
Dominicanish, 65
Dona Maria I., 200
Dozy, Reinhart, 109
Dreyzin, I., *Russish-Yudishes verter bukh*, 186
Drivaud, Marie-Hélène, 83–92
Du Bellay, Joachim, *Défense et illustration de la langue française*, 84
Duden dictionaries, 30, 37
Dunash Ben Labrat, 121
Duramazwi Guru reChiShona (the advanced Shona monolingual dictionary), 161, 164
Duramazwi reChiShona (Shona monolingual dictionary), 161
Dutch, 157, 168
DWB2, 34

Early Modern Danish, 249
Early Modern Irish, 147
East Scandinavian (Danish and Swedish) languages, 249
East Slavic languages, 228, 230, 239
East Slavic lexicography, genesis of, 228
Ecuador, language policies of, 246
eDIL, 151, 152, 153
Edwards, Keri, *Dictionary of Tlingit*, 137
Eggleston, Keri, *Online Tlingit Verb Dictionary*, 137
Eijirō 英辞郎, 215–16
electronic dictionaries, Japanese, 210, 213, 214–16
e-lexicography, 166
Elichay, Yochanan, 127
Eliot, John, 135
ELL (English language learning), 58
Encanto, 69
endangered languages, 184
  dictionaries for, 162
  documenting, 162, 167
England, 235
English, 2, 23, 60, 68, 72–82, 96, 108, 115, 126, 148, 153, 157, 163, 168, 169, 207, 249, 258
  American, 60–61, 78, 81, 82
  in Canada, 133
  development of, 60
  Esperanto and, 19
  in Japan, 210
  lack of academy, 267–68
  Spanish and, 81
  spoken in Israel, 129
  varieties of, 78
English lexicography, global aspect of, 72–82
English-Arabic dictionaries, 115
English-Irish dictionaries, 147, 153
English-Japanese dictionaries, 210–14
  influence of British and American dictionaries on, 210–13
  unabridged, 213–14
English-Japanese glossaries, 210
English-Yiddish dictionaries, 185, 187
  Lilliput, 192
Enlightenment, 83, 126, 134, 200, 234, 235
Ernesti, Johann, 5
Erya 尔雅/爾雅, 223
Escher, M. C., 13
Espanglish, 65
Esperanto, 16–27, 68–69
  as agglutinative language, 20, 22
  in Asia, 23–24
  as bridge language, 21
  in China, 23

290   Index

Esperanto (cont.)
  as Eurocentrist language, 16, 23
  Francophone lexicographers and, 24
  gender-neutral language and, 21
  ideology and, 25
  International Dictionary of, 19
  Language Committee and, 26
  as lingua franca, 25
  as literary language, 21–22
  neologisms and, 22–23
  as neutral language-movement, 20
  poetry and, 21, 22–23
  as political, 25
  social movements and, 20
  specialized lexicons and, 21
  translation and, 21–22
Esperanto dictionaries, 21
Esperanto language-movement, 17
Estienne, Henri, 6, 10
  Thesaurus Graecae Linguae, 6
Estienne, Robert, 6, 84, 85, 88
  creates student versions of dictionaries, 85
  Dictionarium Latino-Gallicum, 86
  Dictionnaire francoislatin, 31, 85, 86
  edition of Calepino's *Dictionarium*, 86
  publishes French translation of Bible, 85–86
  Thesaurus Linguae Latinae, 6, 85, 86
ethnocide, 180
ethnographic work, 28
Etruscan, 4
etymology **104**, 127
  etymological dictionaries, 104, 127
  internet and, 104
euphemism, 10
evangelization, 158, 173, 177, 197, 220, 243, 244
Even-Shoshan, Avraham, *HaMilon HeHadash* (The new dictionary), 125–26
exegesis, 42
Explanatory Combinatorial Dictionary of Modern Russian (*Толково-комбинаторный словарь русского языка*), 236
Explanatory Dictionary of the Living Great Russian Language (*Tolkovyj slovar' zhivogo velikorusskogo yazyka*), 232
Explanatory Dictionary of the Russian Language (*Большой толковый словарь русского языка*), 233–34

Faba, Guido, 98
Fagius, Paul, 186
Falen, James E., 231
Fang, 168
Fangyan 方言, 49
fanqie 反切 phonetic notation method, 48, 55

Faroe Islands, 248, 256, 257
Faroese, 249, 257, 258
Faroese dictionaries, 249, 257–58
Faroese-Danish dictionaries, 258
Farsi, 26
al-Fayrūzābādī, *al-Qāmūs al-muḥīṭ*, 108, 114
Fernández de Avellaneda, 64
Ferreira, Aurélio Buarque de Holanda, *Novo Dicionário da Língua Portuguesa (Dicionário Aurélio)*, 195, 199
Finland, dialects in, 248, 249, 256–57
Finn, Shemuel Yosef, *Ha-Otzar* (The treasure), 123
Finnish, 249, 256–57, 258
Finnish dictionaries, 256
Finnish War of 1808–1809 256
Finnish-Swedish dictionaries, 256
First Nations, 133
Fischer, August, 109
The Five Confucian Classics, 45
Flemish, 96
Florentine vernacular, 98
folktales, 28
Foras na Gaeilge, 145
Forcellini, Egidio, 31
Føroysk-donsk orðabók (Faroese-Danish dictionary), 258
Forro, 169
Forvo, 169
France, 19, 24, 101, 235
France, Anatole, 3
Franco, Francisco Manoel de Mello, 199
François I, 84
La Francophonie, 91
Franglais (French and English), 58, 61, 65, 68, 245
free dictionary search sites, 215
French, 2, 6, 23, 68, 83–92, 96, 108, 115, 126, 157, 163, 167, 168, 169, 249
  in Canada, 133
  Esperanto and, 19
  le français classique, 83
  le français moderne, 83
  La Francophonie, 91
  as language of European diplomacy, 83
  as literary langauge, 84
  spelling change in, 90
French dictionaries, 32
  as communicating vessels between France and La Francophonie, 91
  evolution of after Estienne, 86–90
  German lexicography and, 32
  history of, 83–88
  language standardization and, 83
  slang in, 91–92

French lexicography, 83–92
  digital technology and, 90–91
  evolution of after Estienne, 86–90
  internet's effect on, 90–91
French spelling, standardization of, 90
French vernacular literature, 84
French wars of religion, 86
French-Arabic dictionaries, 108, 115
Freytag, Georg Wilhelm Friedrich, *Lexicon Arabico-Latinum*, 108
Fries, Johannes, 29, 31
Frisch, Johann Leonhard, 32
Frommer, Paul, 67
Fruchtman, Maya, 126
Fula, 156
Fundação para a Ciência e Tecnologia, 195, 202
Fuon Souzu Eiwa Jii 附音挿図英和字彙, 210, 222
Furetière, Antoine, 32, 87, 88
  Dictionnaire universel, 32, 87, 88
  expulsion from Académie, 88

Gabon, 165
Gaeilge, 145
Galen, 115
Galicia, Faustino Chimalpopocatl, *Silabario de idioma mexicano*, 174
Gammeldansk Ordbog (Old Danish dictionary), 254
Gananders, Christfid, *Nytt Finskt Lexicon* (New Finnish lexicon), 256
Garavelli, Bice Mortara, 103
García Márquez, Gabriel, 268
ġarīb (raria), 111–12
Ġarīb al-Qur'ān, 111
Garner, Bryan A., 274
Gates, Henry Louis Jr., 65
GDLI "Battaglia," 100
GENIUS English-Japanese Dictionary, 213
genus proximum, 32
German, 2, 23, 81, 96, 157, 168, 184, 186, 249
  Esperanto and, 19
  history of, 29
  Latin and, 30
  regional variants of, 31
  Yiddish and, 17
German lexicography, 28–39, 123
  French dictionaries and, 32
  future of, 39
  history of, 28–29, 30
  Italian dictionaries and, 32
  place of dictionaries in, 30
  regional vs. national dictionaries, 38
  rich history of, 38–39
  Spanish dictionaries and, 32

Germanic languages, 248, 249, 252
  history of, 102
  North Germanic languages, 249
  Yiddish and, 19
German-Latin dictionaries, 29
Germany
  linguistic regions of, 37–38
  tradition of philological/historical dictionary making in, 38–39
Gerson, Rimmona, 127
Gesenius, Wilhelm, *Hebräisch-deutsches Handwörterbuch über die Schriften des Alten Testaments mit Einschluß der geographischen Nahmen und der chaldäischen Wörter beym Daniel und Esra* (The Hebrew-German Hand Dictionary on the Old Testament Scriptures including Geographical Names and Chaldean Words, with Daniel and Ezra), 123, 130
Gheel, Joris van, 158
Giles, Herbert A., 56
  A Chinese-English Dictionary, 56
Gilliver, Peter, 72–82
Glare, Peter, 9, 10
Glasser, Paul (Hershl), 192
globalism, 28
globalization, bilingual dictionaries and, 115–16
glossaries. *See also specific languages*, 7, 28, 30, 54, 95, 145, 146, 249
glossing, 6, 197
Glottolog, 137
Glückel of Hameln, 184
Godfrey, Reverend Robert, 159
  A Kafir–English Dictionary, 158
Goethe, Johann Wolfgang von, 2, 28
Golius, 108
Goncalves, Manuel Da Luz, *Cape Verdean Dictionary*, 168
Gonçalves, Rebelo, *Vocabulário da língua portuguesa*, 201
Gonzales, Odi, 136, 241–46
González Holguín, Diego, 244
goo Dictionary, 215
Google, 170
Google Translate, 151, 152, 153, 154, 216
Gothic, 134
Gouws, R. H., 164, 165, 169
Gove, Philip B., *Webster's Third New International Dictionary*, 275
Graecum Lexicon Manuale, 5
Grammatisch-kritisches Wörterbuch der Hochdeutschen Mundart, 31, 33
Gran Diccionario Nahuatl, 177

Index

Granada, Fall of, 108
Le Grand Robert, 89, 90, 91
Grande dizionario della lingua italiana (GDLI), 99, 100
Grass, Günter, 39
Graywolf Press, 66
The Great Academic Dictionary of the Russian Language, 227
Great Books Summer Program, 3
The Great Dictionary of the Yiddish Language, 189
The Greater Dictionary of isiXhosa, 160, 163
Greek dictionaries, 7
Greek, ancient, 4–14, 75, 85, 96, 146, 153, 230, 249, 274
  Esperanto and, 18
  loanwords from, 37
  online lexicons, 11–13
A Greek–English Lexicon, 7–10
Greek-Spanish Dictionary project, 10–11
Greenland, 248, 249
Greenlandic, 249
Grimm, Jacob, 32
Grimm, Wilhelm, 28
Grolier Club, 274
Grot, Jacob, *Dictionary of the Russian Language*, 227
Groyser Verterbukh fun der Yidisher Shprakh, 187–88
Grundtvig, Svend
  Dansk Haandordbog, 252–53
  Dansk Retskrivningsordbog (Danish spelling dictionary), 252
Guamán Poma, 243, 245
Guardia Mayorga, César, 245
Guoyin Dictionary (Guoyin zidian 国音字典), 53
Gur, Yehuda (Yehuda Leib Grozovski), *Millon Ivri*, 125
Gustav III, King, 253

Hachette, 24
Hakubunkan 博文館, 208
al-Halīl b. Aḥmad al-Farāhīdī, 111
  Kitāb al-ʿAyn, 107, 109, 112–13
Hamzé, Hassan, 107–17
Han people, 54
Hanagid, Samuel, 121
Hanlin Academy (Hanlinyuan 翰林院), 52
Hannan, Michael, *Standard Shona Dictionary*, 160
Hansen, Z. S., 258
Haoran Tong, 42–56
Haredim, 129, 193–94
Harkavy, Alexander, 127, 184, 185, 186–87
  "Yidisher folks-verterbukh" (unpublished), 192

Harm, Volker, 28–39
Harrio, Thomas, 135
Hasidim, 188, 193
Haskalah (Jewish Enlightenment), 122–23, 186
Haß, Ulrike, 32
Hausa, 156, 157, 161, 167
headwords, 250, 274
Hebrew, 2, 85, 119, 146, 166, 184, 186
  Arab, 128
  Arabic, 128
  biblical, 119, 123, 124, 129
  English and, 129
  Haredi, 128
  medieval, 124
  Modern, 124, 125, 129
  Sages' scripts, 124
  Talmudic, 119
  Yiddish and, 17
Hebrew dictionaries, 19
  bilingual, 126–27
  descriptive, 126
  verb entries, 126
Hebrew lexicography
  11th century, 121–22
  in Israel, 127–28
  period of the Sages (Leshon Hahamim), 120
Hebrew Scriptures, 4, 13, 21, *see also* Septuagint
Hebrew University, 188
Heck, Ellen, *A Is for Bee: An Alphabet Book in Translation*, 59
Hederich, Benjamin, 5
Heine, Bernd, *Ik Dictionary (Nilo-Saharan)*, 167
Hepburn, James Curtis, *Waei Gorin Shūsei* (和英語林集成), 210, 222
Herodotus, 7
Hibríya, 245
Hindi language, 91
hiragana, 207, 218
Hispanic lexicography, 268
Historian Zhou, 45
historical dictionaries, 104
Historical Dictionary of the Republic of Cape Verde, 168
Holocaust, 61
Homer, 21
Hornby, A. S., 211
Horowitz, Zina (Paula), 192
Houaiss, Antônio, 199
  Dicionário Houaiss da língua portuguesa, 195, 198–99
Humboldt, Alexander von, 265
Ḥunayn b. Isḥāq, 115
Huron, 135

Index

hybrid languages. 65, 128, 173, 245 *See also specific languages*,
hybrid words, 207
Hybriya (Hebrew and Arabic), 61, 184

Iberian lexicography, 198
Iberian Peninsula, 134
Ibn ʿAbbās, *Ġarīb al-Qurʾān*, 111
Ibn Durayd, *al-Jamhara*, 114
Ibn Ezra, 122
Ibn Fāris, *Maqāyīs al-luġa*, 114
Ibn Janah, 122
Ibn Manẓūr, *Lisān al-ʿarab*, 108, 114
Ibn Sīda, *al-Muḥkam*, 114
Ibn-Janah, Yonah, *Kitab al-usul* (The book of roots), 121
Ibn-Saruk, Menachem, 121, 122
  Machbarot Menachem (Menachem's notebooks), 121
Ibsen, Henrik, 255
IC&DT Project Competition, 202
Iceland, 248, 256, 257
Icelandic dictionaries, 256
Icelandic, survival of, 249, 257, 258
ideographic constructions, 44
IDIEZ (The Zacatecas Institute for Teaching and Research in Ethnology), 172
Idiomatic and Syntactic English Dictionary (ISED) (Palmer), 211, 212
idiomology, theory of, 211
Idriss, S., *al-Manhal*, 116
Igbo, 156, 168
Ik, 167
immigration, language and, 62
Imperial Academy of Science, 233
imperial languages, 243
Inca Empire, 241
India, 54
Indiana University Press, 191
Indigeneity, definitions of, 133
indigenism, 270–71
Indigenous languages. 132–42, 241–46, 265
  See also specific languages,
  attempts to catalogue, 135
  Colombian, 135
  defining, 132–33
  documentation of, 135
  extinct, 134
  Mexican, 135
  missionary linguists and, 135
  of Northern South Asia, 138–42
  online dictionaries and, 137
  in South Africa, 163–64
Indigenous lexicography, collaboration and, 132, 136, 137–38, 140–42

Indigenous peoples, Hispanicization of, 265
Indigenous, capitalization of, 134
Infopédia. Dicionários Porto Editora, 198
Inka Garcilaso, 243, 245
Inoue Yorikuni 井上頼圀, 211
Inouye Jūkichi 井上十吉, 221
Institut de la recherche agronomique (INRA), 91
Institute for Kiswahili Studies, 162, 166
Institute for Research in English Teaching (IRET), 211
Institute of Theoretical and Computational Linguistics (ILTEC), *Vocabulário ortográfico do português*, 201
Instituto de Lexicologia e Lexicografia da Língua Portuguesa (ILLLP), 200, 204
integrated circuit (IC) electronic dictionaries, 214
Interior Tlingit Noun Dictionary, 137
interlanguage, concept of, 188
Interlingua, 16
Intermediate Lexicon (Liddell and Scott), 10
International Dictionary Day, 170
Introito e porta, 95
Inuit, 133
Inuit languages, 249
Irish, 145–54
  Corca Dhuibhne (West Kerry), 150
  dialectical relationship between oral and written, 150–51
  dialects of, 150
  Dunquin, 150
  early interest in vernacular, 146
  Modern, 151–52
  standardization of, 150
  West-Kerry, 150
Irish dictionaries
  17th century, 147
  digitized, 151
  medieval, 146–47
Irish Franciscans, 147
Irish glossaries, 145, 146
Irish grammars, 147
Irish language enthusiasts, 154
Irish lexicographers, 152
Irish lexicography, 145–54
Irish Script on Screen project, 148
Irish Texts Society, 149, 151
Irish-English dictionaries, 147, 148, 149
Irish-Government Department of Education, 150, 152
Iroha Jiruishō 色葉字類抄, 219
Iroquoian languages, 135
Isabel La Católica, 63, 264
Isamu Hayakawa, 210
Ishikawa Masamochi 石川雅望, *Gagen Shūran* 雅言集覽, 220

Isichazamazwi SesiNdebele (Ndebele monolingual dictionary), 161
isiNdebele, 164
isiXhosa, 160
isiXhosa dictionaries, 163
isiXhosa National Lexicography Unit, 163
Íslex and Íslensk nútímamálsorðabók (Icelandic contemporary dictionary), 258
Italian, 2, 68, 84, 96, 105, 126
  as literary language, 84
  spelling of, 103
Italian dictionaries, 32, 105
Italian lexicography, 105
Italian vernacular, 96–99, 104
Italo-Romance vernacular varieties, 98–99
Italy, 83, 84, 86, 235
Ives, David, 24
ivrit israeli, 125–26, see also Hebrew:Modern
Iwanami Shoten 岩波書店, 208, 219

Jacobsen, Lis, 259
Jakobsen, Jakob, 258
al-Jamhara (Ibn Durayd), 114
Janney, Christine Mladic, 241
Japan, 23
Japan Knowledge, 215
Japanese, 207–23
  characters sets of, 218
  writing system of, 207, 216
Japanese dictionaries
  electronic, 214–16
  graphically vs. semantically organized, 218–20
  online, 214–16
  phonetically organized, 219–20
  post-World War II era, 208–10
Japanese lexicography, 207–23
  Edo period, 219, 220, 221
  Heian period, 217–19
  history of, 216–18
  Kamakura period, 219
  Meiji period, 210, 219, 221–22
  mid-Muromachi period, 219
  Shōwa period, 211
  Taishō period, 211
Japanese-English dictionaries, 210–14, 222
Japanese-Portuguese dictionaries, 220
jargon, 17, 19
Jastrow, Marcus, 123
al-Jawharī, *Ṣiḥāḥ*, 114, 115
Jensen, Oliver, 275
Jerome, 85
Jesuit Mission Press, 220
Jewish Arabic, 121
Jewish diaspora, 119
Jewish Enlightenment, 186
Jewish languages, 184–94
Jewish Theological Seminary, 189
Jewish-Moroccan, 126
jibiki 字引 (character dictionary), 210
Jien 辞苑, 208
Ji-ga 爾雅, 220
Joensen, H., 258
Joffe, David, 166
Johann Gottlob Schneider's Handwörterbuch der griechischen Sprache, 8
Johnson, Samuel, 1, 2, 32, 67, 72, 80, 164
  definition of *lexicographer*, 274
  A Dictionary of the English Language, 19, 74, 75, 87, 210, 251, 275, 276
  Plan of a Dictionary of the English Language, 275, 276
Joint Committee for University Cooperation (CMCU), 117
Jones, Henry Stuart, 7, 9
Jopara (Guaraní and Spanish), 61
Jordan, 117
Joyce, James, 72
Juana Inés de la Cruz, Sor, 265
Judeo-Arabic, 184
Judeo-Aragonese, 134
Judeo-Catalan, 134
Judeo-German, 184
Judeo-Persian, 184
Judeo-Portuguese, 134, 184
Judeo-Spanish, 22, 184
al-Jurjānī, *at-taʿrīfāt*, 110
Jutland, 260
Jysk Ordbog (Jutlandic dictionary), 260

Kabbalah, 122
al-Kabīr, 110
al-Kafawī, *al-Kulliyyāt*, 110
Kaiseijo 開成所, 221
Kaitakusha, 212
Kalkar, O., *Ordbog over det ældre danske Sprog (1300–1700)* (Dictionary of the older Danish language, 1300–1700), 254
Kamusi Project, 168
Kamusi ya Kiswahili. A Swahili-Swahili Dictionary, 162
kana, 208, 219
kana literature, 220
Kanembu, 167
Kangxi, 52
Kangxi Dictionary (*Kangxi zidian* 康熙字典), 51, 55
kanji (Chinese characters), 207, 208, 218, 219
kanji dictionaries, 217, 220
Kannas, Claude, 90

Index

Kanuri, 167
kan-wa jiten 漢和辞典, 218
Karaite tradition, 121, 122
Karamzin, Nikolai, 230–31
Karamzinist movement, 230–31
Karelian dialects, 260
Karttunen, Frances, *An Analytical Dictionary of Nahuatl*, 176, 178, 179
Kashghari, *Diwān luġat at-turk*, 115
Kaššāf iṣṭilāḥāt al-ʿulūm wa l-funūn (at-Tahānawī), 110
katakana, 207, 218, 219
Kavanagh, Séamas, 150
Kazimirski, A., 109
Kenkyūsha
    New Collegiate English-Japanese Dictionary, 212, 213
    New English-Japanese Dictionary, 213, 214
    New Japanese-English Dictionary, 214
    TR-700, 214
Khoisan language, 162
Kichwa, 246
Kielitoimiston verkkosanakirja (Online dictionary of the language institute), 257
Kikongo, 158, 168
Kindaichi Kyōsuke 金田一京助, 209
Kingtoin, Miles, *Let's Parler Franglais*, 65
Kirishitan-ban キリシタン版 (Christian editions), 220
Kirkness, Alan, 34
al-Kisāʾī, *Ġarīb al-Qurʾān*, 111
Kiswahili, 156, 157, 166
Kiswahili dictionaries, 162
Klein, Ernest, 127
Klingon, 67
Knudsen, Knud, 255
Köhler, Ludwig, 123
Kōjien 広辞苑, 208
Kojiki 古事記, 216–17
Kokugo, 215
kokuji 国字, 217
Konstantinovich, Konstantin, 233
Kopotev, Mikhail, 227–39
Korea, 23
Kosugi Sugimura 小杉榲邨, 221
Kotobank, 215
Koyasu Takashi 子安峻, 210, 222
Kritisches griechisch-deutsches Handwörterbuch, 4
Kropf, Reverend Albert, *A Kafir-English Dictionary*, 159, 160, 161
Kūkai 空海, 217–18
Kukanda, V., 165
Kunama, 167
kun-yomi 訓読み readings, 217

Ladino, 22, 184
Lane, Edward, *The Arabic-English Lexicon*, 108
Lang, Sonja, 21
Langenscheidt dictionaries, 30
language 'stocks', 134
language academies. *See also specific academies*, 26
    lack of English, 267–68
    polycentrism in, 269
    Portuguese, 199–201
    Spanish, 267–68
language history, 38
language innovation, 68
language interference, 67
language learning, 58, 197, *see also* mother-tongue education
language policies
    lexicography and, 164
    pan-Hispanic, 267
    unification of variants and, 246
language(s)
    pre-Hispanic, 241–46
language(s). *See also specific languages and languages families*
    alphabetic, 43
    ancient, 4
    birth of new, 69
    bridge, 21
    definition of, 156
    distinguishing from dialects, 134
    endangered, 136, 142, 162
    extinct, 134
    feminist, 21
    global, 4
    government use of, 84
    historiography of, 42
    hybrid, 128
    Indigenous, 132–42
    international, 16–27
    Jewish, 17
    living/dead binary, 5
    logographic, 43
    mixed, 58
    official, 157
    policing of, 63, 87
    preservation of, 142
    revitalization of, 132, 136–37, 161, 162, 167
    Romantic conception of as embodiment of national identity, 75
    standardized, 26, 58, 59, 150, 185, 197, 199, 252, 253, 267
    universalist, 16–27
    vernacular, 147
Lapin, Chava, 192

296   Index

Larouche-Claire, Yves, *Évitez le franglais, parlez français*, 65
Larousse, 88, 90, 91
Latin, 6, 28, 30, 63, 68, 84, 86, 94, 96, 107, 108, 115, 145, 146, 148, 153, 184, 186, 230, 249, 250, 257, 258, 265, 274
    classical, 197
    emancipation of German from, 29
    Esperanto and, 18
    German and, 30
    loanwords from, 37
    as metalanguage, 250
    as model of perfection, 87
    Vulgar, 197
Latin America. *See also specific countries*, 160
Latin-Arabic dictionaries, 108
Latin-Danish glossaries, 249
Latin-English dictionaries, 147
Latin-French dictionaries, 29
Latin-German dictionaries, 29
Latin-Irish dictionaries, 147, 153
Latin-Old Portuguese glossaries, 196
Latinos, 66
Latin-vernacular glossaries, 95, 197
Laurentian, 135
Le Jeune, Paul, 135
Le Robert. see Dictionnaires Le Robert
A Learner's Dictionary of Current English, 212
Lebanon, 117
Lebensgeschichte, 8
Lee, John A. L., *A History of New Testament Lexicography*, 13, 14
Leksikon vokabulam novym po alfavitu (Лексикон вокабулам новым по алфавиту), 229
lemmata, 29–30, 31, 32, 124, 250
lengua del inka (the language of the Inca), 242
lengua general (general language), 242
Lenz, Rodolfo, *Diccionario etimológico de las voces chilenas derivadas de lenguas indígenas americanas*, 271
Lessico Etimologico Italiano, 39
Levi, Jacob, 123
Levita, Elia, *Shemot Devarim* ("Names of Things"), 186
lexical functions, concept of, 236
lexicographers, 2, 4, 5, 7, 36, 72–82
    diversity among, 90, 192, 259, 263, 268–69
    explorers as, 159, 163
    how they became, 103–4, 153
    Irish, 149
    Israeli, 129
    Johnson's definition of, 274
    models used by, 159–60

    need for sufficient feedback, 169
    recruitment of, 38
    what they do, 36–37
lexicography, 195, 266
    as academic and professional discipline, 163
    ancient Greek, 4–14
    bilingual, 29, 35–36, 95, 100
    comparative, 31
    corpus-based, 166
    the Enlightenment and, 83
    French, 6
    Hebrew, 14
    history of, 14, 30–31, 79–80
    language policy and, 164
    Latin, 6
    lexicographic training, 165
    literary language and, 272
    prescriptive vs. descriptive, 251–52
    specialized, 165–66
    technology and, 269–70
lexicology, 195
Lexicology, Terminology, Translation (LTT) network, 117
Lexicon of New Words (*Лексиконъ вокабуламъ новымъ по алфавиту*), 229
Lexikos journal, 164
lexilalia, concept of, 278
Lexis (Лексис сирѣчъ реченїѧ, въкратьцѣ събранны), 228
Lhuyd, Edward, 147
Li Si 李斯, 45
Liddell and Scott, 7–10, 12
Liddell, Henry George, 7–10, 12
    A Greek–English Lexicon, 7–10
    Intermediate Lexicon, 10
Lifshits, Y., *Rusish-Yudisher verterbukh*, 186
Lightfoot, Sheryl, 140
Lin, T. Y., 17
Linear B, 10
Lingala, 156, 168
linguistic diversity, 162
linguistic evolution, 197
linguistic gaslighting, 134
linguistic hegemonies, struggle against, 267
linguistic polycentrism, 269
Linguistics Research Centre of NOVA University Lisbon (NOVA CLUNL), Digital Edition of the Vocabularies of the Academy of Sciences project, 201
Lira, Jorge, 245
Lisbon Academy of Sciences, 201
literary language, popular language and, 272
Littré, Émile, 75, 88, 89, 222
Living Tongues Institute for Endangered Languages, 161

Index

loanwords (*Fremdwörter*), 37, 125, 228
Lockhart, James, 180
logocentrism, 120
logographic languages, 43
Lomavren (Armenian and Indo-Aryan), 61
Lombard, F. J., 165
Lommatzsch, Erhard, 38
Longman, 103, 166, 212
Longman Dictionary of Contemporary English (LDOCE), 212
Lönnrot, Elias, *Suomalais-Ruotsalainen Sanakirja/Finskt-Svenskt Lexikon* (Finnish-Swedish Dictionary), 256
López, Jennifer, 69
Lorenzana y Buitrón, Antonio, 265
Louis XIV, 87
Low German, 38
Lowenstein, Anna, 22
LSJ, 9, *see also A Greek–English Lexicon; Greek-English Lexicon (Liddell and Scott)*
LSJM, 9, 10, 13, *see also A Greek–English Lexicon;Greek-English Lexicon* (Liddell and Scott)
Lu Erkqui 陆尔奎, 53
Lu Fayan 陆法言, *Qieyun* 切韵, 48–49
Lynch, Jack, 274, 278

Maaler, Josua, *Die Teütsch Spraach*, 29
Maasai, 167
Mac Aodhagáin, Baothghalach, 147
Mac Cruitín, Aodh Buidhe, 148
maʿājim al-mawḍūʿāt, 112
maʿājim mubawwaba, 112
MacLean, Edna Ahgeak, *Iñupiatun Uqaluit Taniktun Sivuniŋit* (Iñupiaq to English dictionary), 137
Macmillan, 103
Maʿlūf, Louis, *al-Munjid*, 117
Mandelkern, Shelomo, 123
Mandereau, Gabriel, 3, 241
al-Manhal (Abdel-Nour and Idriss), 116
manyō-gana 万葉仮名, 217
Mar'i, Abed Rachman, *Walla Bseder*, 128
Marazzini, Claudio, 105
Marazzini, Salvatore Battaglia, 100
Marello, Carla, 105
Marguerite de Navarre, 84
Marien Ngouabi University, 165
Mark, Yudel, *Groyser Verterbukh*, 187, 188, 191
Marstrander, Carl, 151
Maskew Miller, 166
mass digitization projects, 202
Massachusett, 135
Matsui Eiichi 松井栄一, 209
Matsui Kanji 松井簡治, 209, 222
Matsui Tadashi 松井驥, 209
Mauritian Creole (Morisyen), 169
Mauritian Creole Pronunciation Dictionary, 169
Mavoungou, Paul Achille, 156–70
Mazia, Aharon, 127
McKenna, Lambert, 153
McKenzie, Roderick, 7, 9
McLaren, James, 159
  A Concise English–Kafir Dictionary, 158
  A Concise Kafir–English Dictionary, 158
McRae, Fiona, 66
Meaning-Text theory, 235
Medici, Cosimo I de', 86
medieval interpreters (*parshanim*), 122
Mei Yingzuo 梅膺祚, *Zihui* 字汇, 51
Meiji Eiwa-Jiten 明治英和字典, 211
Meiji period, 210
Mel'čuk, Igor, 235, 236
Melingo, 129
Merriam-Webster, 60, 62, 72, 78, 83, 92, 132, 269, 270
  as commercial enterprise, 78
  online, 26
mestizo culture, 59
mestizo languages, 61
mestizos, 244
Métis, 133
Mexican National Institute of Indigenous Languages, 172, 180
Mexican National System of Researchers (SNI), 180
Middle English Dictionary, 78
Middle Irish, 147, 151
Midrash, 120, 123
Midrashic literature, 123
Milog, 129
Milson, Menachem, 127
Minamoto no Shitagō 源順, 218
Minsheu, John, *The Guide into the Tongues*, 274
Mirda, 16
Mishna, 120
missionary lexicography, 135–36, 137, 159, 197, 220
missionary linguists, 135
mixed languages, 58
Mizrahi Jews, 129
Modern Irish, 151–52, 153
Modern Irish Dictionary (Foclóir Stairiúil na Gaeilge) project, 152
Modern Standardized Arabic (MSA), 116–17
Modern Swedish, 254
modernity, 18, 235
Molbech, Christian, *Dansk Ordbog* (Danish dictionary), 251, 254

Molina, Alonso de
  Vocabulario en lengua castellana y mexicana, 135, 175, 176, 178, 179
  Vocabulario en lengua mexicana y castellana, 178, 179
Moliner, María, 263, 268
monolingual dictionaries
  in Africa, 163, 164
  Chinese, 216–17
  Finnish, 257
  importance of, 161–62, 181
  of Nahuatl, 179, 181
  for Niger-Congo languages, 168
  in South Africa, 164
  in Spanish, 264
  of Yiddish, 187–88
  in Zimbabwe, 164
Montagnais (Cree dialect), 135
Montaigne, Michel de, 84
Montanari, Franco, *Vocabolario della lingua greca*, 12
Montemerlo, Stefano, *Frasi toscane*, 94, 95
Morais Silva, Antonio de, *Diccionario da lingua portugueza*, 201–3
Moran, Pádraic, 146
MORDigital – Digitalização do Diccionario da Lingua Portugueza de António de Morais Silva project, 195, 202
Morisyen-English-français/diksyoner kreol morisyen, 169
Morohashi Tetsuji 諸橋轍次, 209
Morrison, Robert, 55
Moth, Matthias, 250–51
mother-tongue education, 165
Mozarabic, 134
al-Muʿjam al-ʿarabī al-ʾasāsī (ALECSO), 109
Muḥammad b. ʿUmar at-tūnusī, *aš-Šudūr ad-dahabiyyat fī al-alfāẓ aṭ-ṭibbiyyat*, 115
multilingual dictionaries.184, 185, 186 *See also under specific languages and language combinations*,
multilingual glossaries, 165
al-Munjid fī al-luġa al-ʿarabiyya al-muʿāṣira, 109, 116
Murray, James A. H., 4, 8, 13, 75, 76, 79, 81, 103, 275

Na'vi, 67
Nahuañol, 173
Nahuatl, 172–81
  online databases of, 176–77
  as *lingua franca*, 177
  other Indigenous languages and, 173
  during Mexican independence period, 174–76
  Spanish and, 173
  survival of, 177
  transcription to Roman alphabet, 172
  variants of, 173
Nahuatl dictionaries, 173–78
  modern, 176–77
  sponsors of, 180
  tourist approach to culture and, 181
Nahuatl grammar, 176
Nahuatl orthography, 178
Nahuatl-Spanish-Latin vocabularies, 173
Napoleon Bonaparte, 17, 107
Natan Me-Romy, *Ha-Aruch* ('The edited' or 'The arranged'), 122
nation-building, 266
national dictionaries, 38
national identities, 156
National Lexicography Units (South Africa), 163–64, 165, 166
National Library of Paris, 115
National Press (China), 53
nationalism
  dictionaries and, 163–64
  Irish dictionaries and, 146–47
  Romanticism and, 256
Nazism, 25
Ndebele, 163, 164, 168
Nebrija, Antonio de, 63, 67, 69, 96, 173, 263, 264
  controversies surrounding, 264
  Gramática de la lengua castellana, 263
  Vocabulario latino-español, 276
Nemere, István, 22
Nemirovsky, Ilya, 3
Nencioni, Giovanni, 103
neologisms, 22–23, 109, 116, 124–25, 191, 228, 244
Nepal, 138–42, *see also* Nepali
Nepali, 139, 140
Nettle, Daniel, 134
New CROWN English-Japanese Dictionary, 212
New Dictionaries (*xinzidian* 新字典), 53
New English Dictionary on Historical Principles, 75, 81
New Spain, 265
New Testament, 5, 7
Ní Mhainín, Siobhán, 153
Ní Mhaonaigh, Tracey, 150
Nicot, Jean, *Thresor de la langue françoyse*, 86, 87, 88
Niger-Congo languages, 167–68
Nihon Hogen Daijiten 日本方言大辞典, 209–10
Nihon Kokugo Daijiten 日本国語大辞典, 208, 209, 210

Index

Nihon Ryōiki 日本霊異記, 218
Nihon Shoki 日本書紀 (the oldest chronicles of Japan), 217
Nihongo Daijiten 日本語大辞典, 208
Niina 新字, 217, 218
Nilo-Saharan languages, 167
Nippo Jisho 日葡辞書, 220
Nkomo, Dion, 156–70
non-Indo-European languages, 249
Nordic Association of Lexicography, 259
Nordic countries, 248
Nordic languages, 249
Nordic lexicography, 259
Nordisk Leksikografisk Ordbog (Nordic lexicographical dictionary), 259
Norsk Ordbok (Norwegian dictionary), 255–56, 259
North Germanic languages, 249
Northern South Asia, 138–42
northernisms, 97
Norway, 248, 249, 250, 256
Norway, dialects in, 259
Norwegian, 249, 255
Norwegian dictionaries, 248, 253, 254–56
Norwegian Dictionary, 248
NOVA CLUNL, 202
Nubian Languages, 167
Nuer, 167
Nuttall, Peter Austin, *Routledge's Diamond Dictionary of the English Language*, 210
Nuyorican, 66
Nykysuomen sanakirja (Dictionary of Modern Finnish), 257
Nynorsk, 248, 255–56, 259
Nytt Finskt Lexicon (New Finnish Lexicon), 256

Ó Beaglaoich, Conchobhar, *The English Irish Dictionary: An Foclóir Béarla Gaoidheilge*, 148
Ó Cíobháin brothers, 150
Ó Conaill, Peadar, 149, 151
Ó Dónaill, Niall, 150, 153
Ó Neachtain, Tadhg, "Foclóir Gaeilbhéarlach," 148
O'Brien, Bishop John, *Focalóir Gaoidhilge-Sags-Bhéarla or an Irish-English Dictionary*, 147
O'Clery's (Ó Cléirigh's) Glossary, 147
O'Curry, Eugene, 151
O'Donovan, John, 151
O'Leary, Father Peter (An tAthair Peadar Ua Laoghaire), 150
O'Mulconry's Glossary, 146
O'Reilly series, 148
obscenities, 10
Obunsha
 Comprehensive English-Japanese Dictionary, 212
 Progressive English-Japanese Dictionary, 212
Office of the Commissioner of Official Languages in Canada, 134
Ogilvie, John
 Imperial Dictionary, 210
 Student's English Dictionary, 210
Okrand, Mark, 67
Ōkubo Hatsuo 大久保初男, 223
Old Cyrillic characters, 232, 233
Old Danish, 249
Old French, 38
Old High German, 28
Old Irish, 145, 147, 151
Old Japanese, 207
Old Norse, 249
Old Rus, 227, 230
Old Russian Languages 11th – 14th centuries (Словарь древнерусского языка (XI–XIVвеков), 239
Olmo, Fray Andrés de, 135
Olmos, Andrés de, 174
Ømålsordbogen, 260
Onkochishinsho 温故知新書, 219–20
online dictionaries, 25, 26, 36, 169, 170
 Finnish, 257
 Japanese, 214–16
 Nahuatl, 176
 Portuguese, 198, 201, 203–4
 retro-digitised, 202
 in Russian, 236
 Spanish, 269
 transition from print to online, 203–4
 Yiddish, 192–93
Online Nahuatl Dictionary, 176
on-yomi 音読み readings, 217
oral testimonies, 245
orality, 244, 245
Ordbog over det danske Sprog (Dictionary of the Danish language, known as ODS), 252, 259
Ordbok över Finlands svenska folkmål (Dictionary of Finland's Swedish vernaculars), 260
Ordonnance de Villers-Cotterêts, 84, 85
orientalism, 107–9
Ormbsy, John, 65
Ornan, Uzi, 127
Oromo, 156
Orthographic Agreement of the Portuguese Language, 201

orthography, 252, 255
    ACK, 179
    African languages and, 159–60
    Danish, 253
    Orthography Act of 1997, 253
    Russian, 232–33
    Soviet, 232–33
    standardized, 253
Orthography Act of 1997, 253
Orwell, George, 25
Ōta Zensai 太田全斎, *Rigen Shūran* 俚言集覧, 221
Ōtomo Hirokimi 大伴広公, 219
Ōtsuki Fumihiko 大槻文彦, 221–22
    Daigenkai 大言海, 222
    Genkai 言海 (The Sea of Words), 221–22, 223
Ottomans, 7
Oxford Advanced Learner's Dictionary of Current English (*OALD*), 212
Oxford Dictionary of the English Language, 280
Oxford English Dictionary (*OED*), 4, 8, 10, 14, 36, 60, 72, 73, 75, 76–78, 132, 222, 223, 269, 270, 275, 278
    abridgements of, 78, 252
    as academic endeavor, 78
    authoritativeness of, 74
    changes over time, 79–80
    as collective approach, 76
    cost of first edition, 79
    first edition of, 80
    genesis of, 74–75
    Hispanic terms in, 65
    longest entry in, 76–78
    as model, 207
    as Platonic model, 72
Oxford Latin Dictionary, 10
Oxford University Press, 56, 65, 78, 103, 166, 212
Ozhegov, Sergey, *Dictionary of the Russian Language*, 227
Ozick, Cynthia, 23, 24

pacifism through language, 27
Palencia, Alonso de, *Vocabulario universal en latin y en romance*, 264
Palestinian Arabic dialect, 127
Palmer, Harold E., 211
    Idiomatic and Syntactic English Dictionary (*ISED*), 212
    Interim Report on Vocabulary Selection, 211
    Second Interim Report on English Collocations, 211

Pan South African Language Board (PanSALB), 164
pan-Hispanic language policy, 267
Paris, France, 25
Passow, Franz, 4, 8, 75
    historical principles of, 8
    Johann Gottlob Schneider's Handwörterbuch der griechischen Sprache, 8, 12
    Vermischte Schriften, 75
Pedersen, Christiern, *Vocabularium ad usum Dacorum*, 249–50
Pedi, 168
pentaglot dictionaries (wuti qing wenjian 五体清文鉴), 55
The People's Tongue: Americans and the English Language, 60
Pérez, Francisco Javier, 263–72
    Estudios sobre nuevos temas de lingüística bellista, 266
    Por una democracia de la lengua: Escritores, filólogos y academias frente al panhispanismo lingüístico, 268
Persian, 115
Peru, 246
Peter the Great, 229, 230
Petersen, N. M., 252
Le Petit Larousse, 91
Le Petit Robert, 89, 90, 91–92, *see also Dictionnaires Le Robert*
Petőfi, Janos Sandor, 103
Petrarch, 84
Petuh (Danish and German), 61
Philip III, 96
Phillipine Hybrid Hokkien (Philippine Hokkien, Tagalog, and English), 61
Philological Society, 8, 78, 103
philologists, 4, 28, 200
philology, 38, 63
Phoenician, 134
phonetic notation systems, 48, 55
phonetic standardization, 42
phraseology, 211
pictophonetic formations, 44
pinyin, 49
Piozzi, Hester Lynch, *British Synonymy*, 275
Piyyut, 120
Plato, 2
Plena Illustria Vortaro (PV), 16, 24
Plena Vortaro (PV), 16, 24
Pliny, 6
Pluincéad, Risdeard, 147, 153
    "Vocabularium Latinum et Hibernum: Foclóir Lainne agus Gaoidheilge," 147

Index 301

Pocket Denyakuki ポケット電訳機 IQ-3000, 214
poetry
  in Esperanto, 22–23
  in Quechua, 245
Pokemon, 209
Polikarpov-Orlov, Fedor, 229–30
Polish, 19
Pomba, Giuseppe, *Grande dizionario della lingua italiana* (*GDLI*), 99
popular language, literary language and, 272
Porto Editora, 198
Portuguese, 55, 68, 157, 163, 168, 169, 195–205, 220
  African variants, 197
  Asian variants, 197
  Brazilian variants, 197
  dialects of, 198
  as global language, 198
  in Portugal vs. Brazil, 197–98
  standardization of, 199
Portuguese creole languages, 198
Portuguese dictionaries
  history of, 196–97
  online, 198, 201, 203–4
  in Portugal vs. Brazil, 198
  transition from print to online, 203–4
Portuguese Language Database Ltd., 199
Portuguese National Funding, 195
Portuguese orthography, 201
Portuguese-lexified creole, 169
Portuñol (Portuguese and Spanish), 58, 61, 65, 67, 68
Poulsen, J. H. W., *Føroysk orðabók* (Faroese dictionary), 258
pre-Hispanic languages, 241–46
prescriptive approach, 267
Priberam, 198
Prinsloo, Danie, 166
print dictionaries, 166
Protestant Reformation, 7, 85, 249
  translation as engine of, 86
Protestant tradition, 86
proto-Quechua, 242
Publication Administration (China), 53
publishing houses, 103, 166
Puquina, 242
Pushkin, Alexander, 227, 230, 231–32
  dictionary of his language, 235
  Eugene Onegin, 231
putonghua 普通话, 54

al-Qālī, *al-Bāriʿ*, 114
Qianlong, Emperor, 52
Qieyun 切韵, 48–49

Quechua, 136, 241–46
  language policies and, 246
  modernization of, 245
  as oral language, 242, 243
  poetry in, 245
  regional variants and dialects of, 246
  Spanish and, 242–43, 245–46
  tension between oral and written forms of, 243
  as written language, 242, 243, 246
Quechua dictionaries, 241
  compared to other Indigenous languages, 245
  history of, 242, 243–44
Quechua/Spanish dictionaries, 244
Quechua/Spanish/English Dictionary, 241–42
Quenya, 67
Qulli, 242

Rabelais, François, 84
Random House Dictionary of the English Language, 214
Rashi, 122
Rask, Rasmus, 252, 257
Rationalist ideology, 230
Rav-Millim, 129
Real Academia Española (RAE), 245
Reconquista, 63, 263
regional dictionaries, 38
Reig, Daniel, *as-Sabīl*, 115
Relational Lexicography project, 132
Renaissance, 83, 84, 85, 115, 249
  Renaissance Humanism, 5, 7
  translation as engine of, 86
Renaissance Italy, 84
Renvall, Kustaa, *Suomalainen Sana-Kirja. Lexicon linguae Finnicae, cum interpretatione duplici, copiosiore Latina, breviore Germanica* (Finnish dictionary. Lexicon of the Finnish language, with a double interpretation, more extensive in Latin, briefer in German), 256
research ethics, 132
research foundations, 238
Restless Books, 59
RetaVortaro, 25
Retskrivningsordbogen (The spelling dictionary), 253
Rey, Alain, 89, 90
Rey-Debove, Josette, 90
Rezeptionsgeschichte, 7, 30–31
rhyming reference books, 48
Ricci, Matteo, *Dizionario portoghese–cinese*, 55
Richardson, Charles, 75
Richelet, Pierre, 87, 88
  burning of his dictionary, 88
  Dictionnaire françois, 87, 88

Richelieu, Cardinal (Armand Jean du Plessis, 1st Duke of Richelieu), 83, 87
Robelo, Cecilio A.
   Diccionario de aztequismos, 175
   Vocabulario comparativo castellano y náhuatl, 174, 176
Robert, Paul, 88–89
Roddenberry, Eugene, 67
Roman alphabet, 172
Roman Empire, fall of, 68
Romance languages, 68, 153
   Esperanto and, 19
   history of, 102
   Yiddish and, 19
Romanesco, 98
Romanian, 68
Romantic Scandinavian movement, 252
Romanticism, 256
Ronsard, Pierre de, 84
roots, 20, 30
roots, dictionaries arranged by, 32, 121
Rosen, Haim, 125
Rosenthal, Ruvik, 119
Rosenthal, Yotam, 129
Ross, William, 4–14
Rosten, Leo, 65
Roth, A., 194
Rowling, J. K., 21
Royal Danish Academy of Sciences and Letters, 251
Royal Irish Academy, *Dictionary of the Irish Language: Based Mainly on Old and Middle Irish Materials*, 145, 152
Rozenshteyn, Avraham (Avraham Even-Shoshan), 125, 126
Rumsien language, 137
Runasimi, 242
Ruphy, J. F., 108
Russian, 126, 227–39, 249
   Esperanto and, 19
   as *lingua franca*, 238
Russian Academy of Science, 230, 231, 232
Russian dictionaries, 232
   business-oriented, 237–38
   government-sponsored, 237–38
   historical, 239
   online vs. print, 236, 239
Russian lexicography, 227–28, 235
   academic lexicographic practice, 237
   foreign traditions and, 237
   in the future, 238–39
   history of, 230
   prescriptive or descriptive approach, 238–39
   technology and, 234, 239
Russian orthography, 232, 233

Russian Romanticism, 230–32
Russianness, concept of, 238

Saadia Gaon, 122
   Egron, 120–21
   Tsahut Ha-Lashon (Clarity of the Language), 121
Sacy, Sylvester de, 108
as-Sadūsī, *Ġarīb al-Qurʾān*, 111
aṣ-Ṣaġān, *al-ʿUbāb az-zāhirī*, 109, 114
Sagard-Théodat, Gabriel, 135
Sages' scripts, 122, 123
Sahagún, Bernardino de, 178, 179
aṣ-Ṣāḥib b. Abbād, *al-Muḥīṭ*, 114
Saʿīd aš-Šartūnī, 116
   Aqrab al-Mawārid, 116
Saitō Hidesaburō 斎藤秀三郎, 211
   Idiomological English-Japanese Dictionary (熟語本位英和中辞典), 211
   Japanese-English Dictionary (斎藤和英大辞典), 211
Sakaibe no Iwatsumi 坂合部磐積, 217
Salgado, Ana, 195–205
Salomon ibn Gabirol, 121
Sami, 249
Sanas Cormaic, 146
Sanders, Daniel, *Wörterbuch der deutschen Sprache*, 34–35, 36
Sanguineti, Edoardo, 100
Sanseidō, 215
Sanskrit, 54
Santa Cruz Pachakuti, 243, 245
Santo Tomás, Domingo de, 242, 244
Sanyo Electric, 214
Sarel, Baruch, 127
Šartūnī, 117
Saucier, Khalil, *Historical Dictionary of the Republic of Cape Verde*, 168
Saucier, Lobban, *Historical Dictionary of the Republic of Cape Verde*, 168
aš-Šaybānī, *Kitāb al-Jīm*, 114
Scandinavian languages. *See also specific languages*, 248–60
Schaechter Viswanath, Arun, 189
Schaechter, Mordkhe, 189–91
   English-Yiddish Dictionary of Academic Terminology, 190
   Plant Names in Yiddish, 190
   Pregnancy, Childbirth and Early Childhood: An English-Yiddish Dictionary, 190
Schaechter-Viswanath, Gitl, 184–94
   Comprehensive English-Yiddish Dictionary, 188, 189–93
Scheller, Immanuel Johann Gerhard, 31
Schiller, Friedrich, 21

Index

Schneider, Johann Gottlob, *Kritisches griechisch-deutsches Handwörterbuch*, 4, 5–6, 8, 12
School of Irish Learning, 151, 152
Schor, Esther, 16–27
   Bridge of Words, 18
Schryver, Gilles-Maurice de, 166
Schulman, Sebastian, 22
Scott, Ridley, 17
Scott, Robert, 7–10, 12
   A Greek–English Lexicon, 7–10
   Intermediate Lexicon, 10
Seán an Chóta ('Seán Óg Ó Caomhánaigh' and 'Seán Mac Murchadha Caomhánach'), 149, 150
Sean-Chaint na nDéise, 149
second-language acquisition, 58
secular humanists, 7
Sefarim, Mendale Mocher, *Sefer Toldot Ha-Teva* (The history of nature), 123
Sefer Yetzirah, 122
Seiko Instruments, 210, 213, 214
Sekelj, Tibor, 22
Seki Shinpachi 尺振八, 211
Séminaire sur la Lexicographie Bantu held at CICIBA (Centre International des Civilisations Bantu), 165
Semitic languages, 121, 166
Senegal, 117
Sennacieca Asocio Tutmonda (SAT), 16, 24
Sephardic Jews, 129
Septuagint, 4, 5, 9, 13
Setsuyōshū 節用集, 219–20
Shakespeare, William
   Hamlet, 2, 21, 22
   neologisms invented by, 23
Shakhmatov, Alexander, 232
Sharp, 213, 214
Sheeran, Fr. Thomas, 147
Shi Zhou pian 史籀篇, 44, 45
Shibata Masayoshi 柴田昌吉, 210
   Fuon Sōzu Eiwa Jii 附音挿図英和字彙, 222
Shigeru Takebayashi, 213
Shin'ar, Pesach, 127
Shinhak, Yosef, *Sefer Ha-Mashbir*, 123
Shinmura Izuru 新村出, 208, 209
Shinsen Jikyō 新選字鏡, 218
Shishkov, Alexander, 230
Shishkovists, 230–31
Shōgakukan 小学館, 209
Shōgakukan Group (Net Advance), 215
Shogakukan Random House English-Japanese Dictionary, 214
Shogakukan 小学館, 223

Shōjū 昌住, 218
Shona, 160, 163, 164
Shorter Oxford English Dictionary, 78
Shōwa period, 212
Shūeisha Kokugo Jiten (集英社国語辞典), 208
Shuowen jiezi 说文解字, 46, 47, 48, 51, 216
Siyiguan 四译馆, 55
Ṣiḥāḥ (al-Jawharī), 108, 114, 115
Simão Thaddeo Ferreira, 202
Siméon, Rémi, 174–75, 176
simplified Chinese, 51
Sindarin, 67
Singer, Isaac Bashevis, 193
slang, 91
slavenorossijskije (lit. Slavonic-Russian, meaning 'Church Slavonic'), 230
Slavic languages, 230
   Esperanto and, 19
   Yiddish and, 17, 19
Slavonic, 230
Slomianski, Hipólito, 83, 107, 263–72
Smith, Henrik, 250
social change, 20
social media, 68
social mobility, 169
social movements, 20
Société du nouveau Littré (SNL), 89
Socrates, 2
Söderwall, K. F., 254
Sokolowski, Peter, 72, 83–92
Solenissimo vochabulista, 95
Solresol, 16
Solzhenitsyn, Aleksandr, 232
Somali, 156
Sona, 16
Songhay, 167
Sony, 213
Soros, Tivadar, 22
Sotho, 168
Sotomayor Valdés, Ramón, 266
   Diccionario hispano-americano, 266
South Africa, 165
South African Centre for Digital Language Resources, 166
South African lexicography, 163–64
Soviet censorship, 232
Soviet dictionaries, 235–36
Soviet lexicographers, 232, 235–36
Soviet lexicography, 233–36
Soviet literary language (литературный язык), 233, 234
Soviet Orthography Reform of 1917, 232–33
Soviet Union, 25, 233, 235
Spain, 101

Spanglish (Spanish and English), 36, 58, 61, 62, 66, 68, 69, 98, 128, 243, 245
  Don Quixote and, 63–65
  as hybrid language, 60
  Mexican-American, 66
  varieties of, 66
Spanglish dictionary, 58
Spanish, 2, 60, 61, 68, 96, 108, 126, 153, 157, 168, 249, 263–72
  19th-century enthusiasts of, 266–67
  American, 66
  English and, 81
  global, 263
  Nahuatl and, 173
  as national language, 63
  Quechua and, 242–43, 245–46
  tension between spoken and written forms of, 243, 263
  Venezuelan, 272
Spanish dictionaries, 32, 96
  anglicisms in, 65
  future of, 271–72
  German lexicography and, 32
  online, 269
Spanish Empire, 177
Spanish lexicography, 10, 13
  Covarrubias as father of, 264, 265
  German lexicography and, 32
Spanish–Nahuatl dictionaries, 135
specialized dictionaries, 166
spelling
  Danish, 252
  French, 90
  Portuguese, 201
  spelling reform, 90
  standardization of, 252, 253
Spielberg, Steven, 69
Spinoza, Baruch, 22
The Spring and Autumn, 45
Squarotti, Giorgio Bàrberi, 100
Stalinism, 25
Stamper, Kory, 192
Stanhope, M., 132
State Language Act, passed in 2005 (and updated in 2024) (Russia), 237
Stavans, Ilan
  Dictionary Days: A Defining Passion, 66–67
  How Yiddish Changed America and How America Changes Yiddish, 61
  on hybrid languages, 58
  Resurrecting Hebrew, 119, 124
  Spanglish: The Making of a New American Language, 63, 64
  translation of *Don Quixote* into Spanglish, 243

Steinbach, Christoph Ernst, 29
Steinberg, Yehoshua, 123
Stellenbosch University, 163
Stephanus, 6, 29, *see also* Estienne, Robert
Stephens, Robert, 6, *see also* Estienne, Robert
Stieler, Johann Caspar, 29
Štimec, Spokmenka, 22
Stutchkoff, Nahum, *Der Oytser fun der Yidisher Shprakh* (The definitive Yiddish thesaurus), 187, 191
Sullivan, John, 172–81
  Tlahtolxitlauhcayotl, 179–80
Summer Institute of Linguistics, 180
Suomen murteiden sanakirja (Dictionary of Finnish dialects), 260
Svabo, Jens Chr., 257
Svensk ordbok (Swedish dictionary), 254
Svenskt dialektlexikon (Swedish dialect lexicon), 260
Swahili, 156, 157, 168
Swazi, 168
Sweden, 248, 249, 260
Swedish, 249, 256
Swedish Academy, 253
Swedish Academy Glossary (*SAOB*), **254**
Swedish Academy Glossary, 248
Swedish dictionaries, 253–54, 259
Swedish Etymological Dictionary, 248
Symbolism, 233

Taa Language (!XÓÕ) Online Dictionary, 162
Tachibana Tadakane 橘忠兼, 219
Tagalog, 60
Tahue, 134
Taiwan, 56
Talboys, David, 8
Talmud, 120, 123
Tanigawa Kotosuga 谷川士清, 221
Tanzania, 166
Tasso, Torquato, 103
tearma.ie, 152
technical field labels, 211
technology
  impact on lexicography, 166, 170
  lexicography and, 269–70
  Russian lexicography and, 234, 239
  Soviet lexicography and, 234
Tecual, 134
Tenmu 天武天皇, Emperor, 217
Tenochtitlan, 172
Tenrei Banshō Meigi 篆隷万象名義, 217–18
Tepanec, 134
terminology, 165, 195

Index 305

Terminology Coordination Section in the Department of Sport, Arts and Culture (South Africa), 165
Teso, 167
Tesoro della lingua italiana delle origini (*TLIO*), 101
testimonies, 245
Teui, 134
Texas Spanglish, 66
Thangmi, 138–42
thematic vocabularies, 112
thesauruses, 275
Thomas, Thomas, 147
Thompson, Anne, 9, 10
Thompson, Emily Fjaellen, 241
Tibeto-Burman language family, 138
Tlahtolxitlauhcayotl, 177
Tlingit, 137–38
Thangmi, 138
Toboso, 134
Toki Pona, 21
Tolkien, J. R. R., 67, 73
Tommaseo-Bellini, *Dizionario della lingua italiana*, 100
Toner, Gregory, 151
Tonkin, Humphrey, 22
Tono, Yukio, 207–23
Totorame, 134
TR-700, 214
traditionalism, 270
translation(s), 6, 85, 197
  of the Bible, 85–86
  dictionaries and, 44, 54, 62
  dictionary-making and, 44
  as engine of Renaissance and Reformation, 86
  Esperanto and, 21–22
  Google Translate and, 152
  as revitalizer of language, 22
  rise of during Abbasid era, 115
Trap-Jensen, Lars, 248–60
Trench, Richard Chenevix, 8
Trésor de la langue française (TLF), 90
Trilingual Lexicon (Лексиконъ треязычный, сирѣчь реченій славенскихъ, еллино-греческихъ и латінскихъ сокровище), 229–30
Tshernichovsky, Shaul, 127
TshwaneLex, 166
Tsonga, 168
Tswana, 168
TswaneLex, 166
Tunisia, 117

Turin, Mark, 132–42
  A Grammar of Thangmi with an Ethnolinguistic Introduction to the Speakers and Their Culture, 139
  Nepali-Thami-English Dictionary, 139–40
Turkish, 115
Turkish-Arabic lexicons, 115
Tuscan vernacular, 84, 97, 98, 104
Twain, Mark, 84
Typographia Lacerdina, 202

Ua Súilleabháin, Seán, 145–54
Ueda Kazutoshi 上田万年, 209, 222
Ugaritic, 4
Ukraine, Russian invasion of, 238
Ukrainian, 239
ʿUmar, Aḥmad M., *Muʿjam al-luġa al-ʿarabiyyat al-muʿāṣira*, 109
Unilingua, 16
Unione Tipografico-Editrice, 99
Universal Esperanto Association, 19
Universidad Autónoma de Zacatecas, 172, 180
Universidad Nacional Autónoma de México, 177
universities. *See also specific universities*, 166
University of Bergen, 256
University of Chicago, 78
University of Fort Hare, 163
University of Gothenburg, 164
University of Michigan, 78
University of Oregon, 177
University of Oslo, 164
University of Pretoria, 163, 166
University of Toronto, 78
University of Zimbabwe, 164
Uralic languages, 249
Ushakov, Dmitry
  Dictionary of the Russian Language or the *Dictionary of Word-Stress for Radio and Television Announcers* (*Словарь ударений для работников радио и телевидения*), 235
  Explanatory Dictionary of the Russian Language, 227, 233
Usṭufān b. Bāsīl, 115
Uto-Aztecan languages, 134
Uyghur, 39

van der Schueren, Gerd, 29
van Schalkwyk, D. J., 165
Vandalic, 134
Varela González, Patricia, 65
Venda, 168
Venetian–Bavarian dictionaries, 95
Venezuelan Spanish, 272

vernacular languages, 147
  embrace of, 94, 96–98
  strategies of vernacular lexicography, 161
Vietnamese, 60
Viking Age, 248
Vilakazi, Bennedict Wallet, *English-Zulu Dictionary*, 158
Villanuova, Alberti di, 100
Villar, Mauro de Salles, 199
Virgil, 6
Vocabolario dantesco, 101
Vocabolario degli Accademici della Crusca, 32, 87, 94, 95, 96, 99, 164
Vocabulário da língua do Japão, 220
Vocabulário ortográfico comum da língua portuguesa, 201
Vocabulário ortográfico da língua portuguesa, 200–1
Vocabulario trilingüe, 173–74
Vocabularios, 135
Vocabularium Latinum, Hispanicum, e Congense, 158
Vocabulista aravigo en letro castellana, 108
Vortaro de Esperanto, 16
vulgar languages, 108
Vulgar Latin, 197
Vulgate, 85

Wade, Thomas Francis, 56
Wade-Giles romanization system, 56
Walsh, Francis, 148
Wamyō Ruijushō 和名類聚抄, 218
Wang Guowei 王国维, 45
Wang Xihou 王锡侯, 52
Wanli, Emperor, 55
al-Wasīṭ (dictionary of the Arabic Academy of Cairo), 110, 116–17
Wealie, M. E., 159
Web Dictionary (a subscription service), 215
Weblio, 215
Webster, Noah, 75, 78, 87, 275
  An American Dictionary of the English Language, 210, 211, 222
Webster's Royal Octavo Dictionary, 221
Wehr, Hans, 115
Wei Jiangong 魏建功, 53
Weil, Roberto, 63
Weinreich, Max, 142, 191
Weinreich, Uriel, 185, 189–90, 191
Wells, H. G., 25
West Scandinavian (Norwegian, Icelandic, and Faroese), 249
White, E. B., 275
Wikipedia Japanese edition, 215
Wilkins, John, 18

Winchester, Simon, 13
Wolof, 156, 168
Wood, Stephanie, 176
Woordenboek der Nederlandsche Taal, 74
word family dictionaries, 34
word selection, 89, 191
wordlists, 235
World Oral Literature Project, 132
Wörterbuch der deutschen Sprache, 35
Wortfamilienwörterbuch, 35
Wortgeschichte digital, 34, 35
Wyld, H. C., 76

Xhosa, 156, 158, 168
Xhosa dictionaries, 163
Xhosa Dictionary Project, 163
xiaozhuan 小篆 (small seal script), 45
Xinhua Dictionary (Xinhua zidian 新华字典), 53, 54
Xitsonga, 164
Xixime, 134
Xu Shen 许慎, 46–48, 50
  Shuowen jiezi 说文解字, 46
Xuan, Emperor, 45
Xuanying 玄应, 54

Yahoo! Dictionary, 215
Yamane, Linda, 137
Yang Xiong 扬雄, 49–50
Ye Shengtao 叶圣陶, 53
Yeats, W. B., 145
Yehuda Halevi, 121
Yehudah ibn Hayyuj, 121
Yehudah ibn Tibon, 121
Yeshiva University, 189
Yiddish (Hebrew and German), 2, 17, 19, 61–62, 69, 126, 184–94
  dialects of, 190
  as endangered language, 184
  Haredi and, 128
  preservation of, 62
  standardization of, 185
  translations in, 22
  as univeralist language, 17
Yiddish Book Center, 61
Yiddish dictionaries, 62, 191–92
  online, 192–93
  terminological, 190
Yiddish immersion retreats (Yidish-vokh), 190
Yiddish lexicography, 193
Yiddish-English dictionaries, 184, 187
Yiddish-English-Hebrew dictionaries, 187
Yiddish-Hebrew dictionaries, 127

Yiddish-Yiddish thesaurus, 193
Ying Zheng 嬴政, Emperor, 53
Yinglish, 58
Yiqiejing yinyi 一切经音义, 54
YIVO Institute for Jewish Research, 186, 187
　Language and Culture Atlas of Ashkenazic Jewry, 190
Yonder, 59
Yoruba, 156, 168
Yoshifuru Kaibara 貝原好古, *Wa-ji-ga* 和爾雅, 220
Yuarcuun Technologies, 137
Yugntruf Youth for Yiddish, 190
Yupanqui, Demetrio Túpac, 241, 243
Yupian 玉篇, 217

az-Zabīdī, *Tāj al-ʿarūs*, 108, 114
Zaliznyak, Andrey, 235–36
Zamahšarī, 115
az-Zamakšarī, *Asās al-balāġa*, 114
Zamenhof, Ludovik Lazarus, 16, 17, 18–19, 20, 21, 23, 68–69
　calls Esperanto politically neutral, 25
　first international dictionary by, 25
　Fundamento de Esperanto, 68
　poems by, 21
　translation of Shakespeare into Esperanto, 22
Zayd b. ʿAlī, 111
Zhang Yushu 张玉书, 52
zhengming 正名, 45, 46
Zholkovsky, Alexander, 236
zidian 字典 (model of characters), 52
Zihui 字汇, 51
Zimbabwe, 164
Zimbabwean languages, 159
Zingarelli, Nicola, 94
Zionist movement, 119, 125
Zouho Gorin Wakun no Shiori 増補語林和訓栞, 221
Zulu, 156, 158, 168

For EU product safety concerns, contact us at Calle de José Abascal, 56–1°,
28003 Madrid, Spain or eugpsr@cambridge.org.

www.ingramcontent.com/pod-product-compliance
Ingram Content Group UK Ltd.
Pitfield, Milton Keynes, MK11 3LW, UK
UKHW020851071025
463690UK00022B/985